Advances in Social Media for Travel, Tourism and Hospitality

This book brings together cutting edge research and applications of social media and related technologies, their uses by consumers and businesses in travel, tourism and hospitality.

The first section addresses topical issues related to how social media influence the operations and strategies of tourism firms and help them enhance tourism experiences: open innovation, crowdsourcing, service-dominant logic, value co-creation, value co-destruction and augmented reality. The second section of the book looks at new applications of social media for marketing purposes in a variety of tourism-related sectors, addressing crowd-sourced campaigns, customer engagement and influencer marketing. The third section uses case studies and new methodologies to analyze travel review posting and consumption behaviors as well as the impact of social media on traveller perceptions and attitudes, with a focus on collaborative consumption and sharing economy accommodation. Finally, the fourth section focuses on hot topics and issues related to the analysis, interpretation and use of online information and user-generated content for deriving business intelligence and enhancing business decision-making.

Written by an international body of well-known researchers, this book uses fresh theoretical lenses, perspectives and methodological approaches to look at the practical implications of social media for tourism suppliers, destinations, tourism policy makers and researchers alike. For these reasons, it will be a valuable resource for students, managers and academics with an interest in information and communication technologies, marketing for tourism and hospitality, and travel and transportation management.

Marianna Sigala is a Professor at the University of South Australia. Her interests include service management, Information and Communication Technologies (ICT) in tourism and hospitality, and e-learning. She is currently the editor of the Journal of Service Theory & Practice and the Journal of Hospitality & Tourism Cases. She is a past President of EuroCHRIE and has served on the Board of Directors of I-CHRIE, IFITT and HeAIS.

Ulrike Gretzel is a Visiting Professor in the Annenberg School of Communication and Journalism at the University of Southern California. She received her PhD in Communication from the University of Illinois in Urbana-Champaign. Her research focuses on persuasion in human-computer interaction, social media, technology adoption, intelligent system design and smart tourism.

New Directions in Tourism Analysis

Series Editor:
Dimitri Ioannides,
E-TOUR, Mid Sweden University, Sweden

Although tourism is becoming increasingly popular both as a taught subject and an area for empirical investigation, the theoretical underpinnings of many approaches have tended to be eclectic and somewhat underdeveloped. However, recent developments indicate that the field of tourism studies is beginning to develop in a more theoretically informed manner, but this has not yet been matched by current publications.

The aim of this series is to fill this gap with high quality monographs or edited collections that seek to develop tourism analysis at both theoretical and substantive levels using approaches which are broadly derived from allied social science disciplines such as Sociology, Social Anthropology, Human and Social Geography, and Cultural Studies. As tourism studies covers a wide range of activities and sub fields, certain areas such as Hospitality Management and Business, which are already well provided for, would be excluded. The series will therefore fill a gap in the current overall pattern of publication.

Suggested themes to be covered by the series, either singly or in combination, include: consumption; cultural change; development; gender; globalization; political economy; social theory; and sustainability.

For a full list of titles in this series, please visit www.routledge.com/New-Directions-in-Tourism-Analysis/book-series/ASHSER1207

Advances in Social Media for Travel, Tourism and Hospitality

New Perspectives, Practice and Cases

**Edited by Marianna Sigala
and Ulrike Gretzel**

LONDON AND NEW YORK

First published 2018 by Routledge

2 Park Square, Milton Park, Abingdon, Oxfordshire OX14 4RN
52 Vanderbilt Avenue, New York, NY 10017

Routledge is an imprint of the Taylor & Francis Group, an informa business

First issued in paperback 2019

British Library Cataloguing-in-Publication Data
A catalogue record for this book is available from the British Library

Library of Congress Cataloging-in-Publication Data
A catalog record for this book has been requested

ISBN: 978-1-4724-6920-5 (hbk)
ISBN: 978-0-367-36916-3 (pbk)

Typeset in Times New Roman
by Apex CoVantage, LLC

Contents

Figures

Tables

Contributors

Marisol Alonso-Vazquez is a teaching and research associate at the University of Queensland, Australia in the Tourism Cluster. She holds a PhD in Management and a Master in Marketing. Her research interests lie in initiating behavioral change in individuals and organizations such as adoption of new technologies, social responsibility, education and entrepreneurship. She has industry experience in predictive analytics as well as data and text mining.

Konstantinos Antoniadis is a PhD candidate at the Department of International and European Studies, University of Macedonia, Thessaloniki, Greece. His research is on the use of Twitter in promoting e-Government services.

Wided Batat is Associate Professor of marketing at the University of Lyon 2 (France) and a United Nations Representative at the UNESCO in Paris. Her works focus on consumption cultures and tourism experience, collaborative consumption, young consumers, vulnerability and well-being, food and sustainable consumption.

Anil Bilgihan is an Assistant Professor in the Marketing department at Florida Atlantic University. He holds a PhD in Education from the University of Central Florida. His research areas include digital marketing, multivariate statistics, customer experience and online social interactions.

Dimitrios Buhalis is an internationally renowned researcher who specializes in eTourism and advises on the use of information and communication technology (ICT) in tourism businesses. He is Director of the eTourism Lab at the Faculty of Management, Bournemouth University and is responsible for driving forward a cross-university initiative to pioneer collaborative research within the theme of the creative and digital economy.

Lorenzo Cantoni is professor and director of the Institute for Communication Technologies at Università della Svizzera Italiana, USI – Lugano (Switzerland), where he also directs the laboratories webatelier.net, New Media in Education Lab and eLearning Lab. He holds the UNESCO chair in ICT to develop and promote sustainable tourism in World Heritage Sites, and is president of IFITT. His research interests are where communication, education and new media overlap.

Silvia De Ascaniis is a postdoctoral researcher and lecturer at the Faculty of Communication Sciences at Università della Svizzera Italiana, USI – Lugano (Switzerland). She is Executive Director and coordinator of the doctoral schools Cross-Field and Argupolis, both founded by the Swiss National Science Foundation (SNSF). Silvia's research interests focus on argumentation dynamics in the online environment and in tourism and pilgrimage.

Ricardo J. Díaz Armas is Professor of Marketing in the Department of Economics and Business Administration at the University of La Laguna, Spain. He has earned degrees in marketing and business. His research focuses on marketing, tourism, social media, wine consumption, resident attitudes and the peer-to-peer economy.

Astrid Dickinger is an Associate Professor at the Department of Tourism and Service Management at MODUL University Vienna. Her research focus lies in the fields of Service and Marketing Management, IT and Tourism and Innovation. Her work is inter alia published in the Journal of Business Research, Journal of Travel Research and Annals of Tourism Research.

Laura Di Pietro is a postdoc fellow in the Department of Business Studies at the University of Roma Tre, Italy. She has a PhD in Quality Management. Her research interests are quality management, customer satisfaction, service innovation, information technology and cultural heritage.

Matthias Fuchs is Full Professor of Tourism Studies in the department of Tourism and Human Geography at Mid-Sweden University. His main research areas include electronic tourism (i.e. mobile services, online auctions, business intelligence and data mining in tourism), and destination management, marketing and branding.

Francisco J. García Rodríguez is Professor of Business Management and Entrepreneurship at the University of La Laguna, Spain. His research includes entrepreneurship, corporate social responsibility, organizational environments and competitiveness.

Fernando J. Garrigos-Simon is an Associate Professor in the Department of Business Organization at the Universidad Politecnica de Valencia, Spain. He holds a PhD in Management. He has published papers in the areas of Tourism Management, Planning, Strategic Management, IT Management and Crowdsourcing.

Jing Ge is a research scientist at the Laboratory for Intelligent Systems in Tourism, California. She has a PhD in tourism and marketing communication and has close to 10 years of online marketing industry experience. Her research focuses on computer-mediated communication and the language use by businesses and consumers on social media.

Ulrike Gretzel is a Visiting Professor in the Annenberg School of Communication and Journalism at the University of Southern California. She received her PhD in Communication from the University of Illinois in Urbana-Champaign. Her research focuses on persuasion in human-computer interaction, social media, technology adoption, intelligent system design and smart tourism.

Roberta Guglielmetti Mugion is a researcher in the Department of Business Studies at the University of Roma Tre, Italy. Her research focuses on customer satisfaction and quality management and has been published in tourism and management journals.

Desiderio Gutiérrez Taño is Professor of Marketing at the University of La Laguna, Spain, where he teaches tourism marketing and innovation in business models and participates in academic research in the field of tourism and entrepreneurship. He is also an Industrial Engineer.

Wafa Hammedi is Associate Professor of service innovation and marketing at the faculty of Economics and Management (University of Namur-Belgium) and academic scholar at Cornell University-(Institute for Healthy Futures) – USA. Her current work focuses on service networks, service design, online consumer behavior, co-creation experiences and service experiences.

Wolfram Höpken is Professor for Business Informatics and eBusiness at the University of Applied Sciences Ravensburg-Weingarten and director of the eBusiness Competence Center eLOUM. His main fields of interest are business intelligence and data mining, semantic web & interoperability and mobile services.

Timothy Jung is a Senior Lecturer in Digital Tourism and Director of Creative Augmented Realities Hub (CARH), Department of Food and Tourism Management at Manchester Metropolitan University, UK. His current research focuses on the application of Augmented Reality (AR), Virtual Reality (VR), multisensory visitor experience in cultural heritage tourism.

Barbara Keller studied Business Economics and Marketing at the University of Augsburg and works as a Researcher and Lecturer at Aalen University.

Lidija Lalicic is a PhD student at MODUL University Vienna supervised by Astrid Dickinger. Her dissertation focuses on innovation opportunities for tourism businesses enhanced by social media. In one of her studies she analyzes the concept of user-driven innovation in tourism triggered by the diverse forms of ICT.

Woojin Lee is an Associate Professor in the School of Community Resources and Development, College of Public Service and Community Solutions, at Arizona State University. Her research focuses on examining the impacts of communication technology on online consumer behavior, measuring attendees' evaluation of meeting facilities and identifying the experiential value of local events/festivals.

Maria Lexhagen is the director at ETOUR within Mid-Sweden University and has a PhD in business administration and tourism with a special interest in marketing and new technology. Her current research interests include the use, impact, potentials and challenges with information technology in the tourism industry, destination management and branding and social media, as well as pop culture tourism induced by film, music and literature.

Michael Möhring studied Business Information Systems at Ilmenau University of Technology and works as a Researcher and Lecturer at the University of Applied Science Munich.

Barbara Neuhofer is Senior Lecturer in Experience Design, Salzburg University of Applied Sciences, Austria. Her research focuses on consumer experiences, co-creation and the use of digital technologies in service settings. Barbara is particularly interested in exploring how technologies transform and shape the way contemporary, consumer-driven and co-created experiences are created.

Yeamduan Narangajavana is a researcher and lecturer in the Department of Business Administration and Marketing at the Universitat Jaume I, Spain. She holds a PhD in Marketing from the same university. Her research interests are related to marketing, tourism and social media.

Fevzi Okumus is a Professor in the Hospitality Services Department in the University of Central Florida's Rosen College of Hospitality Management. His research areas include sustainability, strategy, competitive advantage, knowledge management, hotel management, lodging operations, crisis management, cross-cultural management, destination marketing, information technology and developing countries. He is the Editor-in-Chief of the International Journal of Contemporary Hospitality Management.

Ahmet Ozturk is an Assistant Professor at the Rosen College of Hospitality Management, University of Central Florida. He holds a PhD in Hospitality Administration with Hospitality Information Systems concentration from Oklahoma State University. His research focuses on information technology adoption, e-commerce, m-commerce and destination marketing.

Eduardo Parra López is Professor of Digital Economy and Social Media, Strategic Management and Tourism at the University of La Laguna, Spain. He has a background in information systems and his research centers on etourism, Innovation, tourism, strategic management in tourism, hospitality and leisure, as well as social media.

Maria Francesca Renzi is a Full Professor in the Department of Business Studies at the University of Roma Tre, Italy. Her main areas of interest are: customer satisfaction management; operations management and lean organization; cultural heritage management visitors attitude, satisfaction and behavior; and, quality management in the public sector.

Saba Salehi-Esfahani is a PhD student, teaching associate and research assistant at the Rosen College of Hospitality Management, University of Central Florida.

Her research interests lie in social media, tourism, information technology and consumer behavior.

Javier Sánchez-García is a full professor in the Department of Business Administration and Marketing at the Universitat Jaume I, Spain. His research interests lie in consumer behavior, marketing and SEM. His research has been published in major tourism and service management journals.

Silvia Sanz-Blas is an Associate Professor of Marketing at the University of Valencia, Spain. Her research focuses on consumer motivations, attitudes and behaviors in relation to Internet and mobile technologies and has been published in tourism, services, marketing, e-Commerce and management journals.

Rainer Schmidt is a Full-Professor of Computer Science at the University of Applied Science Munich. He holds a PhD in Computer Science from the University of Karlsruhe. His research focuses on business information systems and business process management.

Marianna Sigala is a Professor at the University of South Australia. Her interests include service management, Information and Communication Technologies (ICT) in tourism and hospitality, and elearning. She is currently the editor of the Journal of Service Theory & Practice and the Journal of Hospitality & Tourism Cases. She is a past President of EuroCHRIE and has served on the Board of Directors of I-CHRIE, IFITT and HeAIS.

M. Claudia tom Dieck is a researcher at the Creative Augmented Realities Hub at Manchester Metropolitan University. Claudia recently received her PhD on digital tourism at Manchester Metropolitan University and her research interests range from social media and customer relationship management to augmented reality and cultural heritage tourism.

Martina Toni is a PhD candidate in Innovation, Quality and Sustainability in the Faculty of Economics at the University of Roma Tre, Italy. Her research interests are focused on quality management, customer satisfaction and cultural heritage.

Justine Virlée is a research and teaching assistant in service management at the Faculty of Economics and Management (University of Namur-Belgium) and member of the Research Center on Consumption and Leisure (Cercle – UNamur). Her primary research interest is open innovation. Her current work focuses on healthcare management, patient participation and healthcare communities.

Vasiliki Vrana is an Associate Professor at Department of Business Administration, Technological Education Institute of Central Macedonia, Serres, Greece. She holds a PhD in Computer Science. She teaches Information Systems and research methods. Her research interests include the study of Web 2.0 in Tourism and Politics.

Kyung-Hyan Yoo is an Associate Professor of Communication at William Paterson University of New Jersey, USA. Her research focuses on electronic word-of-mouth, online trust, social media communication, persuasive technology, online information search and decision-making and other issues related to the role of information communication technology in tourism.

Kostas Zafiropoulos is an Associate Professor at the Department of International and European Studies, University of Macedonia, Thessaloniki, Greece. He holds a PhD in Quantitative Methods and he teaches statistics and research methods. His research interests include the study of Web 2.0 in Tourism and Politics.

Introduction

Marianna Sigala and Ulrike Gretzel

Social media have significantly changed the way people create, share and discuss content as well as with whom, how, when and why they network and interact. Thus, social media tremendously affect consumer behavior and decision-making processes and subsequently, the ways that firms need to communicate, develop relations with and provide services to their customers. One of the fundamental changes brought about by social media is the transformation of customers from passive receivers and consumers of services to active participants and co-creators of information, offerings and value. The rise of crowdsourcing and collaborative commerce (or the so-called sharing economy) are only some examples of customer empowerment in the social media era (Egger et al., 2016).

Information and interactions are at the core of tourism and hospitality experiences, and so, tourism is not an exception from such technology trends. On the contrary, social media advances and applications have been a major driving force defining and redefining the way that information and services related to tourism offerings and destinations are being communicated and delivered as well as the ways in which tourists select, evaluate, participate and define the image and identity of tourism businesses and destinations. Social media have provided the technological platforms but also an open marketplace for various tourism actors (i.e. customers, suppliers, communities, partners, distributors etc.) to network, interact and exchange resources for co-creating value. Through their online actions and by using images and language that shape experience meanings and values, these actors affect the way tourism offerings and destinations are imagined, perceived, produced, consumed and evaluated after consumption. In other words, the production and consumption of tourism experiences are no longer characterized by "push" processes controlled, initiated and managed by tourism suppliers. Instead, tourism experiences emerge from a dynamic, multi-actor, interactive and dialectic process of creating, sharing, disseminating and exchanging content and resources, which in turn (re)-defines, shapes and forms tourism markets (Sigala, 2016).

Social media also represent a dynamic socio-material phenomenon whose evolution, usage and impacts are continuously affected and shaped by technological, economical and socio-cultural forces. In this vein, research and practice of social media always need to follow, catch-up but also foresee changes. It is the aim of this book to provide an update and in-depth insights into the latest developments and trends in relation to social media in travel, tourism and hospitality. Since the first version of the book (published in 2012), several things have changed about the use and impacts of social media, and many other developments and advances are predicted for the near future. In particular, the book aims to address four major areas in which research and industry practice have evolved and changed within the travel, tourism and hospitality social media context. To that end, the book chapters are structured and clustered according to the following four topics: co-creation of tourism experiences; marketing applications; consumer behavior; and last but not least, social media analytics and big data.

The first part of the book titled "*Social media applications for co-creating customer value and experience*" includes five chapters that aim to provide both theoretical but also practical evidence of how and why social media advances influence and shape tourism experiences (Sigala, 2017a). Past research has been mainly descriptive in terms of identifying how tourists and tourism suppliers use social media within their daily lives, work practices, decision-making processes and value chain operations, as well as explorative in terms of measuring the impacts of the former on consumer behavior and firm performance. However, apart from conducting social media usage and impact studies, research should also unravel the reasons motivating and empowering both the tourism supply and demand to integrate social media into their social practices. Such insight is required so one can better understand and predict the drivers of the social media-enabled transformations as well as have a theoretical framework for more effectively exploiting and managing available social media tools. To that end, the chapters in Part 1 adopt the theoretical lenses of Service-Dominant-Logic (SDL) and value co-creation and adapt them within the context of social media for showing how their functionality and affordances can support and empower actors to become more creative, ultimately supporting business and customer value co-creation. Fostering customer engagement and elevating it to co-creation is critically important as studies increasingly show that deep customer engagement can significantly affect customer loyalty, relationship quality, value perceptions and trust (Harrigan et al., 2017; Prebensen et al., 2016). In addition, as more research has been devoted to advantages of customer participation and engagement in value co-creation through social media (Sigala, 2017b;p Dolan et al., 2016), one chapter also looks into the issue of value co-destruction and, by using the TripAdvisor as a case study, it shows how actors can also co-destroy or diminish value. To that end, the first part of the book contributes to the field by providing crucial theoretical underpinnings but also practical examples of both the dark and the bright side of value co-creation through social media.

Social media are also transforming the marketing practices of firms. Given the changing travellers' behavior and the demand "pull" for more personalized, co-created tourism experiences, tourism suppliers also have to shift from customer-centric to customer-driven marketing strategies that place travellers at the control and empower them to design, co-produce and co-promote their tourism experiences. It is the aim of the second part of the book titled "*Marketing using social media applications and concepts*" to identify and illuminate some of the most important social media marketing strategies that the industry needs to adopt and become aware of. To that end, the second part includes five chapters looking into the following topics: social media marketing in the context of destinations; Facebook marketing by hotel groups; social media marketing in China; crowdsourcing strategies as valuable tools for tourism and hospitality businesses; and influencer/opinion leader marketing strategies. Part 2 therefore shows that there is no uniform social media marketing strategy that fits all platforms, cultures and businesses; rather, it illustrates the complexity of social media marketing and points to the many gaps that still exist in the literature.

The third part of the book titled "*Social media: travellers' behavior*" is dedicated to analyzing issues related to the social media changes occurring in travellers' behavior. It includes five chapters providing important theoretical backgrounds and findings related to the following specific issues: the diversity of content creation and consumption behaviors; the reasons and the contextual factors driving engagement and participation in contributing online reviews; the way tourists evaluate different hospitality experiences online; the profile and motivations of tourists participating in the collaborative economy; and the role of social media use in changing people's behavior and perceptions of waiting time. Although the chapters focus on different aspects of travel behavior, they all share and provide evidence of common issues: first, that people transfer and adopt behavior from the offline world to the online social media sphere (Simon et al., 2016). For example, social media are used to satisfy and meet basic human needs such as self-promotion, identity construction and starving off boredom. What social media change are the tools and the ways in which humans try to satisfy these needs and the contextual factors in which humans live and operate. And second, that social media use behaviors are nuanced. For example, lurkers are not lurkers across all platforms and content creators vary in the types of contents they produce as well as their posting behaviors. And often, there are generational differences in social media behaviors. Overall, the chapters clearly show that social media contents need to be understood within the context of the motivations and needs of their creators and sharers.

One cannot manage what does not get measured. The pluralization of social media tools, devices and applications has mushroomed the opportunities to capture and analyze data in order to better understand human behavior and derive critical market intelligence. Big data in tourism has been characterized as the fuel of smart tourism (Gretzel et al., 2015), and scholars have also recently started to look into the multitude of opportunities social media analytics provides (Xiang & Fesenmaier, 2017). Thus, the aim of the last part of the book titled "*Market research, business intelligence and social media analytics*" is to provide an overview but also practical examples of the use of various social media metrics and methods for collecting, analyzing and interpreting social media generated data for solving business problems. Big and social media data have been argued to be the next frontier for innovation, competition and productivity and have been identified to create a new paradigm of knowledge assets (Wedel & Kannan, 2016). The exploitation of social media data enables firms to adopt more data-driven strategies which in turn can increase their efficiency and effectiveness (Wamba et al., 2017). This part of the book includes five chapters that discuss various social media metrics and analytical methods /frameworks (e.g. sentiment analysis, social network analysis, machine-learning, and rhetorical analysis) and show how tourism firms can use them to solve specific business problems. Although the book chapters cannot cover the plurality of the social media metrics and analytical methods currently available, the book chapters do provide important definitions, perspectives and theoretical frameworks that tourism suppliers need to adopt for effectively implementing big data strategies.

One book cannot cover all the topics related to the ongoing social media revolution and transformation; however, the book has managed to consolidate under one cover a great number of chapters contributed by leading scholars in the field that represent and discuss some of the most critical topics that currently influence and will continue to influence tourism demand and supply. Furthermore, the book chapters have also identified, analyzed and applied major theoretical foundations and concepts (e.g. customer engagement, co-creation, SDL, social media data, value co-destruction, crowdsourcing) that can guide and enlighten research in the future.

We hope that you will enjoy reading this book and find its chapters valuable in directing your research or deriving strategic insights for your travel, tourism or hospitality business.

References

Dolan, R., Conduit, J., & Fahy, J. (2016). Social media engagement: A construct of positively and negatively valenced engagement behaviours. In Brodie, R., J., Hollebeek, L. D., & Conduit, J. (eds.), *Customer Engagement: Contemporary Issues and Challenges*, Oxon, UK: Routledge, pp. 102–123.

Egger, R., Gula, I., & Walcher, D. (Eds.). (2016). *Open Tourism: Open Innovation, Crowdsourcing and Co-Creation Challenging the Tourism Industry*. New York: Springer.

Gretzel, U., Sigala, M., Xiang, Z., & Koo, C. (2015). Smart tourism: Foundations and developments. *Electronic Markets*, 25(3), pp. 179–188.

Harrigan, P., Evers, U., Miles, M., & Daly, T. (2017). Customer engagement with tourism social media brands. *Tourism Management*, 59, pp. 597–609.

Prebensen, N. K., Kim, H. L., & Uysal, M. (2016). Cocreation as moderator between the experience value and satisfaction relationship. *Journal of Travel Research*, 55(7), pp. 934–945.

Sigala, M. (2016). Learning with the market: A market approach and framework for developing social entrepreneurship in tourism and hospitality. *International Journal of Contemporary Hospitality Management*, 28(6), pp. 1245–1286.

Sigala, M. (2017a). Social media and the co-creation of tourism experiences. In M. Sotiriadis & D. Gursoy (eds.) *Managing and Marketing Tourism Experiences: Issues, Challenges and Approaches*. Bingley, UK: Emerald Publishing, pp. 85–111.

Sigala, M. (2017b). How bad are you? Justification and normalization of online deviant behavior. Proceedings of the ENTER 2017 eTourism Conference, 24–26 January, 2017, Rome, Italy.

Simon, C., Simon, C., Brexendorf, T. O., Brexendorf, T. O., Fassnacht, M., & Fassnacht, M. (2016). The impact of external social and internal personal forces on consumers' brand community engagement on Facebook. *Journal of Product & Brand Management*, 25(5), pp. 409–423.

Wamba, S. F., Gunasekaran, A., Akter, S., Ren, S. J. F., Dubey, R., & Childe, S. J. (2017). Big data analytics and firm performance: Effects of dynamic capabilities. *Journal of Business Research*, 70, pp. 356–365.

Wedel, M., & Kannan, P. K. (2016). Marketing analytics for data-rich environments. *Journal of Marketing*, 80, pp. 97–121.

Xiang, Z., & Fesenmaier, D. R. (2017). Big data analytics, tourism design and smart tourism. In Z. Xiang & D. R. Fesenmaier (eds.) *Analytics in Smart Tourism Design*. New York, Springer International Publishing, pp. 299–307.

Part 1

Social media applications for co-creating customer value and experience

Marianna Sigala

The bright and the dark side of social media in co-creating tourism experiences

Social media advances empower tourists by changing: the way they access, share, distribute, discuss and create information; with whom, how and when they interact; and how and when they participate in business operations (Sigala, 2017a). Customer experience is defined (Gentile et al., 2007, p. 398) as

> "a set of interactions between a customer and a product, a company, or part of its organization, which provoke a reaction. This experience is strictly personal and implies the customer's involvement at different levels (rational, emotional, sensorial, physical and spiritual)".

As experiences are formed, shaped and co-created through interactions and participation, the use of social media for interacting, sharing and discussing information amongst a plethora of actors (i.e. tourists, virtual communities, firms, social networks) influence experience co-creation on an unprecedented scale and scope. The literature has mainly identified the following ways in which social media influence and form tourism experiences:

- Generation and use of big data for personalizing experiences
- Customer empowerment for participating in experience customization
- Mushrooming of the digital touchpoints whereby tourists can interact with firms, travellers, communities and other actors for shaping their experiences. Social media empower all actors to own and operate a touchpoint. Thus, touchpoints can be categorized as: brand-owned (firms' pages on social media, mobile applications); partner-owned (e.g. distribution partners' channels, marketing agents' channels); customer-owned (e.g. customers' blogs and social media profiles); and social/external (e.g. online communities). This plethora but also diversity of touchpoints implies that firms cannot any more control and influence customers' experience alone, and that travellers'

experiences are shaped by numerous factors external to the firm and the customers' resources.

- Influence of customer experience at all stages of the customer journey; in fact, the use of social media shifts and changes tourists' behavior during various trip stages. For example, by using social media, many tourists: plan their trips while at the destination and last minute rather than during the pre-trip stage; share their tourism experiences and spread word of mouth while consuming the tourism experience and not after their trip; the tourism experience is not mainly influenced by factors and actors existing at the time and location of the experience but also by actors located at other places but interacting through social media as well as by information generated and stored in social media well in advance of the real tourism experience. In other words, there is increased evidence that social media amplify and support an interplay and spillover effects of tourism experiences and expectations across all the stages of the customer journey, while the boundaries of behaviors and practices of tourists at each stage are getting blurred.
- The multimedia content generated and shared through social media (e.g. videos, customer reviews, photographs, travel suggestions, maps) influence all the dimensions of tourism experiences namely, emotional, cognitive, sensorial, physical and spiritual. Tourists have access to and generate a plethora of tourism information that significantly influences the way they feel, what they know, what they do and what they think about tourism destinations and offerings.

Sigala (2017a) summarized the ways in which social media facilitate the transformation, but also the formation and creation of new types of tourism experiences as follows:

- Social media-assisted and facilitated tourism experiences (when tourists share travel resources for assisting others' travel planning processes)
- Social media-enriched and augmented tourism experiences (when online travel resources enable tourists to make experiences more personalized, meaningful, imaginative and emotional)
- Social media-formed tourism experiences (when social media interactions amongst various actors enable an iterative co-construction process of experience meaning, understanding and evaluation)
- Social media-mediated tourism experiences (the virtual experience of a destination)
- Social media as the tourism experience itself (the use of the social media while travelling is the core and major purpose of having a tourism experience, i.e. the social media become a tourism experience)
- Social media-empowered tourism experiences (when customers are empowered to participate and engage in the value co-creation processes of the firm, i.e. the customer is embedded within the firm's value system)
- Social media-enabled tourism experiences (i.e. the use of social media for creating new types of tourism experiences, e.g. when the customer uses the

social media for becoming a tourism entrepreneur providing tourism experiences, e.g. sharing economy, the customer uses the firm's infrastructure and value system for providing – marketing tourism experiences)

However, although research has already recognized and described the types of tourism experiences co-created and influenced by social media, little is known on why and how social media form and shape tourism experiences. Service-Dominant-Logic (SDL) and value co-creation are increasingly being used as theoretical lenses for developing a better understanding of the processes influencing the co-creation of tourism experiences (Campos et al., 2015), but there is still limited knowledge on how these perspectives are applied and function in a social media and digital ecosystem (Neuhofer et al., 2012). The few existing studies on social media tourism experiences are also limited in investigating co-creation from a single actor/tourist approach. On the contrary, based on the principles of the SDL, there is an increased need to start examining value co-creation in social media through a subjective, interactive and dialectic approach amongst multiple actors exchanging resources within an ecosystem rather than a dyadic relationship level (Vargo & Lusch, 2015; Sigala, 2017b). The phenomenological and subjective nature of value (Vargo & Lusch, 2008) also implies that value co-creation practices may mean value creation for one actor but value co-destruction for another actor. Thus, actors' interactions do not always lead to positive outcomes for all actors. Value co-destruction (VCD) (Plé & Chumpitaz-Caceres, 2010) has emerged as an important way to conceptualize the non-positive outcomes from actor-to-actor interactions. However, most of the studies have focused on examining the positive aspects of value co-creation practices, ignoring the hidden and dark sides of actors' participation in co-creation, which may also diminish and/or destroy value.

Overview of part 1

The first part of the book includes five chapters aiming to provide both a theoretical underpinning and practical evidence on how the use of social media influence and shape the co-creation of tourism experiences. The first two chapters illuminate the bright and the dark side of the role of social media in forming tourism experiences by discussing the theoretical foundations of both value co-creation and co-destruction. The third chapter illuminates on tourists' innovation capability to use social media for enriching and augmenting their tourism experiences. The last two chapters provide practical examples and a case study showing how social media and their enhancement with augmented reality enrich tourism experiences.

Analytically, the first chapter – written by Barbara Neuhofer and Dimitrios Buhalis and titled as "*Service-dominant logic in the social media landscape: new perspectives on experience and value co-creation*" discusses the SDL as a new perspective for experience and value co-creation in a social media-enabled tourism context. To achieve that, the chapter discusses and contextualizes the key assumptions of the SDL in the context of social media by discussing case studies showing how the former can be applied for value co-creation practices and experience formation in tourism.

In chapter 2 titled "*Value co-destruction in service ecosystems: findings from TripAdvisor*", Marianna Sigala discusses the dark side of customer review websites in destroying value in a tourism setting. The chapter provides a critical review of existing research in VCD and uses TripAdvisor as an ecosystem for collecting data about the forms, conceptualizations and antecedents of value co-destruction from a multi-actor perspective. The findings revealed that value co-destruction can stem from all TripAdvisor ecosystem actors, i.e. "known" and "unknown" actors such as travellers, marketing agencies, tourism firms, anonymous actors with fake profiles) by uploading fake and/or inaccurate reviews. Findings also confirmed the phenomenological and socially constructed conceptualization of VCD, i.e. the practice adopted by marketing agencies being paid to write positive reviews for hotels creates value for themselves, the hotels (positive reviews enable hotels to charge higher price and receive more bookings), and TripAdvisor (a greater number of reviews provides more "content" for potential travels), but it destroys value for travellers (biased and inaccurate information).

In the third chapter titled "*Tourist-driven innovations in social media: an opportunity for tourism organizations*", Astrid Dickinger and Lidija Lalicic elaborate on how social media enable and support tourism-driven innovation, a concept not adequately addressed in the tourism literature (Sigala, 2012). Social media advances do not only increase the numbers of touchpoints, actors and the network of the tourist experience, but they also create a high level of consumer independence, power and creativity to manage these touchpoints. In this vein, this chapter uses several examples to demonstrate how tourists managing their own touchpoints lead to a shift from co-creation to user-driven creation. To achieve this, the chapter structures and exemplifies user-driven innovations within the experience network communicated and accumulated through the means of social media. The discussion section of the chapter provides a holistic understanding of the benefits enterprises can gain through user-driven innovations and provides recommendations for marketers managing this concept for their own benefit.

In their chapter titled "*Enhancing wearable augmented reality visitor experience through social media: a case study of Manchester Art Gallery*", Timothy Jung and M. Claudia tom Dieck identify and discuss how wearable augmented reality (AR) integrated with social media can contribute and support visitors' experiences in a gallery context. Findings are collected through exploratory interviews of visitors of the Manchester Art Gallery and they reveal that technology advances influence both individual as well as social experience factors. Visitors' experiences are heavily influenced by social media functionality enabling people to take, share and discuss photographs amongst their peers and other social media networks. Hence, the case study clearly shows that although wearable AR is a form of personal technology, it can also be designed to be interactive and social in order to enrich and facilitate tourism experiences. The findings also show that wearable AR applications need to be educational, enriching, smooth and intuitive, personal and exciting in order to enhance the tourists' individual experience.

Finally, Barbara Keller, Michael Möhring and Rainer Schmidt in their chapter titled "*More than a technical feature: insights into augmented reality with social media integration in the travel industry*" further elaborate on the role and impact of augmented reality integrated with social media in relation to tourism experiences. To achieve this, the chapter first describes the functionality of these technological advances and then provides several examples showing how these applications can create value for both the tourists and the tourism providers.

Although these five chapters do not provide an exhaustive list of examples and social media technologies and platforms affecting tourism experiences, they identify and discuss the theoretical lenses and constructs that researchers could use for further examining both the dark and the bright side of social media and their effects on tourism experience formation.

References

Campos, A. C., Mendes, J., Valle, P. O. D., & Scott, N. (2015). Co-creation of tourist experiences: A literature review. *Current Issues in Tourism*, 8, pp. 1–32.

Gentile, C., Spiller, N., & Noci, G. (2007). How to sustain the customer experience: An overview of experience components that co-create value with the customer, *European Management Journal*, 66(2), pp. 395–410.

Neuhofer, B., Buhalis, D., & Ladkin, A. (2012). Conceptualising technology enhanced destination experiences. Journal of Destination Marketing & Management, 1(1), 36–46.

Ple, L., & Chumpitaz Caceres, R. (2010). Not always co-creation: Introducing interactional co-destruction of value in service-dominant logic. *Journal of Services Marketing*, 24(6), pp. 430–437.

Sigala, M. (2012). Social networks and customer involvement in New Service Development (NSD): The case of www.mystarbucksidea.com. *International Journal of Contemporary Hospitality Management*, 24(7), pp. 966–990.

Sigala, M. (2017a). Social media and the co-creation of tourism experiences. In M. Sotiriadis & D. Gursoy (eds.) *Managing and Marketing Tourism Experiences: Issues, Challenges and Approaches*. Emerald Publishing, pp. 85–111.

Sigala, M. (2017b). How bad are you? Justification and normalization of online deviant behavior. Proceedings of the ENTER 2017 eTourism Conference, Rome, Italy, 24–26 January, 2017.

Vargo, S. L., & Lusch, R. F. (2008). Service-dominant logic: Continuing the evolution. *Journal of the Academy of Marketing Science*, 36(1), pp. 1–10.

Vargo, S. L., & Lusch, R. F. (2015). Institutions and axioms: An extension and update of service-dominant logic. *Journal of the Academy of Marketing Science*, 44(1), pp. 5–23.

1 Service-dominant logic in the social media landscape

New perspectives on experience and value co-creation

Barbara Neuhofer and Dimitrios Buhalis

Introduction

Consumers are increasingly empowered, connected and engaged in the co-creation of their service and tourism experiences. Creating experiences together with consumers rather than for consumers has become a prominent notion in the recent services marketing literature. The service-dominant (SDL) logic has emerged as a theoretical lens that has re-defined how experiences and value are created. This development has gone hand in hand with the proliferation of ever-more social and mobile information and communication technologies (ICTs). Social media and mobile applications have become a catalyst of change which has enabled consumers to connect, engage, participate and co-create their own experiences and value on an unprecedented scale (Ramaswamy, 2011; Xiang & Gretzel, 2010).

With distinct advances in service and tourism marketing thought, consumer society and the field of technology alike, traditional roles and processes of experience creation have changed. In moving towards technology-enhanced experience environments (Neuhofer et al., 2012), we are faced with new realities for academic discourses on and practical implementation of experience creation. For the tourism, travel and hospitality context this means that we need to revise existing approaches and identify new perspectives that allow for more contemporary, dynamic and consumer-driven experience and value creation. While the role of social media in experience co-creation has been acknowledged, there is still a limited understanding how exactly these tools allow consumers to connect and co-create their tourist experiences.

It is with this premise in mind that the chapter aims to explore and discuss the SDL as a new perspective for experience and value co-creation in a social media-enabled context. This discussion seeks to appraise current perspectives and practices for an understanding of contemporary experience and value creation in the wider service and tourism setting. The chapter is divided into three main sections. The first section provides a theoretical fundament by reviewing the evolution of services marketing and introducing the SDL perspective. The second section contextualizes the key assumptions of the SDL in the context of social media and showcases, through the presentation of case studies, how these can be applied for co-creation creation practices. The third section offers theoretical and practical implications of this development for marketing and tourism research and practice and concludes with an outlook into the future. This chapter contributes by conceptualizing the SDL in the social media landscape that shall offer a novel theoretical and practical starting point for experience and value co-creation.

Evolution from product to service and experience economy

Consumer empowerment and social media have not only brought major advances for consumer society but have also changed the way services and experiences are created (Frochot & Batat; 2013; Grönroos & Ravald, 2011; Vargo & Lusch, 2008). Conventional practices focusing on mere "service delivery" and economically-driven "experience staging" (Pine & Gilmore, 1999) have evolved. This has led to new theoretical and practical realities for service and tourism settings that have forced us to re-think the ways more consumer-driven, personalized and added-value experiences can be facilitated (Binkhorst & Den Dekker, 2009; Prahalad & Ramaswamy, 2004; Vargo & Akaka, 2012). This section reviews the theoretical perspectives underpinning experience and value co-creation. The S-D logic is grounded in a long evolution of services marketing, moving from the early product economy and "value-for-money" to the SDL thinking and "value-in-use" as the core concept that prevails to date.

Product economy: products, goods and value for money

The roots of the service-dominant logic can be dated back to the early product economy in the late 18th century, in which agricultural, manufacturing and goods-centric thoughts centered the debate (Vargo et al., 2008). In this era, tangible goods (e.g. food and machines) were considered as productive, while services (e.g. provided by doctors and lawyers) were predominantly seen as unproductive (Vargo & Lusch, 2004; Vargo et al., 2008). Towards the 20th century, the idea of selling and delivering tangible products to consumers became more prominent (Palmer et al., 2005). In this goods-dominant logic (G-D logic), as the main mode of thought, value was considered as embedded in goods and determined by the market price. The core tenet was "value for money", created when money was exchanged for products and goods (Vargo & Lusch, 2006). The consumer society still played a minor role at the time and was primarily seen as the end of the production chain. The relationship between companies and consumers was distinct and marketing was introduced as a key tool to bridge this gap (Vargo et al., 2006). It fast became a strategic means create for creating and filling demand and emphasizing the value of goods (e.g. cars and washing machines). While the GD-logic continued to prevail until the first half of the 20th century, the post-war economic prosperity induced a radical change in marketing practices, both academically and practically (Vargo & Lusch, 2004). With growing consumer purchasing power and demand, market competition experienced a rapid increase. Companies gradually shifted from simple product orientation towards a stronger focus on consumer behavior (Sheth & Gross, 1988). These advances were primarily driven by the underlying premise to meet and satisfy consumer needs, while fostering consumer satisfaction and loyalty (Kotler et al., 2009) to increase the increasing the firm's competitive advantage, profits and growth (Vargo & Lusch, 2004; Vargo et al., 2006).

Service economy: services and value exchange

With the shift in consumer behavior, society became increasingly characterized as a service-driven economy (Vargo et al., 2006). While the academic practical interest in services has experienced a peak within the SDL most recently, the concept entered the marketing discourses as early as the late 20th century (Vargo & Lusch, 2004). In the 1980s, thinking logic advanced from marketing management towards marketing as a social and economic process (Vargo & Lusch, 2004). Several seminal concepts shaped the discourses that current knowledge builds on, including services marketing (Grönroos, 2000), relationship marketing (Palmer et al., 2005), value, resource and network oriented views (Vargo & Lusch, 2008). The sum of these concepts contributed to an inherently service-centric orientation that recognized products as merely functional means to assist the purpose of service and value exchange (Vargo &Lusch, 2004; Vargo et al., 2008). In this era, Kotler et al. (1996, p. 588) captured services as "any activity or benefit that one party can offer to another which is essentially intangible and does not result in the ownership of anything. Its production may or may not be tied to a physical product".

Experience economy: experiences and economic value progression

The advances of the service-oriented economy have fostered new thinking logics, emphasizing the increased provision of services and experiences. In this changing mindset, consumers did no longer want to simply buy services, but instead, buy into experiences obtained through the consumption of services (Morgan et al., 2010). At the end of the 1990s, several theoretical concepts emerged, conceptualizing this trend within the frame of the dream society (Jensen, 1999), the entertainment economy (Wolf, 1999) and the experience economy (Pine & Gilmore, 1999). Pine & Gilmore (1999) shaped the term experience economy, which has subsequently become one of the most significant concepts for marketing to date. In a market characterized by global competitiveness and use of technology, it has become more critical than ever before for companies to differentiate their services and create unique experiences that stand out from the competition (Prahalad & Ramaswamy, 2004). The experience economy suggests that consumers pursue memorable experiences and companies need to stage such experiences for the progression of economic value. The underlying principles propose that while products are tangible and services are intangible, experiences have the potential to become memorable. Despite its popularity in theory and practice over more than two decades, the experience economy has evolved as its businesses-oriented approach of staging became increasingly challenged (Boswijk et al., 2007).

A new theoretical perspective for experience and value creation: SDL

With the proliferation of social ICTs, consumers have become more active, powerful and involved in the experience production and consumption processes (Ramaswamy, 2009a). This development has fostered a change of relationship between companies and consumers and advanced our understanding of *how* and *by whom* experiences and value are created (Vargo & Lusch, 2004; Vargo et al., 2006; Sfandla & Björk, 2013). As consumers adopt a bigger role as connected and socially-engaged "prosumers", the orchestrated design and staging of experiences (as prevalent in the experience economy), is considered no longer suitable to reflect the needs, wants and roles of today's consumers. This has led to a main paradigm change in the services marketing field, introducing the SDL.

Vargo & Lusch (2004) and Prahalad & Ramaswamy (2004) were among the first scholars to recognize this change and to establish the SDL perspective. The SDL can be understood as a "convergence of contemporary marketing thought" (Vargo et al., 2006, p. 40) that offers a new starting point for experience and value creation. In contrast to previous paradigms, this new logic regards the consumer not merely as a consumer, but as a central actor participating in the own creation of experiences. This has led to a redefined interaction between companies and consumers. Companies no longer design and deliver experiences, but instead facilitate the necessary prerequisites and value propositions that allow consumers to get involved and co-create and generate their own value (Vargo et al., 2008). Particularly driven by the developments in the ICTs sector, this has implied that the role of the consumer has expanded significantly (Neuhofer & Buhalis, 2013). Consumers embody multiple roles as:

- the active co-creators of the experience and value
- the co-creators of the extended physical offline and virtual online experience space
- the extractors and judges of the value.

Based on the assumption that consumers essentially co-create value, the concept of value-in-use has emerged. Compared to previous paradigms, it postulates that value is a phenomenological construct (Helkkula et al., 2012) and hence does not pre-exist in products and services, but needs to be co-created by the consumer situations of use. In other words, "value can only be created with and determined by the user in the 'consumption' process and through use" (Vargo & Lusch, 2006, p. 284). This presents businesses with a changed reality that value cannot be simply delivered, but consumers are needed to integrate their own resources (e.g. social media) to co-create experiences and value (Ramaswamy, 2009a; Grönroos & Ravald, 2011; Wieland et al., 2012). Through the use of ICTs, the collaborative process of co-creation has reached a new level, as it no longer occurs only between companies and consumers (B2C), but also in a wider customer-to-customer (C2C) (Baron & Warnaby, 2011) and actor-to-actor (A2A) network (Vargo & Lusch, 2011). Table 1.1 summarizes the theoretical evolution and

Table 1.1 Evolution of experience and value co-creation

Assumption	From			To
	Product Economy	*Service Economy*	*Experience Economy*	*Experience and ValueCo-Creation (SDL)*
Driver of Economy	Product	Service	Experience	Experience
Economic Function	Make	Deliver	Stage	Co-Create
Nature of Offer	Tangible	Intangible	Memorable	Meaningful
Key Attribute	Standardized	Customized	Personalized	Individualized
Method of Supply	Inventoried after production	Delivered on demand	Revealed over duration	Co-created in-use/context
Role of Company	Manufacturer	Seller	Stager	Facilitator and co-creator
Role of Consumer	User	Client	Guest	Co-Creator
Interaction	B2C	B2C	B2C	A2A
Role of Goods	Main output	Means for services	Means for experiences	Basis for operant resources
Resources	Operand resources	Operand resources	Operand resources	Operant resources
Factor on Demand	Features	Benefits	Sensations	Value
Role of Value	Value-for-money	Value-in-exchange	Economic value	Value-in-use

Source: after Pine and Gilmore, 1999; Neuhofer and Buhalis, 2013

highlights the main shift in assumptions from the product, service and experience economy towards the S-D logic for a changed experience and value co-creation.

Conceptualizing the SDL in the social media landscape

Due to the proliferation of the Web 2.0 and social media, it has become evident that consumer empowerment and co-creation have been inextricably linked to one factor, namely technology (Neuhofer et al., 2012). The significance of ICTs is not only prevalent in society but especially critical across the service, tourism and hospitality sectors. With a plethora of ICTs available, tourists are always connected, which unfolds new possibilities to proactively co-create experiences and value in every step of the consumption (Neuhofer et al., 2014; Wang et al., 2012). Subsequently, it has been of particular interest for academia and practice to understand how to exploit the full potential of ICTs to enable, facilitate and enhance experience and value creation. In interlinking SDL and social media, this chapter now takes a closer look at conceptualizing its synergies for theory and practice.

Social media: a game changer for tourism

ICTs have caused a drastic impact, by changing not only consumer society and various industries (Buhalis & Law, 2008), but also by transforming the nature of how tourist experiences are created (Lamsfus et al., 2013; Tussyadiah & Zach, 2011; Yovcheva et al., 2013). In particular, with the advances of the Internet from the Web 1.0 to the Web 2.0, one of the most transformative technological developments has occurred (Dwivedi et al., 2012 ;Fotis et al., 2011; Leung et al., 2013; Sigala, 2011; Xiang et al., 2014). The Web 2.0 and social media have turned the Internet into an immense space of networking and collaboration (Sigala, 2009). Unlike any other medium before, social media have embraced different people, technologies and new practices, which support consumers and their experiences (Xiang & Gretzel, 2010). The variety of tools available, comprising blogs, videos, wikis, chatrooms, folksonomies and podcasts have empowered individuals to connect, interact and generate user-content on an unprecedented scale (Sigala, 2011; Tussyadiah & Fesenmaier, 2009). In addition, social media have paved the way for new ways of collaboration that have caused a transformation of traditional service design, production and marketing (Sigala, 2009), consumer behavior and tourism (Fotis et al., 2011).

Empowered by the interactive nature of the Web 2.0, consumers have taken an active part in designing services with companies. Through a variety of applications, they have not only altered how services are consumed on the Internet, but also changed how consumers locate, share, read, create and produce information (Sigala, 2009; Sigala, 2011). By enabling connectivity, mass collaboration and networking, social media have thus become key tools for tourism businesses and tourists to dynamically engage, interact, comment and create experiences with each other (Dwivedi et al., 2012; Hays et al., 2012; Leung et al., 2013). These developments have enabled consumers to become "co-marketers, co-producers and co-designers of their service experiences by providing them a wide spectrum of values" (Sigala, 2009, p. 1345). With this potential for collaboration, the key question is how can social media become an effective resource for experience and value co-creation?

Social media: a resource for experience and value co-creation

One of the foundational premises of the SDL is the integration and use of so-called resources. Consumers integrate a wide range of operand and operant resources in experience and value creation processes (Vargo & Lusch, 2011). The role of IT as a resource has been discussed as early as in the 1990s. However previous studies have only provided an incomplete picture of technology, which predominantly portrayed IT as an artefact and outcome of human action (Orlikowski, 1992). Only most recently, scholarship has started to investigate ICTs in service systems, value co-creation propositions and innovation (Lusch & Nambisan, 2015; Maglio et al., 2009), while a deeper knowledge of ICTs, and particularly social media, remains missing. By drawing upon the structurational model of technology by Orlikowski

(1992), social media could be conceptualized as an operant resource. If we suggest that they have the capability to act upon other resources and influence human action (e.g. tourist behavior and experiential activities), social media can ultimately create value for its user (Akaka & Vargo, 2014). As such, they can act "as a means of satisfying higher-order needs (i.e. enhancing the customers' own operant resources*)*" (Cantone & Testa, 2014, p. 507).

In their role of operant resources, social media have enabled a massive space of online collaboration (Sigala, 2009), allowing for a myriad of actor-to-actor relations. Tourists have become interconnected individuals who interact in a physical and virtual technology-enabled experience environment extended to the pre/during/post stages of travel (Neuhofer et al., 2012). They use social media to connect, communicate, generate content, share their experiences and in turn co-create and co-live their experiences with others more than ever before (Ramaswamy, 2009b). As a result, it has become evident that the Web 2.0 and social media have been instrumental to foster actor-to-actor interactions to explode on "an unprecedented scale everywhere in the value creation system" (Ramaswamy, 2009b, p. 17). In fact, recent studies confirm that ICTs support co-creation experiences in a number of different ways (Gretzel & Jamal, 2009; Tussyadiah & Fesenmaier, 2007; Tussyadiah & Fesenmaier, 2009).

For instance, tourists might engage in traditional B2C co-creation in the pre/during/post tourist experience for hotel booking, information exchange at destination, relationship building and experience sharing post-travel. Beyond this dyadic relationship, consumers also seek to engage with their close and extended social networks and engage in C2C co-creation on all levels (e.g. sharing experiences, asking for advice and opinions, examining rankings and reviews). With new forms of social applications emerging over the past few years, tourists are now able to connect to a wider A2A network more than ever before. For instance, tourists are able to use latest social platforms and applications (e.g. AirBnB, Eatwith, Uber) to connect with locals and get expert insights and co-create services with a private local peer rather than an official service provider. To get a better understanding of the "new generation" of co-creation, Table 1.2 offers an outline of social media application in the tourist value creation system. By bringing together S-D logic theory and social media practice, it provides an overview of how different types of social media (resources) are applied (integrated) for different purposes (use context) by different actors in the value creation system (travel process).

Social media: best-practice cases in travel, tourism and hospitality

The understanding and application of co-creation in the travel, tourism and hospitality industry is still scarce (Binkhorst & Den Dekker, 2009) and even more rare with ICTs in place (Neuhofer et al., 2012). Several firms have pioneered the industry by recognizing the new marketing paradigm and putting the principles of the SDL into practice. To provide a better understanding of how co-creation can be realized in practice, valuable insights can be gained by analyzing current industry best-practice cases. Table 1.3 offers an overview of examples that shall assist other

Table 1.2 Social media for experience and value co-creation

Travel Process (Value Creation System)	Tourist Activities (Context of Use)	Social Media Type (Resource)	Interaction (Actors)	Application/Example (Resource Integration)
Pre-Travel Stage	Inspiration Information search Planning Comparison Decision-making Booking	Social networks UGC review sites Video-sharing sites Blogs Virtual worlds	Multi-level engagement: Companies Consumers Friends Locals Service providers	TripAdvisor reviews Pinterest picture inspiration Facebook posts YouTube videos Travel blogs AirBnB site booking
During Travel Stage	Experience consumption Accommodation Transport Visitor attractions Information search Experience sharing Navigation Sharing	Recommender systems LBS-apps UGC review sites Social networks Social augmented reality games and apps	Multi-level engagement: Companies Friends Locals Consumers Service providers	Facebook sharing Real-time Twitter information retrieval Social gaming TripAdvisor reviews Real-time social sharing
Post-Travel Stage	Post-experience engagement Sharing Reviews Interaction Experience re-living	Blogs Social provider networks UGC review sites Text/video/photo-sharing sites	Multi-level engagement: Companies Friends Locals Consumers Service providers	TripAdvisor review writing Facebook experience and album posts Travel blog entries

Table 1.3 Industry best-practice: social media for experience and value co-creation

Industry Best-Practice (Sector)	Social Media Resource Integration (Application)
Marriott Travel Brilliantly (Hospitality)	Co-creation initiative based on crowdsourcing. Individuals can submit innovative ideas through social platform with the potential to enhance the hotel and experience environment for fellow co-travellers.
Hotel Lugano Dante (Hospitality)	Social media engagement and co-creation through a smart mobile customer-relationship platform, enabling enhanced engagement, opportunities for co-creation through hotel experience personalization.
Sol Melia's Sol Wave House (Hospitality)	The world's first Twitter hotel. Innovative use of social media (Twitter) throughout the hotel environment to foster B2C and C2C co-creation, communication and engagement in the experience environment on-site.
KLM Social Seating Initiative (Travel)	KLM introduced a KLM social seating initiative called "Meet and Seat". It tested the idea to connect people, allow C2C interaction and facilitate a more socially-rich in-flight experience.
EatWith (Tourism)	Based on the idea of the sharing economy, EatWith is a social platform allowing for A2A engagement as tourists and locals connect and co-create eating experiences, replacing traditional B2C service provision.

tourism practitioners as a reference guide of how social media could be successfully applied for experience and value co-creation. The five presented industry cases underline the potential in travel, tourism and hospitality environments to allow engaging, personalizing, building with relationships and co-creating experiences together with empowered consumers.

Outlook, implications and future perspectives

The proliferation of social media and the arrival of the SDL as a marketing paradigm have offered new starting points and realities for experience and value creation practices in tourism service settings and beyond. This chapter had the aim to discuss the SDL as a novel theoretical perspective for experience and value co-creation in the social media landscape. It first presented the theoretical advances that underpin services marketing and management, leading from the early product economy to experiential and SDLs, which are recognized as the state-of-the-art thinking for contemporary experience and value creation debates and practices today. The chapter also has shown that with the empowerment of consumers and the widespread use of modern digital technologies, in particular social media, consumers have turned into active prosumers who connect, engage and co-create experiences in wide network of connected actors and service contexts. For tourism academia and practice, this has implied the need for re-conceptualization and re-thinking of how experiences and value can be facilitated. While several principles of the experience economy undoubtedly still apply, the main challenge for businesses will pose the notion of "letting go", as companies are no longer the unique and primary experience creator, but rather are a mere facilitator, or an "invited participator" who tourists might seek to co-create experiences. As a myriad of interactions occur outside the company domain, businesses should facilitate resources and social platforms that allow tourists to connect and collectively co-create experiences and value in a network of actors in the wider service eco-system. Practitioners will thus need to develop strategies that:

- adopt a SDL-driven approach to experience and value creation
- facilitate the resources and environments to create a compelling value proposition
- offer social media tools and platforms as a key resource for enhanced co-creation

To innovate co-creation practices in the long-term, an agenda is necessary that synergizes theoretical, technological and practical advances for competitive experience creation. As ICTs continue to emerge and evolve at a fast pace, we can foresee several key areas that will shape experience and value creation in the near future. Smart tourism and technology, SoCoMo (social, context and mobile) marketing and the peer-to-peer sharing economy (Boes et al., 2015; Buhalis & Foerste, 2015; Gretzel et al., 2015; Neuhofer et al., 2015) are only three exemplary areas in which we will see radical change and major opportunities for co-creation to happen. As these developments gain further momentum, we enter an unprecedented era of social collaboration, smartness, massive resource and data integration, and situation- and context-aware systems that put consumer-centric experience and value extraction at the center stage. While these fields only provide a fragment of possibilities, it can be expected that the application of the SDL in this context will become magnified. This will open a dynamic area to investigate through further research and tap into in tourism marketing and practice.

References

Akaka, M. A., & Vargo, S. L. (2014). Technology as an operant resource in service (eco) systems. *Information Systems and E-Business Management*, 12, pp. 367–384.

Baron, S., & Warnaby, G. (2011). Individual customers' use and integration of resources: Empirical findings and organizational implications in the context of value co-creation. *Industrial Marketing Management*, 40, pp. 211–218.

Binkhorst, E., & Den Dekker, T. (2009). Agenda for co-creation tourism experience research. *Journal of Hospitality Marketing & Management*, 18, pp. 311–327.

Boes, K., Buhalis, D., & Inversini, A. (2015). Conceptualising smart tourism destination dimensions. In I. Tussyadiah & A. Inversini (eds.) *Information and Communication Technologies in Tourism 2015*. Vienna, Austria, Springer, pp. 391–403.

Boswijk, A., Thijssen, T., & Peelen, E. (2007). *The Experience Economy: A New Perspective*, Amsterdam, Pearson Education.

Buhalis, D., & Foerste, M. (2015). SoCoMo marketing for travel and tourism: Empowering co-creation of value. *Journal of Destination Marketing & Management*, 4 (3), pp. 151–161.

Buhalis, D., & Law, R. (2008). Progress in information technology and tourism management: 20 years on and 10 years after the Internet: The state of eTourism research. *Tourism Management*, 29, pp. 609–623.

Cantone, L., & Testa, P. (2014). Latent theoretical constructs of service dominant logic. In L. Freund & W. Cellary (eds.) *AHFE Conference*. Krakow, Poland, pp. 499–514.

Dwivedi, M., Yadav, A., & Venkatesh, U. (2012). Use of social media by national tourism organizations: A preliminary analysis. *Information Technology and Tourism*, 13, pp. 93–103.

Fotis, J., Buhalis, D., & Rossides, N. (2011). Social media impact on holiday travel planning: The case of the Russian and the FSU Markets. *International Journal of Online Marketing*, 1, pp. 1–19.

Frochot, I., & Batat, W. (2013). *Marketing and Designing the Tourist Experience*, Oxford, Goodfellow Publishers.

Gretzel, U., & Jamal, T. (2009). Conceptualizing the creative tourist class: Technology, mobility, and tourism experiences. *Tourism Analysis*, 14, pp. 471–481.

Gretzel, U., Sigala, M., Xiang, Z., & Koo, C. (2015). Smart tourism: Foundations and developments. *Electronic Markets*, 25, pp. 179–188.

Grönroos, C. (2000). *Service Management and Marketing: A Customer Relationship Approach*, Chichester, John Wiley & Sons.

Grönroos, C., & Ravald, A. (2011). Service as business logic: Implications for value creation and marketing. *Journal of Service Management*, 22, pp. 5–22.

Hays, S., Page, S. J., & Buhalis, D. (2012). Social media as a destination marketing tool: Its use by national tourism organisations. *Current Issues in Tourism*, 16, pp. 211–239.

Helkkula, A., Kelleher, C., & Pihlström, M. (2012). Characterizing value as an experience. *Journal of Service Research*, 15, pp. 59–75.

Jensen, R. (1999). *The Dream Society: How the Coming Shift from Information to Imagination Will Transform Your Business*, New York, McGraw-Hill.

Kotler, P., Armstrong, G., Saunders, J., & Wong, V. (1996). *Principles of Marketing: The European Edition*, Hemel Hempstead, Prentice Hall.

Kotler, P., Keller, K. L., Brady, M. K., Goodman, M., & Hansen, T. (2009). *Marketing Management*, Harlow, Pearson Education.

Lamsfus, C., Xiang, Z., Alzua-Sorzabal, A., & Martin, D. (2013). Conceptualizing context in an intelligent mobile enviornment in travel and tourism. In L. Cantoni & Z. Xiang (eds.) *Information and Communication Technologies in Tourism 2012*. Vienna, Springer, pp. 1–11.

Leung, D., Law, R., Van Hoof, H., & Buhalis, D. (2013). Social media in tourism and hospitality: A literature review. *Journal of Travel & Tourism Marketing*, 30, pp. 3–22.

Lusch, R. F., & Nambisan, S. (2015). Service innovation: A service-dominant (S-D) logic perspective. *Management Information Systems Quarterly*, 39(1), pp. 155–175.

Maglio, P., Vargo, S. L., Caswell, N., & Spohrer, J. (2009). The service system is the basic abstraction of the service science. *Information Systems and E-Business Management*, 7, pp. 395–406.

Morgan, M., Lugosi, P., & Ritchie, J. R. B. (2010). *The Tourism and Leisure Experience: Consumer and Managerial Perspectives*, Bristol, Channel View.

Neuhofer, B., & Buhalis, D. (2013). Experience, co-creation and technology: Issues, challenges and trends for technology enhanced tourism experiences. In S. Mccabe (ed.) *Handbook of Tourism Marketing*. London, Routledge, pp. 340–350.

Neuhofer, B., Buhalis, D., & Ladkin, A. (2012). Conceptualising technology enhanced destination experiences. *Journal of Destination Marketing & Management*, 1, pp. 36–46.

Neuhofer, B., Buhalis, D., & Ladkin, A. (2014). Co-creation through technology: Dimensions of social connectedness. In Z. Xiang & I. Tussyadiah (eds.) *Information and Communication Technologies in Tourism 2014*. Vienna, Austria, Springer, pp. 339–352.

Neuhofer, B., Buhalis, D., & Ladkin, A. (2015). Smart technologies for personalized experiences: A case study in the hospitality domain. *Electronic Markets*, 25, pp. 243–254.

Orlikowski, W. J. (1992). The duality of technology: Rethinking of the concept of technology in organizations. *Organisational Science*, 3, pp. 398–427.

Palmer, R., Lindgreen, A., & Vanhamme, J. (2005). Relationship marketing: Schools of thought and future research directions. *Marketing Intelligence & Planning*, 23, pp. 313–330.

Pine, J. B., & Gilmore, J. H. (1999). *The Experience Economy: Work Is a Theatre and Every Business a Stage*, Cambridge, Harvard Business School.

Prahalad, C. K., & Ramaswamy, V. (2004). Co-creation experiences: The next practice in value creation. *Journal of Interactive Marketing*, 18, pp. 5–14.

Ramaswamy, V. (2009a). Co-creation of value: Towards an expanded paradigm of value creation. *Marketing Review St. Gallen*, 26, pp. 11–17.

Ramaswamy, V. (2009b). Leading the transformation to co-creation of value. *Strategy & Leadership*, 37, pp. 32–37.

Ramaswamy, V. (2011). It's about human experiences and beyond, to co-creation. *Industrial Marketing Management*, 40, pp. 195–196.

Sfandla, C., & Björk, P. (2013). Tourism experience network: Co-creation of experiences in interactive processes. *International Journal of Tourism Research*, 15, pp. 495–506.

Sheth, J. N., & Gross, B. (1988). Parallel development of marketing and consumer behavior: A historical perspective. In T. Nevett & R. A. Fullerton (eds.) *Historical Perspectives in Marketing: Essays in Honor of Stanley C. Hollander*. Lexington, Lexington Books, 9–33.

Sigala, M. (2009). E-service quality and Web 2.0: Expanding quality models to include customer participation and inter-customer support. *The Service Industries Journal*, 29, pp. 1341–1358.

Sigala, M. (2011). Special issue on Web 2.0 in travel and tourism: Empowering and changing the role of travelers. *Computers in Human Behavior*, 27, pp. 607–608.

Tussyadiah, I. P., & Fesenmaier, D. R. (2007). Interpreting tourist experiences from first-person stories: A foundation for mobile guides. In *15th European Conference on Information Systems*. Switzerland, St. Gallen, pp. 2259–2270.

Tussyadiah, I. P., & Fesenmaier, D. R. (2009). Mediating the tourist experiences: Access to places via shared videos. *Annals of Tourism Research*, 36, pp. 24–40.

Tussyadiah, I. P., & Zach, F. J. (2011). The role of geo-based technology in place experiences. *Annals of Tourism Research*, 39, pp. 780–800.

Vargo, S. L., & Akaka, M. A. (2012). Value co-creation and service systems (re)formation: A service ecosystems view. *Service Science*, 4, pp. 207–217.

Vargo, S. L., & Lusch, R. F. (2004). Evolving to a new dominant logic for marketing. *Journal of Marketing*, 68, pp. 1–17.

Vargo, S. L., & Lusch, R. F. (2006). Service-dominant logic: Reactions, reflections and refinements. *Marketing Theory*, 6, pp. 281–288.

Vargo, S. L., & Lusch, R. F. (2008). Service-dominant logic: Continuing the evolution. *Journal of the Academy of Marketing Science Review*, 36, pp. 1–10.

Vargo, S. L., & Lusch, R. F. (2011). It's all B2B and beyond: Toward a systems perspective of the market. *Industrial Marketing Management*, 40, pp. 181–187.

Vargo, S. L., Lusch, R. F., & Morgan, F. W. (2006). Historical perspectives on service-dominant logic. In R. F. Lusch & S. L. Vargo (eds.) *The Service-Dominant Logic of Marketing: Dialog, Debate, and Directions*. Armonk, M.E. Sharpe, 29–42.

Vargo, S. L., Maglio, P. P., & Archpru-Akaka, M. (2008). On value and value co-creation: A service systems and service logic perspective. *European Management Journal*, 26, pp. 145–152.

Wang, D., Park, S., & Fesenmaier, D. R. (2012). The role of smartphones in mediating the touristic experience. *Journal of Travel Research*, 51, pp. 371–387.

Wieland, H., Polese, F., Vargo, S. L., & Lusch, R. F. (2012). Toward a service (eco)systems perspective on value creation. *International Journal of Service Science, Management, Engineering, and Technology*, 3, pp. 12–25.

Wolf, M. J. (1999). *The Entertainment Economy: How Mega-Media Forces Are Transforming Our Lives*, New York, Times Books, Random House.

Xiang, Z., & Gretzel, U. (2010). Role of social media in online travel information search. *Tourism Management*, 31, pp. 179–188.

Xiang, Z., Wang, D., O'leary, J. T., & Fesenmaier, D. R. (2014). Adapting to the Internet: Trends in travelers' use of the web for trip planning. *Journal of Travel Research*, 54(4), pp. 511–527.

Yovcheva, Z., Buhalis, D., & Gatzidis, C. (2013). Engineering augmented tourism experiences. In L. Cantoni & Z. Xiang (eds.) *Information and Communication Technologies in Tourism 2012*. Vienna, Springer, pp. 24–35.

2 Value co-destruction in service ecosystems

Findings from TripAdvisor

Marianna Sigala

Introduction

The co-creation of value through actors' interactions is widely established. However, most studies emphasize the positive aspects and outcomes of actors' interactions, while very few studies recognize the negative and dark side of value co-creation (Heidenreich et al., 2014; Chowdhury et al., 2016) that are usually hidden and include potential risks during co-creation (Prior & Marcos-Cuevas, 2016). Yet, it should not be taken for granted that actors' interactions always lead to mutual value co-creation, because actors have different (or conflicting) interests and representations of realities, that in turn influence their co-creation practices and understandings of value outcomes (Echeverri & Skålén, 2011). This one-sided research focus on value co-creation shapes a naïve and simplistic perception of the existence of harmonious actors' interactions and positive value co-creation outcomes (Ple & Chumpitaz-Caceres, 2010; Lindgreen et al., 2012). Therefore, research should also consider the phenomenological nature of value and the dynamic interplays amongst actors, which mean that value creation for one actor may mean value destruction for another actor.

During the last years, value co-destruction (VCD) (Ple & Chumpitaz-Caceres, 2010) has emerged as an important way to conceptualize the non-positive outcomes from actor-to-actor interactions. However, research does not provide clear understanding of the conceptualization and manifestation of VCD as well as of the actors' roles and engagement behaviors in interactive value formation, because past studies have primarily studied value co-creation from (Sigala, 2017): a dyadic B2C perspective that ignores the complex interactions amongst multiple actors taking place within service ecosystems (Lindgreen et al., 2012; Stieler et al., 2014; Chowdhury et al., 2016); and a customer-oriented approach that ignores the phenomenological conceptualization of value, as it fails to unravel how other interacting actors contribute to and perceive the outcomes of value co-creation (Prior & Marcos-Cuevas, 2016; Smith, 2013). As value formation is heavily determined by multiple actors interacting as an aggregate social entity, it has to be studied at two levels of aggregation (Vargo & Lusch, 2015): actor-to-actor; and service ecosystem.

To address these gaps, this study adopted an ecosystem approach for examining and understanding how multiple actors conceptualize and contribute to VCD. Due to lack of previous research and knowledge on the topic, an explorative case study was adopted by using TripAdvisor and its actors' ecosystem as an appropriate context to conduct this study. To achieve these aims, the chapter provides a theoretical underpinning and practical evidence about the conceptualization, drivers and actors' practices leading to VCD by reviewing the existing literature and collecting data from various TripAdvisor actors. The chapter also considers and analyzes the field and research in fake/inaccurate online reviews as a form of online VCD. The findings unravel: what value is co-destroyed (the actors' phenomenological interpretation of VCD); who destroys value; how actors co-destroy value (i.e. the actors' practices manifesting VCD); and why actors engage in VCD (i.e. the actors' drivers and the ecosystem factors leading and/or constraining the actors' VCD behavior). Finally, the practical and theoretical implications of the findings are discussed.

Conceptualization, occurrence and drivers of VCD

A small but increasing number of studies (Worthington & Durkin, 2012; Robertson et al., 2014; Gebauer et al., 2013; Stieler et al., 2014) show how actors participating in value co-creation can deliberately (dark side) and/or inadvertently (downside) destroy value in various online and offline contexts. Actors' intentions are found to determine whether VCD happens intentionally, unintentionally or accidentally, planned or unplanned, because actors may be aware or not aware of the outcomes of their value co-creation activities (Vartiainen & Tuunanen, 2016). Actors are also found to demonstrate passive or active opportunism (Ertimur & Venkatesh, 2010) and/or change from creative to destructive intentions or vice versa according to the success or failure of resource integration (Echeverri & Skålén, 2011). However, VCD is distinguished from service failure and product harm (i.e. value destruction), because it focuses on collaborations and interactions between actors rather than a one-way fault service delivery from the supplier to the customer (Prior & Marcos-Cuevas, 2016).

Plé & Cáceres (2010, p. 431) also acknowledge the interactional nature of VCD and consistent with Vargo & Lusch's (2008, p. 149) definition of value as "'an improvement in system well-being", they defined VCD as: "an interactional process between service systems that results in a decline in at least one of the systems' well-being, which: given the nature of a service system, can be individual or organizational"; and it is due to "misuse" by a system of its own resources or those of another system. Hence, VCD is seen as an interactional, subjectively interpreted process that occurs because of a lack of congruence in actors' expectations related to resource use and it results in diminished actors' well-being. Many other researchers have also adopted a resource and interactional approach for conceptualizing VCD as diminished well-being. Robertson et al. (2014) found that lack of appropriate resources in actors' exchanges can inhibit value creation and instead lead to reduced actors' well-being. Smith (2013) and Stieler et al. (2014) suggested that a loss of well-being resulting from resource losses and/or unmet value expectations is a key indicator of VCD, as the former contribute to negative emotional states causing psychological stress that in turn diminishes subjective well-being. McColl-Kennedy and Tombs (2011) conceptualized and explained VCD occurrence, not as a perceived loss of personal resources, but as a violation of personal needs by others. Echeverri and Skålén (2011) found that VCD happens collaboratively when there is incongruence of social practices elements (namely, procedures, under-standings and engagements) between customers and providers during the interac-tion process. These two last studies clearly recognize the interactional and actors' perspective dimension of VCD. Prior and Marcos-Cuevas (2016) also highlighted the resource-based and interactional nature of VCD, as they claimed that VCD occurs when customers develop perceptions of resource losses, due to two major reasons: a) goal prevention (actors' belief of their inability to achieve their desired outcomes from engaging in a collaborative process with other actors); and b) net resource deficits between the customers' perceived benefits and perceived costs from the interaction/collaboration.

Resources whose loss, lack, inappropriate use and/or mismatch during actors' interactions can lead to VCD are found to include (Smith, 2013; Ple et al., 2010): material (functional, tangible and/or intangible objects); financial (monetary costs); condition (e.g. social status); relational inputs (safety, credibility, security benefits); self (e.g. self-esteem, self-efficacy); social (e.g. peer support); "energies" (e.g. time, money and knowledge); and leisure (i.e. expected/anticipated experi-ence and intrinsic value such as fun, enjoyment) and hope (i.e. perceived ability to achieve something).

Overall, research has used a resource- and practice-based approach for concep-tualizing VCD as an actor's perceived diminished well-being occurring as a result of unmatched and/or unmet personal perceptions and expectations related to lack, (mis)-use, loss of, incongruence and/or unbalanced exchange of resources and/or of social practice elements taking place in actors' interactions. Consequently, the literature views VCD conceptualization and occurrence based on an interactional/ collaborative, phenomenological/inter-subjective and resource exchange perspective.

Fake online reviews: research insights and gaps

Both industry and consumers are increasingly becoming aware of potentially deceptive online reviews (Munzel, 2016; Luca & Zervas, 2016). By adopting a VCD perspective, research shows that fake reviews can be considered as a resource exchange and interacting process amongst actors that may create value (e.g. repu-tation, ability to charge higher prices) for one actor (e.g. a tourism supplier lobby-ing customers to write inaccurate positive reviews for them or negative reviews for competitors), but also destroy value for several other actors, such as: jeopardize the credibility and competitiveness of review websites as important information sources for consumers; mislead consumers' decision-making processes; endanger the reputation, image and sales potential of service providers; and destroy a valu-able source for firms willing to use the internet for gathering marketing intelli-gence. In other words, fake reviews can be considered as a social practice of interactive value co-formation through resources exchanges amongst actors, whose value outcomes are phenomenologically interpreted by each actor.

Despite the increasing importance and occurrence of online fake reviews in tourism (Sigala, 2017; Yoo & Gretzel, 2009; Luca, 2011; Munzel, 2016; Schuckert et al., 2016), research has primarily focused on examining the impact of online (fake) reviews on travellers' behavior and the firms'/destinations' performance variables (e.g. Filieri et al., 2015; Liu et al., 2015; Banerjee & Chua, 2016; Schuckert et al., 2015) ignoring the phenomenological interpretation of the occurrence and results of this social practice from various stakeholders' perspective. Moreover, research about reviews' fraud comes from computer science, psychology and computational linguistics aiming to develop algorithms and methodologies that can detect fake reviews (Feng et al., 2012; Akoglu et al., 2013), while very few studies explore online fake reviews from a social science approach. Thus, research is required to examine the phenomenon of fake online reviews from a value co-formation approach that considers its interpretation, occurrence and value results from an actors' perspective. Findings will provide useful results in determining proactive and customized strategies to address and prevent the occurrence of "fake" online reviews from the perspective of every actor involved.

Research methodology

Aims and data collection methods

The study aimed to address the role of actor subjectivity in VCD and the call for research to investigate VCD from all actors' perceptions within an ecosystem. The study also aimed to address the gaps related to the role of contextual factors, network dynamics and interrelations amongst the ecosystem actors that can influence value formation practices. Due to limited previous research and understanding of VCD from an ecosystem/multi-actor perspective, an exploratory, theory-building case study approach was adopted as an appropriate methodology for obtaining a deeper understanding of VCD from the perspective of each actor and generating new insights and knowledge about contemporary phenomena within real-life contexts (Yin, 2003, p. 13). In this vein, TripAdvisor was selected as an appropriate ecosystem to study VCD from a multiple actor perspective, because: its two-sided business model creates an ecosystem consisting of multiple actors, who are interconnected through different (and sometimes conflicting) value propositions; and although numerous publications discuss the value destruction caused by travellers writing fake and/or negative reviews, no study has considered the perceptions and behaviors of other actors towards this VCD process. Data were collected from various TripAdvisor's actors about their conceptualizations, assessments and behaviors in VCD as well as about the factors supporting and/or constraining them to engage in VCD practices. The sample of actors interviewed included and represented: 13 travellers, 17 tourism firms/destinations and eight of their employees, as well as three marketing companies. The type of TripAdvisor actors to be approached was based on anecdotal evidence and publications about the type of people involved in the TripAdvisor model. The number of actors being approached for an interview was stopped when additional interviews did not provide additional new data or access to other actors was not possible (i.e. the case of marketing companies).

A critical incident technique (CIT) was adopted for asking various TripAdvisor's actors to describe their salient past experiences of VCD occurred within the TripAdvisor ecosystem. CIT was previously used (e.g. Echeverri & Skålén, 2011), Stieler et al., 2014; Smith, 2013) as an appropriate method for investigating the phenomenological nature of VCD, because: critical incidents result in threats to personal goals or loss of well-being (Bacharach & Bamberger, 2007), which is the nature of VCD; and CIT requires respondents to tell a story about an experience they have had in order to gain understanding of the incident from the individual's perspective, taking into account cognitive, affective and behavioral factors (Chell, 2004). Similarly to studies examining value co-creation from a network perspective (Jaakkola & Hakanen, 2013; Chowdhury et al., 2016), the ARA (Actors – Resources – Activities) framework (Håkansson & Snehota, 1995) was also used as a conceptual basis for studying the actors' experiences and interpretations in VCD processes, because it allows to capture: which actor (who) is involved and how he/she interprets VCD; what causes VCD (i.e. resource approach); and how VCD happens (activities reflecting actors' engagement in VCD social practices).

Research context: TripAdvisor's ecosystem

Primary data were collected from actors participating in the TripAdvisor ecosystem. The latter was selected as an appropriate network context for this study, because its two-sided business model (B2C and B2B) represents an interesting ecosystem of various actors who are interconnected through different value propositions. Overall, TripAdvisor crowdsources reviews from travellers and travellers can use the platform for exchanging/reading reviews and interacting with each other (a free B2C model), but TripAdvisor provides this market intelligence and other services to tourism firms and marketing companies, so that they can develop their marketing and competitive strategies accordingly (a fee based B2B model). Figure 2.1 visualizes: the major actors participating in the TripAdvisor ecosystem; the major value propositions connecting actors; and the major resources exchanged amongst actors. Figure 2.1 visualizes TripAdvisor at the center of the ecosystem, as TripAdvisor is the focal and initiator actor of this ecosystem, and its business model includes value propositions for getting it connected with many actors. Moreover, the direct dyadic relations amongst TripAdvisor and its actors also spur a multiplicity of other (indirect via TripAdvisor) relations amongst the actors which in turn expand the ecosystem into a complex and dynamic network of actors' interrelations. For example, a relation between marketing firms and tourism firms (indirect via TripAdvisor) is developed (dotted lines in Figure 2.1), since marketing firms rely on content provided by TripAdvisor for gaining market intelligence, analyzing and using it for providing tourism firms with marketing services for a fee (e.g. online advertising, handling of customer feedback, search engine optimization, SEO, service improvement consulting). Similarly, travellers can form a relation with tourism firms and/or other travellers (indirect via TripAdvisor, dotted lines in Figure 2.1), since they can use TripAdvisor as a platform for providing their feedback to and interacting with tourism firms and/or other travellers. In practice, these indirect actors' interrelations reinforce the TripAdvisor's business model, because they strengthen the importance of its value propositions to its actors. In other words, the more customer reviews and travellers' interactions are posted online, the more value travellers get from using TripAdvisor in order to find and share travel content and peer support; as more and more travellers, travel content and market intelligence are collected on TripAdvisor, the more value tourism firms and marketing companies get from producing and promoting more and better personalized advertising and marketing content on TripAdvisor, which in turn attracts more travellers to read and share travel content on TripAdvisor and so on. This inter-connectivity but also inter-dependency of the value propositions and relations amongst all actors confirm the dynamic and complex network of the TripAdvisor's ecosystem.

Recently, TripAdvisor added some more actors into its ecosystem (highlighted red in Figure 2.1) including several online intermediaries (e.g. Hotels.com,

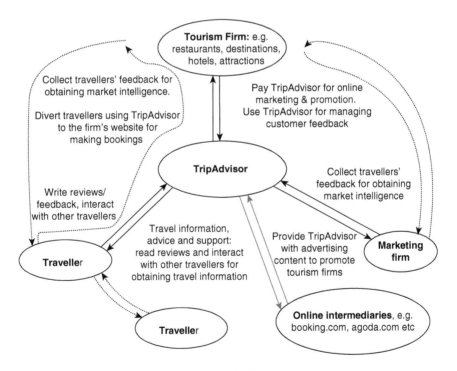

Figure 2.1 TripAdvisor ecosystem: actors and value propositions

Note: TripAdvisor is visualized in the center only because it is the primary actor enabling all other inter-actor interactions; however, the ecosystem can be visualized by placing any other actor in the center

booking.com, agoda.com, Qantas.com, expedia.com) in order to enable its users to also compare hotel prices across multiple online channels and facilitate bookings. As new actors are added in the ecosystem, actors are afforded with many new opportunities to get interconnected through new value propositions (e.g. marketing firms developing the tools and expertise for supporting the tourism firms to get distributed on TripAdvisor through online intermediaries). In other words, Figure 2.1 gives only a very simplistic representation of the TripAdvisor's ecosystem and its complex actors' interrelations that can dynamically and continuously develop.

However, the value and importance of TripAdvisor is not just based on the number of users and reviews, but also on the reliability of this information. The increasing awareness and occurrences of fake and/or inaccurate reviews concern not only TripAdvisor, but also all the tourism firms whose reputation and brand image is threaten by counterfeit and malicious reviews. The phenomenon of fake reviews has a severe impact on the sustainability of the TripAdvisor's business model, because it is not only the reality but even the suspected presence of fake reviews (Jeacle & Carter, 2011) that threatens the reliability of TripAdvisor and its interrelations with other actors. Consequently, TripAdvisor claims to undertake many measures for preventing and identifying such attempts of fraud (TripAdvisor, 2016) such as:

- Filtering of incoming reviews through sophisticated behavior modelling tools that can identify reviews with suspicious patterns
- A TripAdvisor fraud investigation team aiming to identify: optimization-hiring sites where users are paid to write reviews; and tourism firms using optimizing-hiring sites for boosting their popularity/rankings
- When hotels are detected to be getting fake positive reviews, TripAdvisor displays a red flag notice on the hotel stating this fact as well as drops the popularity ranking of this firm
- Tourism firms are allowed to reply to reviews as well as request for suspected fake reviews to be deleted
- TripAdvisor operates a crowdsourcing possibility asking all firms to report any suspected action and/or malicious actor

By informing but also engaging its actors to participate in the detection of fake reviews, TripAdvisor does not only want to delegate tasks to other actors. Instead, TripAdvisor also aims to highlight that the phenomenon of fake reviews can only be effectively managed and prevented through the development of a culture of shared action and responsibility amongst its ecosystem actors.

Analysis and discussion of the findings

The findings provide useful insights and understandings about the nature, processes and factors supporting the occurrence of VCD. Specifically, findings reveal information about: who (actor) is involved with VCD; what VCD means for each actor; how VCD happens (engagement social practices per actor leading to VCD); and the contextual factors and rivers leading actors to engage in VCD practices.

Actors engaging in VCD: their motivations and contextual factors supporting the actors' engagement in VCD (who and why engage in VCD)

All the interviewed actors perceived VCD within the TripAdvisor context as writing fake or inaccurate reviews, which can then result in lower or bad value for another actor(s). All interviewees reported that travellers are the most obvious actors engaged in VCD either intentionally (e.g. retaliate for bad service) or unintentionally (e.g. because customers have wrong or unreasonable service expectations and understandings). Few interviewees (n = 8) also reported that VCD is also when an actor (i.e. firm, traveller or TripAdvisor) does not do something in order to correct a fake review of which that he/she might be aware.

The findings also revealed that VCD in an ecosystem can derive from all its "known" and "unknown suspects" actors (e.g. travellers, marketing agencies, tourism firms/destinations, unknown blackmailers) as well as from anonymous users and/or actors who create fake profiles for uploading fake or inaccurate reviews. The majority of the interviewees recognized that the following contextual factors increase the actors' tendency to participate in VCD, and this is what several actors admitted to have done, i.e. create a fake or anonymous profile for uploading fake or inaccurate reviews: the possibility to "cover" or "hide" one's identity in an online environment; the lack of policing or systems to identify and punish actors engaging in VCD; and the technical features of TripAdvisor not requiring someone to have made a booking for sharing an online review.

Not all of the interviewed actors gave examples to show that they were "aware" of all other potential actors that could be engaged in VCD. Because of the existence of these unknown suspects and the fact that many actors are not aware of their existence and practices, few websites have emerged (www.TripAdvisor-warning.com and www.TripAdvisorwatch.wordpress.com) with the purpose to create awareness about the former by sharing information and/or allowing actors (i.e. travellers and firms) to share and report their experiences of VCD (e.g. blackmailing cases).

Table 2.1 summarizes the findings about the types of actors reported and/or found to engage in VCD (based on other actors' declarations). The majority of the interviewed actors reported that they believed that more than 40% of online reviews on TripAdvisor are fake or inaccurate.

Findings also showed that VCD is implemented by actions of individual actors, but also by concerted and orchestrated synergy and collaborative actions amongst many actors. For example, three travellers declared that in one instance they have asked from their friends' network to go online and write a fake negative review about a firm with which they had been dissatisfied. Another hotelier mentioned

Table 2.1 Actors engagement practices in VCD, resources and motivations for engaging in VCD

ACTORS	MOTIVATION, ENGAGEMENT PRACTICE, RESOURCES
Known actors	
Travellers	• Dissatisfaction with service standards and/or the process of addressing their complaint or service failure and travellers' willingness to: help others to avoid going to the firm; and/or retaliate/punish the firm • Travellers writing fake or inaccurate reviews because they are not aware of service standards and/or have unreasonable and/or wrong service expectations • Travellers reading fake or inaccurate reviews and not replying – posting online to provide evidence that these reviews are not true • Firms reported that customers were threatening that they were going to write a negative review about them, if the firm would not satisfy their demands (i.e. upgrade, discount, free services) • Travellers being rewarded (free services, upgrades, discounts) for writing fake or inaccurate reviews for firms • Travellers (called travel activists by two interviewees) posting online fake – inaccurate reviews for showing to everyone that the "system" has bugs, i.e. the TripAdvisor platform has technical problems allowing fake/inaccurate reviews in order to "help" others understand that they should not totally trust TripAdvisor and to increase their self-esteem, self-satisfaction and pride.
Tourism firms/ destinations and their competitors	• Firms/destinations writing negative reviews for their competitors • Firms/destinations writing positive reviews about themselves for improving their online ratings, image and replying to reviews in a "polite" appropriate way (e.g. claiming that they have improved processes although this is not true)
TripAdvisor	• TripAdvisor being perceived by the majority of the actors not to take corrective and proactive sufficient action to address the phenomenon of fake or inaccurate reviews
Unknown suspects/actors	

Marketing companies (some interviewees called them review farms)	• Marketing companies paid by tourism firms to write fake/ inaccurate reviews and online content in order to:
	  • improve the firms' ranking and image in online customer review websites
	  • improve the SEO of firms
	  • reply in an appropriate but fake way to online customer reviews on behalf of their firms (client)

Firm employees	• Employees blackmailed, rewarded, motivated or demanded by their firms (i.e. loose their job, get a bonus) to write fake – inaccurate positive reviews for their employee • Employees who wrote fake replies to online reviews in order to increase the hotels' ranking, influence online hotel impressions and show that they are doing their job well (i.e. in terms of replying to online reviews, providing good service standards and/ or learning from complaints and improving business practice)
Unknown blackmailers	• An hotelier shared this online published story: hoteliers blackmailed to pay a bride to an unknown person in order to receive positive reviews and avoid getting negative reviews (http://tripadvisor-warning.com/tripadvisor-accepts-bribes

about a case that was published online (BBC News, 2013) whereby a group of users created a fictional restaurant in Brixham and by writing numerous extremely positive reviews, they placed this property amongst the best in the TripAdvisor's rankings. The latter finding also highlights how the characteristics and affordances of social networks can support and empower individual actors to collaborate for engaging in VCD.

The findings also confirmed that VCD should also be perceived as a phenomenological and socially constructed term, as it is evaluated within the context and idiosyncrasy of every actor. Findings providing evidence of the phenomenological and socially constructed conceptualization of VCD include: interviewees reported that by creating fake profiles and writing positive reviews for hotels, marketing agencies generate value for themselves (hotels pay them to write reviews, value-in-exchange), the hotels and the TripAdvisor (as more content is provided in the platform reflecting web traffic and increasing the value-in-exchange of the brand TripAdvisor), but they destroy value for the travellers (biased in their travel decisions). Similarly, "travel" activists writing fake reviews on TripAdvisor create value for themselves (i.e. take power, control and feel proud of themselves that they unraveled the vulnerability of the TripAdvisor system and helped others to understand not to trust TripAdvisor), but they destroy value for the travellers, TripAdvisor (decrease in brand name and value-in-exchange) and market agencies (who in the long-term may lose their business, as no firm will be willing to pay them to write fake reviews if everyone knows that online reviews are fake and should not be trusted).

In addition, the characteristics of the online environment and platform (i.e. anonymity and lack of rules, systems policing and punishing VCD), the following ecosystem network effects amongst actors were also found to motivate actors to engage in VCD: the actors' perceptions that other actors are engaged in VCD (e.g. hoteliers writing positive reviews for their properties because they believed that their competitors are writing positive reviews for their properties anyway or because they thought that they are under attack by fake negative reviews and wanted to compensate for the latter). In this vein, VCD was perceived as a retaliation to others' perceived activity (which might or not might be taking place) and as a value co-creation and not a value co-destruction activity (i.e. protecting oneself, getting justice). This finding again confirms the phenomenological nature and understanding of VCD and its occurrence based on actors' perceptions and interpretations. The findings also show that VCD occurs not only when actors mis-use social practices but also when they have a mis-match and mis- or wrong understanding of other actors' engagement in social practices. Moreover, the impact of these perceptions to drive actors to engage in VCD can lead to perpetual exchanges of VCD processes amongst the ecosystem actors, and in the long-term this "accidental" or "intentional" misuse may become formalized and over time become intentional use. Thus, the findings show as well that deterrence and stop of VCD is not just a technical or legislative issue, but a socially constructed and determined problem as well. Future research should thus investigate the normalization/routinization process of VCD processes and how one can influence and re-direct such social practices from VCD to value co-creation.

Actors' interactions and engagements in VCD (what and how value is co-destroyed)

Findings in Table 2.1 also provide examples and insight into the social practices in which actors engage and co-destroy value. The findings also reveal that VCD is an interactional, resource exchange process amongst actors whereby resources are exchanged for motivating and driving VCD. In this vein, findings confirm the interactional and resource-based perspective of VCD.

Resources being exchanged for motivating and driving VCD were found to include all type of previously stated resources, i.e.: material (free services, career advancement); financial (discounts, marketing fees, bonuses); condition (e.g. social status, pride); relational inputs (self-protection and self-security); self (e.g. self-esteem, self-efficacy, self-benefit); social (e.g. peer support, provide common benefit altruists motives); "energies" (e.g. time, money and knowledge); and lei-sure (i.e. expected/anticipated experience and intrinsic value such as fun, enjoy-ment) and hope (i.e. perceived ability to achieve something). Findings show that it is not only the loss, lack or mis-use of resources causing VCD but also the actors' perceptions of not achieving or being allowed to achieve the expected resources (i.e. customers not getting sufficient service for the money paid, firms not able to protect their online image/reputation) as well as their perceptions that their per-sonal needs and benefits are violated (firms' perceptions that competitors act against their benefits) (Smith, 2013; Ple et al., 2010). Similar to previous studies, the findings confirmed that the following factors can lead actors to engage in co-destruction: expectations for resource achievement – gain, inability to use resources, lack of information/resources, disagreement – conflict of value proposi-tions amongst actors, perception of unfairness in resource exchanges, service dissatisfaction.

These findings confirm the theory explaining the occurrence of VCD as a resource exchange interaction process amongst actors and its conceptualization as loss of well-being (financial, psychological, physical, social) due to loss, mis-use and lack of achievement of expected resources. The interactional approach of VCD is based on the inter-dependencies and value proposition (resource exchanges) linking the ecosystem actors together. Moreover, the findings also show how the inter-dependencies of the value propositions connecting the various actors of an ecosystem (i.e. the business model of one depends on the business model of the other) may reinforce, motivate and support the continuation of VCD practices (repercussions circle effects, review farms producing fake reviews for a fee, Tri-pAdvisor benefits as more content is created online to drive more online traffic, firms writing fake reviews to compensate for this competitive disadvantage in relation to competitors having more reviews etc.). This repercussion and reproduc-tion of value co-destruction activities – practices may ultimately be normalized and routinized and become intentional actions.

Findings show that actors have also a phenomenological interpretation of the time horizon of well-being and trade-off of resource exchanges in VCD processes. For example, some travel activists also claimed that what they do also creates value for TripAdvisor, because by identifying the system bugs, TripAdvisor can further improve its platform and value proposition in the future and so, travellers can also benefit in the long-term by having a more reliable platform (although they lose short-term by trusting and planning trips based on fake reviews). Hence, the findings revealed that value formation (co-creation and co-destruction) processes occur because of the actors' understandings of the long-term value and well-being creation and implications and the short-term vs. long-term trade-offs and dynamics on value-in-exchange (the money one system gives to the other for obtaining its value proposition).

Findings also revealed cases of actors using resources intentionally and planned for lobbying or pressing other actors to engage in VCD (e.g. restaurants providing free drinks to customers and hoteliers pressing their employees in order to write positive reviews for them, travellers threatening hotels with negative evaluation on TripAdvisor unless they are upgraded or compensated). Thus, the findings add to the field that VCD within ecosystems can happen not only accidentally (travellers not knowing the hotel star system and evaluating hotels inaccurate) or intentionally, but it can also be manipulated and negatively imposed from one actor to another by mis-using the resources and configurations (actors' inter-dependencies) of the ecosystem (platform). Thus, findings reveal that actors use VCD as a way to develop a value proposition and a "service" that they can use as a resource and value-in-exchange in order to link with other actors in a service ecosystem setting. In other words, the findings also confirm that VCD as a resource-based approach does not only pre-exist but it is being formed through actors' interactions.

Conclusions and implications for future research

The study contributes to research that has neglected the dark side of value co-creation, namely VCD. It confirms our understanding of VCD as an interactional, resource based and phenomenological concept and phenomenon, but it also expands it because:

- It provides insights into the concept and occurrence of VCD from an eco-system multi-actor approach and not a dyadic actor-to-actor approach (as adopted by previous research); findings show that VCD is not the opposite of value-co-creation and a zero-sum game. Within a service ecosystem, value co-creation and VCD can simultaneously co-exist, as value creation for one actor can be VCD for another actor. Indeed, the findings revealed that it is the interconnections and value propositions amongst the various actors that may also perpetuate and drive the continuation of VCD.
- VCD does not occur as a result of exchanges, losses, lack, mis-use or not achieving resources. VCD can also become a resource in itself for being exchanged and traded amongst actors (e.g. actors threatening other actors that they will engage in VCD unless paid money)
- The phenomenological nature of VCD means that the same social practices for one actor may be interpreted as value creation by one actor and VCD by another actor. VCD is a social practice driven by actors' perceptions of

value, benefits and understandings of practice elements such as, actors' engagement in procedures. It is the actors' perceptions (which may be true, false or even virtual) that drive and motivate their engagement in social practices of value formation as well as interpret the result of co-creation practices.

- The phenomenological nature of VCD also means that actors have a long-term and not only short-term understanding of resources and trade-offs
- The context of VCD (online anonymous and not easily regulated environment) motivates and fosters VCD
- VCD can be not only an active but also a passive social practice
- VCD can be (un)intentional, (un)planned and/or accidentally occurring social practice

Thus, overall, VCD is not just a technical but also a social practice problem whose deterrence requires customized action and measures that address the perceptions and actions of each actor engaged in value formation. One-size-fits all approach is not an appropriate strategy to address VCD specifically within dynamic and multi-actor ecosystems. Future research should be conducted in order to better understand: the short-term value vs. long-term value dynamics and trade-offs of value formation activities that actors perceive and the way they trade them off; whether and how accidental misuse and VCD (i.e. wrong or false perceptions) become formalized over time to become intentional and routine – expected use of resources; and VCD processes at various levels (individual micro-level and community macro-level).

References

Akoglu, L., Chandy, R., & Faloutsos, C. (2013). Opinion fraud detection in online reviews by network effects. *ICWSM*, 13, pp. 2–11.

Bacharach, S. B., & Bamberger, P. A. (2007). 9/11 and New York City firefighters' post hoc unit support and control climates: A context theory of the consequences of involvement in traumatic work-related events. *Academy of Management Journal*, 50(4), pp. 849–868.

Banerjee, S., & Chua, A. Y. (2016). In search of patterns among travellers' hotel ratings in TripAdvisor. *Tourism Management*, 53, pp. 125–131.

BBC News. (2013). TripAdvisor removes fake Brixham restaurant Oscar's. Available at: www.bbc.com/news/uk-england-devon-23504081 [Accessed 17 August 2015].

Chell, E. (2004). Critical incident technique. In C. Cassell & G. Symon (eds.) *Essential Guide to Qualitative Methods in Organizational Research*, London, Sage publications, pp. 45–60.

Chowdhury, I. N., Gruber, T., & Zolkiewski, J. (2016). Every cloud has a silver lining: Exploring the dark side of value co-creation in B2B service networks. *Industrial Marketing Management*, 55, pp. 97–109.

Echeverri, P., & Skålén, P. (2011). Co-creation and co-destruction: A practice-theory based study of interactive value formation. *Marketing Theory*, 11(3), pp. 351–373.

Ertimur, B., & Venkatesh, A. (2010). Opportunism in co-production: Implications for value co-creation. *Australasian Marketing Journal*, 18(4), pp. 256–263.

Feng, S., Xing, L., Gogar, A., & Choi, Y. (2012). Distributional footprints of deceptive product reviews. *ICWSM*, 12, pp. 98–105.

Filieri, R., Alguezaui, S., & McLeay, F. (2015). Why do travelers trust TripAdvisor? Antecedents of trust towards consumer-generated media and its influence on recommendation adoption and word of mouth. *Tourism Management*, 51, pp. 174–185.

Gebauer, J., Fuller, J., & Pezzei, R. (2013). The dark and the bright side of co-creation: Triggers of member behavior in online innovation communities. *Journal of Business Research*, 66, pp. 1516–1527.

Håkansson, H., & Snehota, I. (1995). *Developing Relationships in Business Networks*, London, Routledge.

Heidenreich, S., Wittkowski, K., Handrich, M., & Falk, T. (2014). The dark side of customer co-creation: Exploring the consequences of failed co-created services. *Journal of the Academy of Marketing Science*, 43(3), pp. 1–18.

Jaakkola, E., & Hakanen, T. (2013). Value co-creation in solution networks. *Industrial Marketing Management*, 42(1), pp. 47–58.

Jeacle, I., & Carter, C. (2011). In TripAdvisor we trust: Rankings, calculative regimes and abstract systems. *Accounting, Organizations and Society*, 36(4), pp. 293–309.

Lindgreen, A., Hingley, M. K., Grant, D. B., & Morgan, R. E. (2012). Value in business and industrial marketing: Past, present, and future. *Industrial Marketing Management*, 41(1), pp. 207–214.

Liu, B., Pennington-Gray, L., Donohoe, H., & Omodior, O. (2015). New York city bed bug crisis as framed by tourists on TripAdvisor. *Tourism Analysis*, 20(2), pp. 243–250.

Luca, M. (2011). Reviews, Reputation, and Revenue: The Case of Yelp.com. Harvard Business School NOM Unit Working Paper (12–016), NY, USA.

Luca, M., & Zervas, G. (2016). Fake it till you make it: Reputation, competition, and Yelp review fraud. *Management Science*, 62(12), pp. 3412–3427.

McColl-Kennedy, J. R., & Tombs, A. (2011). When customer value co-creation diminishes value for other customers deliberately or inadvertently. Naples Forum on Service-Service Dominant logic, network & system theory and service science: integrating three perspectives for a new service agenda, Capri, Italy. 14th–17th June.

Munzel, A. (2016). Assisting consumers in detecting fake reviews: The role of identity information disclosure and consensus. *Journal of Retailing and Consumer Services*, 32, pp. 96–108.

Ple, L., & Chumpitaz Caceres, R. (2010). Not always co-creation: Introducing interactional co-destruction of value in service-dominant logic. *Journal of Services Marketing* 24(6), pp. 430–437.

Prior, D. D., & Marcos-Cuevas, J. (2016). Value co-destruction in interfirm relationships: The impact of actor engagement styles. *Marketing Theory*, 16(4), pp. 533–552.

Robertson, N., Polonsky, M., & McQuilken, L. (2014). Are my symptoms serious Dr Google? A resource-based typology of value co-destruction in online self-diagnosis. *Australasian Marketing Journal (AMJ)*, 22(3), pp. 246–256.

Schuckert, M., Liu, X., & Law, R. (2015). Hospitality and tourism online reviews: Recent trends and future directions. *Journal of Travel & Tourism Marketing*, 32(5), pp. 608–621.

Schuckert, M., Liu, X., & Law, R. (2016). Insights into suspicious online ratings: Direct evidence from TripAdvisor. *Asia Pacific Journal of Tourism Research*, 21(3), pp. 259–272.

Sigala, M. (2017). How "bad" are you? Justification and normalisation of online deviant customer behaviour. In Stangl, Brigitte et al., (eds.), *Information and Communication Technologies in Tourism 2017*. Springer, Cham, pp. 607–622.

Smith, A. (2013). The value co-destruction process: A customer resource perspective. *European Journal of Marketing*, 47(11–12), pp. 1889–1909.

Stieler, M., Weismann, F., & Germelmann, C. C. (2014). Co-destruction of value by spectators: The case of silent protests. *European Sport Management Quarterly*, 14(1), pp. 72–86.

www.tripadvisor.com [Accessed 23 March 2016].

Vargo, S. L., & Lusch, R. F. (2008). Service-dominant logic: Continuing the evolution. *Journal of the Academy of Marketing Science*, 36(1), pp. 1–10.

Vargo, S. L., & Lusch, R. F. (2015). Institutions and axioms: An extension and update of service-dominant logic. *Journal of the Academy of Marketing Science*, 44(1), pp. 5–23.

Vartiainen, T., & Tuunanen, T. (2016, January). Value co-creation and co-destruction in an IS artifact: Contradictions of geocaching. In *2016 49th Hawaii International Conference on System Sciences (HICSS)*. IEEE, pp. 1266–1275.

Worthington, S., & Durkin, M. (2012). Co-destruction of value in context: Cases from retail banking. *The Marketing Review*, 12(3), pp. 291–307.

Yin, R. K. (Ed.). (2003). *Case Study Research: Design and Methods* (Vol. 5), London, Sage.

Yoo, K. H., & Gretzel, U. (2009). Comparison of deceptive and truthful travel reviews. In *Information and Communication Technologies in Tourism 2009 Proceedings of the International Conference in Amsterdam, The Netherlands, 2009*, Vienna, Springer-Verlag, pp. 37–47.

3   Tourist-driven innovations in social media

An opportunity for tourism organizations

Astrid Dickinger and Lidija Lalicic

Introduction

The tourist journey is a dynamic chain of various actors and services provided (Aldebert et al., 2011; Sundbo et al., 2010). Tourists have different touchpoints throughout their journey of travelling, such as the flight experience, overnight stays and visiting a site (Zomerdijk & Voss, 2009). In general, services present many customers touchpoints which act as discrete sub-experiences (Berry et al., 2006). The introduction of Information and Communication Technologies (ICT) increased the numbers of touchpoints, actors and network of the tourist experience (Berry et al., 2006; Libai et al., 2010; Lamsfus et al., 2014). On the one hand, the technological developments allow for higher cross-over channel experiences of these touchpoints. On the other hand, the touchpoints can be separated into smaller steps and managed on a more individual level. In fact, the tourist experience can be seen as interrelated small steps leading to optimal touchpoints building the overall experience. Therefore, the concept of touchpoints represents what actually happens from the customer point of view and thus, places the customer at the heart of the service design (Zomerdijk & Voss, 2009). Several authors have been referring to the concept of "co-creation" where the customer together with the service provider creates and optimizes a specific touchpoint (Vargo & Lusch, 2004). In a setting such as tourism the concept of co-creation has been used to efficiently manage the tangible aspects and better understand how consumers interact with a destination.

However, the availability of ICT creates a high level of consumer independence, power and creativity to manage these touchpoints (i.e. Labrecque et al., 2013; Couture et al., 2015; Dickinson et al., 2014). Consumers are becoming independent players acting, working and interacting through platforms such as TripAdvisor, Everplaces and Yelp. Hence, peer-to-peer networks, acting as social hubs where peers meet to exchange knowledge related to tourists' experiences, slowly start to dominate the information-source market in tourism. On top of that, the functionalities of ICT-related devices, such as smartphones and mobile travel communities (apps), support tourists to act as self-regulating creative actors on the go continuously linked to social media. Tourists are, thus, managing their own touchpoints where a shift from co-creation to user-driven creation is emerging. Von

Hippel and Katz (2002) refer to user-driven innovation as a way consumers modify, adapt and create products and/or services to satisfy their own needs. Clearly, in tourism this trend is becoming more evident. Hjalager and Nordin (2011) show how companies can take advantage of the internet to understand this phenomenon in tourism. Werthnes and Klein (1999) illustrated how the tourism industry operates as a network and its effect on the actors. Furthermore, there is continuous research on the usage of social media used by tourists and tourism businesses.

Nevertheless, the concept of user-driven innovation enhanced by ICT in tourism is hardly integrated, illustrated and/or tested. Firms should realize that the ideas from users and their combination with tourism experiences are crucial inputs for their innovation strategies (Sundbo et al., 2010). Social media offers tourism organizations untapped opportunities provided by innovative customers, and helps them to understand the innovation diffusion process among tourists. Lastly, social media sheds light on user-driven innovation and serves as an integral part of the tourism experience network. Hence, this paper structures and exemplifies user-driven innovations within the experience network communicated and accumulated through the means of social media. The results provide a holistic understanding of the benefits enterprises can gain through user-driven innovations. This paper aims to identify the concept of user-driven innovation in tourism and to provide recommendations for marketers managing this concept for their own benefit.

Tourist-driven innovations in an experience network

The tourist experience consists of a system of customer interactions with service personnel, the servicescape and other customers. Van der Duim (2007) refers to tourismscape, which is similar to servicescape that brings together people, organizations, objects, technologies and spaces for tourists (Van der Duim, 2007). Stickdorn and Frischhut (2012) refer to an ecosystem of experiences consisting of several layers. Therefore, often tourism is considered a hybrid collective in perceptual movement, forming a network including actors (e.g. customers and service providers), non-human entities (e.g. restaurants), and stakeholder interactions (Paget et al., 2010). Likewise, the tourism industry can be perceived as a knowledge and information intensive sector which is sensitive to the impact of new technologies for knowledge creation, and alters the relationship dynamics among actors (Larsen et al., 2007). The new technologies allow, especially consumers, to act and interact with the tourismscape on a more self-sufficient manner. Neuhofer et al. (2013) furthermore indicate the role of technology mediating the tourist experience. Tussyadiah and Fesenmaier (2009) show how videos positively mediate tourists' experiences. Hence, technologies allow tourists to find new ways to combine different service experience elements and engage in forms of cooperation (i.e. direct and informal user-to-user communities) (Von Hippel, 2007). The ideas, needs and actions derive directly from customers themselves to enhance their travel experiences (Hjalager and Nordin, 2011).

A typical characteristic of user-driven innovators is the modification and development of products without direct collaboration or support of the service provider

(Von Hippel, 2005). Often the ingredients to create user-driven experiences are provided by the service provider. Services that firms provide can act as ingredients for consumers to create their own unique experiences (Sundbo et al., 2010). Consumers are able to fulfill their needs of interacting with the service rather than how providers aim to fulfill customers' needs (Fuglsang et al., 2011). As a result, tourists reach higher levels of satisfaction and, furthermore, they enjoy the creative problem-solving process (Von Hippel et al., 2011; Von Hippel, 2005). Consumers steering their own innovation work without firms' direct support, are highly motivated, often reveal their innovation and the diffusion is low cost, easy and competitive with commercial production and distribution (Von Hippel, 2007). The easiness and speed of ICT effectively increases the numbers of user-driven innovations in tourism. Generally, user-driven innovations enabled by social media can take various forms. One example is providing feedback and support to create entirely new products, services and systems (Fuglsang et al., 2011). Given the unique environment of tourism, the concept of *tourist-driven innovation* is introduced. Tourist-driven innovation can be defined as a form of innovation emerging from tourists needs, supported and enhanced by the different forms of ICT-related devices and the peer-to-peer network effects. Unlike products and many other services-focused industries, tourism is produced in a network of businesses and service providers. Hence, the format of tourist-driven innovation can occur on multiple moments through various available social media platforms. Especially in tourism where a high number of small touchpoints are a part of the overall customer journey, the concept of tourist-driven innovation dominates throughout. Thus, social media are the focus of tourist-driven innovation in this paper; see Figure 3.1 for an illustration.

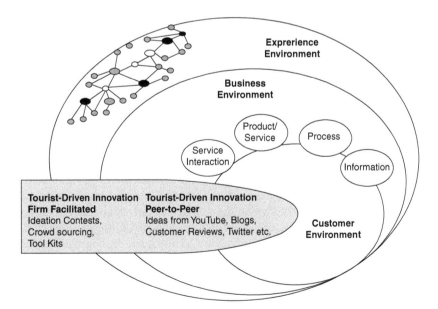

Figure 3.1 Tourist-driven experience network enabled by social media

However, there is no explicit theory in tourism research illustrating the concept of tourist-driven innovation enhanced by social media as a part of the experience network. Therefore, a conceptual framework provided in this chapter offers companies a simple, yet effective, system to find ways to tap tourist-driven innovations. Employing social media, the goal is to identify what tourists are suggesting to companies and to other peers. The systematic orientation towards users' external ideas and their experiences is crucial for innovation in this field (Sundbo et al., 2010). The framework distinguishes the types of innovation environments, which are the experience environment where the tourist experience is created, the business environment where individual firms create a component of the experience, and the customer environment where customers co-create the experience. Tourist-driven innovation capacity also exists in the latter. Tourist-driven innovations can influence any of these environment layers. The framework breaks down the creative capacity of individual customers to innovate in different areas of the business environment such as the product/service, process, service interaction and information. These areas are part of the business environment where firms create their products. The conceptual framework hereby highlights the dynamic movement of the tourism industry facilitated by different forms of digital media (see Figure 3.2 for an overview).

The experience environment

As discussed before, tourists operate in a dense network. The tourism's network environment includes manifold service providers such as transport (e.g. airlines, trains, buses) accommodation (e.g. hotels, camping, hostels), sights, activities, destination marketing organizations, cultural offers and the local community. By definition, the tourists are always co-creators of value and part of the experience network (gray-shaded area in Figure 3.1). The co-creation occurs, firstly, through the tourist's interaction with all elements in the experience network, and, secondly, through the tourist as part of the network impacting the other tourists' experiences. For the online world, Werthnes and Klein (1999) suggest an interconnected view of technology, service providers and customers. Furthermore, social media affects the linearity and direction of information and purchase flow from service providers to customers. As the figure depicts, the experience network consists of customers (shaded gray in Figure 3.1), ICT (white in Figure 3.1), service providers and the local community (both in black in Figure 3.1). Prahalad and Ramaswamy (2003) propose a model of experience innovation networks. These experience networks display the non-sequential, nonlinear interactions between businesses, customers, and institutions (Prahalad & Ramaswamy, 2003). Consequently, literature addressing tourism as a system, dealing with constant change and activity, introduces the sectorial system of innovation production, where change activates the co-evolution of elements of the tourist experience (Malerba, 2001). The availability of social media strengthens this change and production of innovations, which also explains plausibly the rise of tourist-driven innovations in the experience environment.

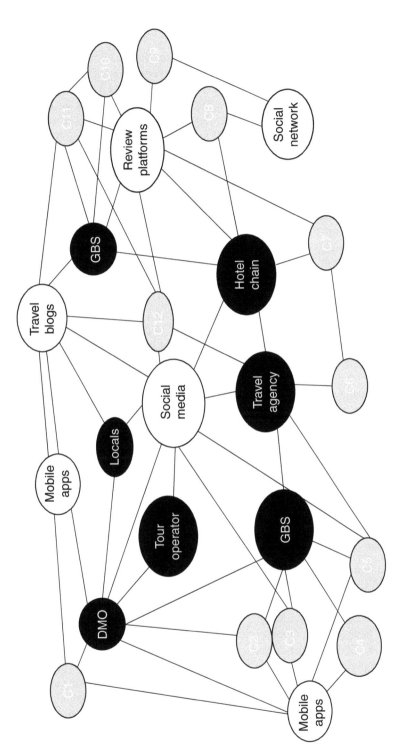

Figure 3.2 Interconnected tourism innovation network

Business environment

The business environment is an integrated element of the model representing the level where the firms create the experience and the innovation area's location. To date little research exists on innovation in tourism. Prior studies focus on the innovativeness of accommodation businesses (Peters & Pikkemaat, 2005), destination marketing organizations (Zach, 2012) and conceptual work on the innovativeness of tourism (Hjalager, 2002, 2015). Radical innovation rarely is discussed in tourism literature; instead, studies tend to address small changes in existing structures (Zach, 2012; Sundbo et al., 2007). Innovations in tourism often originate from individual players in this networked service economy (e.g. airlines) (Brooker & Joppe, 2013). However, innovative experience design likely will become a successful firm's core capability in tourism and hospitality because competitors offer close substitutes (Su, 2011). The literature highlights product/service innovations based on modifications, processes, organizational structures, methods and management (Gallouj, 1998). Schumpeter (1939) distinguishes between five different types of innovation: product, methods of production, way of supply, markets and new business models. Innovations in the experience economy tourism are predominant at the product level (70.7%), process level (19.2%) and in marketing (9.2%) (Aldebert et al., 2011; Sundbo et al., 2010). Other authors identify product or service innovation, process innovations and marketing innovations as the three innovation types relevant for an experience network (Hjalager, 2010; Sundbo et al., 2010).

For the conceptual framework at hand, the relevant innovation types are product/service, process, service interaction and information. Products/services comprise the core of the tourism experience. The processes and service interactions are vital in co-production settings such as tourism. Finally, information regards the interactive nature of the tourism experiences and the advances in ICT. Not surprisingly, this area is the one completing the framework. Social software demonstrates information's role in supporting the innovation process (Mayer, 1997). Accordingly, suggestions to harvest social media for innovations are proposed below.

Customer environment and the tourist as innovator

The nested part of the model refers to the customer environment where tourist-driven innovations emerge. User innovation communities are not a new phenomenon (Franke & Shah, 2003; Von Hippel, 1998); however, ICT advances new ways to interact, and harvest, user ideas. The marketing and business literature investigates users, as innovation drivers or innovators (Von Hippel, 1998; Franke et al., 2010; Lüthje, 2004). Tourist-driven innovation in this conceptual framework represents an independent workforce driven by tourists. Nevertheless, supporting tourist-driven innovation is the perception that tourist-driven firms have higher innovation capabilities and, thus, generate more innovative ideas. Further, tourist-driven innovations provide a higher degree of novelty and customer benefit, while the feasibility of the new product is lower (Schreier et al., 2012). In order to increase the feasibility of tourist-driven innovation, firms can support them with toolkits and communities. Subsequently, this study introduces the concept of Tourist-Driven Firm Facilitated Innovation (TDFF). In addition, ICT also enables platforms that are facilitated and initiated by peers referred to as Tourist-Driven Peer-To-Peer Innovation (TDPP).

Tourist-Driven Firm Facilitated Innovation (TDFF)

The literature suggests different approaches to user-driven innovation. One stream compares lead-users as innovators to conventionally developed products (Lilien et al., 2002). Expert users create ideas for product modification or product innovation. A more collaborative approach is crowdsourcing. In crowdsourcing the idea generation develops through interactions between a very large group (the crowd). Sometimes this process happens as a competition between users who self-select and contribute (Poetz and Schreier, 2012). The group activated through crowdsourcing is obviously much richer and bigger than the lead-user approach. Mass-customization through toolkits allows all users to self-design their products (Franke et al., 2010). The above-mentioned concepts assume that customers innovate in environments such as communities or toolkits for user innovation which are at least partly facilitated by the firm.

Firms use TDFF innovations to improve their processes, products/service, service interaction and information (see Figure 3.1). Convenient tools such as idea contests, crowdsourcing and toolkits gather knowledge for this innovation type. The firms delivering components of the experience benefit by offering new forms of service interaction, product/service, processes and information. The following examples illustrate how firms can facilitate tourist-driven innovations in different solution spaces. This allows for systematic integration into the firms' business environment (see Table 3.1 for examples).

Product

In this setting a firm provides an environment for tourists to innovate. For example, a hotel uses Second Life to develop new products and services. The idea is to observe how the avatars use the hotel, which furniture they use and what they dislike as a repository of ideas for product innovation (Kohler et al., 2008). Electronic guestbooks offer customers a platform to provide innovative ideas similar to review pages. However, firms control their guestbooks and the risk of negative comments is lower (Hjalager & Nordin, 2011). Tourism Flanders organizes annual festivals. To create the ultimate festival destination, they initiate a competition to engage music blogging communities, requesting the bloggers to share their thoughts and ideas as valuable information to create the optimal festival experience (D'Haen, 2014). Considering that Flanders wants to increase awareness, stimulate conversation, inspire people and activatie the brand, these competitions also serve as examples for information innovation.

Process

The use of mobile technology allows companies to track and extract knowledge from tourists about consumption and their activities, relevant to space and time movement at the destination (Sundbo et al., 2010). The data collection derives from mobile technology and serves as valuable input for process innovation. An example is the destination Åre equipping tourists with GPS technology to learn from their movements (Hjalager & Nordin, 2011).

Service interaction

The Catalan Tourist Board called for a photo competition on Instagram, a photo-sharing platform. Travellers and locals uploaded their photos of Catalonia's distinct and outstanding sights and viewpoints. This contest had various effects. Tourists showed their images of Catalonia, the tourism organization learned what visitors find special about the destination and interacted with tourists. Similarly, the Viennese tourist board ran a video competition on YouTube; local people uploaded videos of their perfect day in Vienna.

Information

Companies use this area most frequently to innovate together with their customers. Popular tools include facilitated communities, forums and guest books. Some firms develop more creative ways to generate tourist-driven information. A very prominent and successful example is Tourism Queensland's 2009 "Best Job in the World" Campaign (bestjobs.australia.com). In the campaign's second run, 330,000 applicants from 196 countries sent their videos. The campaign's results was world-wide media coverage worth 100M dollars (Kahrvi, 2009). Given the potential of tourist-driven innovations, firms need to recognize the multiple and interlinked forms of innovation triggered by the diverse solution spaces. Nevertehless, the areas of innovation are also present in the customer environment; this study introduced the Tourist-Driven Peer-to-Peer Innovation (TDPP) context.

Tourist-Driven Peer-to-Peer Innovation (TDPP)

A peer-to-peer network acts as a tool for tourists exchanging their knowledge related to their travels. Social media facilitates the peer-to-peer network with a wide range of portals, communities, wikis, social networks, collaborative tagging and shared files on YouTube and Flickr (Xiang & Gretzel, 2010). In the peer-to-peer network, consumers can act as role models for less experienced customers, shape actual experiences and provide a sense of the community (Füller et al., 2008; Kohler et al., 2008). Social media allows for environments where customers interact and discuss products in forums and blogs. Tourists can share their information in blogs, online review websites, social networking sites and

Table 3.1 Examples of TDPP and TDFF

Innovation area	Tourist-Driven Peer-to-Peer Innovation (TDPP)	Tourist-Driven Firm Facilitated Innovation (TDFF)
Product / service	• Review pages for implicit research on product improvement (tripadvisor.com) • Travel communities and local people providing innovative product suggestions	• Flanders Festival Express ideation contest based on crowdsourcing • Hotel improvements based on virtual worlds such as second life • Electronic guestbook for improvement suggestions
Process	• Travel communities, blogs, mobile applications suggesting guided tours and guidebooks free for download (tripwolf.com)	• Mobile GPS tracking for product innovation in tourist regions around Aare
Service interaction	• Mobile applications impacting the tourist experience on-site • Review pages giving suggestions for improved service interaction	• Mobile applications • Catalan tourist board uses crowdsourcing on photo-sharing platform • YouTube video competition for perfect day in a given city
Information	• Mobile applications, travel websites initiated by tourists or locals to provide insider tips (likealocalguide.com) • Compilation of restaurant evaluations for download (Zagat.com) • YouTube videos and pictures on Instagram on destinations/hotels/favorite spots	• Crowdsourced marketing campaign by Tourism Queensland • Any guestbook and platforms developed for traveller feedback can be harvested for innovative ideas

electronic communities (Hjalager & Nordin, 2011; Tussyadiah, 2014). It should be acknowledged that TDPP innovations can be highly successful and used by many travellers without the firm commercializing the innovations. Therefore, they are located on the borderline between customer environment and business environment in Figure 3.1. Hence, these sources of TDPP offer a wealth of customer-designed innovations for products, processes and service interactions, and information (see Table 3.1).

Product

The solution spaces like review platforms and communities allow for tourists' ratings and reflection upon elements of the service experience. This platform offers important information usable for product innovation (Hjalager & Nordin, 2011) such as recommendation for hotels offering complimentary Wi-Fi, accommodations needing refurbishment, and availability of tourist information at the hotel. Examples from TripAdvisor.com read as follows:

> ". . . place for improvement is the lack of tourism information
> first hand info from the taxi driver is not the best way to plan ones trip!"
> "Rusty ironwork on balconies needs attention!"

Process

Blogs offer tourists' in-depth reporting of their holiday experiences. Travel blogs provide information essential for product and process innovation (Hjalager & Nordin, 2011). Communities such as Tripwolf show how peer interaction helps tourists to innovate. Peers' insights about their trips provide elaborate descriptions on sights, activities and experiences. These descriptions even connect to maps, showing an ideal route through the city. Travellers can download these individual user-generated guidebooks for free. This information delivery changes the trip-planning process and also the information source used for the on-trip phase. A similar approach is provided by www.journiapp.in where travellers design perfect trips for other travellers with in-depth information and pictures.

Service interaction

Mobile technology is an important tool for tourists to gather and exchange information during trips (Tussyadiah, 2014). Thus, customers exchange experiences with peers which enable innovative service interaction. Travellers can receive location-based information on their mobile phones and interact with the experience network at the destination. Hotels can collect tangible advice for service interaction innovation from hotel review pages:

> Given how expensive this hotel is, it shocks me that they are not able to do a better job training their staff. Until their customer service (and management sincerity) improves, I can't see recommend this hotel.

Information

Social media offers a wide range of information to be found in peer-to-peer networks. Some of the previous examples overlap with the information area. Additionally, locals sometimes engage in solution spaces and provide valuable information. On mobile applications or websites travellers receive innovative information from locals to create a unique travel experience (e.g. www.likealocal-guide.com). The examples illustrate the creative capacity of peers for peers. Naturally, the innovation areas overlap, exemplifying the interactive and networked nature of the tourist experience.

Conclusion

The development of Web 2.0, social media platforms and mobile computing communities allowed tourists to become independent actors in the experience network. This chapter refers to the concept of tourist-driven innovation. This concept demonstrates the new ways tourists are travelling and acting as a part of the experience network supported by social media. Subsequently, this chapter illustrates a solid framework towards developing new perspectives about tourist-driven innovation for tourism organizations. Various forms of business model innovations are identified for businesses to optimally deal with this phenomenon in a strategic way. In order to so companies first need to realize the changing nature of tourists' positions, their interdependence as actors in the network, and their creative and innovative nature facilitated by ICT toolkits. Second, firms need to go beyond a linear market view and aim for innovative flexible mindsets understanding what tourists are doing in their own network of experiences. In fact, firms need to embrace tourists as true innovators, supporting them by allocating the right resources. Third, companies should realize that the unique characteristics of a tourist experience seize their opportunities to innovate. Therefore, as this chapter highlights, the future of innovation processes of tourism firms starts with learning from the independently acting tourists. Consumer-centric thinking cannot be ignored any longer by practitioners when aiming for effective business model innovation.

Researchers and practitioners need to further explore the concept of tourist-driven innovation. Issues such as value creation, failures, responsibilities and issues that occur during the process of tourist-driven innovations need to be investigated. The role of different stakeholders in the network and the perception of tourist-driven innovation can help the industry to create supportive platforms and toolkits enabling extraordinary tourist experiences.

References

Aldebert, B., Dang, R., & Longhi, C. (2011). Innovation in the tourism industry: The case of Tourism@. *Tourism Management*, 32(5), pp. 1204–1213.

Berry, L., Wall, E., & Carbone, L. (2006). Services clues and customer assessment of the service expierence: Lessons from marketing. *The Academy of Management Perspectives*, 20(2), pp. 43–57.

Brooker, E., & Joppe, M. (2013). Developing a tourism innovation tyology: Leveraging liminal insights. *Journal of Travel Research.*, 53(4), pp. 500–508.

Couture, A., Arcand, M., Sénécal, S., & Ouellet, J. (2015). The influence of tourism innovativeness on online consumer behavior. *Journal of Travel Research*, 54(1), pp. 66–79.

D'Haen, T. (2014). *Flanders Is a Festival: Blogger Campaign*. Retrieved February 10, 2014, from Digital Tourism Think Tank http://thinkdigital.travel/best-practice/flanders-is-a-festival/

Dickinson, J. E., Ghali, K., Cherrett, T., Speed, C., Davies, N., & Norgate, S., (2014). Tourism and the smartphone app: Capabilities, emerging practice and scope in the travel domain. *Current Issues in Tourism*, 17(1), pp. 84–101.

Franke, N., Schreier, M., & Kasier, U. (2010). The "I designed it myself" effect in mass customization. *Management Science*, 56(1), pp. 125–140.

Fuglsang, L., Sundbo, J., & Sørensen, F. (2011). Dynamics of experience service innovation: Innovation as a guided activity: Results from a Danish survey. *The Service Industries Journal*, 31(5), pp. 661–677.

Füller, J., Matzler, K., & Hoppe, M. (2008). Brand community members as a source of innovation. *Journal of Product Innovation Management*, 25(6), pp. 608–619.

Gallouj, F. (1998). Innovating in reverse: Services and the reverse product cycle. *European Journal of Innovation Management*, 1(3), pp. 123–138.

Hjalager, A. M. (2002). Repairing innovation defectiveness in tourism. *Tourism Management*, 23(5), pp. 465–474.

Hjalager, A. M. (2010). A review of innovation research in tourism. *Tourism Management*, 31(1), pp. 1–12.

Hjalager, A. M. (2015). 100 innovations that transformed tourism. *Journal of Travel Research*, 54(1), pp. 3–21.

Hjalager, A. M., & Nordin, S. (2011). User-driven innovation in tourism: A review of methodologies. *Journal of Quality Assurance in Hospitality & Tourism*, 12(4), pp. 289–315.

Kahrvi, V. (2009, July 20). *Case Study: "Best Job in the World" Campaign Winner of the Inaugural PR Award at Cannes 2009*. Retrieved February 14, 2014, from PR Next http://prnext.wordpress.com/2009/07/20/case-study-best-job-in-the-world-campaign-winner-of-the-inaugural-pr-award-at-cannes-2009/

Kohler, T., Matzler, K., & Füller, J. (2008). Avatar-based innovation: Using virtual worlds for real-world innovation. *Technovation*, 29, pp. 395–407.

Labrecque, L. I., Mathwick, C., Novak, T. P., & Hofacker, C. (2013). Consumer power: Evolution in the digital age. *Journal of Interactive Marketing*, 27(4), pp. 257–269.

Lamsfus, C., Wang, D., Alzua-Sorzabal, A., & Xiang, Z. (2014). Going mobile defining context for on-the-go travelers. *Journal of Travel Research*, 54(6), pp. 691–701.

Larsen, J., Urry, J., & Axhausen, K. (2007). Network and tourism, mobile social life. *Annals of Tourism Research*, 34(1), pp. 244–262.

Libai, B., Bolton, R., Bügel, M. S., De Ruyter, K., Götz, O., Risselada, H., & Stephen, A. T., (2010). Customer-to-customer interactions: Broadening the scope of word of mouth research. *Journal of Service Research*, 13(3), pp. 267–282.

Lilien, G. L., Morrison, P. D., Searls, K., Sonnack, M., & Hippel, E. V., (2002). Performance assessment of the lead user idea-generation process. *Management Science*, 48(8), pp. 1041–1059.

Lüthje, C. (2004). Characteristics of innovating users in a consumer goods field: An empirical study of sport-related product consumers. *Technovation*, 24(9), pp. 683–695.

Malerba, F. (2001). Sectoral systems of innovation and production. *Research Policy*, 31(2), pp. 247–264.

Neuhofer, B., Buhalis, D., & Ladkin, A. (2013). A typology of technology-enhanced tourism experiences. *International Journal of Tourism Research*, 16(4), pp. 340–350.

Paget, E., Dimanche, F., & Mounet, J. (2010). A tourism innovation case: An actor-network approach. *Annals of Tourism Research*, 37(3), pp. 828–847.

Peters, M., & Pikkemaat, B. (Eds.). (2005). *Innovation in Hospitality and Tourism*, London: Routledge.

Poetz, M., & Schreier, M. (2012). The value of crowdsourcing: Can users really compete with professionals in generating new product ideas? *Journal of Product Innovation Management*, 29(2), pp. 245–256.

Prahalad, C., & Ramaswamy, V. (2003). The new frontier of experience innovation. *MIT Sloan Management Review*, 44(4), pp. 12–18.

Schreier, M., Fuchs, C., & Dahl, D. (2012). The innovation effect of user design: Exploring consumers' innovation perceptions of firms selling products designed by users. *Journal of Marketing*, 76(5), pp. 18–32.

Schumpeter, J. (1939). *Business Cycles: A Theoretical, Historical and Statistical Analysis of the Capitalist Process*, Philadelphia, Porcupine Press.

Stickdorn, M., & Frischhut, A. (2012). *Service Design and Tourism*, Hamburg, Books On Demand.

Su, C. (2011). The role of service innovation and customer experience in ethnic restaurants. *The Service Industries Journal*, 31(3), pp. 425–440.

Sundbo, J., Orfila-Sintes, F., & Sørensen, F. (2007).The innovative behaviour of tourism firms: Comparative studies of Denmark and Spain. *Research Policy*, 36(1), pp. 88–106.

Sundbo, J., Sørensen, F., & Fuglsang, L. (2010). *Innovation in the Experience Sector*. Center for Service Studies, Roskilde University Denmark.

Tussyadiah, I. (2014). Social actor attribution to mobile phones: The case of tourists. *Journal of Information and Technology and Tourism*, 14(11), pp. 21–47.

Tussyadiah, I. P., & Fesenmaier, D. R. (2009). Mediating tourist experiences: Access to places via shared videos. *Annals of Tourism Research*, 36(1), pp. 24–40.

Van der Duim, R. (2007). Tourismscapes an actor-network perspective. *Annals of Tourism Research*, 34(4), pp. 961–976.

Vargo, S. L., & Lusch, R. F. (2004). Evolving to a new dominant logic for marketing. *Journal of Marketing*, 68(1), pp. 1–14.

Von Hippel, E. (1998). Economics of product development by users: The impact of "sticky" local information. *Management Science*, 44(5), pp. 629–644.

Von Hippel, E. (2005). Democratizing innovation: The evolving phenomenon of user innovation. *Journal für Betriebswirtschaft*, 55(1), p. 6378.

Von Hippel, E. (2007). Horizontal innovation networks: By and for users. *Industrial and Corporate Change*, 15(2), pp. 293–315.

Von Hippel, E. A., Ogawa, S., & de Jong, J. (2011). The age of the consumer-innovator. *MIT Sloan*, 1, p. 53.

Von Hippel, E., & Katz, R. (2002). Shifting innovation to users via toolkits. *Management Science*, 48(7), pp. 821–833.

Werthnes, H., & Klein, S. (1999). ICT and the changing landscape of global tourism distribution. *Electronic Markets*, 9(4), pp. 256–262.

Xiang, Z., & Gretzel, U. (2010). Role of social media in online travel information search. *Tourism Management*, 31(2), pp. 179–188.

Zach, F. (2012). Partners and innovation in American destination marketing organizations. *Journal of Travel Research*, 51(4), pp. 412–425.

Zomerdijk, L. G., & Voss, C. A. (2009). Service design for experience-centric services. *Journal of Service Research*, 31(1), pp. 67–82.

4 Enhancing wearable augmented reality visitor experience through social media

A case study of Manchester Art Gallery

Timothy Jung and M. Claudia tom Dieck

Introduction

Augmented reality (AR) is thought to be the next big thing on the technology market and increasingly tourism destinations and visitor attractions recognize opportunities of this new and innovative way of visitor engagement (Uricchio, 2011). In particular, the rapid advancement and availability of smartphones and more recent wearable technologies has led to an increased popularity of AR (Jung et al., 2015a). The cultural heritage sector has started to focus its interactive strategies on integrating AR in the museum and art gallery experience. In fact, de los Ríos et al. (2014) acknowledged that one of the biggest challenges within the cultural heritage sector is the attraction, engagement and retention of visitors. Utilizing new approaches to visitor engagement can attract new target markets that generally are difficult to reach.

The staging of tourism experiences is regarded as an important part of tourists' value perception (Hallmann & Zehrer, 2015). Nowadays, technologies play an important role in the pre-, during and post-tourism experience (Neuhofer et al., 2014). Social media networks have thoroughly been discussed to be an effective way of staging the tourism experience (Magasic, 2016) and creating value for both tourists and tourism suppliers. With the advancement in mobile technologies, new devices have emerged that allow for the use of social media networks while travelling (Leue et al., 2015). Previous tourism literature investigated the effects of using mobile AR to enhance visitor experience and engagement (Chang et al., 2015; Han et al., 2014; Jung et al., 2015a; Yovcheva et al., 2012); however, studies focusing on wearable AR within the tourism context and the cultural heritage sector in particular are scarce. Taking into account the novelty and scarcity of wearable AR research, it is important "to provide organizations with a useful set of principles for creating the experience for consumers" (Leask et al., 2014, p. 9). Therefore, the present study aims to explore the concept of wearable AR as an enhancer of the visitor experience in art galleries by examining the "ideal" experience associated with using Google Glass and the role of social media in sharing experience.

Literature review

Using technology to enhance the visitor experience

The core of the tourism industry lies in the development and delivery of the visitor and tourist experience (Ritchie et al., 2011). According to Oh et al. (2007), the experience economy belongs to the fastest growing sectors, and especially in tourism, the focus has shifted from the delivery of experiences to a staging of experiences. Nowadays, tourists are more interested in receiving unique experiences instead of simply consuming services and products that led to the idea of "experience economy" (Pine & Gilmore, 1999). The idea of "ideal" or "optimal" experience roots back to 1975, when Csikszentmihalyi proposed that an enjoyable experience can be achieved when individuals use their skills, while being met with a decent amount of challenges. Csikszentmihalyi (1975) proposed that too little challenges result in boredom, while too little skills end up in anxiety. Therefore, developing and delivering experiences that involve the right amount of skills and challenges were proposed to result in an "ideal experience" (Csikszentmihalyi & LeFevre, 1989).

Latest advancements in information technologies have the opportunities to enhance the visitor experience within museums and art galleries through enhanced provision of interactive and enjoyable content (Leue et al., 2015). Over the past decade, social media took the place of an interactive platform that allowed tourists to capture and share experiences. In fact, Magasic (2016) referred to "social media tourism" as a way of using social networks to plan, support and augment the travel experience. The idea of augmentation, overlaying digital content onto tourists' real environment, links nicely to the focus of this study as social media platforms can be used to provide AR applications for tourists' value creation (tom Dieck & Jung, 2016). Pine and Gilmore (1999) confirmed the importance of delivering a unique tourist experience as it creates a signature moment of the experience and also allows tourists to remember their experience at a later time. However, Meecham and Stylianou (2014) cautioned a quick and easy implementation of technology into the visitor experience. Although latest technologies such as mobile application may be successful in enhancing the visitor experience, it was identified that often applications fail to succeed due to a lack of research on what visitors actually want (Meecham and Stylianou, 2014). Therefore, considering the early stage of wearable AR and the scarcity of research in the tourism and art gallery context, exploratory qualitative investigation needs to identify visitors' perception with regards to the implementation of this new technology into the visitor experience and the role of social media in sharing experience.

Wearable Augmented Reality in tourism

AR has changed the way tourists are able to experience destinations and visitor attractions (Jung et al., 2015a). Traditionally more developed for smartphones and tablets, latest developments allow for the emergence of wearable AR (Krevelen & Poelman, 2010). AR allows the projection of digital content into the real environment, adding a tool of information enhancement in various contexts (Han et al., 2014; Yovcheva et al., 2012). Tourism destinations started to develop AR applications such as "Tuscany+" or "Augmented Reality for Basel" (Kounavis et al., 2012) and also researchers explored a number of cases of mobile AR applications integrated into the tourism experience including Jeju themepark in South Korea (Jung et al., 2015a), Dublin AR (Han et al., 2014) or the AR application for the

Italian Alpulia region (Fiore et al., 2014). These studies found that AR has the potential to create a realistic experience, aiming to enhance the tourism experience through informative, interactive and enjoyable content. The re-enactment of historical events and bringing history to life are just some advantages destinations and tourism attractions can benefit from (Herbst et al., 2008).

Recently, museums and art galleries started to explore opportunities of integrating and offering wearable computing devices for the visitor experience (Rhodes & Allen, 2014) and also the use of wearable AR has started to become a focus-point among certain museums and art galleries (e.g. Manchester Art Gallery, Imperial War Museum London) (Leue et al., 2015). Advantages compared to traditional mobile AR lie in the uncumbersome and hand-free approach to visiting museums and art galleries, allowing for an undisturbed and traditional experience (Leue et al., 2014). During the Manchester Art Gallery project, Leue et al. (2014) found the incorporation of social media functions and interactivity to be most important in an art gallery application. Visitors identified that the sharing of content should be a key feature of a wearable AR application linking to enjoyment and interaction factors. These findings are not surprising, considering the increased importance of social media networks for today's society (Munar & Jacobsen, 2014).

Case study background and methods

The initiative to utilize Google Glass as an enhancement tool for visitor experience at Manchester Art Gallery started in January 2014. Being among the first in Europe to test Google Glass in an art gallery environment, the test of the wearable AR application aimed to explore how the usage of Google Glass can enhance the visitor experience. A prototype application was developed, providing information (audio and visual) on the artist, paintings and related paintings. The aim was to use the idea of an audio guide but making it more interactive and engaging for the visitor. Functionalities of the application included reading aloud content and sharing it via social media networks. In order to use Google Glass in the gallery (see Figure 4.1), visitors had to follow the following steps:

1   Taking a picture of the painting
2   Sharing it with the application (image recognition)
3   Receiving information

The aim of the study was to identify which factors would contribute to an ideal experience for visitors when using these new and innovative devices through exploratory interviews. The identification of these factors aims to help future application development and museum and art gallery professionals to develop and implement wearable AR into the visitor experience. The exploratory research approach was considered most appropriate as it is concerned with the discovery of new phenomena and theories (Jupp, 2006). The study was conducted on 10th and 11th of April 2014 at Manchester Art Gallery with 29 art gallery visitors.

Figure 4. 1 Google Glass test at Manchester Art Gallery

Purposive quota sampling method was used to collect data and Table 4.1 shows the profile of participants. Purposive quota sampling is a sampling technique whereby participants are selected based on certain characteristics (age, gender, knowledge etc.) (Daniel, 2011; Tongco, 2007). This sampling technique is often used in preliminary studies (Tongco, 2007). For the present study, suitable participants were selected to encompass a wide range of the target market ranging

Table 4.1 Profile of participants

Participant	Gender	Age	Recruitment channel
P1	Male	30–39	Art Gallery
P2	Female	Over 60	Art Gallery
P3	Female	Below 20	Art Gallery
P4	Male	20–29	Art Gallery
P5	Male	20–29	Art Gallery
P6	Male	40–49	Art Gallery
P7	Female	20–29	Art Gallery
P8	Female	Over 60	Art Gallery
P9	Male	Below 20	Art Gallery
P10	Female	20–29	Art Gallery
P11	Female	Below 20	Art Gallery
P12	Female	Below 20	Art Gallery
P13	Male	50–59	Social Media
P14	Female	20–29	Social Media
P15	Male	20–29	Social Media
P16	Female	20–29	Social Media
P17	Male	40–49	Social Media
P18	Male	30–39	Social Media
P19	Male	30–39	Social Media
P20	Female	30–39	Social Media
P21	Female	30–39	Social Media
P22	Male	20–29	Social Media
P23	Male	20–29	Social Media
P24	Male	20–29	Social Media
P25	Male	30–39	Social Media
P26	Female	20–29	Social Media
P27	Female	50–59	Art Gallery
P28	Female	60 and above	Art Gallery
P29	Male	20–29	Art Gallery

from teens to visitors in their eighties. A total of 29 art gallery visitors were recruited and half of the participants were recruited in the Art Gallery during the day of testing and the other half were recruited through social media by the official profile of Manchester Art Gallery.

Prior to the experiment, functionalities of Google Glass such as swiping, voice commands and taking pictures were explained to and tested by participants for 15 minutes. After the initial familiarizing with the device, the experiment moved on to testing the application. Participants took a picture of paintings, shared it with the application and were able to receive further information about the painting, artist as well as related paintings. After this test, participants were asked to participate in a semi-structured interview. In order to achieve the aim of the present study, the following four questions were asked:

- Before testing Google Glass today, have you ever heard of it and were curious of using it?
- What's your overall opinion about using Google Glass?
- What words or phrases would you use to describe an ideal experience with this application?
- Do you think an application such as this can enhance the experience of visitors in the Art Gallery?

The interview aimed to identify whether participants perceived the experience to be enhancing to their art gallery visit and what would constitute an ideal AR experience. The obtained data were analyzed using content analysis which is considered an appropriate technique for exploratory analysis (Weiler and Davis, 1993).

Findings

Throughout the interviews, eight factors emerged which were perceived to contribute to an ideal wearable AR art gallery experience.

Individual experience

Smooth and intuitive experience

More than half of the participants revealed that an ideal experience using wearable AR in the art gallery should be intuitive (Participants 1, 4, 6, 7, 8, 9, 10, 12, 17, 19, 21, 22, 23, 24, 25). P1 and P24 agreed that the application should feel natural and there should be "a better natural way of using it" (P1). In addition, the importance of responsiveness and sleekness was identified (P22). Intuition fits very well into the overall purpose of wearables, providing a hands-free, uncumbersome and easy to use alternative to traditional mobile devices (Due, 2014). The importance of an intuitive experience using wearable AR in the gallery becomes clear from a quote by P4:

> In a gallery it takes so long to go around anyway, for it to be intuitive so it kind of guides you smoothly around the gallery, so that you can make the best of it.

Throughout the interviews, the study revealed that participants found it to be a much easier and intuitive approach to visit Manchester Art Gallery when using wearable AR as it enabled them to receive information on paintings they were interested in, viewing related paintings and thus, create their own sleek experience. However, P7 revealed that "It is very much still the prototype stage to a degree, even so you would hope the equipment to be a little bit nimbler and a little bit lighter and less intrusive".

Enriching experience

Ideally, a wearable AR application would make the museum and art gallery experi-ence more enriching, according to a number of participants (P12, 13, 14, 17, 22, 24, 26, 25, 28). There are several ways in which a wearable AR application could be enriching. P13 for instance found that information should be enriching to make the entire experience more useful and interesting:

> I found it was enriching because I do go through the art gallery quite often and I find I feel a sense that I am missing a lot without having a guided tour, that I am missing something. [Google Glass] is like having an expert.

As far back as 1995, Bederson found that tour guides utilizing basic ideas of AR have the capability of enriching the museum visitor's experience and Anderson (1999) confirmed that technology allows for an easy retrieval of information from the past. More recently, Chang et al. (2015) investigated the use of mobile AR guidance systems and confirmed that these new forms of visitor engagement enrich the experience and increase interaction with historical contexts. All of this was confirmed within the wearable AR art gallery context by P25 summarizing that "You would want it to be rich, to actually enrich your experience" and P24 added "It needs to add value and enhance what you are doing".

Educational experience

The facilitation of the learning experience was considered an important factor of an ideal wearable AR experience (Participants 5, 14, 15, 18, 22, 27). Museums and art galleries are increasingly asked to provide evidence of their strategies and efforts towards facilitating visitor learning (Hooper-Greenhill et al., 2003). A number of participants confirmed that wearable AR is an ideal device and should be used in order to enhance the learning experience. Audio guides and interactive displays have proven to be beneficial for an interactive and exciting learning atmosphere (Hawkey, 2004; Linzer, 2013) and also wearable AR was perceived as a future device for the learning experience. P14 was curious about using it as [she] is quite interested in technology in terms of learning in art galleries and museums and P22 confirmed that Google Glass enhanced the flow of information which "for educational purposes for somewhere like a museum is actually great". In addition, personalization adds value to the learning and educational experience as visitors are enabled to tailor the learn-ing to their needs and wants, making it more enjoyable and memorable (Falk et al., 2012; Leue et al., 2015). This was confirmed by P14 saying:

> I definitely think it would be good as a learning tool to tailor your own tour around the gallery I guess. You would be able to do it in a way you wanted.

Exciting and fresh experience

Wearable AR has the potential to create more exciting and fresh art gallery experi-ences according to few participants (P3, 11, 18, 25, 26, 27). While visitors seem to be interested in experiencing museums and art galleries in a new and exciting way, Meecham and Stylianou (2014) remarked that museums and art galleries are often reluctant to allow new approaches of visitor engagement into their walls due to concerns of "disneyfication" and removing the traditional atmosphere from historic buildings and artefacts. Nonetheless, previous research has shown that using innovative technologies such as Google Glass can attract new target markets into museums and art galleries (Leue et al., 2015). Considering recent cuts for public organizations, footfall numbers are important for museums and art galleries to continue operations (Goulding, 2000); and therefore, creating fresh and exciting opportunities for visitor engagement can be an important strategy. P3 confirmed that:

> Normally, I don't go to galleries but if it is something new, something fresh I would definitely go to the gallery and use it. I am not very good with new technology, but still if there is an opportunity, I will always try to use one. This is the kind of thing I would be really interested in.

As wearables offer the opportunity for an unobtrusive experience, other visitors are not disturbed in their experience and thus, it could be considered as a fresh and exciting way of attracting the younger market or those less interested in art galleries and museums.

Personal experience

Technologies enabled museums and art galleries to increasingly focus on a customized and personalized experience (Linge et al., 2012). Implementing personal tours through audio guides, PDAs or smartphones have enhanced the interaction with art and museum displays, adding a dimension of interactivity (Beltrán et al., 2014). A small number of participants (P14, 21, 26) picked up this trend of utilizing technology devices to personalize the visitor experience. It was revealed that wearables devices such as Google Glass would be ideal devices to enable visitors to view paintings they are most interested based on selected criteria of interest (P21, 26). In addition, P14 raised an important point by comparing a wearable application to the "Wikipedia principle":

> I would like it to be personal, I would like to really go down the rabbit hole with what I was viewing. I would like to have lot of options.

P14 revealed that a normal visitor or a tourist who comes into the gallery will most likely be interested in basic information; however, returning visitors or art fanatics could use the application to find out always new content through interlinking the application with galleries around the world.

Social experience

Sharing experience via social media

The review of previous literature briefly noticed the importance of social media networks and interactivity of applications for the enhancement of the visitor experience (Leue et al., 2014), and a number of participants confirmed these assumptions (P1, 3, 16, 17, 18, 24, 26, 29). P1 would welcome

> To open [the application] to different social networks definitely, Facebook and Whatsapp and so on, and to link it with a mobile device so maybe I could send [the content of the painting] to my phone.

P14, however, differed with this opinion revealing that social media should not take every aspect of daily life. On the contrary, P16 saw the value in sharing content between glasses and friends while being in the gallery to make it a more interactive and social experience. This is in line with previous research assessing an increased importance of social media networks within the tourism industry (Fountoulaki et al., 2015). One participant enjoyed the idea of saving content on social media for the after-experience; allowing him to access and remember information (P17).

Social acceptance

Social acceptance is an important factor for the wearable experience in galleries according to few participants (P6, 9). Interestingly, P6 (in the 40–49 age range) raised the idea of "social etiquette", questioning whether art galleries are the right places to walk around with a wearable device in your face. Therefore, he concluded:

> "What would prevent me from using it, I suppose social acceptability is the main thing.

This was confirmed by various media articles covering Google Glass and its development which revealed users are often mocked and excluded (Gaudin, 2015). This contributes to limited acceptance and perceived usefulness. In fact, the few participants who raised their concerns about Google Glass confirmed they had heard negative news coverage from the media.

Discussion and conclusion

Wearable AR in the tourism context has just recently started to be explored by academia and industry and only few studies focused on the potential of these new and innovative devices (Jung et al., 2015b; Leue et al., 2014, 2015). Therefore, the present study aimed to explore the concept of wearable AR as an enhancer of the visitor experience in art galleries by examining the "ideal" experience associated with using Google Glass and the role of social media in sharing experience. Throughout the exploratory interviews with art gallery visitors, seven factors were found that would help to create an ideal wearable AR art gallery experience as shown in Figure 4.2.

As Figure 4.2 presents, the seven identified factors can be classified as individual and social experience factors. This clearly shows the link of wearable AR

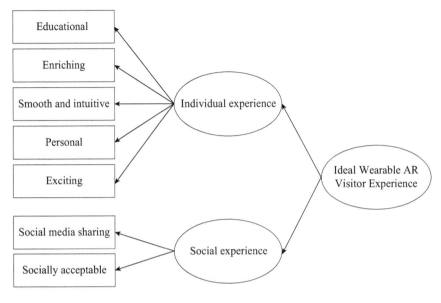

Figure 4.2 Factors of ideal wearable augmented reality experience

being a form of personal technology while being interactive and social. As discussed throughout the literature, social media networks were an important medium for the tourism experience throughout the last decade and continue to be so in the future. However, the devices through which social media networks are being accessed are changing. While originally tourism organizations could only reach tourists through desktop computers or laptops, the development of mobile devices allowed a dialogue with tourists everywhere at any time. Latest devices such as wearable headsets created an even more interactive platform for the sharing and accessing of social media content. The findings have shown that wearable AR applications need to be educational, enriching, smooth and intuitive, personal and exciting in order to enhance tourists' individual experience. In addition, social media sharing needs to be included and social acceptability ensured in order to enhance the social experience. A focus on these areas is proposed to create an ideal wearable AR experience in the art gallery context. Therefore, the identified seven factors are proposed to be considered by art gallery professionals for future wearable AR application design. Cuts in public funding have forced museum and art gallery managers to find new ways of visitor engagement in order to enhance the overall experience, thus to retain existing visitors, create positive word-of-mouth and attract new visitors (Goulding, 2000). Mobile applications in general and in particular mobile AR applications have proven to be successful in facilitating learning, interactions with artefacts among visitors and the enhancement of the visitor experience (Charitonos et al., 2012; Han et al., 2014). The study found similar factors to Charitonos et al. (2012) and Han et al. (2014) and therefore, all these factors should also be considered and facilitated when creating wearable AR in order to create an ideal visitor experience. This shows that identified factors from the present study do not much differ from the previous mobile AR study by Han et al. (2014) on user requirements for an AR application; however, social acceptability and social sharing are important factors influencing the experience that emerged from the interviews specifically applicable to wearable devices. Recent research in the tourism domain has confirmed that social media is strongly embedded within the travel experience and in fact "part of daily touristic routines and experiences" (Magasic, 2016, p. 178). According to Vu et al. (2016), the sharing of content via social media provides important implications for destination management with regards to planning of the tourist experience for the enhancement of value. The sharing of images and videos does not only capture the actual experience but creates an online journey for tourists' social network friends and family (Magasic, 2016, p. 178). As findings of this study revealed, art gallery visitors suggested that wearable AR is an ideal tool for the sharing of the museum experience with a wider circle of friends. Social media networks have been the trend of the past 10 years and continue to influence tourism behavior. Our study has shown that new and innovative technologies such as wearable AR do not replace the idea of social media but embrace it. Using devices such as Google Glass to capture experiences from a tourist's perspective and sharing it on social networks seems to be the trend ahead according to our findings. Nevertheless, Gaudin (2015) agreed that wearable devices such as Google Glass have received negative attention from the public and media which ultimately influences the acceptance and success of these devices. However, as found in the current study, visitors accept using wearable AR for specific purposes, such as the museum visit. Museum and art gallery visitors perceive wearable AR to be beneficial if the application runs smoothly, content is enriching and exciting, interactive, educational, and personalized as well as allows for social sharing. If museum and art gallery managers are aware of the drawback of wearable AR but keep in mind its strengths and potential possibilities, then museum and art galleries can truly benefit from these new and innovative devices. Implementing wearable AR allows them to offer a unique visitor experience and differentiate themselves from other tourism organizations (Leue et al., 2014). Therefore, it can aid the attraction of new target markets and increase footfall numbers. In addition, the visitor satisfaction is believed to result in positive word-of-mouth, again aiding the acquisition of new target markets. In particular, the sharing of content on social media networks is believed to create value through the online sharing of information and reaching of a wider audience. According to Prahalad and Ramaswamy (2013), value is created when tourists are able to exercise choice, and Neuhofer et al. (2012, p. 36) added that the co-creation of value in the tourism domain created "rich and memorable experiences". Especially, social media networks can facilitate the co-creation of value by the sharing of personal experience. However, Binkhorst (2006) argued that tourism organizations have to create compelling experience for tourists to be willing to engage in the value co-creation process.

For museum and art gallery managers as well as application developers, findings from this study provide important implications for the functionalities and areas required to create and implement a successful wearable AR application for the staging of an ideal experience. For academia, the model presented in Figure 4.2 can be considered a starting point of a theoretical foundation for the enhancement of the visitor experience through wearable AR. Quantitative research should be conducted to support the identified factors. In addition, the model and proposed factors should be considered for further theory development and testing. The present study used qualitative interviews to explore which factors should be considered in order to develop and implement wearable AR for an ideal visitor experience. The identified factors are solely based on qualitative perceptions and future research should test them on a larger scale to generalize findings to a wider population. In addition, the present study focuses on the art gallery context and future research is required to extend the scope to the wider tourism industry. Finally, the link between wearable AR and social media networks was supported within the present study and future research could investigate how mixed realities can incorporate social media networks for the co-creation of value and the enhancement of the tourism experience.

Acknowledgements

This research has been supported by Knowledge Exchange Innovation Fund, MMU and the authors would like to thank Manchester Art Gallery for providing all contents for the development of the Google Glass AR application and 33Labs and Digital Sense Technologies for the development and hosting of the application.

References

Anderson, M. L. (1999). Museums of the future: The impact of technology on museum practices. In *Daedalus*. pp. 129–162.

Beltrán, M. E., Ursa, Y., de los Rios, S., Cabrera-Umpiérrez, M. F., Arredondo, M. T., Páramo, M., & Pérez, L. M. (2014). Engaging people with cultural heritage: Users' perspective. In C. Stephanidis & M. Antona (eds.) *Universal Access in Human-Computer Interaction: Universal Access to Information and Knowledge*. Heidelberg, Springer International Publishing, pp. 639–649.

Binkhorst, E. (2006). *The co-creation tourism experience*. Paper presented at XV International Tourism and Leisure Symposium, Barcelona.

Chang, Y. L., Hou, H. T., Pan, C. Y., Sung, Y. T., & Chang, K. E. (2015). Apply an augmented reality in a mobile guidance to increase sense of place for heritage places. *Journal of Educational Technology and Society*, 18(2), pp. 166–178.

Charitonos, K., Blake, C., Scanlon, E., & Jones, A. (2012). Museum learning via social and mobile technologies: (How) can online interactions enhance the visitor experience? *British Journal of Educational Technology*, 43(5), pp. 802–819.

Csikszentmihalyi, M. (1975). Play and intrinsic rewards. *Journal of humanistic psychology.*

Csikszentmihalyi, M., & LeFevre, J. (1989). Optimal experience in work and leisure. *Journal of Personality and Social Psychology*, 56(5), pp. 815–822.

Daniel, J. (2011). *Sampling Essentials: Practical Guidelines for Making Sampling Choices*, Thousand Oaks, CA, Sage Publications.

de los Ríos, S., Cabrera-Umpiérrez, M. F., Arredondo, M. T., Páramo, M., Baranski, B., Meis, J., & del Mar Villafranca, M. (2014). Using augmented reality and social media in mobile applications to engage people on cultural sites. In C. Stephanidis & M. Antona (eds.) *Universal Access in Human-Computer Interaction: Universal Access to Information and Knowledge*. Heidelberg, Springer International Publishing, pp. 662–672.

Due, B. L. (2014). The future of smart glasses: An essay about challenges and possibilities with smart glasses. *Working Papers on Interaction and Communication*, 1(2), pp. 1–21.

Falk, J., Ballentyne, R., Packer, J., & Benckendorff, P. (2012). Travel and learning: A neglected tourism research area. *Annals of Tourism Research*, 39(2), pp. 908–927.

Fiore, A., Mainetti, L., Manco, L., & Marra, P. (2014). Augmented reality for allowing time navigation in cultural tourism experiences: A case study. In L. de Paolis and A. Mongelli (eds.) *Augmented and Virtual Reality*. Heidelberg, Springer International Publishing, pp. 296–301.

Fountoulaki, P., Leue, M. C., & Jung, T. (2015). Distribution channels for travel and tourism: The case of Crete. In I. Tussyadiah & A. Inversini (eds.) *Information and Communication Technologies in Tourism 2015*. Vienna, Springer, pp. 667–680.

Gaudin, S. (2015). Company pulls glass out of the limelight to rework it. Available at: www.computerworld.com/article/2868471/google-tries-to-reset-glass-embarrassment-with-cooler-wearable.html [Accessed 10 June 2015].

Goulding, C. (2000). The museum environment and the visitor experience. *European Journal of Marketing*, 34(3–4), pp. 261–278.

Hallmann, K., & Zehrer, A. (2015). Limits of modelling memorable experiences: How authentic shall events be? In H. Pechlaner and E. Smeral (eds.) *Tourism and Leisure*. Wiesbaden, Springer Fachmedien, pp. 269–286.

Han, D., Jung, T., & Gibson, A. (2014). Dublin AR: Implementing Augmented Reality (AR) in tourism. In Z. Xiang & I. Tussyadiah (eds.) *Information and Communication Technologies in Tourism*. Vienna, Springer, pp. 511–523.

Hawkey, R. (2004). *Learning with Digital Technologies in Museums Science Centres and Galleries*, Bristol, FutureLab.

Herbst, I., Braun, A., McCall, R., & Broll, W. (2008). TimeWarp: Interactive time travel with a mobile mixed reality game. In H. Hofte & I. Mulder (eds.) *Proceedings of the 10th International Conference on Human Computer Interaction with Mobile Devices and Services*, New York, ACM, pp. 235–244.

Hooper-Greenhill, E., Dodd, J., Moussori, T., Jones, C., & Pickford, C. (2003). *Measuring the Outcomes and Impact of Learning in Museums, Archives and Libraries*. University of Leicester, Research Centre for Museum and Galleries, pp. 1–24.

Jung, T., Chung, N., & Leue, M. C. (2015a). The determinants of recommendations to use augmented reality technologies: The case of a Korean theme park. *Tourism Management*, 49, pp. 75–86.

Jung, T., Leue, M. C., Lee, H., & Chung, N. (2015b, June 25–27). Examining offline to online service using augmented reality: Theory of reasoned action perspective moderating. In *World Hospitality and Tourism Forum, WHTF 2015*. Seoul, Republic of Korea, 2015.

Jupp, V. (2006). *The SAGE Dictionary of Social Research Methods*, London, Thousand Oaks.

Kounavis, C. D., Kasimati, A. E., Zamani, E. D., & Giaglis, G. M. (2012). Enhancing the tourism experience through mobile augmented reality: Challenges and prospects. *International Journal of Engineering Business Management*, 4(10), pp. 1–6.

Krevelen van, D. W. F., & Poelman, R. (2010). A survey of augmented reality technologies, applications and limitations. *International Journal of Virtual Reality*, 9(2), pp. 1–20.

Leask, A., Barron, P., Ensor, J., & Fyall, A. (2014). Generation Y: The Impact of Generational Changes in Consumer Behaviour on the Marketing of Tourist Attractions. Edinburgh Napier University, Edinburgh. Working Paper.

Leue, M. C., Jung, T., & tom Dieck, D. (2015). Google glass augmented reality: Generic learning outcomes for art galleries. In I. Tussyadiah & A. Inversini (eds.) *Information and Communication Technologies in Tourism 2015*, Vienna, Springer, pp. 463–476.

Leue, M. C., Han, D., & Jung, T. (2014, June 26–28). Google Glass Creative Tourism Experience: A Case Study of Manchester Art Gallery. In *World Hospitality and Tourism Forum, WHTF 2014*. Seoul, Republic of Korea.

Linge, N., Bates, D., Booth, K., Parsons, D., Heatley, L., Webb, P., & Holgate, R. (2012). Realising the potential of multimedia visitor guides: Practical experiences of developing mi-Guide. *Museum Management and Curatorship*, 27(1), pp. 67–82.

Linzer, D. (2013). Learning by doing: Experiments in accessible technology at the Whitney museum of American art. *Curator: The Museum Journal*, 56(3), pp. 363–367.

Magasic, M. (2016). The "selfie gaze" and "social media pilgrimage": Two frames for conceptualising the experience of social media using tourists. In A. Inversini & R. Schegg (eds.) *Information and Communication Technologies in Tourism*, Heidelberg, Springer, pp. 173–182.

Meecham, P., & Stylianou, E. (2014). Interactive technologies in the art museum. *Designs for Learning*, 5(1–2), pp. 94–129.

Munar, A. M., & Jacobsen, J. K. S. (2014). Motivations for sharing tourism experiences through social media. *Tourism Management*, 43, pp. 46–54.

Neuhofer, B., Buhalis, D., & Ladkin, A. (2012). Conceptualising technology enhanced destination experiences. *Journal of Destination Marketing & Management*, 1, pp. 36–46.

Neuhofer, B., Buhalis, D., & Ladkin, A. (2014). A typology of technology-enhanced tourism experiences. *International Journal of Tourism Research*, 16(4), pp. 340–350.

Oh, H., Fiore, A. M., & Jeoung, M. (2007). Measuring experience economy concepts: Tourism applications. *Journal of Travel Research*, 46(2), pp. 119–132.

Pine, B. J., & Gilmore, H. J. (1999). *The Experience Economy: Work Is Theatre and Every Business a Stage*, Boston, Harvard Business School Press.

Prahalad, C. K., & Ramaswamy, V. (2013). *The Future of Competition: Co-Creating Unique Value with Customers*, Boston, Harvard Business Press.

Rhodes, T., & Allen, S. (2014). *Through the Looking Glass: How Google Glass Will Change the Performing Arts*. Arts Management and Technology Laboratory, pp. 1–12.

Ritchie, J. R., Wing Sun Tung, V., & Ritchie, R. J. (2011). Tourism experience management research: Emergence, evolution and future directions. *International Journal of Contemporary Hospitality Management*, 23(4), pp. 419–438.

Tom Dieck, M. C., & Jung, T. (2016). Value of augmented reality to enhance the visitor experience: A case study of Manchester Jewish museum. *E-Review of Tourism Research*, 7, pp. 1–5.

Tongco, M. D. C. (2007). Purposive sampling as a tool for informant selection. *Ethnobotany Research & Applications*, 5, pp. 147–158.

Uricchio, W. (2011). The algorithmic turn: Photosynth, augmented reality and the changing implications of the image. *Visual Studies*, 26(1), pp. 25–35.

Vu, H., Leung, R., Rong, J., & Miao, Y. (2016). Exploring park visitors' activities in Hong Kong using geotagged photos. In A. Inversini & R. Schegg (eds.) *Information and Communication Technologies in Tourism*. Heidelberg: Springer, pp. 183–196.

Weiler, B., & Davis, D. (1993). An exploratory investigation into the roles of the nature-based tour leader. *Tourism Management*, 14(2), pp. 91–98.

Yovcheva, Z., Buhalis, D., & Gatzidis, C. (2012). Smartphone augmented reality applications for tourism. *E-Review of Tourism Research*, 10(2), pp. 63–66.

5 More than a technical feature

Insights into augmented reality with
social media integration in the
travel industry

*Barbara Keller, Michael Möhring
and Rainer Schmidt*

Introduction

The power of the internet initiates technical advances, thus changing the market conditions in almost every business sector. The tourism industry is no exception, because here the circumstances have also dramatically changed (Buhalis & Law, 2008), with the digitization (Markovitch & Willmott, 2014) of the branch in full swing (McAfee, 2014). There exist a number of technical opportunities – like the service to book travels on a website (Olsen & Connolly, 2000) – that could be implemented to change the strategy in tourism regarding the changing situation (Buhalis & Law, 2008). Besides, other more futuristic technologies might be a good response to the changing circumstances, although they are not commonly introduced at present. The following achievements attend to this gap in the tourism sector and focus on two emerging technologies that could be an appropriate measure to adapt to the new and changed circumstances, namely augmented reality and social media: more precisely, the concept of augmented reality and its integration of social media.

Augmented reality, as well as social media, has gained significant attention in different contexts in the recent past. Moreover, both technologies are discussed as very important approaches to face the upcoming challenges in the travel sector (Keller et al., 2015; Sigala, 2007). Augmented reality can help to enhance customers' experience (Azuma, 1997; Carmigniani et al., 2011; Kipper & Rampolla, 2012). Travellers can gain assistance and information for their whole trip by using this technology, before booking their travel, during their journey and even afterwards. For instance, the use of AR glasses at travel agents can help customers to gain insights into the hotel or the landscape, while providing useful information such as the distance to the next bus stop. This benefit can be further developed by combining this application with social media. The integration of social media (e.g. travel blogs in the internet, Facebook, Twitter, etc.) into an augmented reality system can support customers with individual-relevant information and consequently improve the evaluation of tourism services.

This chapter provides insights into how these different modern technologies can be combined and implemented in a value-creating manner in terms of increasing the individual value from the perspective of both the suppliers and customers. In the following sections, the basic technologies are described. In this context, we particularly explore the concept of augmented reality with social media integration. We show more clearly the possibilities and opportunities offered by combining the technologies with examples related to the tourism center. Furthermore, we aim to provide an outlook of the expected benefits for both sides, namely suppliers in the travel agencies and customers.

Basic technologies

Artificial environments: virtual reality vs. augmented reality

The concept of Virtual Reality (VR) is not uniquely defined and thus has to be differentiated (Steuer et al.,1995). From a technical perspective, VR is a technological system that simulates an artificial environment implemented by employing a compounded system of different IT systems, including hardware (Steuer et al., 1995) as well as software. Besides, a further definition is established that is more related to people's emerging experience while using the application (Steuer et al., 1995). Therein, VR is defined as a "real or simulated environment in which a perceiver experiences telepresence" (Steuer et al., 1995, p. 39). Rather than experiencing the environment directly, the user is immersed in an artificial environment without any touchpoints to the real world, whereby their perception is mediated by other media; for instance, additional hardware such as data glasses (Azuma, 1997).

The fields in which VR applications could be introduced are broad and wide. For instance, one already common field is the education of pilots, whereby the technical progress and digitization facilitate the use of forward-looking technologies and make their implementation attractive for different areas. In literature, approaches related to VR are discussed along with business economies (Williams et al., 1994; Williams & Hobson, 1995). Some authors argue that VR might be an effective marketing tool. This assumption has been even extended to the travel industry (Williams et al., 1994; Williams & Hobson, 1995), and a positive influence of this application has been supposed (Guttentag, 2010).

Another concept in the context of artificial environments is augmented reality (AR). Just like VR, it is determined in different ways. A well-established definition is provided by Azuma (1997), who states that AR is a version of VR and very similar to this technology (Azuma, 1997). However, an AR system enables the user to experience the real world as well as added virtual entities at the same time (Azuma, 1997). This aspect clearly contrasts with VR. Therefore, AR not only combines the real environment with a virtual aspect but also gives users the opportunity to interact in real time and in three dimensions (Azuma, 1997). Consequently, the user of AR is better involved in the application, has a better experience of the environment and can gather more individual-relevant information.

In summary, it is conceivably that both presented technologies – VR as well as AR – could make a contribution in terms of grasping the opportunities of the altered circumstances in the travel sector. Nevertheless, the concept of AR seems more advantageous regarding the remarks above. The customers are much better integrated into the AR system compared to a VR application, because the former provides the possibility to interact with the real world in real time via touchpoints. For this reason, customers' experience of the use (or service) provided by the application is much higher and thus from the customer's perspective the individual value might be increased by using the AR system. The touchpoints between the artificial and the real environment enable the user to interact with the system along the individual preferences (i.e. gain information about the position of the hotel in relation to the beach). Furthermore, the benefit of the AR system lies not only on the customer's side but also emerges on the supplier's side (e.g. travel operator). While using the technology, the customer provides the supplier with insights into their preferences and needs. Moreover, important criteria for the customer's decision-making are revealed. The supplier could use this valuable information for its own strategic purpose and improve the offer and customer approach accordingly.

Social media

Social media can be defined as "a group of Internet-based applications that build on the ideological and technological foundations of Web 2.0, and that allow the creation and exchange of User Generated Content" (Kaplan & Haenlein, 2010, p. 61). It includes social media with medium and high social presence like Facebook and Second Life, as well as with low social presence like blogs (Kaplan & Haenlein, 2010).

The list of activities is created by social production (Benkler, 2006) and it is open to new entries. By providing endorsements of interesting activities, collective intelligence (Bonabeau, 2009) is implemented. Furthermore, it is possible to enter into contact with other people providing content to the website, thus creating weak ties (Granovetter, 1973).

Platforms such as TripAdvisor[1] or Facebook are examples of social media in the travel industry. Everybody can join and contribute to the community. Therefore, an amount of different relevant information and facts about a specific and highly relevant topic (here: travel/holidays) of the community arise. This information implements a collective intelligence. Everyone can enlarge it and also benefit by using it for taking personal decisions. For example, even if a person had never visited a country, she/he can make the decision based on the information and experiences of a person who has already visited because of the collective intelligence of the community. Furthermore, persons can interact with each other and assist them on a peer-to-peer base.

Data analytics approaches and technologies

In relation to the considerations above, the benefit of an AR application could be increased by enriching with information gained from social media. The following section describes different basic approaches that can be used for the integration of data and the respective combination of the two technologies, as well as the analysis of data from internal sources like travel agents' databases and external data from sources such as Facebook or Twitter.

Big Data (Zikopoulos & Eaton, 2011; McAfee et al., 2012) significantly extends the set of data available for decision-making by integrating structured data (e.g. turnover data from tourism office or hotels) as well as unstructured data (e.g. customer travel reviews). A high volume of data can be analyzed in a short period (Zikopoulos & Eaton, 2011; McAfee et al., 2012). Therefore, tourism-related decision-making – e.g. for the customer and the travel agency – can be improved and may offer an example concerning how decisions can be taken easier and better with big data.

Text Mining denotes another useful concept, which can be applied to analyze textual information by extracting interesting patterns or knowledge from texts (Tan, 1999). Text Mining can also be defined as an extension of data mining (Tan, 1999; Fayyad et al., 1996; Simoudis, 1996). Textual data are very important sources of data in the tourism sector, as well as in the business process life cycle of various other sectors (Schmidt et al., 2015; Möhring et al., 2014). Nowadays, this data is largely not manually or semi-automated processed; rather, text mining can help to process this data, e.g. from social media sites like Facebook or Twitter.

Furthermore, other interesting sources of data for the tourism sector exist. For instance, it could be also favorable to gather and analyze the opinions of customers (or travellers), e.g. from holiday reviews on TripAdvisor or a hotel's Facebook fanpage. This data could be used in a beneficial manner by conducting sentiment analytics. *Text sentiment analysis* attempts to "determine the attitude of a speaker or a writer with respect to some specific topic" (Li & Wu, 2010, p. 354). Sentiment analyses use techniques of Text Mining or opinion lexica to understand the writer's opinion about a specific theme (Gräbner et al., 2012). There are some studies in the field of text classification and sentiment analytics in the context of tourism management (e.g. Gräbner et al., 2012; Lu et al., 2011; Kasper & Vela, 2011; Duan et al., 2013).

The mentioned basic technologies can be very useful to integrate social media and particularly user-generated content into other ICT applications. It is easily conceivable that this integration of such content and the associated combination of social media and AR can be very advantageous in terms of increasing the individual value on behalf of both suppliers and customers in a value-creating manner. Therefore, this opportunity is further discussed in the following section.

Potentials of the integration of social media and AR

According to Keller et al. (2015), AR generates different values for tourists as well as the travel industry, all of which grow out of the acceptance of the value proposition that the involved parties (entities) give to each other and the integration of their resources. Accordingly, the value is always co-created as described in the SDL (Lu et al., 2011; Kasper & Vela, 2011).

The resources that must be integrated in the case of booking and having pleasant holidays are primarily different kinds of information and knowledge. From the suppliers' perspective, there exists a need to know what customers really want and what they think about the different options. Accordingly, customers want to know whether the offer fits their preferences and whether the given information is true. This lack of information on both sides can be reduced through the integration of ICT and the associated potentials. Modern technologies have a vast number of interfaces to each other. Hence, they can assist the process of value co-creation by enabling the collection of information from various sources and disseminating it geared to the target group.

An AR application can be identified as a system that can be beneficially used. Therefore, AR systems facilitate the integration of different data sources, whereby information becomes more up-to-date as well as customer-centric, because user-generated data through social media is often more up-to-date than data provided by tourism providers. Furthermore, it provides more insights independent of the tourism operator's perspective. This approach is already implemented and used in other industry sectors; for instance, retailers use social data for improving local service processes (Schmidt et al., 2015).

For the integration of information from social media, a huge amount of unstructured data like textual posts must be analyzed. Furthermore, provider-generated content like general hotel and airport information as well as weather forecast can also be integrated in an augmented reality tourism application. To support of these steps, technologies and approaches like Big Data, Text Mining and sentiment analysis (see previous section) must be applied. The relations between the different data sources and the data processing, analytics and integration are illustrated in the following figure:

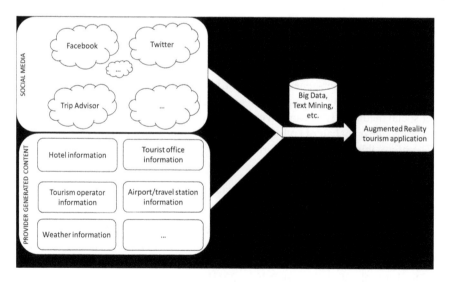

Figure 5.1 Augmented reality tourism application

Source: figure created and extended according to Milano et al. (2011), Maedche et al. (2002), Knoblock et al. (2001), Schmidt et al. (2015)

The integration of social media data can enrich customer shopping as well as tourism experience (Yuen et al., 2011), for example, by sharing likes on Facebook. Several other examples can be provided showing the advantages of integrating social media. This approach can also be integrated into AR applications to support customers' decision-making process related to the tourism industry (Sigala, 2007). For instance, the representation of one's friends' locations with information taken from Facebook (current or in the past) can provide customer value (Furht, 2011). Moreover, the symbolization of the satisfaction of different customers with a bar, museum, place or hotel (Furht, 2011; Ebling & Cáceres, 2010) can represent favorable information and facilitate tourists' decision-making. Other studies (Balduini et al., 2013) have also shown how to analyze data from social media about large city events (such as festivals, sporting events or expos) to investigate various issues and support decision-making, for instance, concerning which are the most attended venues or what visitors think about the events.

Based upon the specific elements of every social media sources,[2] the following attributes of social media (Table 5.1) could be integrated with AR:

Thus, by combining AR technologies with various social media information types and sources, people can use more current information to connect with others. For instance, if a customer evaluates a hotel with the assistance of an AR system, the customer would not only be able to see the hotel's swimming pool in 3D, but they would also be able to gather other additional information such as the opinions of other customers posted on Twitter or Facebook. By collecting more personalized and varied information, tourists can take better decisions (e.g. if there are negative reviews about the water quality, customers might decide to choose another hotel).

Moreover, user-specific profiles and preferences (e.g. about hotel and restaurants preferences) can also be taken into consideration for further improving customer value from a customer perspective. Furthermore, other information sources can also be identified and used for providing a more customer-oriented service. For instance, information from online travel sites (e.g. TripAdvisor[3]) can be

Table 5.1 Social media attributes

Social Media	*Attributes/Types of information*	*Example*
Facebook	• Posts (text, picture, video) on fan pages, groups or personal timelines • Socio-demographics and states (Users age, gender etc.) • Likes of fan pages • Etc.	• e.g. display opinions of different users of a special place (e.g. swimming pool). These opinions can be sorted by socio-demographic factors like age (e.g. young travellers vs. families) etc.
Twitter	• Socio-demographics (user's gender etc.) • Tweets • Followers • Etc.	• e.g. show current tweets for a special place (e.g. opinions about the current atmosphere of a club)

integrated into the illustration of the AR. User-generated reviews trough TripAdvisor or Hotels.com are very popular and can be used to extract the opinion of the guests (Duan et al., 2013).

This new kind of integrated service can be used in different areas of the tourism industry. First, travel agencies can use it to generate value and support possibilities of co-creation, according to Keller et al. (2015). Therefore, local travel agencies might be more competitive against the internet holiday booking sites and customers will gain a better view about their holidays before booking. Second, customers can use this solution during their holiday trip to explore the destination context. Furthermore, hybrid models of both (e.g. local tourist offices etc.) can offer this service to generate value.

These considerations are better illustrated in the following tourism scenario:

> *Envision yourself booking a holiday: how would you respond to the proposition to reduce the probability of a negative and disappointing trip? Would you agree to it?* If you respond favorably to this option, you might book your next holiday at a travel agent with an AR system. The implementation such an application supports you as a customer in your decision-making by not only providing more information about the holidays but also more individual-relevant information. For instance, before the travel has even started, you can check out whether your individual requirements for a favorable holiday (e.g. bus station next to the hotel, calm and quiet position of the hotel) are fulfilled. Therefore, you can reduce your individual risk of booking a holiday that you will not enjoy, simply by using the service offered by travel agents.

This example clarifies the advantage of the implementation of an AR system for customers as well as travel agents. However, this benefit could be enhanced by the combination of the technology with social media. The critical aspect here might be the integration of various information sources. Information can be differentiated according to information that customers want and need, respectively. Customers are commonly well-supplied with the information that they need; for example, prices or photos of hotel rooms. This information is readily available and can even be used in classical media like travel brochures. However, AR can enable the user not only to obtain this information but also make it possible to experience a hotel room. Thus, the technology application can assist to improve the customer's experience and service. Moreover, the major advantage of the implementation of an AR system can be seen in the integration of the other kind of information mentioned above, namely information that customers do not necessarily need to have but rather that they strongly desire. This information largely includes customer-generated content, namely not only official information but also experiences that travellers have previously gained, e.g. evaluations of the hotel, nearby restaurants, sightseeing etc. Customers' wish to gather this special kind of information can be clarified by social media (e.g. TripAdvisor) with an ever-growing community. Therefore, it is easily conceivable that customers especially cherish the further details provided by other customers, potentially because they take the truthiness of such content for granted. They assume that normally the informants do not expect any advantage from manipulating their statements.

Figure 5.2 shows an example of an AR system with social media integration related to the tourism industry:

Figure 5.2 Example of an AR application with social media integration

The picture (Figure 5.2) shows an impression of scenery in Barcelona seen through AR glasses, for example. At the edge are depicted possible interfaces to other applications, such as social media. Even before a customer books the travel or arrives at the travel destination, the application enables him/her not only to gain a first impression about the position of the hotel but also to gain valuable information (i.e. evaluations of restaurants nearby via TripAdvisor). Besides this example, there exist a number of further possibilities – as mentioned above – to integrate social media (e.g. Facebook) into the application and enhance the service provided and benefit for both parties.

Opportunities, chances and benefits: a marketing's perspective

The rise of the internet and the involved technological revolution have dramatically changed the market situation and the conditions in the travel industry (Buhalis & Law, 2008). Based upon this accelerated development of modern information and communication technologies, new marketing channels such as internet travel agencies and travel report forums have been formed and thus the information available to the customer has continuously improved (Buhalis & Law, 2008). Consequently, the offerings become more interchangeable and imitable (Carey et al., 2012), as well as transparent for the customers. Besides the information customers can get through the description of the hotelier or evaluate platforms run by internet travel agencies (Schegg & Fux, 2010; Buhalis & Mamalakis, 2015), travellers can interchange information and experiences quick and directly on a peer-to-peer basis (Sigala, 2007). As a result, the travel industry cannot create any further value by providing information about the holidays and travel options, because in fact the customer can already gather sufficient needed as well as desired information, although the way of obtaining this information is very time-consuming and could be difficult. Nevertheless, the progress also opens up new chances of opportunities. The considerations in the prior sections indicate beneficial starting points to exploit (see previous section). Hence, a change of the business and marketing strategy towards the customer is necessary (Carey et al., 2012) to implement a target-aimed customer approach.

A promising opportunity in service intensive industries – such as the travel industry – can be seen in a service-oriented development of the marketing. It is conceivable that a suitable approach could be to apply marketing from a SDL perspective according to the remarks of Vargo and Lusch. Contrary to former concepts, their approach focuses on the exchange of services and the co-creation of value and no longer even strictly on the exchange of goods (Vargo & Lusch, 2004; Lusch et al., 2006). Their "service-dominant" perspective is founded upon 10 foundational premises (Lusch et al., 2006; Vargo et al., 2008), which are described in Table 5.2:

Table 5.2 Premises of the SDL lean on Vargo et al. (2008)

Foundational premises	Modified/new declaration
FP 1	Service is the fundamental basis of exchange
FP 2	Indirect exchange masks the fundamental basis of exchange
FP 3	Goods are a distribution mechanism for service provision
FP 4	Operant resources are the fundamental source of competitive advantage
FP 5	All economies are service economies
FP 6	The customer is always a co-creator of value
FP 7	The enterprise cannot deliver value, but only offer value propositions
FP 8	A service-centered view is inherently customer-oriented and relational
FP 9	All social and economic actors are resource integrators
FP 10	Value is always uniquely and phenomenologically determined by the beneficiary

In summary, service is the essential factor in all economies and all exchanges are fundamentally based upon the interchange of service between entities. Both of them can only offer value propositions and cannot deliver the value by themselves. Therefore, value is always a co-production with a uniquely determined use, which arises from the integration of the resources of the social and economic actors.

In the context of the travel industry, agencies could establish a consumer-oriented technological application like an AR system to improve their service in a service-dominant perspective (s. FP 1; FP 5). Through the possibility to gain more useful and additional information, the travel provider offers the customer a value (s. FP 7), for instance, by simplifying decision-making and/or reducing the probability of having a negative holiday. However, the value only arises if people accept the value proposition and became a co-creator of the value (s. FP 6). Accordingly, the customer him-/herself has to use the technical application offered by the travel agent. Therefore, the value is always individual and unique; for instance, if a travel agent implements an AR application, customers are offered more and even more individually desired information. If people use the system – for example, by wearing the data glasses, they accept this proposition and become a co-creator of their own individual value. The integration of the information that is relevant and useful for themselves can reduce the uncertainty before the booking decision (Buhalis & Law, 2008). The offer of this technology and the improvement of extraordinary information make the supplier more customer-oriented (s. FP 8) and offer an advantage compared to other online and offline competitors. Although almost all suppliers sell almost the same product, the situation is different because it focuses not on the product itself and the direct exchange, but rather on the service and the indirect exchange (s. FP 4). Both customers as well as suppliers are interested in increasing their value and thus both are keen to interact with each other to improve their individual advantage (s. FP 9; FP4). As an example, it can be seen that people are willing to use the AR system (e.g. data glasses) proposed by the travel agent because they want to improve their value of having a pleasant holiday. Vice versa, the supplier is determined to implement the system because it could help to create an advantage through the interaction with the customer, focusing not on the product but rather the service. As a result, a very beneficial situation is developed by the interaction of both parties. As a possible consequence, the supplier can continuously gain information about consumer needs and preferences and incorporate this knowledge to improve its customer approach and marketing strategy. The integration of this information into the marketing strategy can help to offer individualized offers, which increases sales and enables remaining competitive regardless of the commonly substitutable product (e.g. travel). On the other hand, the customer can derive useful and unique value by using the AR application and interacting with the supplier while showing one's preferences. Using such a system and integrating the information of the own preferences in the creation of the value enables the supplier to make him/her a suitable offer. Furthermore, it increases the value of the customer by improving the probability of having a pleasant holiday by reducing uncertainty; thus, ICT simplifies the decision-making (Sigala et al., 2001).

Therefore, AR with touchpoints to social media could be implemented to redesign a marketing strategy from a service-dominant perspective. It can be a beneficial value proposition of a supplier to the customer. The use and consequently the interaction have an individual value for both parties. Customers obtain information that they want to have and are supported to make a decision that satisfies themselves. Suppliers can improve the marketing strategy in a customer-oriented manner regardless of the substitutable product. Therefore, they can offer the customer an individualized travel experience, which leads to increased sales and a competitive market position.

AR in the travel industry: empirical evidence

In relation to the considerations above, the logical deduction is that the use of the mentioned technologies could have a positive impact on the travel industry. The opinion to use modern application is a widespread consensus even in research. In the literature, it can be found that the use and integration of modern information technologies reflects a good approach to improve marketing concepts in the service industry (Vargo et al., 2008). Besides the theoretical findings, the customer's perspective must also be considered and integrated in an appropriate manner.

Keller et al. present research on AR in the travel industry (Keller et al., 2015), which forms the basis of this section. A qualitative research approach was used to develop a theory about the use of AR in the travel industry, adapted from the customers' perspective based upon Grounded Theory (Glaser, 1998; Glaser & Strauss, 2009). The research was conducted in the fourth quarter of 2014 and the first quarter of 2015 (Keller et al., 2015).

The authors conducted a qualitative study to include the customer's perspective in the approach to use modern and innovative technologies to improve customer service as the marketing strategy. In the survey, participants were shown an example of an artificial environment. In particular, the interviewees were introduced to the concept of AR and its possibilities in the context of travelling. Therefore, the participants were shown a short video (WELT, 2015) and informed about how this application could be implemented in practice (e.g. glasses) to develop customer service. For instance, participants were informed that in an AR scenery they can gather additional information such as distances or proportions of a hotel room. In semi-structured interviews, participants expressed their opinions about the conditions under which they would use the technology and respond to the value proposition of gathering more relevant information to avoid unfavorable holidays. Furthermore, they commented on the value that they could gain in use for themselves from their perspective. Additionally, they evaluated how the improved service could have an impact on their behavior in context with a travel agency offering this kind of service.

Figure 5.3 shows the final model, which was developed in the qualitative research by Keller et al. (2015):

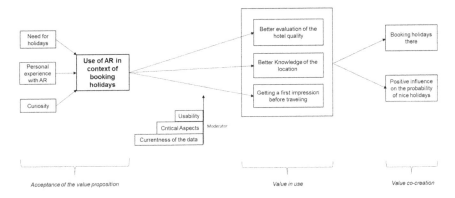

Figure 5.3 Model of the use of AR

Source: *Keller et al. (2015)*

In the qualitative research, three influencing factors for people's attitudes towards adopting an AR application as a service in the context of booking holidays were found (Keller et al., 2015). Furthermore, three moderators are identified that could enhance or weaken the supposed coherencies.

First, the "personal experience people took with AR", their individual "curiosity" and their "need for holidays" have a positive impact on acceptance of the value proposition given by the technology (Keller et al., 2015). This means in fact that the factors are not stringently inquired, but rather if they existent people are more likely to use the application while gathering information and making a decision.

The second moderator is that people were enabled to generate value in use through the implementation of this modern information technology (Keller et al., 2015). The tool offers the consumer additional and more detailed information, acknowledging that people are gaining a first impression before travelling, a better evaluation of the hotel and better knowledge of the location. The interviewees mentioned this benefit of the system consistently and confirmed the assumption and expectations hereby.

In the context of the second influencing factor, moderating factors are also mentioned by the participants of the study (Keller et al., 2015). If the "currentness of data", the "usability" (e.g. for spectacle wearer) and other "critical aspects" (e.g. the truthiness of the given information) are not guaranteed, the possible benefit could be weakened by these facets.

The third factor is that while adopting the application, people could co-create a value, which appears in an increasing "probability of nice holiday" and the heightened attitude to "book the holidays" at the point of sale, where they can use the AR application (Keller et al., 2015).

The findings indicate that from a customer's perspective the implementation of an AR system is very beneficial (Keller et al., 2015). The proposal of this service could be a kind of unique selling proposition in the highly competitive market of the tourism industry. As mentioned by the interviewees in the study, the system increases the probability of having a pleasant holiday and thus it offers them an advantage that classical and also online travel agencies cannot offer. For this reason, they are more willing to book at suppliers who can offer the service of such a system.

Conclusion and outlook

AR applications have become increasingly interesting and relevant for the tourism industry. For instance, customers can evaluate different services (hotel rooms, bars, museum etc.) from a more realistic perspective. Research has shown that customers are willing to use this technology because they anticipate that information systems applications like AR can help them to increase their individual value. Besides, the benefit of the integration arises not only for one of the both parties but for both of them. While using the application as well as social media, customers continuously reveal their preferences and true opinions, which facilitates the travel agent to offer travel options that are in demand and customer-oriented services at all times. Consequently, there is a rise in customers' probability of having a pleasant holiday and an increase in revenue on the supplier's side. Furthermore, there exists evidence that people are more likely to book their holidays where such an information system can provide their decision-making. In this manner, the pointed use and integration of technology and information gathered not only from official positions (e.g. travel agents, tour operators) but also from the target group itself can be used to strengthen and expand one's own market position. Online travel booking pages and local travel agencies might use this approach to become more competitive and increase their customer service level. Additionally, local tourist offices and museums can offer new services for travellers.

Social media sites like Twitter or Facebook can also be used to enable the use of more personal and actual data. Therefore, the use of different technologies like Big Data, Text Mining and sentiment analytics is needed. Current research shows how this data can be analyzed. Social media can be integrated through different specific attributes like visits to places of friends, posts at local locations, timelines or tweets about hotel or places.

For practical application, we recommend an AR app for smartphones as an easily implementable and applicable first step in the direction of implementing virtual environments in a marketing strategy. As an example, we refer to the AR application that IKEA has implemented with their catalog from 2014. The app enables customers to see the furniture of their choice embedded in their own apartment. For instance, they can test whether the couch from the catalog fits their living room and whether the measurements are suitable, as well as whether the color fits their other furnishing. Such an application could also be implemented for the tourism sector, for instance, allowing customers to see the room of a hotel via an AR app already at the travel agency before booking, simply by using simply an app on their smartphone. Therefore, the travel agent can offer an improved service and increase the probability of selling the travel option through supporting the decision-making of the customer. The implementation of a smartphone app can also be very beneficial for both parties even if the holiday has already started and the customers are at the travel destination. The app helps the customers quickly to find out interesting facts about the destination; for example, a new and fancy restaurant that is also favorably evaluated by other tourists. The supplier can track these and gain information about the customer and use it for a further customer approach. Furthermore, the customer can interpret the app as an advanced service of the travel agent and could incorporate this favorable evaluation for the future booking of holidays

Future research should empirically investigate the use and customer acceptance of this integration. Therefore, field or laboratory experiments in which persons can actively use the technology are conceivable. Besides testing an app, it is conceivable – as a further example – to enable people to discover a hotel while using data glasses. In this situation, an observation can help to discover critical aspects and improve the usability of the technology. Subsequently, a survey could be conducted to specify the relevant needs and to investigate additional requirements. Furthermore, different domain-specific adoptions (e.g. tourism sector etc.) are needed.

Notes

1 www.tripadvisor.com
2 www.facebook.com; www.twitter.com
3 *www.tripadvisor.com*

References

Azuma, R. T. (1997). A survey of augmented reality. *Presence*, 6(4), pp. 355–385.

Balduini, M., Valle, E. D., Dell'Aglio, D., Tsytsarau, M., Palpanas, T., & Confalonieri, C. (2013). Social listening of city scale events using the streaming linked data framework. In *The Semantic Web: ISWC 2013*. pp. 1–16.

Benkler, Y. (2006). *The Wealth of Networks: How Social Production Transforms Markets and Freedom*, New Haven, CT, Yale University Press.

Bonabeau, E. (2009). Decisions 2.0: The power of collective intelligence. *MIT Sloan Management Review*, 50(2), pp. 45–52.

Buhalis, D., & Law, R. (2008). Progress in information technology and tourism management: 20 years on and 10 years after the Internet: The state of eTourism research. *Tourism Management*, 29(4), pp. 609–623.

Buhalis, D., & Mamalakis, E. (2015). Social media return on investment and performance evaluation in the hotel industry context. In *Information and Communication Technologies in Tourism 2015*. pp. 241–253.

Carey, R., Kang, D., & Zea, M. (2012). The trouble with travel distribution. *McKinsey Quarterly*.

Carmigniani, J., Furht, B., Anisetti, M., Ceravolo, P., Damiani, E., & Ivkovic, M. (2011). Augmented reality technologies, systems and applications. *Multimedia Tools and Applications*, 51(1), pp. 341–377.

Duan, W., Cao, Q., Yu, Y., & Levy, S. (2013). Mining online user-generated content: Using sentiment analysis technique to study hotel service quality. In *System Sciences (HICSS), 2013 46th Hawaii International Conference*. pp. 3119–3128.

Ebling, M. R., & Cáceres, R. (2010). Gaming and augmented reality come to location-based services. *IEEE Pervasive Computing*, (1), pp. 5–6.

Fayyad, U., Piatetsky-Shapiro, G., & Smyth, P. (1996). From data mining to knowledge dicovery in databases. *AI Magazine*, 17(3), p. 37.

Furht, B. (2011). *Handbook of Augmented Reality*, Vienna, Austria: Springer Science & Business Media.

Glaser, B. G. (1998). *Doing Grounded Theory: Issues and Discussions*, Sociology Press.

Glaser, B. G., & Strauss, A. L. (2009). *The Discovery of Grounded Theory: Strategies for Qualitative Research*, Transaction Publishers.

Gräbner, D., Zanker, M., Fliedl, G., & Fuchs, M. (2012). Classification of customer reviews based on sentiment analysis. In *Information and Communication Technologies in Tourism 2012*. pp. 460–470.

Granovetter, M. S. (1973). The strength of weak ties. *American Journal of Sociology*, 78(6), pp. 1360–1380.

Guttentag, D. A. (2010). Virtual reality: Applications and implications for tourism. *Tourism Management*, 31(5), pp. 637–651.

Kaplan, A. M., & Haenlein, M. (2010). Users of the world, unite! The challenges and opportunities of social media. *Business Horizons*, 53(1), pp. 59–68.

Kasper, W., & Vela, M. (2011). Sentiment analysis for hotel reviews. *Computational Linguistics-Applications Conference*, 231527, pp. 45–52.

Keller, B., Möhring, M., & Schmidt, R. (2015). *Augmented reality in the travel industry: A perspective how modern technology can fit consumer's needs in the service industry*. Presented at the Naples Forum on Services 2015, Naples.

Kipper, G., & Rampolla, J. (2012). *Augmented Reality: An Emerging Technologies Guide to AR*. London: Elsevier.

Knoblock, C. A., Minton, S., Ambite, J. L., Muslea, M., Oh, J., & Frank, M. (2001, April). Mixed-initiative, multi-source information assistants. In *Proceedings of the 10th International Conference on World Wide Web*, ACM, pp. 697–707.

Li, N., & Wu, D. D. (2010). Using text mining and sentiment analysis for online forums hotspot detection and forecast. *Decision Support Systems*, 48(2), pp. 354–368.

Lu, B., Ott, M., Cardie, C., & Tsou, B. K. (2011). Multi-aspect sentiment analysis with topic models. In *Data Mining Workshops (ICDMW), 2011 IEEE 11th International Conference on*. pp. 81–88.

Lusch, R. F., Vargo, S. L., Bolton, R. N., & Webster, F. E. (2006). *The Service-Dominant Logic of Marketing: Dialog, Debate, and Directions*, Armonk, NY, ME Sharpe.

Maedche, A., Staab, S., Wöer, K., Frew, A. J., & Hitz, M. (2002). Applying semantic web technologies for tourism information systems. In *Information and Communication Technologies in Tourism 2002*. Springer, pp. 311–319.

Markovitch, S., & Willmott, P. (2014). *Accelerating the Digitization of Business Processes*, McKinsey & Company.

Milano, R., Baggio, R., & Piattelli, R. (2011). The effects of online social media on tourism websites. In *ENTER 2011*. pp. 471–483.

McAfee, A. (2014). *I Have Glimpsed the Future of Commercial Aviation. There Were Fewer Workers There*. Retrieved April 19, 2015.

McAfee, A., Brynjolfsson, E., Davenport, T. H., Patil, D. J., & Barton, D. (2012). Big data: The management revolution. *Harvard Business Review*, 90(10), pp. 61–67.

Möhring, M., Schmidt, R., Härting, R.-C., Bär, F., & Zimmermann, A. (2014). Classification framework for context data from business processes. In F. Fournier & J. Mendling (eds.) *Business Process Management Workshops*, Springer, pp. 440–445.

Olsen, M. D., & Connolly, D. J. (2000). Experience-based travel: How technology is changing the hospitality industry. *The Cornell Hotel and Restaurant Administration Quarterly*, 41(1), pp. 30–40.

Qiang, Y., Law, R., & Gu, B. (2009). The impact of online user reviews on hotel room sales. *International Journal of Hospitality Management*, 28(1), pp. 180–182.

Schegg, R., & Fux, M. (2010). A comparative analysis of content in traditional survey versus hotel review websites. In *Information and Communication Technologies in Tourism 2010*. pp. 429–440.

Schmidt, R., Möhring, M., Härting, R.-C., Keller, B., & Zimmermann, A. (n.d.). Enabling social-data driven sales processes in local clothing retail stores. In *BPM Work-Shops 2015*, Lecture Notes in Business Information Processing, Springer, forthcoming.

Schmidt, R., Möhring, M., Härting, R.-C., Zimmermann, A., Heitmann, J., & Blum, F. (2015). Leveraging textual information for improving decision-making in the business process lifecycle. In R. Neves-Silva, L. C. Jain, & R. J. Howlett (eds.) *Intelligent Decision Technologies*, Springer International Publishing.

Sigala, M. (2007). WEB 2.0 in the tourism industry: A new tourism generation and new e-business models. ICT-Working Papers. Retrieved from http://hdl.handle.net/123456789/386

Sigala, M., Lockwood, A., & Jones, P. (2001). Strategic implementation and IT: Gaining competitive advantage from the hotel reservations process. *International Journal of Contemporary Hospitality Management*, 13(7), pp. 364–371.

Simoudis, E. (1996). Reality check for data mining. *IEEE Intelligent Systems*, 11(5), pp. 26–33.

Steuer, J. (1995). Defining virtual reality: Dimensions de-termining telepresence. In Biocca, F., & Levy, M.R. (eds.), *Communication in the Age of Virtual Reality*. pp. 33–56.

Tan, A. (1999). Text mining: The state of the art and the challenges. In *Proceedings of the PAKDD 1999 Workshop on Knowledge Discovery from Advanced Databases*. pp. 65–70.

Vargo, S. L., & Lusch, R. F. (2004). Evolving to a new dominant logic for marketing. *Journal of Marketing*, 68(1), pp. 1–17.

Vargo, S., Maglio, P., & Akaka, M. (2008). On value and value co-creation: A service systems and service logic perspective. *European Management Journal*, 26(3), pp. 145–152.

WELT. (2015). WELT-DE TV Video: ITB Gadgets. Retrieved April 27, 2015, from www.facebook.com/WELTVideo/videos/805365332844414

Williams, P., & Hobson, J. P. (1995). Virtual reality and tourism: Fact or fantasy? *Tourism Management*, 16(6), pp. 423–427.

Williams, P., Hobson, J. P., & Seaton, A. V. (1994). Tourism: The next generation: Virtual reality and surrogate travel, is it the future of the tourism industry? In *Tourism: The State of the Art*. pp. 283–290.

Yuen, S., Yaoyuneyong, G., & Johnson, E. (2011). Augmented reality: An overview and five directions for AR in education. *Journal of Educational Technology Development and Exchange*, 4(1), pp. 119–140.

Zikopoulos, P., & Eaton, C. (2011). *Understanding Big Data: Analytics for Enterprise Class Hadoop and Streaming Data*. London: McGraw-Hill Osborne Media.

Part 2

Marketing using social media applications and concepts

Ulrike Gretzel

Social media marketing

Web 2.0 technologies are in essence about easy and decentralized multimedia content creation and sharing and therefore require a different marketing mindset from the traditional company-controlled mass media communication paradigm (Gretzel & Yoo, 2013). While Web 2.0 applications create a wonderful toolset for tourism and hospitality marketers and social media platforms offer access to wider but also more easily targeted audiences, they also bring with them enormous challenges. A recent report on the social media marketing industry suggests that 35% of social media marketers are unsure whether their marketing efforts are actually effective (Stelzner, 2016). Marketers constantly face the danger of losing control over their brands and as soon as they figure out how marketing on a particular social media platform works, new platforms emerge or old ones revamp their algorithms.

Despite these challenges, social media marketing spending continues to grow. Worldwide spending on social media marketing is forecast to reach US$ 31 billion in 2016, almost double what it was in 2014 (Statista, 2016). Statista (2016) further reports that the global share of businesses taking advantage of social media marketing is 97% and that Facebook continues to be globally the most used platform by marketers. Forbes.com (2016), however, warns that growth in spending is not as high as predicted and shows that spending in some areas like blogging and podcasts has been drastically reduced. Social media are fundamentally about connecting people with people and ever more about connecting marketers with consumers. Yet, many marketers are now realizing that simple connections like getting consumers to follow a page are not enough. "Success in the social world of marketing requires a deep connection to the customer and the ability to drive a transformation of the company to embrace a whole new type of customer engagement" (Forbes.com, 2016, n.p.). These connections between marketers and consumers are increasingly mediated by so-called influencers and social media marketers in general are struggling to develop effective strategies to take advantage of this phenomenon.

Despite its central role in social media marketing, customer engagement remains ill-defined and under-researched. Pansari and Kumar (2017) argue that customer engagement results from committed relationships, trust, satisfaction and emotional bonding. Harrigan et al. (2017) suggest that customer engagement with tourism brands is comprised of three dimensions: 1) identification; 2) absorption and 3) interaction. While there is growing literature on how customers engage with brands, not so much is currently known about how tourism and hospitality organizations stage such engagement. Social media afford a variety of persistent, customized and triggered engagement opportunities (Cabiddu et al., 2014), and tourism and hospitality organizations currently have little empirical information on which they can base their strategic social media marketing decisions. This part of the book therefore tries to shed light on some of the phenomena that are pertinent to contemporary social media marketing.

Overview of part 2

The chapters included in this section of the book present interesting cases and discuss social media marketing phenomena from a variety of perspectives and covering different geographic areas, suggesting that social media marketing approaches vary across platforms, organization types and markets.

The first chapter, *Social media and destination marketing* by Ozturk, Salehi-Esfahani, Bilgihan and Okumus, deals with social media marketing for destination marketing organizations (DMOs) and argues that DMOs have shifted from wondering whether they should market on social media to struggling to identify how they should market on various platforms in order to achieve high returns on their investments. The authors claim that the roles of DMOs as social media marketers are not clear and that many DMOs have yet to define their social media marketing strategies. A short case study presenting the social media efforts of the Visit Orlando DMO illustrates various customer engagement efforts implemented by the DMO across several platforms. The chapter argues that sophisticated measurement is needed to ensure that these initiatives are actually effective.

Ge and Gretzel paint a detailed picture of China's internet and social media landscape in the following chapter titled *A new cultural revolution: Chinese consumers' internet and social media use* and provide insights into the latest travel-related trends regarding Chinese independent travellers. The chapter illustrates the many unique opportunities but also challenges tourism marketers face when wanting to promote their destinations or tourism products in the complex and crowded Chinese social media space. The authors argue that a technological orientation, careful analysis of the latest travel trends and intricate understanding of Chinese social media use conventions are needed in order to successfully market to Chinese travel consumers.

The chapter *Crowdsourcing in travel, tourism and hospitality: practical cases and possibilities* by Garrigos-Simon, Narangajavana, Sanz-Blas and Sanchez-Garcia discusses crowdsourcing as a valuable marketing practice. Defined as taking a function once performed by employees or contractors and outsourcing it to an undefined public through an open call on social media, crowdsourcing is identified as a particularly useful tool for tourism and hospitality organizations. The chapter discusses different application types of crowdsourcing and identifies a four-stage process that is common to most crowdsourcing efforts. The case studies presented in the chapter illustrate how crowdsourcing can be used to develop brands and create marketing contents.

Yoo and Lee's chapter *Facebook marketing by hotel groups: impacts of post content and media type on fan engagement* deals with Facebook marketing by hotel groups and focuses on customer engagement. Arguing that social media marketing requires a new, more conversation-focused paradigm, they analyze and compare the strategies of eight different hotel groups in terms of the type of posts used to encourage engagement on their Facebook pages. Specifically, they look at the content of the post as well as its media modality. Whether the hotel group responds to Facebook posts was also examined. The research measures engagement through a variety of variables but emphasizes "comments" as the most active and visible form. The results of the study indicate that conversational posts in text-only forms as well as responses by the hotel groups encourage consumers to leave comments on the hotel Facebook page more so than other strategies. The authors conclude that it is important for marketers to invite consumers into conversations and to help manage and maintain them through company responses.

In the last chapter of this section, *Influencer marketing in travel and tourism*, Gretzel provides an overview of influencer marketing. While the Web 2.0 initially promised decentralized communication, opinion leaders in the form of early bloggers started to emerge rather quickly, resulting in a tiered communication structure. Indeed, the chapter illustrates how the very nature of Web 2.0 with its opportunities to easily amass and display a following facilitated the emergence of the influencer phenomenon. Influencers play a critical role in aggregating and processing contents for end users and therefore help marketers reach their targeted end consumers. However, rather than just focusing on the opportunities and latest trends related to influencer marketing, the chapter also discusses the inherent challenges tourism and hospitality marketers face when selecting and working with influencers.

Together, the chapters in this section illustrate not only the complexity of social media marketing but also its dynamic nature due to continuing changes in Web 2.0 technology and in the social media platforms built on it. Stelzner (2016) reports that 40% of surveyed marketers agree that social media marketing has become more difficult in the past 12 months. How to best market in this environment therefore remains a puzzle that tourism and hospitality marketers have to perpetually solve. Research that focuses on social media marketing is critical in informing their practice.

References

Cabiddu, F., De Carlo, M., & Piccoli, G. (2014). Social media affordances: Enabling customer engagement. *Annals of Tourism Research*, 48, pp. 175–192.

Forbes.com. (2016). Social media spending triples but falls short of expectations. Retrieved online December 1, 2016 from www.forbes.com/sites/christinemoorman/2016/08/23/social-media-spending-triples-but-falls-short-of-expectations/#78d24bf47cff

Gretzel, U., & Yoo, K. H. (2013). Premises and promises of social media marketing in tourism. In S. McCabe (ed.) *The Routledge Handbook of Tourism Marketing*. New York, Routledge, pp. 491–504.

Harrigan, P., Evers, U., Miles, M., & Daly, T. (2017). Customer engagement with tourism social media brands. *Tourism Management*, 59, 597–609.

Pansari, A., & Kumar, V. (2017). Customer engagement: The construct, antecedents, and consequences. Journal of the Academy of Marketing Science, 45(3), 294–311.

Statista. (2016). Social advertising spending worldwide from 2014 to 2016 (in billion U.S. dollars). Retrieved online November 30, 2016 from www.statista.com/statistics/495115/social-ad-spend-worldwide/

Stelzner, M. A. (2016). 2016 Social media marketing industry report. Social media examiner. Retrieved online December 15, 2016 from www.socialmediaexaminer.com/wp-content/uploads/2016/05/SocialMediaMarketingIndustryReport2016.pdf

6 Social media and destination marketing

*Ahmet Bulent Ozturk, Saba Salehi-Esfahani,
Anil Bilgihan and Fevzi Okumus*

Introduction

Advancements in information communication technologies (ICTs) and internet tools have transformed the way businesses are run in the service and manufacturing industries. The tourism industry is no exception to this transformation; and with its increased accessibility, travellers have become more dependent on the internet not just for seeking out basic information, but for planning an entire trip. Today, travellers can easily access information about any destination in the world, plan and book their trips, and share memories of their vacations via their computers and mobile devices. For instance, a recent study conducted by Google (Google/ Ipsos Media, 2014), which surveyed 3,500 US leisure travellers who made at least one trip for personal reasons, revealed that travellers routinely turn to the internet during the early stages of trip planning.

One major development in the evolution of the internet is the increasing popularity of social media platforms. In the past, it was sufficient for internet users to visit a website and access desired information through their browser, where information was disseminated predominantly via one-way broadcasting methods (Web 1.0). Today, however, the latest version of the Web (Web 2.0) is much more interactive, where collaboration, exchange and two-way communication are possible through a variety of social media platforms. This new internet has drastically transformed how individuals communicate within our modern society (Hays et al., 2013).

Social media are particularly essential for travellers, as tourism involves information-intensive activities and consists of products and services that are intangible in nature where consumers do not have a chance to test or experience prior to consumption (Hays et al., 2013; Gretzel et al., 2000). Social media allows travellers to access user-generated information that can aid in the process of travel planning and allow them to make sound decisions regarding the selection of tourist destinations and different types of tourism-related products (Popesku, 2014). Thus, today's tourists are more sophisticated and independent, planning their own trips and booking vacations without the help of professionals, as used to be the norm. According to the Google/Ipsos Media (2014) study, 83% of leisure travellers were inspired by social networking, video or photo sites to consider personal or leisure trips. Social media has become an integral and seamless part of the modern travel experience; it allows travellers to search and plan their trips, interact with others throughout their travels, and even provide post-trip memories and feedback. Accordingly, the question for travel marketers and destination management organizations (DMO) has shifted from "Should we consider using social media?" to "How can we use social media more effectively?".

Destination marketing and DMOs

The tourism industry has been recognized as one of the main sources of economic growth in both developed and developing countries. Over the past few decades, many new tourism locations have emerged to supplement the traditional destinations of Europe and North America (Ozturk et al., 2015; Ozturk & Hancer, 2008). As a result, competitiveness among tourism destinations has increased significantly and today, marketers find themselves in a position where they must compete directly with other destinations in order to survive in this competitive environment (Ozturk & Qu, 2008; Wang, 2011). In this regard, the development and implementation of an effective marketing strategy has become critically important for destinations to gain and maintain competitive advantage.

In general, marketing activities at the destination level are primarily associated with strategies to entice potential tourists to visit a destination. More specifically, destination marketing is the process of communicating with potential tourists in an attempt to influence their decision-making in favor of a particular destination. Destination management organizations (DMOs) play a significant role in marketing and development activities for a destination (Wang, 2011). In general, DMOs are responsible for representing a specific destination and assisting the long-term development of a community by acting as organizers and facilitators of tourism (Wang, 2011; Destination Marketing Association International, 2016).

Morrison (2013) argues that destination management and destination marketing are two highly interrelated concepts. Destination management involves all the roles that a DMO should perform, such as planning and research, product development, leadership and coordination and community relations. Destination marketing is merely one responsibility of a DMO and mainly focuses on marketing and promotional activities, which are very important and well-accepted functions. Wang (2011) examined the roles of DMOs and focused particular attention on destination marketing. Based on interviews with 37 tourism businesses and a number of local DMO personnel in a small town in Indiana, Wang (2011) found that DMOs play the following marketing roles.

- *Community brand builder:* one of the most important responsibilities of a DMO is to market the destination as one complete entity. The DMO can market the destination as a wide geographical area through local- and regional-level partnerships.
- *Organizer of destination marketing campaigns*: the DMO is responsible for developing feasible marketing activities and appropriately implementing the promotional strategy with the support of local residents and partners.

- *Funding agent for collective marketing activities:* the DMO takes a leading role in a variety of collaborative marketing activities, especially those involving the collective marketing and promotion of the destination at a large scale.
- *Partner and team builder:* the DMO ensures that all partners involved in collaborative marketing activities share resources, responsibilities, risks, and gains so that mutually respectful and trusting relationships are established.
- *Network management organizer*: the DMO creates marketing networks wherein individual local businesses work in partnerships that provide value to the local community in ways that would be impossible to accomplish through uncoordinated individual efforts.

Social media and destination marketing

Social media refers to the various web applications that allow users to post and share content (Lange-Faria & Elliot, 2012). Safko & Brake (2009) define social media as the

> activities, practices, and behaviors among communities of people who gather online to share information, knowledge, and opinions using conversational media. Conversational media are Web-based applications that make it possible to create and easily transmit content in the form of words, pictures, videos, and audio (p. 6).

Social media applications include a mix of different types of ICT tools; as such, it is very difficult to categorize different social media applications in a systematic way, especially considering that a new social networking site appears on the internet seemingly every day. However, some researchers have attempted to classify the various social media types. Based on the theories in the field of media research and social processes (Short et al., 1976; Daft & Lengel, 1986), Kaplan and Haenlein (2010) utilized two dimensions, namely (1) social presence/media richness and (2) self-presentation/self-disclosure, to classify social media into six types. These types include blogs and microblogs, collaborative projects, virtual social worlds, content communities, social networking sites and virtual games (Table 6.1).

Table 6.1 Classification of social media

		Social presence/Media richness		
		Low	*Medium*	*High*
Self-presentation/ Self-disclosure	*High*	Blogs	Social networking sites (e.g. Facebook)	Virtual social worlds (e.g. Second Life)
	Low	Collaborative projects (e.g. Wikipedia)	Content communities (e.g. You Tube)	Virtual game worlds (e.g. World of Warcraft)

Source: adapted from Kaplan and Haenlein, 2010

Regarding social presence and media richness, collaborative projects and blogs score "low," as they are often text-based and permit only a limited amount of information exchange. Content communities and social networking sites score "medium," as users are able to share pictures, videos and other types of media in addition to text-based messages. However, as virtual games and social worlds attempt to replicate various dimensions of face-to-face interaction in a virtual environment, these forms of social media score "high" on the social presence and media-richness level. Along similar lines, social networking sites allow for greater self-disclosure than content communities. Last but not least, as virtual game worlds are administrated according to specific guidelines and rules that compel users to behave in a certain way, their self-disclosure levels are generally lower than those of virtual social worlds (Kaplan & Haenlein, 2010).

As previously mentioned, the current marketplace demands that an organization develop an effective marketing strategy to maintain its competitive advantage. Although the overall number of users has leveled off in recent years, social media has become one of the cornerstones of modern marketing strategy (Marketing Challanges International, 2013). In many industries, marketing strategies have shifted from traditional marketing practices to online, and online to social media campaigns. It is important to note that social media marketing differs from traditional marketing in that the former concept largely involves participation, sharing and collaboration, whereas the latter mainly deals with more straightforward advertising and selling practices (Kaplan & Haenlein, 2010). In a social network environment, marketers act as conversation managers who continuously communicate with potential customers through various social media channels (Yoo & Gretzel, 2010). Yoo and Gretzel (2010) argue that active consumer participation in marketing conversations has altered expectations, which in turn requires the application of new approaches. Based on this argument, the researchers identified specific marketing functions brought about by the shift in marketing strategy from traditional to Web 2.0-appropriate methods. These marketing functions include customer relationship management, product development, promotion, pricing, distribution, market research and performance measurement. Table 6.2 summarizes the differences between traditional marketing and Web 2.0 marketing. Overall, their study results demonstrated that customer relationships must be engaging and targeted and suggested that product development should involve active consumer participation. Additionally, in Web 2.0 marketing, companies have quick and easy access to their customers' feedback; this allows them to use this feedback as promotional material. However, a greater amount of accessible feedback and visible communication with potential customers leads to greater transparency, which can present challenges for the pricing of goods and services (Yoo and Gretzel, 2010).

As most other organizations, DMOs have realized the benefits of social media marketing and have begun to extensively utilize the platforms as viable marketing tools. In the recent past, it may have been sufficient to disseminate information via websites; today, however, DMOs cannot afford to resist the inclusion of social media in their marketing strategies, as it has become one of the most efficient

Table 6.2 Marketing functions extended with Web 2.0 technologies

Marketing Functions	Traditional Marketing	Web 2.0 Marketing
Customer Relations	• One-way communication • Offline customer service centers • Limited customer data • Limited C2C communications • Delayed response	• Feedback from customers • Online customer service • Customer identification via data mining • Virtual customer communities • Real-time communication
Product	• Limited product information • Mass products for mainstream markets • Company-created products	• Value added information on products: pictures, videos, catalogs, consumer reviews etc. • Product customization • Co-creation with consumers • Digital/virtual products
Price	• One-price pricing • Limited payment options	• Flexible pricing (price transparency) • Online payment
Promotion	• Offline promotions • One promotion message • Partnerships with traditional partners • Targeted customers • Mediated through mass media	• Online promotions • Customized promotion messages • Non-traditional partnerships • Customer participation • Facilitated by Web 2.0 tools
Place	• Intermediaries • Time required to process orders/bookings • Offline distribution of products	• Dis-/ Re-intermediation • Real-time ordering and processing • Online distribution of products
Research	• Delayed results • Encouraged through incentives • Push • No follow-up • Mediated • Sporadic • Costly • Response limited to numbers and text	• Real-time information through RSS or email alerts • Pull • Based on altruistic motivations • Immediate reactions • Unmediated • Continuous • Free data • Multiple formats
Performance Measurement	• Leads • Discrete times • Hard sales/visitor numbers	• Conversations • Continuous • Consumer sentiments

Source: Yoo and Gretzel, 2010

methods of modern marketing. Therefore, current DMOs include various forms of social media marketing activities, utilize different types of social media tools and approach assorted social networking channels to promote their destinations.

According to Morrison (2013), some of the most important social media marketing activities that a DMO can pursue are as follows (p. 385):

• *Building and maintaining communities of interest:* as social networks are likely to group people according to similar interests, a DMO can take advantage of social networks to build a strong community that shares an interest in its specific destination.

- *Collecting user-generated content:* through social networking sites, a DMO can collect user-generated content, as people post blogs, comments, videos and photographs of trips to its destination.
- *Distributing topical news stories:* through social networking channels, a DMO can distribute news stories about its destination to those who have indicated an interest in the destination.
- *Emphasizing current events and campaigns:* as millions of people constantly check their various social networks, these sites provide a DMO with the opportunity to inform potential tourists about upcoming events and campaigns.
- *Encouraging word-of-mouth recommendations:* a DMO can use social networking tools to disseminate positive recommendations from previous visitors to influence others to visit the destination.
- *Getting feedback:* social networking sites present platforms for a DMO to conduct pools and surveys to obtain valuable feedback.

The way in which DMOs establish their presence in a social media environment and utilize modern marketing strategies may differ significantly from destination to destination (Hays et al., 2013). There is no one-size-fits-all social media marketing strategy that every DMO can adopt and apply to effectively market its destination. Some researchers have attempted to provide insight into the social media practices and strategies utilized by DMOs. For example, a study conducted by Munar (2012) identified three strategies that DMOs frequently apply to their social media marketing practices: mimetic, advertising and analytic. According to the mimetic strategy, a DMO will copy the style of a social networking site and apply it to their own website. For example, a DMO might ask visitors to write about their previous experience at the destination and/or upload photos and videos from their travels, thus creating an artificial social network. The advertising strategy views social media channels as advertising conduits and promotional platforms. As per this strategy, a DMO will redirect advertising campaigns and news to social media sites such as Facebook or YouTube, which increases the DMO's social media presence and raises awareness of its destination brand. Finally, the analytic strategy adopts a data mining approach and analyzes, selects, classifies, monitors and evaluates visitor-generated content that is already available on the Web (Munar, 2012).

Influencer marketing is another strategy that DMOs have begun to adopt in recent years. Influencer marketing involves the practice of identifying individuals who have influence over a target audience. Influencers can be buyers, users or recommenders of products or services both online and offline. Influencers may also be trusted third parties such as bloggers, journalists, academics, public figures or celebrities. In social media marketing, influencers may also be real people, not traditional celebrities (Appinions, 2012). For example, DMOs might identify social travellers, invite them to the destination and ask them to share their experiences on various social media channels; for example, the traveller may be asked to upload videos on YouTube, post photos on Instagram or send out tweets on Twitter.

CASE STUDY: VISIT ORLANDO

Visit Orlando is an official organization that provides tourists with information on the city of Orlando. The website provides information for tourists to utilize during the preliminary stages of trip planning; potential travellers can visit the site to find a travel agent, access weather and climate forecasts, see what events will be taking place in Orlando, purchase tickets and enjoy discounts on attractions. Additionally, Visit Orlando launched a marketing campaign called "Orlando – The Never Ending Story," a universal platform that allows visitors to tell their stories and share memories of the region. This campaign focuses on the emotional connections made during tourists' visits (Myers, 2015). The campaign maintains a website, OrlandoStories.com, where people can tell their stories and post photos of themselves enjoying Central Florida. The campaign also promotes the use of the #MyOrlandoStory social media hashtag for all domestic and international visitors to share their memories via communication venues such as Twitter, Facebook, and Instagram. When visitors post content that includes the #MyOrlandoStory tag, Visit Orlando might pick it up and repost the content on their official website (Myers, 2015). The following section explains the social media platforms officially used by Visit Orlando in its online marketing campaign.

Facebook

Facebook was first introduced in 2004 and currently has 170,694,747 users. Facebook is a major component of the lives and daily practices of its users; a typical user spends about 20 minutes per day on the site, and two-thirds of users sign into their Facebook page at least once a day (Ellison et al., 2007). In 2006, Facebook introduced "profiles" for commercial organizations. As of November 2006, almost 22,000 organizations had Facebook pages (Ellison et al., 2007). Visit Orlando's Facebook page includes information regarding its initial founding (1984), the company's purpose (to promote the city of Orlando), their address and phone number, and a direct link to their official website. The Visit Orlando Facebook page has 824,719 followers and includes 14,310 reviews about the city. Additionally, people are given the opportunity to rate their Orlando experience on a scale of one to five stars; one star indicates a very negative ordeal and five stars denotes a very positive experience. On its Facebook page, Visit Orlando provides visitors with the opportunity to click on a sign up button to be redirected to another page where they can register their email address to receive updates about Orlando. Visit Orlando's Facebook page also includes photo albums with pictures of events, tourist attractions, theme parks and restaurants to convey to potential visitors a sense of the Orlando experience. The page also provides visitors with two options to improve communication between travellers and the organization: (1) visitors can contact Visit Orlando directly via Facebook message, and (2) visitors can post pictures and write a post on the organization's virtual wall.

Twitter

Twitter is a popular online social media platform that was introduced in 2007. Twitter users can write and post short messages, called tweets, comprised of only 140 characters. Twitter boasts 100 million daily visitors who use the platform for various purposes, such as learning about breaking news, keeping up with their favorite sports team, and finding employment. Twitter is an online network that allows users to connect with people who share similar interests and enables individuals to instantly broadcast a piece of information around the world (Mcheyzer-Williams & Mcheyzer-Williams, 2016). Twitter also has a feature called the "hashtag," which allows users to self-categorize their messages and join a virtual discussion on a given topic (An & Weber, 2016). Visit Orlando's Twitter page, created in 2009, has a direct link to Visit Orlando's official website. Currently, it has 103k followers and 16.2k likes, and has uploaded 2,134 photos and videos. Moreover, Visit Orlando itself follows 1,331 people and businesses, thus staying up-to-date on the tweets posted by those parties. The Visit Orlando Twitter page distributes information on Orlando-area events, attractions and restaurants and utilizes the opportunity to participate in a virtual conversation with people who seek out topics relating to Orlando, travel, Harry Potter and the like. Notably, the top of the Visit Orlando Twitter page features a static photo that encourages people to share their stories about Orlando with others using #MyOrlandoStory on OrlandoStories.com.

YouTube

YouTube is a "content community" that was founded in 2005. YouTube allows users to post, watch, comment on and share original videos via a URL link. YouTube is one of the most popular social media platforms; every minute of every day, more than 35 hours of video is uploaded to the site (O'Neill, n.d.). Dehghani et al. (2016) conducted a study on YouTube advertising and found that YouTube videos contribute to increases in people's brand awareness and purchase intention. The terminology of the "viral video" has become prevalent and refers to a concept in which a video clip attracts significant attention and is distributed to others in a virus-like manner. The viral video concept has caused companies to realize that they can take advantage of this marketing avenue to reach potential customers; therefore, many companies have created their own YouTube channels to post marketing videos (O'Neill, n.d.). Visit Orlando has its own YouTube channel which features a direct link to its other social media domains. The Visit Orlando YouTube page currently has more than 3,500 subscribers and contains various videos about events, theme parks and outdoor activities.

Pinterest

Pinterest was launched in 2010 as a means to connect people around the world based on shared tastes and interests using images and photographs. Users not only post original pictures and images, but also "like" and/or "repin" the images posted by other users into categorized albums (Hemant & Avan, 2015). Spitznagel (2013) states that in 2013, Pinterest was the third most popular website after Facebook and Twitter. Visit Orlando has a Pinterest account with the following motto: "Official Pinterest boards of Visit Orlando filled with plenty of Orlando inspiration." The Pinterest page includes several albums with information on Orlando vacation tips, dining, lodging, events and sports. As of 2016, the Visit Orlando Pinterest page had 27 boards (albums), 662 pins, 58 likes, and 3.5k followers. Followers are also able to access links to the Visit Orlando Twitter page and official website via the Pinterest page.

Instagram

Instagram is a relatively new mobile application that was introduced in 2010. Instagram users can easily upload photos and add captions; users can publicly and virtually share those photos using hashtags (#) to bring together users with common interests. Instagram users can share their life moments via pictures and can address a person directly using the @ symbol (Manikonda, 2014). Instagram users also have the option to specify where a given picture was taken. The Visit Orlando Instagram account has 64.1k followers and has posted 716 photos. At the top of Visit Orlando's Instagram homepage, people are encouraged to share their stories with the following statement: "Share your Orlando vacation memories using #MyOrlandoStory." Additionally, those individuals who are interested in sharing a more in-depth look into their Orlando experience are encouraged to follow a link to the Visit Orlando YouTube channel.

Conclusion and discussion

Web 2.0 is constantly evolving and social media is characterized by ever-changing tools and up-and-coming platforms; thus, it is difficult for DMOs to adopt a long-term strategic perspective (Munar, 2012). It is becoming increasingly important for DMOs to adopt social media marketing strategies, as public sector funding budgets have been cut and companies must ensure that marketing budgets are spent appropriately (Hays et al., 2013). With limited resources, social media strategies are especially important for tourism – an information-intensive industry – as they allow DMOs to reach global audiences.

DMOs should accept the fact that this is the era of technology and that they must adopt an online presence or risk losing their competitive advantage (Popesku, 2014). However, the only thing more damaging than not understanding or refusing to adopt social media marketing practices is their poor or ineffective use (Schegg et al., 2008).

One major concern often prevents companies from adopting social media marketing strategies during the early stages of social media utilization: measuring the return on investment (ROI). Marketing experts are under considerable pressure to measure the outcomes of their policies. However, measuring the effectiveness of social media is extremely difficult (Hays et al., 2013). That said, there are multiple metrics that can be used to measure social media impact. Companies might measure "audience size (e.g. number of followers), reach (e.g. viral impact), engagement (e.g. number of comments), sentiment (e.g. consumer response) and outcomes (e.g. resulting traffic, conversions)" (Schetzina, 2010). Qualitative measurements are typically required for social media assessment; however, online marketers are neither comfortable nor familiar with those methods (Fisher, 2009).

Many DMOs often have an ambiguous and diverse understanding of social media. The rights and wrongs of general marketing are barely defined, and the rules of social media marketing are even more vague and imprecise. Consequently, social media is still not widely accepted or appreciated as a vital tool in marketing strategies and is frequently underfunded and/or disused. Researchers have suggested that the main factor that contributes to the development of an advanced social media strategy is leadership; strong leadership can exercise great influence and support high levels of social media activity (Hays et al., 2013). DMOs must address the various difficulties associated with processing their online presence through social media. Many DMOs could enhance their position by recognizing and acknowledging social media as a viable marketing means in its own right rather than merely using social media as if it were like any other marketing tool. Following that realization, DMOs should focus on developing official yet flexible strategies. DMOs should pay careful attention to opportunities and threats to ensure that they are using social media effectively and are exercising its full potential to initiate informal conversations (Hays et al., 2013). DMOs must apply the Kaplan and Haenlein (2010) list of five key actions: "be active, be interesting, be humble, be informal, and be honest." Though this list was originally created for web marketing, it is applicable to social media marketing as well.

There are certain tasks that DMOs must undertake. DMOs must be interactive on their social media platforms, as involvement and the encouragement of contribution are two keys to attracting and keeping users (Hays et al., 2013). DMOs should encourage people to share their blogs, comments, stories, videos and pictures of their trips to a destination on various social media platforms; users should be urged to post videos on YouTube and Vimeo and photos on Instagram, Pinterest or Flickr (Popesku, 2014). Furthermore, DMOs must remain up-to-date and aware of the social media approaches of other tourism experts and organizations so that they may learn from their successes and failures. DMOs also need to distinguish social media from other marketing tools by recognizing it as a distinct and powerful instrument and must establish innovative and flexible approaches and strategies to utilize social media. In doing so, the long-term success of social media marketing will be all but guaranteed (Hays et al., 2013). Munar (2012) also suggests that there should be sufficient formalization and synergy between organizational cultures and social media initiatives to facilitate success. She also argues that it is crucial for top-level management to focus attention on the strategic value of social media and the importance of Web 2.0.

Based on the above discussion, Visit Orlando must recognize social media as a distinct marketing tool and must strive to effectively utilize social media. The organization must develop a good understanding of their performance by applying the previously-discussed metrics to assess the effectiveness of their efforts. These metrics include measurements of audience size, rate of audience growth and the number of visits to social media pages. Visit Orlando must continue to involve social media and encourage visitors and tourists to share, post and spread the word of their experiences through various media. Finally, it is critical for Visit Orlando to correctly and precisely use social media to maintain its competitive advantage. Otherwise, it will likely lose the game that has become so popular in this fast-paced era of technology.

Visit Orlando could identify the tourists' characteristics visiting Orlando by interviewing them to have a better understanding of what their needs and wants are, why they chose Orlando as their vacation destination, and what their experiences have been like so far. Then, they can address the negative experiences of tourists and reinforce the positive aspects of their experience through social media. In addition, Visit Orlando should watch its usage; meaning that they should know when, how and how often prospective tourists use their social media. For instance, they could use Google Analytics which is one of several services that can provide extensive information on traffic to web services such as blogs, such as information on how people are referred to their site, how long they stayed, and what they viewed and what they clicked on. It is a great way of scrutinizing what the prospective visitors finds interesting and useful from what they ignore.

References

An, J., & Weber, I. (2016). # greysanatomy vs.# yankees: Demographics and hashtag use on Twitter. *Proceedings of The Tenth International Conference on Web and Social Media*, Palo Alto, CA: AAAI Press, pp. 523–526.

Appinions. (2012). Basics of influence marketing [Online]. *Appinions*. Available at: http://blog.appinions.com/?s=basics+of+influence+ [Accessed 5 May 2016].

Daft, R. L., & Lengel, R. H. (1986). Organizational information requirements, media richness and structural design. *Management Science*, 32(5), pp. 554–571.

Dehghani, M., Niaki, M., Ramezani, I., & Sali, R. (2016). Evaluating the influence of YouTube advertising for attraction of young customers. *Computers in Human Behavior*, 59, pp. 165–172.

Destination Marketing Association International. (2016). What is a destination marketing organization? [Online]. *Destination Marketing Association International.* Available at: www.destinationmarketing.org/faq [Accessed 5 May 2016].

Ellison, N. B., Steinfield, C., & Lampe, C. (2007). The benefits of Facebook "Friends": Social capital and college students' use of online social network sites. *Journal of Computer-Mediated Communication,* 12(4), pp. 1143–1168.

Fisher, T. (2009). ROI in social media: A look at the arguments. *Journal of Database Marketing & Customer Strategy Management,* 16(3), pp. 189–195.

Google/Ipsos Media. (2014). *The 2014 Traveler's Road to Decision* [pdf]. Available at: https://think.storage.googleapis.com/docs/2014-travelers-road-to-decision_research_studies.pdf

Gretzel, U., Yuan, Y. L., & Fesenmaier, D. R. (2000). Preparing for the new economy: Advertising strategies and change in destination marketing organizations. *Journal of Travel Research,* 39(2), pp. 146–156.

Hays, S., Page, S. J., & Buhalis, D. (2013). Social media as a destination marketing tool: Its use by national tourism organisations. *Current Issues in Tourism,* 16(3), pp. 211–239.

Hemant, C. S., & Avan, R. J. (2015). Why do college students use Pinterest? A model and implications for scholars and marketers. *Journal of Interactive Advertising,* 15(1), pp. 54–66.

Kaplan, A. M., & Haenlein, M. (2010). Users of the world, unite! The challenges and opportunities of social media. *Business Horizons,* 53(1), pp. 59–68.

Lange-Faria, W., & Elliot, S. (2012). Understanding the role of social media in destination marketing. *Tourismos: An International Multidisciplinary Journal of Tourism,* 7(1), pp. 193–211.

Manikonda, L., Hu, Y., & Kambhampati, S. (2014). Analyzing user activities, demographics, social network structure and user-generated content on Instagram, *CoRR abs/1410.8099* (November 2014), pp. 1–5.

Marketing Challenges International. (2013). *Social Media Marketing for Global Destinations in the Meetings and Conventions Industry* [pdf]. New York: Marketing Challenges International. Available at: http://library.constantcontact.com/download/get/file/1103328861222-343/MCIntl++Social+Media+in+the+Meetings++Conventions+Industry_final_090413.pdf

Mcheyzer-Williams, L. J., & Mcheyzer-Williams, M. G. (2016). Our year on Twitter: Science in #SocialMedia. *Trends in Immunology,* 37(4), pp. 260–265.

Morrison, A. M. (2013). *Marketing and Managing Tourism Destinations,* London and New York, Routledge.

Munar, A. M. (2012). Social media strategies and destination management. *Scandinavian Journal of Hospitality and Tourism,* 12(2), pp. 101–120.

Myers, B. (2015). Visit Orlando using social media to entice visitors [Online]. *News 13.* Available at: www.mynews13.com/content/news/cfnews13/news/article.html/content/news/articles/cfn/2015/5/31/visit_orlando_visito.html [Accessed 5 May 2016].

O'Neill, S. n.d. What is YouTube? [Online]. *Diginital Unite.* Available at: www.digitalunite.com/guides/tv-video/what-youtube [Accessed 5 May 2016].

Ozturk, A. B., & Hancer, M. (2008). Exploring destination satisfaction: A case of Kizkalesi, Turkey. *Tourism Analysis,* 13(5–1), pp. 473–484.

Ozturk, A. B., Ozer, O., & Çaliskan, U. (2015). The relationship between local residents' perceptions of tourism and their happiness: A case of Kusadasi, Turkey. *Tourism Review,* 70(3), pp. 232–242.

Ozturk, A. B., & Qu, H. (2008). The impact of destination images on tourists' perceived value, expectations, and loyalty. *Journal of Quality Assurance in Hospitality & Tourism*, 9(4), pp. 275–297.

Popesku, J. (2014). Social media as a tool of destination marketing organizations. *Singidunum Journal of Applied Sciences*, pp. 715–721.

Safko, L., & Brake, D. K. (2009). *The Social Media Bible: Tactics, Tools, and Strategies for Business Success*, Hoboken, NJ, John Wiley & Sons.

Schegg, R., Liebrich, A., Scaglione, M., & Sharifah Fatimah Syed, A. (2008). An exploratory field study of Web 2.0 in tourism. In O'Connor, P., Hoepken, W., & Gretzel, U. (eds.), *Information and Communication Technologies in Tourism 2008: Proceedings of the International Conference in Innsbruck, Austria, 2008*. Vienna, Springer Vienna, pp. 152–163.

Schetzina, C. (2010). *Introduction to Social Media Analytics*, New York, PhoCus Wright.

Short, J., Christie, B., & Williams, E. (1976). *The Social Psychology of Telecommunications*, London: John Wiley & Sons.

Spitznagel, E. (2013). Dude! The battle to become the "Male Pinterest" [Online]. *Bloomberg*. Available at: www.bloomberg.com/news/articles/2013-04-10/dude-the-battle-to-become-the-male-pinterest [Accessed 5 May 2016].

Wang, Y. (2011). Destination marketing and management: Scope, definition and structures. In W. Youcheng & P. Abraham (eds.) *Destination Marketing and Management Theories and Applications*. Wallingford, Oxfordshire; Cambridge, MA, CABI, pp. 1–20.

Yoo, K. H., & Gretzel, U. (2010, June 20–22). Web 2.0: New rules for tourism marketing. In Beeton, S. & Hsu, C. (eds.), *The 41st Annual Conference of the Travel and Tourism Research Association*. San Antonio, TX: Lake Orion: Travel and Tourism Research Association.

7 A new cultural revolution

Chinese consumers' internet and social media use

Jing Ge and Ulrike Gretzel

Introduction – a look behind the great firewall

Much has been written over the past decade about internet surveillance and censorship in China, a phenomenon often referred to as the Great Firewall. Scholars and Western media have attempted to position online China within a discourse of media control, as government policy has, for instance, blocked popular social media sites, such as Facebook, Twitter and YouTube. As a result of this government policy, it seems the Chinese internet and its users remain largely separated from the World Wide Web (Fong, 2009). However, though the metaphor of the Great Firewall has unveiled some aspects of China's internet situation, it fails to acknowledge the reality of the prosperous and dynamic Cyber-China that has evolved despite government constraints. By the end of 2015, the number of Chinese netizens reached 668 million, making China the largest internet population in the world, according to the China Internet Network Information Center (CNNIC, 2016). Further, the fractional internet penetration rate in China is increasing. While internet penetration in urban areas was more than 64% in 2015, rural areas were catching up, reaching more than 34% (CNNIC, 2016).This momentum in growth shows that China is experiencing rapid popularization of the internet in rural areas, while its overall internet growth also shows no sign of slowing down.

China's prosperous internet landscape is characterized by vibrant home-grown internet services, ranging from search engines and web portals to a large array of social media sites. Social media users make up 95% of total Chinese netizens (ChinaInternetWatch, 2015c), meaning that those Chinese who are online, are also on social media. Mobile applications and digital wearable devices are new engines further stimulating internet growth (CNNIC, 2016). This advancement of internet mobility allows Chinese netizens to access social media sites anytime and anywhere.

One phenomenon that warrants particular mention is that the adoption of specific types of social media platforms is completely different from patterns that can be seen in other parts of the world. Location-based services (LBS), social networking service (SNS), Weibo (the Chinese version of microblogs), instant messaging service (i.e. WeChat) and bulletin board systems (BBS) are the major social media categories, and 88% of the users are active on at least one social media site

(GoGlobe, 2013). Among them, instant messaging and Weibo represent more than 90% and nearly 80% Chinese social media users, respectively (CNNIC, 2016).

Through much of the West, Facebook, Twitter and YouTube hold sway as default social media platforms, attracting a wide range of demographics (Gretzel et al., 2010). Yet the same does not hold true in China's complex social media landscape, as a variety of channels attract very different users. Douban (www.douban.com), Kaixin 001 (www.kaixin001.com) and RenRen (www.renren.com) are Facebook-like sites. While users of Douban connect according to their personal hobbies, such as art, books and movies, Kaixin 001 attracts white-collar professionals who often share information relating to health, relationships and professional advancement. RenRen is another platform, designed for university students to connect with class-mates (Chong, 2013). Moreover, the video-sharing sites space in China is occupied by Youku and Tudou, with both resembling YouTube. Ba Ba Bian and Ba Bi Dou are recognized as popular photo-sharing sites, characterized by similar features to those offered by Flickr. The competitive microblog sites, Sina Weibo, Souhu Weibo, Netease Weibo and Tencent Weibo, combine many features of Facebook and Twitter, and have surpassed SNS in terms of use, becoming one of the most popular social media services in China (ChinaInternetWatch, 2015d). While SNS users keep in touch with friends, a majority of Weibo users engage with the social media platform to acquire the latest information, record feelings and experiences, keep track of celebrities, discuss topical issues and share personal opinions (iRe-search, 2012). In addition to these so-called "equivalent" sites, China also offers social media services that are not available in the West. For instance, WeChat is a mobile messaging app that affords intimate and private communication among close friends, which means it is essentially a tool for one-on-one interaction. On the other hand, it also contains a "Moments" feature that allows its users to broad-cast updates to those that are in their friend circle and comment on their friend's updates. In addition, it is now also used by companies to push promotional mes-sages to users and to offer customer service.

The emerging trends in internet and social media adoption also offer new per-spectives on China's indigenous innovations. China is becoming increasingly adept at attracting and profiting from technological advances and networks world-wide in order to satisfy the different preferences of its netizens and to tailor tech-nology to local consumer needs. As a result, Chinese social media foster particular usage conventions, which also reflect specific cultures (Gretzel & Yoo, 2013). Thus, business worldwide needs to acknowledge the complex use of social media by Chinese consumers in order to intrinsically understand social media use pat-terns and culture in modern China.

In recent literature, social media have been described as a mega trend that has substantially impacted the tourism system (Leung et al., 2013), and China, of course, is not excluded. As the world's largest outbound tourist market (ChinaIn-ternetWatch, 2015a), Chinese tourists have created a new wave in terms of the way they travel. This opens up an avenue for intricate linkages between social media adoption and an emergent outbound tourism phenomenon. This chapter will ini-tially address the new trends related to Chinese general consumers' as well as tourists' internet and social media usage, and will present significant implications for marketing tourism to Chinese consumers.

Chinese culture 2.0 – the Weibo dynasty

Economic growth, social progress, cultural change, along with technological advancement and access make social media platforms increasingly the shared commons where an ever growing number of Chinese consumers convenes to engage in various online activities, from information search and online shopping to social sharing and online entertainment. The result is a Chinese online economy with distinct characteristics. Importantly, the development of e-commerce in China is much higher than the global average, and it is the world's largest online market (Nielsen, 2016). The idea of globalization and the very nature of commercial culture lead to Chinese consumers experiencing a transition away from the Confucian tradition to a modern norm. Although deeply influenced by Western culture, Chinese consumers are modernizing, but are not becoming Western (Doctoroff, 2012). Doctoroff (2012) explains that the modern Chinese consumers live in a continuum between propagating Western material lifestyles and maintaining traditional local culture. On one hand, they are ambitious and like to boldly show off status. The moral characters of modesty and self-sacrifice no longer matter, as they want to stand out from the crowd, to act and express themselves individually. On the other hand, Chinese consumers are cautious and self-protective. They are obsessed with preserving face, maintaining harmonious social connections, looking for a sense of group belonging and expecting affirmation from peers. Due to a proliferation of social shopping, online sharing and cyber entertaining activities, this typical modern consumer culture is fully manifested in China's social media landscape, representing a so-called "Chinese culture 2.0". Weibo (Mandarin for microblogging) is the most influential social media site (ChinaInternetWatch, 2015d); its distinctive culture, the unique characteristics of its users and the widespread use of complex language on this popular social media platform (Yu et al., 2011) demonstrate how modern Chinese consumer culture manifests in today's digital era. The Chinese consumers are also first in line when it comes to shopping through online social networks, leaving reviews of what they buy, and how they were treated (Wu & Pearce, 2014). Therefore, to have an intrinsic understanding of consumers in China, one has to examine their online culture and social media use conventions.

Chinese consumer culture on the Web 2.0

Chinese consumers are modernizing, as the Confucian culture is deeply influenced by Western culture. They endorse what some have termed Westerners' hedonism (Gerth, 2003), and treat the internet as a form of interactive media through which they entertain themselves, chat and poke fun at their peers. They are also engaged in online gaming. Compared to Western countries, online gaming in China is experiencing a faster growth. Chinese consumers consider 3D and action role play

games as their most favored gaming options due to their fun and futuristic characteristics (Millward, 2014). Moreover, that Chinese consumers engage to a great
extent with hedonistic Web contents is also demonstrated by the top accounts on
Weibo with millions of followers, such as "Weibo Funny Ranking", "We like to
tell jokes", and "Laugh too much to be pregnant". Akin to their Western counterparts, Chinese consumers are eager for their voice to be heard, through fully leveraging BBS, SNS and Microblogging sites. In particular, Weibo is viewed as a
platform where they can fully express their individual opinions on any topics in
which they are interested (iResearch, 2013a), including entertaining news, movies,
social issues and trivial things in their routine life. They may spout philosophy of
life, such as "what is love or happiness", or discuss trivial questions, such as "is it
normal for a person to not eat green onions, ginger and garlic". Topical social
issues such as "opinion for legalizing homosexuality" are also engaging online
topics. For some of the Chinese, just speaking out on Weibo cannot satisfy their
ambition – the huge trend of online celebrity culture shows that social media can
give Chinese a chance to stand out from the crowd and that becoming such a social
media celebrity has become a goal for many social media users (Goldstein & Yang,
2016). Many social media celebrities – from pop stars to professional experts,
business tycoons to ordinary users- can attract substantial online followers/fans
due to their active online presence. For instance, the user called "Homework" is
an ordinary post-80s boy – he attracts a substantial number of followers due to a
large amount of online posts reflecting life philosophy. Another one called "Super
Lady Yu Ying" is a doctor – she regularly publishes a post sharing her work experiences in a humorous way.

At the same time, Chinese consumers still maintain their traditional perspectives
and values to some extent. Despite expressing their often socially and culturally
bold ideas individually, they do these things in a manner that ensures some degree
of protection. They are more likely than Western users to hide themselves behind
avatars and pseudonyms. To quote one online gaming fan: "I can be gay; I can be
king of darkness. I can be whoever I want to because no one knows who I am"
(Doctoroff, 2012, p. 69). Moreover, Chinese consumers are still communally constructed – they take advantage of online social networks to manage their "guanxi"
(relationships/connections) (Ong and du Cros, 2012). This may be best illustrated
by the Chinese tradition of gift-giving on people's smartphones. The Spring Festival of 2014 saw a peak cash rush as the tradition of red envelopes moved into the
virtual world. Users of WeChat can swap virtual red envelopes by directing money
transfers to individuals. They can also do it in a more interesting way, putting cash
up for grabs in a designated chat group. Furthermore, Chinese consumers remain
cautious and they care about their peers' opinions, which is illustrated by a large
number of looking-for-advice posts on BBS.

Profiling the social media generation

China's young consumers, who are under the age of 30, are standing at the center
of the changes (ChinaInternetWatch, 2013). In contrast to their Western

counterparts, the profiles of these young people are characterized by contradiction – they are looking for both a sense of belonging and individualism and subscribe to both materialism and spiritual value. Chinese young consumers were born under China's One-Child Policy; therefore, they have grown up in a degree of isolation from peers, and making a living is not easy for them. About 60% of migrant workers in cities are young people who describe themselves as sandwiched between urban and rural areas due to a lack of sense of belonging. Adding to the pressure they feel is their realization that they may need to work for 30 to 40 years before they can afford an apartment (Yang, 2011). Against this backdrop, Weibo offers an attractive space where they can express their emotions, release pressure and relax. As opposed to an offline domain, cyberspace gives these youths a sense of security, which leads them to speak and behave much more wildly than many of their peers in other countries (Herold & Marolt, 2011). The pressures of modern Chinese life and a sense of insecurity further encourage these young people to embrace a 'me-culture' (Sima & Pugsley, 2010) – they label themselves, choose their own lifestyle and make bold decisions. Young graduates who rent and squeeze into a small apartment together call themselves "The Ant Tribe". Young Chinese women do not shy away from appearing vain. As one girl starkly stated, she would rather cry in a BMW than smile on a bicycle; in other words, she prefers money over love. In contrast, some young couples claim to value "Naked Marriage", which does not mean they wear nothing at their wedding, but that they are ready to get married without houses, cars, diamond rings or a wedding banquet because they are committed to true love.

The language of Chinese social media

The capabilities that social media offer facilitate different kinds of casual and interpersonal interactions: various channels, including "posting publicly", "reply", "tag users", "repost" and "hashtags", allow users to check in with and chat to others (Ge et al., 2014), and foster the proliferation of slang. In particular, the way slang develops and is used on Weibo is unique to China's socio-technological and cultural milieu. While Twitter largely relies on text/hyperlinks, and Facebook offers explicit emoticons for anger, disgust, joy, love, surprise and sadness, on Weibo the emoticons are animated, and express a wider range of emotions. These emoticons, along with affective gestures, contain implicit meanings. For instance, "V5" is universally used as "Awesome", because V and 5 have a similar pronunciation to the Chinese translation of "awesome" (Wei Wu).

　　Futher, while phonetic writing, prefixial accretion, initialisms and non-standard spelling are widely identified as "slanguage" on Western social media (Crystal, 2001), the playful language alterations used on Weibo are particularly creative and innovative. They are largely coined from conversations in television dramas, a quote in a news story or a line from a song, or could simply be made up. These popular phrases perform an important role in phatic communication, as they contribute to solidarity and the construction of ambient affiliation (Zappavigna, 2012). Some slang is used to poke fun at each other and create intimacy. "Alexander", transliterated as "yalishanda", a phrase describing a huge amount of pressure, could be used for showing sympathy. "Zan", a word showing support or praise that is similar to the thumbs-up "like" button on Facebook, might convey a compliment. Other phrases, such as "keng die", meaning "cheating your father", might be used to accuse people of dishonesty; meanwhile, it may also serve to create a sense of solidarity with people who have had the same experiences. Other slang is group-related, such as that used for self-deprecation or to laugh at others. For instance, "bai fu mei" (a rich and gorgeous woman) and "gao fu shuai" (a tall, rich and handsome male) are widely used to refer to attractive people who are privileged, powerful and well-connected. In comparison, "diao si" is used by youths to describe themselves as struggling to make a living, with humble origins, ordinary looks and poorly paid jobs; its use helps build group cohesiveness and identity. Furthermore, important social functions of social media are probing the "hive mind" (Zappavigna, 2012) and creating and expressing a desire for social status, and this can be seen in the slang "tu hao". Loosely translated as "nouveau riche", it has appeared more than 100 million times on Chinese social media since early September 2013 (ChinaDaily, 2013). It is used to express Chinese netizens' desire for wealth and is associated with things they cannot have in their offline lives (BBCNEWS, 2013). Given this, businesses in China have introduced gold phone covers to give old phones a new look and attain the status of "tu hao".

The above discussion suggests there are three issues resulting from and at the same time fuelling Chinese culture in the Web 2.0 era: the massive adoption of online shopping and online social networks, the distinctive online behaviors and the unique chracteristics of Chinese online consumers. Further, it becomes clear that Chinese Web 2.0 culture is not only driven by technological trends but also encompasses a huge cultural and social shift. Importantly, as an increasing number of consumers moves online, social media provide the Chinese a desired space where they can shift their behavior and culture freely.

The role of technology in Chinese travel planning – unleashing the dragon

A Chinese proverb says, "It is better to travel ten thousand miles than to read ten thousand books." According to the Chinese National Tourism Administration, in 2013, 97 million Chinese visitors went abroad, making China the world's largest outbound tourism market (He, 2014). In 2014, Chinese outbound tourists reached 109 million (ChinaInternetWatch, 2015b). One of the factors of this explosive growth has been a shift of the stereotype of busloads of group travellers toward new breeds of Chinese tourists who prefer free and independent travel (FIT) (Xu, 2013). Increasing disposable income, the relaxation of government restrictions on foreign travel and social and demographic factors are underlying drivers of this new wave (He, 2014), but the proliferation of digital devices, social media and networking technologies significantly assist Chinese FIT tourists set to spread their wings to foreign countries. Their extensive online preparation, dubbed "doing homework", has become a travel-planning pattern during the pre-trip stage. Taking electronic word of mouth, or e-WOM, as the most credible information source, they seek out extensive information across multiple online platforms. While on the road, "information-on-the-go" and staying connected, facilitated by mobile technology and social media, occur in a broader interaction framework than in the Western context. In addition to this mobile sociality, the sophisticated use of social media by FIT travellers also builds online travel hotspots that are characterized by specific interaction paradigms.

FIT as a new wave

Organized package tours, often described as "travelling three countries in seven days", are now outdated. The stereotypical Chinese outbound tourists with matching hats have been replaced by self-organized tourists who prefer free and independent travel (Xu, 2013). Middle-class tourists, who are younger and more highly educated, play a major role in this emerging phenomenon (ChinaInternetWatch, 2014b). Unlike traditional tourists, FIT tourists prefer to spend quality time on sightseeing, and value learning foreign culture through leisure and enjoyment (ITB, 2012), rather than just trying to earn the status of being able to say "I was there". The popularity of FIT suggests that today's Chinese outbound tourists are more demanding and sophisticated, and have a stronger desire than previous generations to explore and deeply experience the outside world.

Descriptions of FITs are often focused on backpackers who prefer budget accommodation, itinerary flexibility, meeting other travellers and involvement in participatory activities (Chen et al., 2014). Though these descriptions are important and valid, they capture an incomplete picture of overseas tourists from China. Different cultural, social-demographic and motivational factors further diversify Chinese outbound FIT tourists. Thus, a greater understanding of new breeds of Chinese outbound FIT tourists is necessary.

First emerging from the Sina Travel Forum, "donkey friends" are an online network of backpackers ambitiously seeking like-minded or hobby-orientated travel companions (Winter et al., 2008). The phrase "donkey friends" (lüyo[Insert symbol Here]) sounds like the word for travel (lÜ˜ yoú), and is a culture-driven wordplay. Donkey friends share personal stories and useful tips and strive to gather enough "positive energy" to make a desperately wanted change in lifestyle through travelling abroad. As a recent forum post illustrated: "If you don't travel, seek out adventure, enter into a relationship or try living a life you have never lived before, but instead you idly play on the Internet all day doing things that an 80-year-old man can do, what the heck are you wasting your youth for?". It can be seen that travelling with "donkey friends" is a good way of realizing oneself while still belonging to a group. On one hand, these "donkey tourists" engage in "I-travelling"; in other words, they prefer self-centered travel by choosing preferred destinations and the way they travel. They frequently publish online travelogues, often titled something like "Non-mainstream overseas itinerary"; some have spent 23 days in Italy only with their backpacks and one cooking pot, whereas others have spent seven days walking through three national parks in the US. On the other hand, they can still enjoy the social aspects of "we-travelling" by actively seeking "donkey friends". They often post their detailed "do-it-yourself" (DIY) travel plans online, including where, when and how to travel together.

Amongst donkey friends, trendsetters who advocate embracing freedom, change and challenge through travel are recognized as "backpacker stars" (Shao and Gretzel, 2011). Like grass-root celebrities, these high-profile backpackers are active social-media users, and their posts attract millions of viewers who marvel at their travel achievements. Thus, backpacker stars may view posting their travel experiences on various social-media platforms as a distinct way of promoting themselves and heightening their own social status in cyberspace. For instance, inspired by Jack Kerouac's *On the Road*, two Chinese hitchhikers, Gu Yue and Liu Chang, made their way from Beijing to Berlin, where Gu's girlfriend was living, on a 16,000-kilometer journey through 13 countries in the summer of 2009. They recorded their three-and-a-half month trip and turned their adventure into a documentary entitled To Berlin by Thumb, which became a big hit on the internet. Similarly, a couple spent four years sailing 30,000 nautical miles, just to fulfill their personal dreams. By telling their story on social media, their behavior influenced thousands of individual backpackers who often publish similar posts on Weibo, saying something like that "we only have one life, so let's set our footprint in the place we dream of".

Another emerging type of traveller prefers the use of Fang Che, or recreational vehicles. Known as Chinese recreational vehicle travellers "Chinese RVers", they have special interest in self-driving and prefer to travel with self-organized RV groups (Wu & Pearce, 2014). Compared to backpacking, RV touring might be seen as a way of symbolizing novel, unconstrained and luxurious travelling experiences. Four wheels make their road trip flow, and self-driving gives them full control over their itineraries. A Chinese RVer posted on Weibo, "An RV tour allows me to make the best things happen. We can choose to stay on the beach, listening to the waves and counting the stars at night, and welcome the sunrise in the morning." In addition to flexibility in travel itineraries, a feature that has been widely recognized in the backpacking context, Chinese RVers have their own characteristics. As RVs have just become widely available in China in recent years, novelty plays a key role in this emerging trend; therefore, experiencing RV tours overseas might be a way of distinguishing themselves from other travellers. Moreover, given that China is still a developing country, owning an expensive car and a house may be understood as emblematic of prestigious social status; thus, an RV tour may support Chinese tourists' materialism and ego-enhancement. As online posts have illustrated, many Chinese RVers compared their RVs to "six-star hotels" that boast beautiful views. Most importantly, however, is that social media critically facilitate the emergence of this sector in that online posts and discussions serve as important information but also a support system and a way for acculturation to this new travel consumer behavior.

Travel planning pattern – "doing homework"

Many researchers have recognized the important role social media have assumed in travellers' planning processes, including need recognition and information search before departure (Xiang & Gretzel, 2010; Yoo & Gretzel, 2010, 2011), along with evaluation of alternatives and making purchase decisions during the trip (Leung et al., 2013). Chinese outbound tourists' travel planning is dominated by the pre-trip stage, and they call the information-collection pattern "doing homework". Prior to departure, Chinese independent tourists spend more time and look much more extensively for travel information than their counterparts from other countries, researching their choice of destinations, arranging their travel itinerary, transportation and accommodation and looking for promotions such as hotel and flight coupons (iResearch, 2013b). "Doing homework" is also the key behavioral difference between FIT tourists and group tourists regarding travel planning. Without tour operators to make arrangements, travel abroad may be hindered by insufficient capability to appreciate destinations and a lack of control over the trip. Thus, in order to relax and enjoy their visit, they undertake "doing homework" as a purposeful approach, which FIT tourists perceive as a distinguishing characteristic of themselves (Xiang, 2013).

"Doing homework" using online sources in China is well above the average across all markets, including those in the West (TourismAustralia, 2013). Chinese FIT tourists start their search on more comprehensive platforms to receive broader information. Search engines (e.g. Baidu and Sousou) offer outbound tourists a clear picture of a destination and access to broad channels, including business organizations' websites and online travel forums. A majority of tourists may visit destinations' official websites to gain overall knowledge about tourist attractions, local events, cuisine and shops (Nelson, 2013). Given that travel agencies provide specific advantages through offering discounted flights and accommodation, their promotional information is more accepted by these middle-class tourists. As for social media, online travelogues, SNS and microblogging sites as well as WeChat provide information access beyond the boundaries of one's immediate social circle (Yoo & Gretzel, 2011) and offer spaces where Chinese travellers can further seek, discuss and confirm information.

While Western tourists still regard traditional word of mouth as having higher perceived credibility than e-WOM because of the difficulty of identifying message sources in online contexts (Leung et al., 2013; Yoo & Gretzel, 2010), 71% of Chinese outbound FIT tourists perceive online information as most trustworthy (ChinaTravelTrends, 2012). They use their own judgment to attach credibility to different information sources, including peer reviews from friends or acquaintances, hobby-orientated groups and admired celebrities as well as from companies actively engaged on Weibo (ChinaTravelTrends, 2012; Y. Xiang, 2013). The reason might be that that they consider these sources more transparent, comparable, realistic, closer to life, up-to-date and interesting.

The use of technology and social media by FIT tourists

While user-to-user interactions facilitated by digital technologies have been widely recognized, Gretzel (2012) argues that one has to think about human-technology interactions, as the use of technology completely changes the way tourists retrieve/

provide information and communicate with other individuals and service providers. Indeed, tourists are increasingly dedicated to using internet technology – they are not just on the road, but also online, on smartphones and on various Wi-Fi enabled devices. As a result of technology-dependence on the move, the way tourists use the internet becomes more sophisticated. According to a CNNIC (2013) report, using voice information search and QR search via mobile phones are emerging trends. Chinese tourists show a relatively high demand for POI information – 69.8% demand detailed shop information in the neighborhood; 53.5% ask for shop coupons nearby; and 69.8% consumers search restaurants on mobile map apps, 58.1% search for tourist sites (ChinaInternetWatch, 2014a). Indeed, smartphones with various mobile apps provide personalized services by which tourists can get whatever they need – information about local restaurants, tourist sites, bus stops and even toilets. Qunar mobile is a full-feature travel app that covers information on flights, hotels, group-buying deals, but also supports searches, payment and booking and location-based services. Without doubt, it performs multiple roles, serving as a tour guide, service provider and local who answers questions, gives travel tips and handles transactions. These mobile apps provide personalized and 24/7 services. Further, interacting with mobile technologies alters the way tourists communicate with others (Gretzel, 2012), making co-presence with dispersed social networks possible (Germann Molz & Paris, 2015). Tourists can use photo-sharing mobile apps to capture and share their travel moments with friends and family while they are experiencing them. For example, Paipai (similar to Instagram) is a mobile app that allows tourists to take a photo, choose a filter to transform its look and feel and add either text or voice message. Mottos like "Wish you were here with me!" are becoming "I am here right now and you are here (virtually) with me".

The convergence and increasing use of social media and mobile technologies are emblematic of emerging forms of mobile sociality and mediated togetherness (Germann Molz & Paris, 2015). The state of posting, viewing, responding to and sharing updates has been referred to as the statusphere, where tourists are empowered by connectivity (Paris, 2011). The case in China is compelling, because sociality and connectivity take place in broader interaction frameworks which are facilitated by a large array of social media platforms. Chinese travellers can share travel stories with a broad audience on Weibo sites, or post on a BBS to share their experiences with like-minded people. Alternatively, they can use WeChat to share with close friends whom they know well through inexpensive text messages or voice messages. Furthermore, they can also discover new friends through "meet-and-greet" features like "Shake" and "Look Around" on WeChat, which provide tourists with more surprises when they are constantly on the move. As one backpacker named "Qi Che Xi Zang" (Cycling in Tibet) stated on his personal blog, when he felt lonely during his journey, he played with "Shake" to find someone else to talk with, or even travel with. Moreover, "Look Around" allows tourists to find people who are close-by geographically. One tourist posted on social media that he felt very excited to find some other travellers from China, and they had a good time together. These observations might be concluded by using O'Regan's

(2008) statement – "in this networked world, people are able to talk to almost anyone, anytime from anywhere; strangers may no longer exist, but are simply connections waiting to happen" (p. 113).

Online hotspots – Qyer and Sina Weibo

Two online travel hotspots – Qyer and SinaWeibo – are outbound Chinese FIT travellers' most used online community and their favorite microblogging site. They are characterized by different interaction paradigms – in other words, different online cultures and value norms. The community culture and values of Qyer make it a space of virtual mooring (Germann Molz & Paris, 2015). Members of Qyer actively interact with each other both online and offline: they establish a community by getting to know new tourists, and maintain it by fostering and preserving existing relationships. As the Qyer slogan says, "Dedicated to travelling abroad; let's help each other and explore the wonderful world together", indicating that the online companionship of Qyer is more close to real life; members are more likely to build intimate interactions through mutual understanding, obligations to help each other and affirmation among peers. For instance, Qyer organizes "voting campaigns": members whose travelogues receive the most comments are recognized as the "best writers", and those who most actively answer others' questions are recognized as the "best helpers". Moreover, when members post their adventures on Qyer, others actively reaffirm and recognize them for their triumphant tours. Most importantly, Qyer also organizes offline events, bridging the virtual with the real world for Chinese travellers (Shao & Gretzel, 2014).

Chinese tourists' engagement on Sina Weibo occurs entirely online, and the companionship is far less like real life compared to Qyer. A majority of tourists focus on word-of-mouth comments, while requests to travel together account for a very small proportion of interactions (Liu, 2013). As opposed to "virtual moorings" in Qyer, the interactivity characterizing Sina Weibo creates a sense of "following" and "being followed" by a broad audience including business organizations. When tourists publish a post on Sina Weibo, they have their imagined audience in mind (Marwick, 2011) – either their own network of followers and those they follow, or the general public. Therefore, their online activities may be understood as broader social interactions focused on "self-presentation" and "self-promotion". On Sina Weibo, tourists may have less sense of obligation for "peer affirmation", but they are more likely to promote peers' travel experiences through commenting and reposting, which could be evidence of paying attention, challenging as well as affirmation.

The rise of independent travel and the emergence of internet technology/social media share a strong connection in China. An increasing ability to rely on technology provides Chinese outbound tourists with more confidence to enjoy free and flexible travelling overseas. At the same time, however, intensive online information search characterized above as "doing homework" suggests that they intend to control their trip as much as possible. In addition, though Chinese outbound tourists desire to be independent, their online sharing activities show their eagerness to be connected as well.

Conclusion – unwrapping the fortune cookie

Looking beyond the Great Firewall, this chapter offers a nuanced picture, showing the prosperity, dynamics and complexity of China's internet and social-media landscape. As the marketing power of Web 2.0 grows, China – as the world's largest internet and social media market, as well as the largest outbound tourism market – provides the tourism industry with attractive opportunities. At the same time, advanced indigenous innovations, different home-grown social media platforms and a unique modern consumer culture suggest knotty challenges for tourism marketers. Against this backdrop, this chapter asserts that in the process of marketing tourism in China, adaptation to China's vibrant and evolving consumer culture, particularly as it is manifest on the internet and across the social media landscape, is crucial.

Given a strong connection between social media and outbound tourism in China, businesses and destinations should take a broad view to look at Chinese social-media-based consumer culture and how it relates to tourism marketing. A few aspects merit particular attention. For example, the popularity of unique types of jokes, online parody, funny pictures and emoticons on Chinese social media suggests that Western forms of discourse will be less successful on Chinese social media. Marketers need to understand how conversations can be made meaningful to Chinese consumers, and adapt to the language of China's social media users. Moreover, to meet the needs of ambitious Chinese consumers for social recognition and prestige, destinations may need to create tailored travel experiences that will impress in the social media statusphere. The online celebrity culture demonstrated by the enormous influence of professional experts, pop stars and grassroots celebrities is a huge trend that cannot be ignored. Prior to making the most of these social media stars' enormous influence in offering advice on trendy destinations and activities, tourism marketers need to identify the specific power exerted by these online celebrities, or key opinion leaders (KOLs) as they are usually referred to by online Chinese marketers (Harca, 2014). In general, the "doing homework" mentality of Chinese consumers suggests that marketers may also need to do their homework to make sure they distribute their marketing information through the right platform while being cognizant of the specific interaction cultures and the needs of various consumer groups. The above also suggests that partnerships with online platforms like Qyer might be a good investment.

A glimpse of the future

Internet technology and social media trends in China will experience a shift from "quantitative change" to 'qualitative change" (CNNIC, 2014). While the growth of the internet population tends to remain steady, Chinese netizens may increasingly depend on advanced technology, and the way they use it may become more sophisticated as they become more demanding. This shift might be the result of improvements in internet infrastructure, advancements in mobile technology, radical innovation in social media applications and the growing popularity of e-commerce. A greater penetration of broadband networks and 3G in the third-tier cities and rural areas directly promotes the use of the internet on a broader geographical scale; on the other hand, the fast development of 4G technology may serve as an important backup for increased adoption of mobile technology and smart devices in the first- and second-tier cities.

Over the next few years, the rapid surge in smartphone penetration and access to mobile internet will generate a much faster and deeper impact in China than in Western markets, according to CIC (2014). As a result, Chinese consumers will tend to increasingly rely on mobile phone applications in every aspect of their lives, from advanced information search (e.g. voice search) and online entertainment (e.g. gaming, video and music) to instant messaging and e-commerce (e.g. online payment and social shopping). In addition to the ubiquitous use of mobile applications, Chinese consumers' strong interest in wearable devices will open up a new booming market on the internet (iResearch, 2014). Personalized and localized functions and affordable prices offered by the Chinese technology giants will accelerate their adoption.

New applications and services will be continuously introduced into the Chinese social media landscape, and adopted at an astonishing pace (CNNIC, 2014). The convergence of mobile internet, online social networks and e-commerce, along with their pervasiveness in consumers' daily lives, may increase the complexity of China's social-media dynamics, making it also more competitive as a market. Given this, new social-media platforms will continue to be launched that specifically target different interest groups, such as Travel Social, Enterprise Social, Light Blog, Photo Social and Short-video Social (CIC, 2014). Meanwhile, existing social-media platforms show no signs of being left behind, as they enhance their innovative capability through constantly introducing new tailored products and functions, such as social shopping, social gaming, online booking/payment and social music/video.

The foregoing discussion suggests that the "Internet technology +" pattern will be changing China (iResearch, 2014) as business and advanced mobile internet technology become increasingly inseparable. The tourism industry, of course, cannot be excluded. To feed the technology addiction and dependence of Chinese outbound travellers, foreign destinations need to create and improve their tourism infrastructure. Moreover, an increasing convergence of social media and e-commerce will make social shopping an essential option for purchasing tourism products. Therefore, foreign destinations need to constantly introduce products and services that support and take advantage of these travellers' heavy use of online transactions. For instance, a proprietary payment system, such as near-field communication (NFC), may be required for mobile payment. Considering the extensive information search that Chinese outbound tourists tend to conduct, tourism businesses should enhance their capability for content distribution: marketing information must "travel" with each device securely, and must be tailored to each channel. Finally, the surge in social sharing suggests that tourism destinations and attractions need to translate "road culture" into "virtual culture".

In conclusion, the development of the Chinese outbound tourism market has to be understood in conjunction with technology-induced/supported cultural shifts that are creating new waves of travellers looking for distinct travel experiences and are increasingly accustomed to using mobile social media to achieve their extraordinary travel goals. Therefore, both researching and marketing to Chinese outbound tourists requires a technological understanding and orientation. More so than any tourist market before, Chinese have embraced internet and mobile-based media in their general lives as well as their travels, and while there are similarities to developments in Western markets, the Chinese media technologies and use conventions are unique in many ways. Government statistics and industry reports provide some insights but theoretical conceptualizations and comprehensive empirical work to better grasp this new cultural revolution is still lacking. As a consequence, there is little concrete guidance for tourism marketers in terms of how to best seize the opportunities with which Chinese social media provide them.

References

BBCNEWS. (2013). #BBCtrending: Tuhao and the rise of Chinese bling. Retrieved from www.bbc.com/news/magazine-24677113

Chen, G., Bao, J., & Huang, S. S. (2014). Segmenting Chinese backpackers by travel motivations. *International Journal of Tourism Research*, 16(4), pp. 355–367.

ChinaDaily. (2013). Chinese buzzwords draw attention. Retrieved from http://usa.china daily.com.cn/china/2013-11/22/content_17122650.htm

ChinaInternetWatch. (2013). China Internet news, trends and stats. CIW China Internet insights 2013. Retrieved from www.slideshare.net/RockyFu/china-internet-stats-insights

ChinaInternetWatch. (2014a). Chinese travelers mobile app search behavior (3 part series). Retrieved from www.chinainternetwatch.com/5320/china-lbs-travel-part3/

ChinaInternetWatch. (2014b). Rise of the China outbound tourism. Retrieved from www.chinainternetwatch.com/8832/outbound-travelers/

ChinaInternetWatch. (2015a). China, the largest outbound tourism market in 3 consecutive years. Retrieved from www.chinainternetwatch.com/13152/the-largest-outbound-tourism-market-3-consecutive-years/#ixzz3XUNFZ4i8

ChinaInternetWatch. (2015b). Chinese outbound tourism insight in 2014. Retrieved from www.chinainternetwatch.com/14869/chinese-outbound-tourism-insight-2014/

ChinaInternetWatch. (2015c). Social media users make up 95 percent of total Chinese netizens Retrieved from www.chinainternetwatch.com/13844/china-social-media-users-insights-2015/

ChinaInternetWatch. (2015d). Weibo search users insights 2015. Retrieved from www.chinainternetwatch.com/16366/weibo-search-users-insights-2015/

ChinaTravelTrends. (2012). Essential China travel trends 2012. Retrieved from http://sete.gr/_fileuploads/entries/Online%20library/GR/120423_Essential%20China%20Travel%20Trends%202012.pdf

Chong, E. (2013). The power of connectedness: How social media usage among China's digital natives is evolving. *Insights China, Collection No. 1*. Retrieved from http://designmind.frogdesign.com/2013/04/power-connectedness/

CIC. (2014). China social media landscape: Where to play and how to play. Retrieved from www.seeisee.com/sam/2014/02/26/p3789

CNNIC. (2013). Statistical report on Internet development in China. Retrieved from www1.cnnic.cn/IDR/ReportDownloads/201310/P020131029430558704972.pdf

CNNIC. (2014). Statistical report on Internet development in China. Retrieved from www1.cnnic.cn/IDR/ReportDownloads/201404/U020140417607531610855.pdf

CNNIC. (2016). The 36th statistical report on Internet development in China. Retrieved from www1.cnnic.cn/IDR/ReportDownloads/201601/P020160106496544403584.pdf

Crystal, D. (2001). *Language and the Internet*, Cambridge, Cambridge University Press.

Doctoroff, T. (2012). *What Chinese Want: Culture, Communism and the Modern Chinese Consumer*, New York: Macmillan.

Fong, C. (2009). "Sea turtles" powering China's Internet growth. Retrieved from http://edition.cnn.com/2009/TECH/09/30/digitalbiz.redwired/index.html#cnnSTCText

Ge, J., Gretzel, U., & Clarke, R. J. (2014). Strategic use of social media affordances for marketing: A case study of Chinese DMOs. In Xiang, Z. & Tussyadiah, I. (eds.) *Information and Communication Technologies in Tourism 2014*. Cham, Switzerland: Springer, pp. 159–173.

Germann Molz, J., & Paris, C. M. (2015). The social affordances of flashpacking: Exploring the mobility nexus of travel and communication. *Mobilities*, 10(2), pp. 173–192.

Gerth, K. (2003). *China Made: Consumer Culture and the Creation of the Nation* (Vol. 224), Cambridge, MA: Harvard University Asia Center.

GoGlobe. (2013). Social media in China: Statistics and trends. Retrieved from www.go-globe.com/blog/social-media-china/

Goldstein, A., & Yang, G. (2016). *The Internet, Social Media, and a Changing China*, Philadelphia, USA: University of Pennsylvania Press.

Gretzel, U. (2012). Tourism in a technology-dependent world. *Future Tourism: Political, Social and Economic Challenges*, 28, pp. 123.

Gretzel, U., Fesenmaier, D. R., Lee, Y. J., & Tussyadiah, I. (2010). 11 narrating travel experiences: The role of new media. In Sharpley, R. & Stone, P. R. (eds.), *Tourist Experience: Contemporary Perspectives*. Oxon, UK: Routledge, pp. 171–182.

Gretzel, U. & Yoo, K.-H. (2014). Premises and promises of social media marketing in tourism. In McCabe, S. (ed.). *The Routledge Handbook of Tourism Marketing*, pp. 491–504. Oxon, UK: Routledge.

Harca, E. (2014). Bloggers, commentators, and KOLs: Harnessing the power of Chinese influencers. Retrieved from www.clickz.com/clickz/column/2322997/bloggers-commentators-and-kols-harnessing-the-power-of-chinese-influencers

He, A. (2014). Outbound tourism set to surge, report says. Retrieved from http://usa.chinadaily.com.cn/epaper/2014-01/22/content_17250130.htm

Herold, D. K., & Marolt, P. (2011). *Online Society in China: Creating, Celebrating, and Instrumentalising the Online Carnival* (Vol. 25), Oxon, UK: Routledge.

iResearch. (2012). China social networking site and microblog users' behavior report. Retrieved from. www.iresearchchina.com/samplereports/4366.html

iResearch. (2013a). 2012–2013 China microblog marketing audience behavior report (Brief Edition). Retrieved from www.iresearchchina.com/samplereports/5021.html

iResearch. (2013b). More enterprises explore outbound self: Driving travel market of Chinese tourists. Retrieved from www.iresearchchina.com/views/5215.html

iResearch. (2014). Ten trends of China's Internet development in 2013. Retrieved from www.iresearchchina.com/news/5375.html

ITB. (2012). 012/2013 ITB world travel trends report. Retrieved from www.itb-berlin.de/media/itbk/itbk_media/itbk_pdf/WTTR_Report_2013_web.pdf

Leung, D., Law, R., Van Hoof, H., & Buhalis, D. (2013). Social media in tourism and hospitality: A literature review. *Journal of Travel & Tourism Marketing*, 30(1–2), pp. 3–22.

Liu, S. (2013). Enhancing China's outbound travel boom using Sina Weibo. Retrieved from http://chinesesocialmedia101.wordpress.com/author/sijieliu/

Marwick, A. E. (2011). I tweet honestly, I tweet passionately: Twitter users, context collapse, and the imagined audience. *New Media & Society*, 13(1), pp. 114–133.

Millward, S. (2014). Let's take a look at China's $13.5 billion online gaming industry (INFOGRAPHIC). Retrieved from www.techinasia.com/about-us

Nelson, C. (2013). Destinations target Chinese tourists on Weibo. Retrieved from www.chinabusinessreview.com/destinations-target-chinese-tourists-on-weibo/

Nielsen, C. (2016). China's E-commerce market: Untapped potential for global companies. Retrieved from http://sites.nielsen.com/newscenter/chinas-e-commerce-market-untapped-potential-for-global-companies/

Ong, C.-E., & du Cros, H. (2012). The post-Mao gazes: Chinese backpackers in Macau. *Annals of Tourism Research*, 39(2), 735–754.

O'Regan, M. (2008). Hypermobility in backpacker lifestyles: The emergence of the internet café. In Burns, P. M. & Novelli, M. (eds.), *Tourism and Mobilities: Local-Global Connections*, Oxfordshire, UK: CABI, pp. 109–132.

Paris, C. M. (2011). Understanding the statusphere and blogosphere: an analysis of virtual backpacker spaces. In Law, R., Fuchs, M. and Ricci, F. (eds.), *Information and Communication Technologies in Tourism* 2011, pp. 443–455. Vienna, Austria: Springer.

Shao, J., & Gretzel, U. (2011, November 28–29). Social media created the Chinese backpacker star. In W. Frost, G. Croy, J. Laing, & S. Beeton (eds.) *International Tourism and Media Conference*. Melbourne, Tourism and Hospitality Research Unit, La Trobe University and Department of Management, Monash University.

Shao, J., & Gretzel, U. (2014, June 18–20). Integrating social media influencers into the marketing strategy of Chinese travel communities. In K. Griffin & M. Joppe (eds.). *Proceedings of the TTRA 2014 International Conference*, Lake Orion, MI: Travel and Tourism Research Association., pp. 1079–1084.

Sima, Y., & Pugsley, P. C. (2010). The rise of A 'Me culture' in postsocialist China youth, individualism and identity creation in the blogosphere. *International Communication Gazette*, 72(3), pp. 287–306.

TourismAustralia. (2013). Tourism Australia's consumer demand research: Understanding the Chinese consumer. Retrieved from http://yarrarangestourism.com.au/wpcontent/uploads/2013/09/Factsheet_CDP_China_Jul13.pdf

Winter, T., Teo, P., & Chang, T. C. (2008). *Asia on Tour: Exploring the Rise of Asian Tourism*, [0]Oxon, UK: Routledge.

Wu, M.-Y., & Pearce, P. L. (2014). Chinese recreational vehicle users in Australia: A netnographic study of tourist motivation. *Tourism Management*, 43, pp. 22–35.

Xiang, Y. (2013). The characteristics of independent Chinese outbound tourists. *Tourism Planning & Development*, 10(2), pp. 134–148.

Xiang, Z., & Gretzel, U. (2010). Role of social media in online travel information search. *Tourism Management*, 31(2), pp. 179–188.

Xu, J. (2013). Affluent tourists "go it alone"; seek culture, good food. Retrieved from http://europe.chinadaily.com.cn/business/2013-08/22/content_16912832.htm

Yang, L. (2011). The generation that's remaking China. TED Speech.

Yoo, K.-H., & Gretzel, U. (2010). *Web 2.0: New rules for tourism marketing*. Paper presented at the Proceedings of the 41th Annual Conference of the Travel and Tourism Research Association.

Yoo, K.-H., & Gretzel, U. (2011). Creating more credible and persuasive recommender systems: The influence of source characteristics on recommender system evaluations. In Kantor, P.B., Ricci, F., Rokach, L., & Shapira, B. (eds.) *Recommender Systems Handbook.*, Vienna, Austria: Springer, pp. 455–477.

Yu, L., Asur., S., & Huberman, B. A. (2011). What trends in Chinese social media. In Ghosh, J. & Smyth, P. (eds.), *Proceedings of the 5th SNA-KDD Workshop*, New York: ACM.

Zappavigna, M. (2012). *Discourse of Twitter and Social Media: How We Use Language to Create Affiliation on the Web*, London: Continuum International Publishing Group.

8 Crowdsourcing in travel, tourism and hospitality

Practical cases and possibilities

Fernando J. Garrigos-Simon,
Yeamduan Narangajavana, Silvia Sanz-Blas
and Javier Sanchez-Garcia

Introduction

In the present innovative environment, new business models and open innovation are becoming critical research matters. Specifically, the development of information and communication technologies, and the spread of social media are changing the way of managing the production processes of firms (Garrigos et al., 2012b). Nowadays, considering different sectors, we can see that the participation of people outside the firms is crucial to improve the competitiveness of organizations. This fact, of course, is profoundly influencing the way of managing travel, tourism and hospitality firms.

Crowdsourcing mechanisms focus on this matter. Specifically, crowdsourcing is conceived as an evolution of traditional outsourcing, which considers the participation of a broad range of stakeholders and other people through the internet, as critical elements to improve the different tasks of organizations. In this chapter, we are going to define, explore, analyze and discuss the importance of crowdsourcing activities to improve the competitiveness of businesses and destinations. In addition, the paper aims to focus on its importance and use in the travel, tourism and hospitality industry as a critical technique which can transform the conception of the businesses, and also the reality of these sectors.

The chapter begins by considering the definition, the benefits and the disadvantages of crowdsourcing in the literature, and it continues by analyzing its implementation. Examples of the application of crowdsourcing in travel, tourism and hospitality are provided by describing its use by various companies and destinations. In particular, the chapter analyzes three specific crowdsourcing cases: Benidorm, Buggl, and Freehand Miami. The chapter concludes by identifying the implications and limitations of this study.

Crowdsourcing definition, advantages and disadvantages

The concept of "crowdsourcing" was coined by Jeff Howe in (2006). "Crowdsourcing represents the act of a company or institution taking a function once performed by employees and outsourcing it to an undefined (and generally large) network of people in the form of an open call". We define crowdsourcing in this chapter as the act of taking a job or task usually performed by an employee of the organization or a contractor (Howe, 2009), and outsourcing it through an open call to a large group of people or a community (crowd or mass) through the internet.

Considered to be a new web-based business strategy (Brabham, 2008), or an innovative business model through the internet (Peng and Zhang, 2010), crowdsourcing processes can integrate users and all types of stakeholders who are not employees of the firm (Garrigos et al., 2012b). The process is used to improve production processes, obtain the solution to problems (Doan et al., 2011), generate open innovations or ideas (Poetz and Schreier, 2012) or broadly execute any of the firm's tasks (Estellés & González, 2012), in almost all the processes of a product or service life cycle (Porta et al., 2008). It could comprise everything from the design of a product or process, product development and configuration, solving technical or other problems, creating content, carrying out corporate R&D, advertising, quality monitoring . . . , to the inclusion of almost every step in an organization's value chain (Garrigos et al., 2012b).

Crowdsourcing consists of the outsourcing of tasks to the general internet public (Kleemann et al., 2008) who are remunerated or motivated through diverse mechanisms (Geiger et al., 2011). Although advantages and disadvantages largely depend on the type of crowdsourcing under consideration (Schenk & Guittard, 2011), we can identify the following general implications. In terms of advantages, Schenk and Guittard (2011) mention relatively low costs and high quality, the crowdsourcing's capacity to foster positive network externalities and the adoption of new technologies, the reduction of the dependence and information asymmetries with suppliers, and the enhancement of motivation and incentives, as crowdsourcing implies voluntary participation. However, crowdsourcing is mainly important, because it may be free, or significantly cheaper than that contribution is worth to the firms (Kleemann et al., 2008), and because of the quality of the solutions provided. Hence, compensations are usually cheaper than those required to satisfy other providers. In addition, the literature shows that crowdsourcing often has the potential to provide faster and higher quality solutions than other alternative mechanisms. In this vein, Brabham (2008) states that the crowd can help to design products, to produce memorable commercials and images, and to outperform industry faster and cheaper than even the top minds in the field.

In relation to the crowdsourcing disadvantages, Schenk and Guittard (2011) mention problems with knowledge appropriability and its applicability in fields that rely strongly on tacit knowledge. Whitla (2009) also points out the ineffectiveness of this method when the information to be gathered or project being worked on is secretive in nature. In addition, crowdsourcing can fail to attract sufficient contributors (Schenk & Guittard, 2011), can suffer from the lack of satisfactory contributors when the request is ill-defined or the task is not focused or clearly explained. This results in potential misunderstandings in advance (Conley & Tosti-Kharas, 2014, Whitla, 2009), or even the problem of evaluation and selection of contributors (Schenk & Guittard, 2011). Hence, a crowd can sometimes return a vast amount of noise that may be of little relevance (Keen, 2007), and generally researchers cannot have feedback, cannot follow up with contributors to clarify or revise problems or information, and crowdsourced contributors cannot discuss and resolve differences when they are anonymous (Conley & Tosti-Kharas, 2014). In addition, we can add some problems regarding the legal ownership of ideas submitted (Stibbe, 2006), or ethical issues mainly regarding low-paid tasks and the question of exploitation of workers (Conley & Tosti-Kharas, 2014, Horton et al., 2011, Whitla, 2009).

Implementation of crowdsourcing

Normally, each crowdsourcing project is developed through a process with four dimensions (Garrigos et al., 2014, Geiger et al., 2011):

- Pre-selection of contributors. This stage is addressed by selecting potential contributions and launching an open call. The firm can opt to maximize the size of the crowd or pre-select the contributors depending on desirable skills (Feller et al., 2009). The destinations of the call can include internal employees (Garrigos et al., 2014), employees of partners of the organization, or a wider group of people, including consumers, online communities or general internet communities (Kleemann et al., 2008, Whitla, 2009).
- Accessibility of peer contributions. In this phase, the crowdsourcing organization must decide how and whether contributors can access the work of other contributors (Garrigos et al., 2014). According to Geiger et al. (2011) there is a range or degree of accessibility by contributors, from cases where the contributors do not see the projects of the other participants, to other situations where contributors can see, evaluate, comment or even modify, complete or delete the work of other contributors. In order to decide about these situations organizations have to understand intellectual property rights and consider security and the security of information.
- Aggregation of contributions. During this stage, the organization has to unify the selected contributions and discard those that do not attain the expected quality. Only the best contributions are selected (Schenk & Guittard, 2011). Monitoring the process is critical, and has to stress the ability to verify the data and to gauge the quality of the work (Estellés & González, 2012).
- Remuneration for contributors. The literature has shown that several motivating factors encourage the crowd to participate in these processes. These include: simple satisfaction, passion, fun, personal achievement, self-esteem (Estellés & Gonzáles, 2012, Leimeister et al., 2009), or social recognition and improvement of personal image and reputation (as in the case of the participation and provision of information in blogs or diverse social media), or even financial compensation (Horton & Chilton, 2010, Geiger et al., 2011, Mason & Watts, 2010). The crowdsourcing organization has to analyze all of them and emphasize the most important ones for its aims.

Types of crowdsourcing processes

There are many types of crowdsourcing processes. For instance, Geiger et al. (2011) used 46 crowdsourcing examples, with 19 distinct types of processes. More recently, Sanz-Blas et al. (2015) stressed several typologies of crowdsourcing: based on the type of task that is crowdsourced (differentiating between crowdwisdom, including crowdcasting, crowdstorming, and market predictions, crowdproduction, crowdvoting and crowdfunding); based on the type of task performed (distinguishing between averaging crowds, datamine crowds, networking crowds, social production crowds, and transactional crowds); based on the problems that crowdsourcing is trying to solve (making a distinction between knowledge detection and management, distributed human intelligence tasking, broadcast searching, and peer-vetted creative production); or based on the motivation to participate (discriminating between communals, utilizers, aspirers and lurkers). In addition to these typologies, and specifically in the tourism sector, Galdon et al. (2016) focused on the use of crowdsourcing in the diverse phases of the tourism value chain in the tourism industry, stressing the importance of crowdsourcing techniques for marketing, sales and services, operations, technology development and company infrastructure.

However, the most widely used typologies concentrate on the types of tasks to be crowdsourced. Focusing on this aspect, Trifu and Croitoru (2014) stress the importance of: crowdvoting, to gather a large group's opinions or judgment on a certain topic; crowdfunding, to gather the necessary financial resources for funding different projects by a multitude of people that contribute with a small amount; creative crowdsourcing, which refers to graphic design, crowdsourcing architecture, apparel design, illustration, writing; or crowdsearching, a general search for answers, solutions, or missing persons, pets or lost items. More recently, Estelles, Navarro and Gonzalez (2015) after comparing several previous typologies, created and integrated typologies that comprise five main types: crowdcasting, where, once the problem or the task is proposed to the crowd, whoever solves it first or does it better is rewarded; crowdcollaboration, where communication between individuals in the crowd occurs (including crowdstorming, or a massive online brainstorming session, and crowdsupport, where the customers themselves solve the doubts and problems of other customers); crowdcontent, where the crowd creates or finds content of various types in a non competitive way (comprising crowdproduction, crowdsearching, and crowdanalyzing); crowdfunding, where the crowd funds initiatives in exchange for a reward; and crowdopinion, where the crowd votes, comments, tags or even shares sales.

The use of crowdsourcing in travel, hospitality and tourism

The use of crowdsourcing is important for the travel and tourism industry, as it can be used to improve almost all the phases of the value chain of organizations, and to develop and promote destinations. Following this point, and although crowdsourcing is a novel area of research in tourism and travel literature, the observation of the praxis shows that within the tourism sector, extensive mechanisms of crowdsourcing have been used for many purposes, especially by firms and tourism organizations. For instance, it has been used to identify new brands and to spread the brand and image of the firms, operational activities such as marketing (e.g. Starbucks idea) or user-generated content for social media websites (e.g. Facebook) (Garrigos et al., 2014, Rieder & Voß, 2010, Sigala, 2012).

Crowdsourcing has been used, for example, to improve the design and installations of hotels (Richard et al., 2016), such as Marriot (Trejos, 2013), to improve the quality of the products and services offered by hotels and hospitality firms such as Starbucks (Müller, 2011, Sigala, 2012), or Sheraton (Sigala & Marinidis, 2009), and can be used to improve the management of inventories of hospitality and airline industries.

Crowdsourcing also includes the participation of the crowd to advise customers, by writing product reviews or the uploading of all kinds of information, in virtual travel agencies, diverse networks, the web pages of tourism organizations or specific sites like TripAdvisor and Wayn.com (Buhalis et al., 2011, Deutch & Milo, 2012, Sigala, 2009). This process is essential in order to evaluate hotels, recommend restaurants (Tzvetan, 2006), and tourist attractions (Bachrach et al., 2014).

In the travel industry, user-generation of advertising content is also used by companies like JetBlue, "hoping to reach young, tech-savvy consumers who will spread their marketing messages [virally] around the Web" (Brabham, 2008, p. 78). Moreover, the use of social media such as Facebook, through citizen participation and contribution via the use of crowdsourcing techniques, has been used to promote tourism destinations, such as in the case of Tourism Australia (Alam & Diamah, 2012). For instance, Della Corte et al. (2013, p. 45) explain that using different formulas and methods in the application of crowdsourcing, the crowd can suggest new ideas to promote destinations; for instance, "in terms of the right things to do in the destinations, the best experiences to live, the place in which they can find tour information or opinions for new tourist services".

Furthermore, crowdsourcing can also help organizations to identify any observable changes in market supply or consumer demand, complementing traditional market search (Conley & Tosti-Kharas, 2014, Kleemann et al., 2008). In this vein, crowdsourcing is essential to satisfy the individual demands of specific segments of customers, or can help in the personalization of the services offered to customers (Garrigas et al., 2012b).

Moreover, although the literature has not focused on these innovations much, in our opinion, the description and enumeration of the possibilities of crowdsourcing used by tourism firms is very extensive. Hence, crowdsourcing could be used to improve operations, marketing, R&D, infrastructures (Galdon et al., 2016), or in general almost all the phases of the value chain of travel and tourism organizations, as we posited above. Following these previous works, in this chapter we are going to concentrate on some cases illustrating the use of crowdsourcing.

Cases of the use of crowdsourcing in travel, hospitality and tourism

Benidorm: new destination image design

Benidorm is the third most important European travel destination and one of the most prominent summer resorts in Spain. The city has the best urban beaches in the Mediterranean, which are visited by national and international tourists year after year. Its sun and beach tourism offer is combined with a wide range of leisure activities, gastronomy and theme parks, which taken together contribute to position Benidorm as an upscale travel destination where perfect holidays can be enjoyed.

Last November 17, 2014 the town of Benidorm launched an international competition to redefine its image through a new logo, slogan and pattern through the Talents United crowdsourcing platform. The main purpose of the competition was to obtain new design ideas which would help to renew the image of the city, strengthening its international prestige in the tourism market. The repositioning of the image of Benidorm was focused on its urban beach which has become a benchmark for the industry (Hosteltur, 2014, VisitBenidorm, 2014). The competition was presented online with the hashtag #BenidormbyTalents.

All those interested in participating had to register in the online platform (www.talentsunited.com) or through the Visit Benidorm website (www.visitbenidorm.es). #BenidormbyTalents consisted of three consecutive challenges: logo, slogan and pattern. A jury of experts and internet voting were to decide the winners of each stage to achieve the aim of #BenidormbyTalents: a new design for the brand of Benidorm. The deadline for the receipt of proposals closed on January 18, 2015, while voting ran until February 1, 2015. The winners were announced on February 28, 2015.

Regarding the first challenge of the new logo of Benidorm, a large number of visual artists, designers and cartoonists took part in the competition. Copywriters from eight different countries presented a total of 159 proposals, from which 11 were shortlisted. Eight of them were selected by the experts, while the other three were nominated by public voting, with more than 3000 registered voters on Facebook (Talents United, 2015, VisitBenidorm, 2014).

The designer of the best logo was awarded €3000 and the two runners-up received 600 Euros each. Regarding the other two challenges, the winners of the best slogan and the best pattern were awarded €1500. In addition, two secondary awards of 300 Euros were given in both of the challenges (VisitBenidorm, 2014).

The winning logo proposal "Benidorm. Things happen here", was inspired by its beach silhouette, sun-drenched by the Costa Blanca sun, and the color of its sunset, which evokes the warmth and heartbeat of the Spanish leisure culture. The logo is composed of the capital letter "B", the first letter of the city's name, which at the same time alludes to the Levante and Poniente beaches (see http://en.visitbenidorm.es/).

The proposed brand is incredibly versatile, as it can be applied in a variety of ways depending on the medium or the target market addressed; it looks like a heart and a speech bubble at the same time, by means of which the brand expresses itself. The logo can be presented in a darker color and contain more volume effects, or, on the contrary, it can be more sober with just an outline. It is a sound, universal, forward-looking icon (Ais, 2014). The new design was introduced across all the communication media and promotional channels of Benidorm Town Council.

Buggl: the insiders guide to travel

Buggl is an application to create and sell travel guides (Buggl, 2015a, b). It is one of the first platforms that rewards travellers for sharing their knowledge (see www.buggl.com/).

Buggl is a website where a user, who has already had a travel experience, can create personalized travel guides and therefore share his/her knowledge with people from all over the world, enrich their travel experiences and inspire other travellers to discover the world in a different way (Buggl, 2015a, b). This web application is similar to an online marketplace, as it is based on the idea that travel recommendations written by users have some monetary value. The travel guides are available to those who appreciate the knowledge they contain (Ortega, 2014). However, the author of the travel guide is the one who decides whether to sell it or share it for free. The price of the guides ranges between $1 and $10.

In this way, by sharing their travel knowledge with others, users can (Buggl, 2015b):

- Earn money: make additional income or turn the love for their place into a business.
- Become global influencers: gain credibility and get noticed worldwide by sharing knowledge with travellers from all over the world.
- Tell their story: enjoy the thrill of helping people, giving them the real story behind a city, country or region.
- Help their community: tell people the best places to go and things to do. Promote lesser-known events and locations off the beaten track.

The application is very easy to use, as it enables users to search for travel guides filtered by places to visit or activities of interest. In this way, users can find travel guides for major travel destinations such as Istanbul, London, Barcelona and many more, as well as travel guides by themes: gastronomy, adventures, architecture, religion etc. (Buggl, 2015a).

Due to the development of this type of crowdsourcing platform, we are witnessing new travel trends, where tourists give more value to online travel guides created by people who share similar tastes and hobbies with them, than to guided tours, whose guides offer general information about the destination and match their interests to a lesser extent.

Freehand Miami: visual storytelling

With the emergence of social media, and visually-rich website experiences, visual storytelling has become a must for hotels to stand out online these days (Leonardo, 2014).

Thanks to the online community, nowadays hotels can access a myriad of inspiring pictures and videos created by their guests, by encouraging them to tag the hotel in their posts in social media channels (Instagram in particular). In this way, hotel owners can successfully "crowdsource" the creation of exciting and convincing visual stories through the web or any social media channel, even when their budget is limited (see http://freehandhotels.com/miami/) (Hosteltur, 2015).

Freehand Miami is an excellent example of a hotel that makes good use of this strategy. The hotel is doing a great job by editing, posting and promoting their guests' pictures on the website. Customers are encouraged to take pictures, make videos and post them on social media channels with the hashtag #FreehandMiami. The hotel staff is also involved in taking pictures of some "hotel moments", so that they can also share them online with a special hashtag. The social media profiles of the hotel, especially the one in Instagram, prove that it is possible to take advantage of the differentiation: young, modern, connected and showcasing an aesthetic outlook (Mora, 2013). All of this means that the hotel owner does not have to obtain fresh content for the website.

However, it should be noted that the core of this strategy does not consist of copying pictures and pasting them on company's website. The shared pictures should tell the story of the hotel, so a careful selection should be made looking for the best, most irresistible photos. Once chosen, the pictures have to be edited and further information should be included on them such as consistent messages and professional details of the company (Leonardo, 2014). In the end, it is all about creating a high-impact visual story about the brand, with its website performing as a showcase. Just like votes or comments in blogs or social networks, pictures uploaded by customers are a valuable source of information, as they show the company from the clients' perspectives and give a clue to what is most important for the customer.

Conclusions and future research

The development of social media and the internet are changing the structures of the hospitality, tourism and travel industries, and the way organizations and users interact. In the new framework, open innovation, promoted by the participation of people, is changing the basis of the competitiveness of these sectors. This chapter focuses on these advances, by concentrating on the importance of crowdsourcing processes.

We define crowdsourcing as the act of taking a job or task usually performed by an employee of the organization or a contractor, and outsourcing it through an open call to a large group of people or a community (crowd or mass) through the internet. The chapter explains diverse processes used with crowdsourcing techniques, and the advantages and disadvantages of these mechanisms. In addition, the work focuses on steps to develop crowdsourcing mechanisms. Moreover, the paper contemplates the main types of crowdsourcing processes analyzed in the literature, explaining diverse typologies, and specifically the possible tasks to be crowdsourced by organizations. More specifically, the paper describes how diverse crowdsourcing techniques have been used in the tourism and hospitality industry.

Finally, the chapter describes three cases of the use of crowdsouricng by tourism and travel organizations and destinations. In this vein, we first analyze how crowdsourcing techniques have been used by the tourist destination of Benidorm in order to design the destination brand, through an open international competition. Secondly, we explain the development of the application Buggl, an instrument to create and sell travel guides, which rewards travellers for sharing their knowledge and travel experiences. Thirdly, we illustrate the case of Freehand Miami, a case of visual storytelling for hotels that allows hospitality organizations to crowd-source the creation of visual stories through the web or social media channels, a fact which permits these organizations to enhance their promotion and also have more information about the tastes and important questions considered by their customers.

Despite its growing importance in the new environment guided by innovation and open knowledge, the study of crowdsourcing is still novel in the hospitality, travel and tourism sectors. Future research should explore its use by different organizations in these and other sectors, and its use for improving diverse tasks of the organizations value chain, in order to enhance competitiveness.

References

Ais, J. (2014). Benidorm: Things happen here. Una 'LoveMark' para benidorm. Available at: http://talentsunited.com/juan-ais/benidorm-things-happen-here [Accessed 15 June 2015].

Alam, S. L., & Diamah, A. (2012, January). Understanding user participation in Australian government tourism Facebook page. In Lamp, John (ed.), *ACIS 2012: 23rd Australasian Conference on Information Systems*, Geelong, VIC: Deakin University, pp. 1–11.

Bachrach, Y., Ceppi, S., Kash, I. A., Key, P., Radlinski, F., Porat, E., & Sharma, V. (2014). Building a personalized tourist attraction recommender system using crowdsourcing. In Lomuscio, A., Scerri, P., Bazzan, A. & Huhns, M. (eds.), *International Foundation for Autonomous Agents and Multiagent Systems: 2014 International Conference on Autonomous Agents and Multi-Agent Systems*, Richland, SC: International Foundation for Autonomous Agents and Multiagent Systems, pp. 1631–1632.

Brabham, D. C. (2008). Crowdsourcing as a model for problem solving: An introduction and cases, convergence. *The International Journal of Research into New Media Technologies*, 14(1), pp. 75–90.

Buggl. (2015a). The insiders guide to travel. Available at: www.buggl.com/ [Accessed 2 June 2015].

Buggl. (2015b). Design a guide. Available at: www.buggl.com/become-an-expert [Accessed 2 June 2015].

Buhalis, D., Leung, D., & Law, R. (2011). eTourism: Critical information and technologies. In Y. Wang & A. Pizam (eds.) *Destination Marketing and Management: Theories and Applications*. Walling Ford, UK, CAB International, pp. 205–224.

Conley, C., & Tosti-Kharas, J. (2014). Crowdsourcing content analysis for managerial research. *Management Decision*, 52(4), pp. 675–688.

Della Corte, V., Del Gaudio, G., & Lavazzi, A. (2013, October). New marketing frontiers: Crowdsourcing theoretical hints and empirical evidences. In *XXV Convegno Annuale di Sinergie: L'innovazione per la competitività delle imprese*. Ancona, Università Politecnica delle Marche, pp. 24–25.

Deutch, D., & Milo, T. (2012). Mob data sourcing. *2012 ACM Sigmod International Conference on Management of Data*, May, pp. 581–584.

Doan, A., Ramakrishnan, R., & Halevy, A. Y. (2011). Crowdsourcing systems on the World-Wide Web. *Communications of the ACM*, 54(4), pp. 86–96.

Estellés, E., & González, F. (2012). Towards an integrated crowdsourcing definition. *Journal of Information Science*, 38(2), pp. 189–200.

Estellés, E., Navarro, R., & González, F. (2015). Crowdsourcing fundamentals: Definition and typology. In F. Garrigos, I. Gil, & S. Estelles (eds.) *Advances in Crowdsourcing.* Cham, Switzerland: Springer International Publishing, pp. 33–48.

Feller, J., Finnegan, P., Hayes, J., & O'Reilly, P. (2009). Institutionalising information asymmetry: Governance structures for open innovation. *Information Technology & People*, 22(4), pp. 297–316.

Galdon, J. L., Garrigos, F. J., & Gil, I. (2016). Improving hotel industry processes through crowdsourcing techniques. In R. Egger, I. Gula, & D. Walcher (eds.) *Open Tourism-Open Innovation, Crowdsourcing and Co-Creation Challenging the Tourism Industry.* Berlin: Springer International Publishing, pp. 95–107.

Garrigos, F. J., Lapiedra, R., & Barbera, T. (2012b). Social networks and Web 3.0: Their impact on the management and marketing of organizations. *Management Decision*, 50(10), pp. 1880–1890.

Garrigos, F. J., Narangajavana, Y., & Galdón, J. L. (2014). Crowdsourcing as a competitive advantage for new business models. In I. Gil, D. Palacios, M. Peris, E. Vendrell, & C. Ferri (eds.) *Strategies in E-Business.* New York: Springer, pp. 29–37.

Geiger, D., Seedorf, S., Schulze, T., Nickerson, R., & Schader, M. (2011, August 4–7). Managing the crowd: Towards a taxonomy of crowdsourcing processes. In *Seventeenth Americas Conference on Information Systems*, Detroit, Michigan, pp. 1–11.

Horton, J. J., & Chilton, L. B. (2010). *The Labor Economics of Paid Crowdsourcing*, In Proceedings of the 11th ACM conference on Electronic commerce, New York: ACM, pp. 209–218.

Horton, J. J., Rand, D. G., & Zeckhauser, R. J. (2011). The online laboratory: Conducting experiments in a real labor market. *Experimental Economics*, 14(3), pp. 399–425.

Hosteltur. (2014). Benidorm será marca chic and cheap: La ciudad encarga la búsqueda de una nueva imagen turística. Available at: www.hosteltur.com/185020_benidorm-sera-marca-chic-and-cheap.html [Accessed 22 June 2015].

Hosteltur. (2015). Técnicas de crowdsourcing para dotar de storytelling visual a la web del hotel. Available at: www.hosteltur.com/140500_guia-buenas-practicas-usar-contenido-clientes-rrss-hotel.html [Accessed 8 July 2015].

Howe, J. (2006). The rise of crowdsourcing. *Wired*, 14(6). Available at: www.wired.com/wired/archive/14.06/crowds.html [Accessed 15 November 2015].

Howe, J. (2009). *Crowdsourcing: Why the Power of the Crowd Is Driving the Future of Business.*, New York: Three Rivers Press.

Keen, A. (2007). *The Cult of the Amateur: How Today's Internet Is Killing Our Culture and Assaulting Our Economy*, London, Nicholas Brealey.

Kleemann, F., Voß, G. G., & Rieder, K. (2008). Un(der)paid innovators: The commercial utilization of consumer work through crowdsourcing. *Technology & Innovation Studies*, 4(1), pp. 5–26.

Leimeister, J. M., Huber, M., Bretschneider, U., & Krcmar, H. (2009). Leveraging crowdsourcing: Activation-supporting components for IT-based ideas competition. *Journal of Management Information Systems*, 26(1), pp. 197–224.

Leonardo. (2014). The do's and don'ts of crowdsourcing content for your hotel. Available at: http://blog.leonardo.com/dos-and-donts-of-crowdsourcing-content/ [Accessed 10 July 2015].

Mason, W., & Watts, D. J. (2010). Financial incentives and the performance of crowds. ACM Sigkdd exploration newsletter, 11(2), pp. 100–108.

Mora, D. (2013). Tu hotel tiene una historia que contra. Available at: www.emoturismo. com/tu-hotel-tiene-una-historia-que-contar/ [Accessed 12 July 2015].

Müller, C. (2011). Social media marketing. A critical and evaluative account on the emergence and principles of social media marketing and its true potential to enhance the marketing initiatives of hotels and other organisations. *Scholarly Essay, 2011*. Available at: www.grin.com/en/e-book/200590/social-media-marketing [Accessed 5 January 2015].

Ortega, C. A. (2014). Buggl, una aplicación para crear y vender guías turísticas. Available at: www.youngmarketing.co/viajeros-expertos-ahora-podran-monetizar-sus-recomendaciones-2/ [Accessed 8 June 2015].

Peng, L., & Zhang, M. (2010). An empirical study of social capital in participation in online crowdsourcing. In Ogunbona, P. and Qin, S. (Eds.), *International Conference on E-Product E-Service and E-Entertainment*, Henan, China, November 7–9, 2010, pp. 1–4. doi: 10.1109/ICEEE.2010.5660804. New York: IEEE.

Poetz, M. K., & Schreier, M. (2012). The value of crowdsourcing: Can users really compete with professionals in generating new product ideas? *Journal of Product Innovation Management*, 29, pp. 245–256.

Porta, M., House, B., Buckley, L., & Blitz, A. (2008). Value 2.0: Eight new rules for creating and capturing value form innovative technologies. *Strategy & Leadership*, 36(4), pp. 10–18.

Richard, B., Ford, R., & Perry, W. (2016). Crowdsourcing in the lodging industry: Innovation on a budget. In R. Egger, I. Gula, & D. Walcher (eds.) *Open Tourism: Open Innovation, Crowdsourcing and Collaborative Consumption Challenging the Tourism Industry*, Berlin: Springer Verlag, pp. 79–94.

Rieder, K., & Voß, G. G. (2010). The working customer: An emerging new type of consumer. *Psychology of Everyday Activity*, 3(2), pp. 2–10.

Sanz-Blas, S., Tena-Monferrer, S., & Sánchez-García, J. (2015). Crowdsourcing: An application of promotional marketing. In F. Garrigos, I. Gil, & S. Estelles (eds.) *Advances in Crowdsourcing*. Cham, Switzerland: Springer International Publishing, pp. 147–161.

Schenk, E., & Guittard, C. (2011). Towards a characterization of crowdsourcing practices. *Journal of Innovation Economics and Management*, 7, pp. 93–107.

Sigala, M. (2009). WEB 2.0 in the tourism industry: A new tourism generation and new ebusiness models. Available at: www.traveldailynews.com/pages/show_page/20554 [Accessed 22 October 2015]

Sigala, M. (2012). Social networks and customer involvement in new service development (NSD). The case of www.mystarbucksidea.com. *International Journal of Contemporary Hospitality Management*, 24(7), pp. 966–990.

Sigala, M., & Marinidis, D. (2009). Exploring the transformation of tourism firms' operations and business models through the use of web map services: European and Mediterranean Conference on Information Systems 2009 (EMCIS 2009), Brunel University, Izmir, 13–14 July.

Stibbe, M. (2006). All contributions welcome. *Director*, 60(4), pp. 76–81.

Talents United. (2015). Logo benidorm. Available at: http://talentsunited.com/reto/logobenidorm [Accessed 15 June 2015].

Trejos, N. (2013). Guests help design the hotel of the future. Available at: www.usatoday.com/story/travel/hotels/2013/11/14/hotel-guests-millennials-designmarriott-holiday-inn/3538573/ [Accessed 5 April 2015].

Trifu, A., & Croitoru, I. (2014). A SWOT analysis of today's crowdsourcing process. *International Journal of Management Sciences*, 2(10), pp. 487–493.

Tzvetan, H. (2006). Using location for personalized POI recommendations. In Otoo Bobbie, P. & Takemura, H. (eds.), *Mobile Environments: Proceedings of the International Symposium on Applications and the Internet*, Phoenix, AZ, Washington, DC: IEEE, pp. 124–129.

VisitBenidorm. (2014). Benidorm lanza un reto online para que creativos de 40 países definan su nueva marca turística. Available at: www.visitbenidorm.es/ver/1424/ benidorm-lanza-un-reto-online-para-que-creativos – de-40-paises-definan-su-nueva-marca-turistica.html/ [Accessed 15 June 2015].

Whitla, P. (2009). Crowdsourcing and its application in marketing activities. *Contemporary Management Research*, 5(1), pp. 15–28.

9 Facebook marketing by hotel groups

Impacts of post content and media type on fan engagement

Kyung-Hyan Yoo and Woojin Lee

Introduction

With the recent surge in social media use for marketing, growing research attention has been paid to examining the role of social media in hospitality and tourism marketing. Several researchers have noted a changing marketing paradigm resulting from increasingly empowered travellers (O'Connor, 2008; Sigala, 2008) and found impacts of social media contents on travellers' information search (Chung & Koo, 2015), sharing (Chung et al., 2015) and decision-making (Litvin et al., 2008; McCarthy et al., 2010; Pan et al., 2007; Yoo & Gretzel, 2008). Witham (2011) claimed that social media offer a golden opportunity for the hospitality industry in terms of guest engagement and branding.

Customer engagement has been defined in many different ways. Some definitions focused on the emotional or psychological connections of customers with a brand (e.g. Forrester Consulting, 2008; Economist Intelligence Unit, 2007), while other definitions place more weight on the customers' intentions and behaviors like the desire to purchase and the time or attention a customer gives to a brand (e.g. Chaffey, 2008). There is currently no standardized definition or metric that definitively measures customer engagement on social media. Most companies use their own metrics to evaluate their social media marketing success. Further, there is still a lack of empirical studies that analyze the social media contents to understand what drives fan engagement. Kwok and Yu (2013) noted that only a few studies have analyzed the Facebook contents of hospitality companies to understand how the companies use the channels for their user engagement and branding. A number of researchers also indicated the need to analyze the social media communication and fan engagement to better assess the effectiveness of social media communication (Bonson Ponte et al., 2015; Mitropoulou et al., 2015; Leung & Bai, 2013). Consequently, this chapter seeks to analyze the Facebook communication of hospitality companies to better understand what makes customers engage with corporate Facebook posts. For that purpose, the Facebook posts published by major hotel groups were analyzed and tested in terms of whether the posts' topics and media types make any differences in encouraging fan engagement.

In the following sections, this chapter will first review relevant studies and theories. Then, this chapter will provide the findings of the content analysis of eight major hotel groups on the following aspects: 1) Facebook contents (topic and media type); 2) The level of fan engagement; and, 3) the influence of Facebook content on the fan engagement. Finally, this chapter will conclude with a discussion of implications for travel practitioners as well as researchers.

Literature review

Social media engagement in tourism and hospitality

Sharing travel experiences through personal narratives or pictures has always been an integral part of tourism experiences (Gretzel et al., 2011). Considering that other travellers' experiences often serve as important information sources for those planning travels, it is not surprising that social media have become popular communication platforms for travellers. On the other hand, social media have opened a new communication and marketing channel for tourism and hospitality practitioners. With emerging social media technologies providing a new tourism marketing framework (Gretzel & Yoo, 2013; Yoo & Gretzel, 2010), a number of previous studies have investigated how social media escalate customers' engagement with products or services, resulting in the enhancement of customers' perceived value and their loyalty (Kabadayi & Price, 2014; Senders et al., 2013; van Doorn et al., 2010). Some studies emphasize that consumer engagement facilitates customers' interactive behaviors with brands and further augments the overall brand value (Brodie et al., 2011). More specifically, those consumers who engage with brands on social media are more likely to become repeat customers (Smith, 2013; Wallace et al., 2012). Casalo et al. (2010) also support that consumers' engagement in online travel communities has a great impact on intentions to use products or services, and further enhances consumers' willingness to spread positive word of mouth. With respect to use of social media in tourism, Leung and Bai (2013) similarly noted that travellers' social media involvement has a positive effect on their revisit intention to social networking sites.

From the perspective of consumer experience management, Sashi (2012) claimed that using the interactive nature of the social media, marketers can fortify relationships with existing as well as new customers and can build communities that support collaborating, understanding and providing solutions together. Nowadays, consumers expand their engagement role to being "co-creators", becoming involved in the whole value-creation process (Kabadayi & Price, 2014). In other words, they help marketers to understand the consumers' needs by participating in product development and delivery, and also providing reviews of the product (Sashi, 2012). Given those aspects, social media play a critical and influential role in encouraging consumers to participate in the value-creation process.

In the context of tourism and hospitality, marketers use social media to get customers to engage more actively through encouraging them to post online reviews, offering room booking technology through Facebook, and facilitating customers' engagement in brand communities, e.g. the Walt Disney World Mom's

Panel, which is a forum where online "Moms" share information about family vacations to Disney (Hudson & Thal, 2013). Much of the literature also indicates that social media have changed the tourism and hospitality marketing paradigm, and thus new marketing approaches should be applied in social media communication (Gretzel & Yoo, 2013). Existing literature has identified several areas of marketing in which the active participation of consumers and the resulting changes in expectations require new approaches. These areas include customer relationship management, product development, promotion, pricing, distribution, market research and performance measurement.

Engaging Facebook content

Existing research indicates that consumer engagement leveraged by social media contributes to the establishment of trust and commitment, which leads the customers to be product advocates and foster interactive relationships (Gummerus et al., 2012, Sashi, 2012, Kabadayi & Price, 2014). Examining consumer engagement across a variety of social networking sites, Kabadayi and Price (2014) emphasize that it is Facebook that is the most heavily used social networking site to drive consumer engagement. From the corporations' management perspective, using Facebook is quite attractive. For example, Facebook allows companies to create their own Facebook page where they can share stories, pictures and links which enable the customer to engage by liking and/or commenting on those posts and messages (Gummerus et al., 2012). It is critically important for tourism and hospitality companies to make this engagement successful and incorporate it with their overall marketing strategies.

The research regarding Facebook functions by Wallace et al. (2012) argues that out of various ways customers engage via Facebook, "Liking" and "Commenting" are the most popular. Clicking "like" on Facebook can contribute not only to increased brand awareness, but can also raise the return on marketing investment (Barnard & Knapp, 2011). In addition, "Comments" on Facebook page are more visible compared to "Likes" in terms of consumers sharing their opinions about or agreement/disagreement with the content especially when showing the users' name and pictures next to his or her comments (Kabadayi & Price, 2014; Wallace et al., 2012). Previous empirical research by Hsu (2012), which examines the Facebook pages of six hotels with five-diamond ranking in Taiwan, demonstrates that Facebook users tend to like and post comments related to guest experiences and satisfaction. Interestingly, research on the impact of "Likes" or "Comments" (Lipsman et al., 2012; Libai, 2011) on Facebook indicates that consumers' commenting behavior on Facebook exposes their feelings, opinions and emotions toward the brand, which expresses their support of the brand, and further influences other peers to visit the brands' Facebook pages (Naylor et al., 2012; Lipsman et al., 2012). The research findings provided by Lee et al. (2012) confirm the argument that Facebook users' emotional connection to Facebook event pages can influence the pages' perceived usefulness, ease of use and enjoyment; ultimately, it can affect consumer decision-making to attend the local events.

The pressing question for tourism and hospitality marketers is, thus, how to encourage engagement on social media. Previous research has not been systematic or comprehensive but, for instance, suggests that posts asking questions to the fans or provide special offers or exclusive discounts and coupons can generate more engagement than average postings on Facebook (Facebook Page Publishing Best Practices, 2011).

Multimedia learning theory & media-richness theory

Multimedia learning theory developed by Mayer (1997) contends that multimedia presentations can foster focused attention and immersion into the content and, consequently, can make it more meaningful. In the context of online tourism marketing, applying multimedia learning theory, it is noted that some verbal and visual presentations on corporate social networking sites have the potential to provide more vivid and imaginative contents for consumers, which possibly lead to profound changes in consumer attitudes (Gobe, 2001; Lee & Gretzel, 2012). Media-richness theory, which was initially posited by Daft and Lengel (1986), establishes the important impact of media type on information processing. With regards to social networking sites, Facebook messages with photos and videos have been found to generate more engagement than the average post (Facebook's Page Publishing Best Practices, 2011). Social media posts typically involve using photographs, videos, emoticons and other linguistic markers (Baym, 2010). Previous empirical research reveals that sharing tourism experiences is typically accomplished by sharing of audio-visual contents such as photos and short videos, while narrative forms in posts are more effective to disseminate information (Munar & Jacobsen, 2013). Understanding the impact of post type in terms of its modality is therefore critical.

Methods

A quantitative content analysis was conducted in May, 2013 to analyze the Facebook communication effectiveness of hotel groups.

Selection of websites and hotel groups

The world's top 10 hotel groups were selected based on the MKG Hospitality's 2013 ranking results (MKG hospitality database, 2013). The hotel groups' official websites were visited to identify the availability of a Facebook page. Since Home Inns and Carlson Rezidor Hotel groups did not have Facebook pages at the time of the data collection, they were excluded from the analysis. A total of 443 posts published from January to March 2013 (1st Quarter of 2013) on the eight hotel groups' Facebook pages were examined. See Table 9.1 for a detailed description of the sample.

Table 9.1 Description of the sample

Names of Hotel Groups	Number of Fans (May 2013)	Number of Posts (Jan. – March, 2013)
IHG	40,916	17
Hilton Hotels	1,024,101	25
Marriott International	148,198	57
Wyndham Hotel Groups	30,039	86
Choice Hotels	151,337	74
Accor	221,904	31
Starwood Hotels & Resorts	62,675	28
Best Western	713,536	125
Total	2,392,706	443

Coding instrument and measurement

A codebook was developed to measure three aspects of Facebook communication: 1) content topic, 2) content media type and 3) fan engagement. Five categories of topics were identified from a pilot study: corporate news/information, marketing/promotion-related messages, conversational messages, entertaining messages and others. Two coders were trained to read each post carefully to identify the major topic and categorize it into a topic category. For example, if a post was entertaining and also contained company-related information, the coders were advised to identify the main purpose of the post and categorize it accordingly. A post was assigned to only one topic category. The media type of the posts was categorized into four categories (Text, Link, Photo and Video) following Kwok and Yu (2013). The text category includes text only posts. The photo category includes the photo only posts and photo posts with text. However, if an image in a post was generated from a shared link, the posts were categorized into the link category. The link category includes all posts with URL links. Posts with videos were categorized into the video category. To assess fan engagement, the number of likes, comments and shares for all individual posts were coded and the level of engagement was further analyzed following the engagement metrics proposed by Bonson and Ratkai (2013) (See Table 9.2). In addition, the engagement of hotel groups with their fans was analyzed by examining whether the hotel groups replied to their fans' comments using the "Reply" feature on Facebook.

Data collection

Two trained coders visited the eight hotel groups' Facebook pages in May 2013 to analyze all posts from the first quarter of 2013. In total, 443 posts were examined.

Table 9.2 Metrics for fan engagement

Popularity	P1	Number of posts liked/total posts	Percentage of Posts that have been liked
	P2	Total likes/total number of posts	Average number of likes per post
	P3	(P2/number of fans) x 1000	Average number of likes per post per 1000 fans
Commitment	C1	Number of posts commented on/total posts	Percentage of posts that have been commented on
	C2	Total comments/total number of posts	Average number of comments per post
	C3	(C2/number of fans) x 1000	Average number of comments per post per 1000 fans
Virality	V1	Number of posts shared/total posts	Percentage of posts that have been shared
	V2	Total shares/total number of posts	Average number of shares per post
	V3	(V2/number of fans) x 1000	Average number of shares per post per 1000 fans
Engagement	E	P3+C3+V3	Stakeholder engagement index

Source: Bonson and Ratkai, 2013

The coders examined the posts in terms of the post topic, post media type and fan engagement. All units were cross-coded by two coders to establish intercoder reliability. Cohen's kappa was used as an index. Cohen's kappa is known to be a conservative index to measure intercoder reliability (Lombard et al., 2010). Fifteen percent of the content was used to calculate the measure. Intercoder agreement averaged .74, which is considered satisfactory or acceptable (Lombard et al., 2010).

Data analysis

Descriptive analyses were employed to examine the content (topics and media types) of hotel groups' Facebook posts and the fan engagement. Kruskal-Wallis tests were conducted to determine whether the fan engagement varied as a function of content topic and media type. Mann-Whitney tests were used to test the relationship between the fan engagement and the interactive communication of hotel groups. Non-parametric Kruskal-Wallis and Mann-Whitney tests were used because the variables were not normally distributed.

Findings

Facebook contents

The findings show that the most shared topics are corporate news/information and marketing/promotion-related contents. About 32.7% of the content

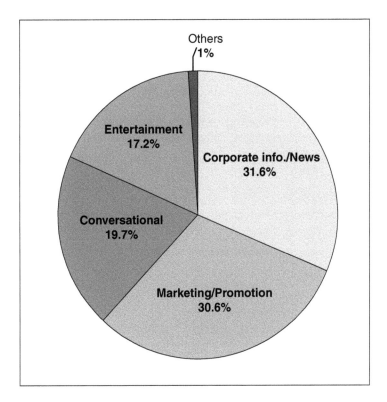

Figure 9.1 Facebook post topics

(145 posts) was related to hotel news or company information (e.g. new partnerships, product information) and about 30% (134 posts) of posts shared marketing information like special offers, discounts or promotion events. The hotel groups sometimes posted conversational messages that asked the fans for comments or feedback (92 posts, 19.7%) or entertaining messages or images (68 posts, 15.3%). See Figure 9.1 for a distribution of the Facebook message topics within the analyzed posts.

It is interesting that there are differences in the topics shared by hotel group. Corporate information or news are the most frequently shared topics for IHG (94.1%), Starwood Hotels (85.7%), Marriott (40.4%) and Wyndham (36%), while marketing/promotion-related contents were most often posted on Hilton Hotels (64%) and Best Western (48.8%) pages. Accor (41.9%) and Choice Hotels (35.1%) tended to post contents that asked questions or sought their fans' feedback. Table 9.3 provides the detailed descriptive findings by hotel group.

In terms of media type, the majority of content was comprised of posts with links (70.9%). About 23% of posts were created with photos. However, text-only (3.2%) or video (2.9%) contents were rarely posted (See Figure 9.2 and Table 9.4).

Table 9.3 Facebook post topics by hotel groups

Hotel Groups	Corporate Info./News	Marketing/ Promotion	Conversation	Entertainment/ Sensation	Other	Total
IHG	**16 (94.1%)**	–	–	–	1 (5.9%)	17 (100%)
Hilton Hotels	6 (24.0%)	**16 (64.0%)**	1 (4.0%)	–	2 (8.0%)	25 (100%)
Marriott	23 **(40.4%)**	5 (8.8%)	18 (31.6%)	11 (19.3%)	–	57 (100%)
Wyndham	**31 (36%)**	21 (24.4%)	11 (12.8%)	23 (26.7%)	–	86 (100%)
Choice	5 (6.8%)	23 (31.1%)	**26 (35.1%)**	20 (27.0%)	–	74 (100%)
Accor	6 (19.4%)	8 (25.8%)	**13 (41.9%)**	4 (12.9%)	–	31 (100%)
Starwood	**24 (85.7%)**	–	3 (10.7%)	–	1 (3.6%)	28 (100%)
Best Western	34 (27.2%)	**61 (48.8%)**	20 (16.0%)	10 (8.0%)	–	125 (100%)
Total	145 (32.7%)	134 (30.2%)	92 (20.8%)	68 (15.3%)	4 (0.9%)	443 (100%)

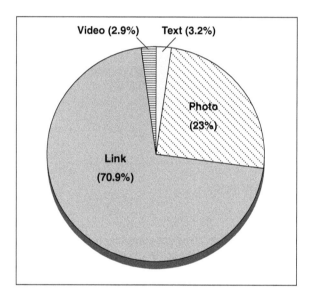

Figure 9.2 Facebook post media types

Table 9.4 Facebook post media types by hotel group

Hotel Groups	Text	Photo	Link	Video	Total
IHG	–	–	15 (88.2%)	2 (11.8%)	17 (100%)
Hilton Hotels	–	–	25 (100%)	–	25 (100%)
Marriott	–	18 (31.6%)	38 (66.7%)	1 (1.8%)	57 (100%)
Wyndham	5 (5.8%)	18 (20.9%)	63 (73.3%)	–	86 (100%)
Choice	5 (6.8%)	28 (37.8%)	38 (51.4%)	3 (4.1%)	74 (100%)
Accor	–	17 (54.8%)	13 (41.9%)	1 (3.2%)	31 (100%)
Starwood	–	3 (10.7%)	25 (89.3%)	–	28 (100%)
Best Western	4 (3.2)	18 (14.4%)	97 (77.6%)	6 (4.8%)	125 (100%)
Total	14 (3.2%)	102 (23%)	314 (70.9%)	13 (2.9%)	443 (100%)

Table 9.5 Message topic by media type

Message Topic	Media Type				Total (% of posts)
	Text	Photo	Link	Video	
Marketing/Promotion	1	6	126	1	134 (30.2%)
Conversation	11	54	27	0	92 (20.8%)
Entertainment/ Sensation	1	30	33	4	68 (15.3%)
Corporate News/Info.	1	12	124	8	145 (32.7%)
Others	0	0	4	0	4 (0.9%)
Total (% of posts)	14 (3.2)	102 (23)	314 (70.9)	13 (2.9)	443 (100%)

The data were further analyzed to determine whether message topic and media type were related. In other words, the data were analyzed to explore whether certain topics were more likely created in certain media types. The findings show that hotel groups are more likely to create their Facebook messages with links when they share marketing-related messages or corporate news/information. However, they are more likely to post in a text-only message or use photos when they try to have a conversation with their fans or seek feedback. The entertaining posts were more likely to be published with photos or links (Table 9.5).

Facebook engagement

The results (See Table 9.6) show that 100% of the posts were liked (P1), 89% were discussed (C1) and 87% of posts were shared (V1) on average. On average, the hotel groups' individual Facebook posts received about 487 likes (P2), 45 comments (C2) and 37 shares (V2) (Medians: 94 likes, 5 comments and 11 shares per post). However, when the numbers were calculated per 1000 fans, each post received on average only 0.2 likes (P3), 0.02 comments (C3) and 0.02 shares (V3) per 1000 fans. This means that there is a small percentage of fans who actively engage with hotel groups on Facebook and many fans had liked the page at some point in the past but have never interacted afterwards. With these engagement metrics, the overall fan engagement index (E) was generated. The average fan engagement level is 0.24 likes/comments/shares per post per 1000 fans. The overall level of fan engagement was higher for the dimension of popularity than commitment and virality. This makes sense because clicking a "Like" button is easier than writing a comment or sharing the post with friends.

The level of engagement was varied by hotel. The posts by Hilton Hotels were most liked and shared by its fans while the fans of Best Western are the most likely to write comments. However, these two hotel groups have the highest number of fans. When we calculated the average level of engagement per post per 1000 fan (Engagement Index), the fans of IHG emerged as the most engaged group with an engagement index of 4.02, followed by Hilton Hotels (3.10),

Table 9.6 Hotel groups' Facebook fan engagement

Popularity	P1	Percentage of posts that have been liked	1
	P2	Average number of likes per post	486.56
	P3	Average number of likes per post per 1000 fans	0.2
Commitment	C1	Percentage of posts that have been commented on	0.89
	C2	Average number of comments per post	44.55
	C3	Average number of comments per post per 1000 fans	0.02
Virality	V1	Percentage of posts that have been shared	0.87
	V2	Average number of shares per post	37.02
	V3	Average number of shares per post per 1000 fans	0.02
Engagement	E	Stakeholder engagement index	0.24

Table 9.7 Fan engagement by hotel group

Hotel Groups	Likes		Comments		Shares		Engagement Index
	Mean	Median	Mean	Median	Mean	Median	
IHG	116.76	71	17.94	4	29.76	12	4.02
Hilton Hotels	2880.72	1458	83.56	60	209.04	181	3.10
Wyndham	73.55	36	5.69	2.5	3.16	1	2.74
Marriott	316.61	267	28.28	12	46.37	33	2.64
Best Western	842.95	165	109.18	13	42.64	14	1.40
Accor	161.84	39	17.94	4	28.23	13	0.93
Starwood	39.25	21.5	2.82	1	5.36	1	0.76
Choice	76.81	51.5	16	3.5	18.88	11	0.73

Wyndham (2.74) and Marriott (2.64). Table 9.7 presents the means and medians of number of likes, comments and shares by hotel group as well as their overall engagement indices.

The hotel groups' engagement was further analyzed. We analyzed whether the hotels replied to any comments from their fans using the "Reply" feature on Facebook. Findings show that a small percentage of hotel groups participated in interactive conversations. Hilton Hotels had the highest level of interaction (24%) followed by Starwood (21.4%) and Wyndham (19.8%). But the average percentage of interactive communication is 14.4% and less than 20% for most hotel groups. This indicates that many hotel groups deliver their messages on Facebook but do not actively participate in the conversations with their fans (See Table 9.8).

Table 9.8 Interactive communication of hotel groups

Hotel Groups	Interactive Communication	
	Number of Posts with Reply	*Percentage of Posts with Reply*
IHG	2	11.8%
Hilton Hotels	6	24%
Marriott	7	12.3%
Wyndham	17	19.8%
Choice	12	16.2%
Accor	6	19.4%
Starwood	6	21.4%
Best Western	8	6.4%
Total	64	14.4%

The influence of post content topic and media type on fan engagement

The results of Kruskal-Wallis tests show that whether the fans write comments on the Facebook posts of hotel groups was related to the post content topic ($H(3) = 67.254$, $p = .000$) and media type ($H(3) = 20.302$, $p = .000$). However, there was no significant relationship between the post content topic/media type and the number of likes and shares on the posts.

Post-hoc comparisons indicate that the mean rank scores among all groups were significantly different. The results show that the number of comments was greater for conversational messages than for posts regarding marketing, entertainment or corporate news/information. When we compared the marketing posts with other groups, the marketing-related posts received a greater number of comments than corporate news/information and entertainment posts. There are a greater number of comments for the corporate news/information posts than for the entertainment posts. The findings suggest that the Facebook fans engage in conversations with hotel groups when the companies begin the conversation. They are also more likely to engage in discussion when they receive incentives. Our findings align with the results of Kwok and Yu (2013) and Bonson Ponte et al. (2015). Kwok and Yu (2013) reported that conversational messages received a higher number of comments than sales/marketing messages. Bonson Ponte and his colleagues found more fan engagement for marketing contents than corporate or community-related contents. They are, however, surprising given Gretzel and Fesenmaier's (2012) research on the motivations to follow travel companies on Facebook, suggesting that most tourism consumers seek special offers and promotions.

In terms of the influence of media type on the number of comments, text-only posts received the highest number of comments followed by photo, link and video posts. This finding agrees with Kwok and Yu (2013)'s study. They also found that text-only posts received more comments than the other three types of messages.

The effect sizes were calculated with the Chi-square values as suggested by Green and Salkind (2005) and the strength of effect size was interpreted following the guidelines by Cohen (1988). Our findings show that there is a large effect of post topic (eta squared = .15) and a moderate effect of post media type (eta squared = .05) on the fans' likelihood to write comments in response to the hotel groups' Facebook posts (See Tables 9.9 and 9.10 for the details).

Table 9.9 Kruskal-Wallis test results for content topic and engagement

Test Variables	Post Content Topic	N	Mean Rank	Chi-square	df	Eta squared	P
Likes	Marketing	134	225.63	5.894	3	.01	.117
	Conversation	92	233.27				
	Entertainment	68	187.03				
	Corporate News/Info.	145	221.83				
Comments	Marketing	134	237.13	67.254	3	.15	.000**
	Conversation	92	296.26				
	Entertainment	68	145.30				
	Corporate News/Info.	145	190.81				
Shares	Marketing	134	234.83	3.022	3	.01	.388
	Conversation	92	220.09				
	Entertainment	68	212.26				
	Corporate News/Info.	145	209.87				

** p<0.01

Table 9.10 Kruskal-Wallis test results for media type and engagement

Test Variables	Post Media Type	N	Mean Rank	Chi-square	df	Eta squared	P
Likes	Text	14	215.36	5.089	3	.01	.165
	Photo	102	245.78				
	Link	314	215.90				
	Video	13	189.88				
Comments	Text	14	318.25	20.302	3	.05	.000**
	Photo	102	256.96				
	Link	314	207.59				
	Video	13	192.15				
Shares	Text	14	147.11	7.232	3	.02	.065
	Photo	102	237.95				
	Link	314	221.49				
	Video	13	189.81				

** p < 0.01

Table 9.11 Mann-Whitney test results for two-way communication and engagement

Test Variables	Two-way Communication	N	Mean Rank	Z	P
Likes	No	379	219.91	−.837	.403
	Yes	64	234.38		
Comments	No	379	210.07	−4.784	.000**
	Yes	64	292.63		
Shares	No	379	218.35	−1.463	.144
	Yes	64	243.60		

** $p < 0.01$

The relationship between the fan engagement and interactive communication (whether hotel groups replied to the fans' comments) was analyzed using Mann-Whitney test. The results indicate that the number of comments was greater when the hotel groups participated in interactive communication. The Z value is -4.78 with a significance level of p = .000 (Table 9.11).

Summary and discussion

Our findings address three aspects of Facebook communication of hotel groups. First, our analysis found that in the first quarter of 2013 the most frequently published topics by hotel groups were corporate information/news and marketing-related messages and the preferred media type was posts with links. Second, in terms of fan engagement, our results indicate that only a small percentage of fans were active hotel group followers and that the fans were more likely to "like" the posts than write comments or share the posts. Lastly, our findings show that the Facebook fans were more likely to write their comments in response to conversational messages than other topics and when the post was created in a text-only format.

A number of implications can be drawn from our findings. It suggests that there is a potential communication gap between the organizations and their fans. While the hotel groups apply traditional marketing approaches to their social media communication, which focus on delivering the company's messages or marketing contents to the target audiences, their fans only reward marketers with comments if they are invited into a conversation. They are more likely to write comments when the company begins the conversation by asking questions or seeking feedback from their fans. O'Connor (2008) noted that industry must apply new thinking to new media. The traditional marketing approach does not only fail but could be considered offensive in social media marketing (McCarthy et al., 2010). Our findings therefore suggest the need for a better understanding of the foundations of strategic social media communication for hospitality companies.

It is also interesting to find that the fans were more likely to write comments to text-only posts than in response to photo, link and video posts. Our study does not provide a definitive reason for this finding but this indicates that the hotel group

Facebook fans seem to read the content prior to engaging on social media. To some degree, this finding is consistent with the findings by Kwok and Yu (2013), which found that text-only posts received more comments than other types of posts. This makes sense given that most text-only posts have a conversational focus according to our data. Yet, the findings stand in contrast to media-richness theory and require further research. With growing popularity of video content on Facebook, research that takes current interactions into account is paramount.

While a growing number of hospitality and tourism companies are present in the social media environment, many marketers often are more concerned with "getting it," instead of "getting it right" (eMarketer, 2012). It is important to understand the changing marketing paradigms and adjust the approach to more effectively communicate with the customers. The findings of this study provide a snapshot of social media use by hospitality marketers on Facebook and found some interesting relationships that can inform our understanding of fan engagement. Further, the social media evaluation metrics used in this study can serve as a building block for developing sound and standardized social media marketing measurement and provide a basis for future research in this area.

References

Barnard, C., & Knapp, S. (2011). Do Facebook likes indicate marketer ROI? *DM News*, 33(7), p. 25.

Baym, N. K. (2010). *Personal Connections in the Digital Age*, Cambridge, Polity.

Bonson, E., & Ratkai, M. (2013). A set of metrics to assess stakeholder engagement and social legitimacy on a corporate Facebook page. *Online Information Review*, 37(5), pp. 787–803.

Bonson Ponte, E., Carvajal-Trujilo, E., & Escobar-Rodriguez, T. (2015). Corporate Facebook and stakeholder engagement. *Kybernetes*, 44(5), pp. 771–787.

Brodie, R. J., Hollebeek, L. D., Biljana, J., & Illc, A. (2011). Consumer engagement: conceptual domain, fundamental propositions and implications for research. *Journal of Service Research*, 14(3), pp. 252–271.

Casalo, L. V., Flavian, C., & Guinaliu, M. (2010). Determinants of the intention to participate in firm-hosted online travel communities and effects on consumer behavioral intentions. *Tourism Management*, 31(6), pp. 898–911.

Chaffey, D. (2008). Customer engagement definition. Available at: www.davechaffey.com/E-marketing-Glossary/Customer-engagement.htm [Accessed March 2011].

Chung, N., & Koo, C. (2015). The use of social media in travel information search. *Telematics and Informatics*, 32, pp. 215–229.

Chung, N., Lee, S., & Han, H. (2015). Understanding communication types on travel information sharing in social media: A transitive memory systems perspective. *Telematics and Informatics*, 32, pp. 564–575.

Cohen, J. (1988). *Statistical Power Analysis for the Behavioural Sciences the Effect Size*, Hillsdale, NJ, Lawrence Erlbaum.

Daft, R. L., & Lengel, R. H. (1986). Organizational information requirements, media richness and structural design. *Management Science*, 32, pp. 554–571.

Economist Intelligence Unit (EIU). (2007). Beyond loyalty: Meeting the challenge of customer engagement, part 1. Available at: www.adobe.com/engagement/pdfs/partI.pdf [Accessed March 2011].

eMarketer. (2012). Social media for travel marketers: Cultivating conversation to capture customer sentiment. [Online]. Available at: www.emarketr.com [Accessed 20 August 2012].

Facebook Page Publishing Best Practices. (2011). Building essential connections: Engaging your audience by publishing to your page. Retrieved 06 June 2012 from www.facebook.com/business/pageposts

Forrester Consulting. (2008). How engaged are your customers?. Available at: www.adobe.com/engagement/pdfs/Forrester_TLP_How_Engaged_Are_Your_Customers.pdf [Accessed March 2011]..

Gobe, M. (2001). *Emotional Branding*. New York, Allworth Press.

Green, S., & Salkind, N. (2005). *Using SPSS for Windows and Macintosh: Understanding and Analysing Data*, Upper Saddle River, NJ, Prentice-Hall.

Gretzel, U., & Fesenmaier, D. R. (2012). Customer relations 2.0 – Implications for destination marketing (abstract). TTRA Annual International Conference, Virginia Beach, VA. 17–19 June, 2012.

Gretzel, U., Fesenmaier, D. R., Lee, Y.-J., & Tussyadiah, I. (2011). Narrating travel experiences: The role of new media. In R. Sharpley & P. Stone (eds.) *Tourist Experiences: Contemporary Perspectives.*. New York, Routledge, pp. 171–182.

Gretzel, U., & Yoo, K. H. (2013). Premises and promises of social media marketing in tourism. In S. McCabe (ed.) *The Routledge Handbook of Tourism Marketing*. New York, Routledge, pp. 491–504.

Gummerus, J., Liljander, V., Weman, E., & Pihlstrom, M. (2012). Customer engagement in a Facebook brand community. *Management Research Review*, 35(9), pp. 857–877.

Hsu, Y. L. (2012). Facebook as international eMarketing strategy of Taiwan hotels. *International Journal of Hospitality Management*, 31(3), pp. 972–980.

Hudson, S., & Thal, K. (2013). The impact of social media on the consumer decision process: Implications for tourism marketing. *Journal of Travel & Tourism Marketing*, 30, pp. 156–160.

Kabadayi, S., & Price, K. (2014). Consumer-brand engagement on Facebook: Liking and commenting behaviors. *Journal of Research in Interactive Marketing*, 8(3), pp. 203–223.

Kwok, L., & Yu, B. (2013). Spreading social media messages on Facebook: An analysis of restaurant business-to-consumer communications. *Cornell Hospitality Quarterly*, 54(1), pp. 84–94.

Lee, W., & Gretzel, U. (2012). Designing persuasive destination websites: A mental imagery processing perspective. *Tourism Management*, 33(5), pp. 1270–1280.

Lee, W., Xiong, L., & Hu, C. (2012). The effect of Facebook users' arousal and valence on intention to go to the festival: Applying an extension of the technology acceptance model. *International Journal of Hospitality Management*, 31(3), pp. 819–827.

Leung, X. Y., & Bai, B. (2013). How motivation, opportunity and ability impact travelers' social media involvement and revisit intention. *Journal of Travel & Tourism Marketing*, 30(1–2), p. 58.

Libai, B. (2011). Comment: The perils of focusing on highly engaged consumers. *Journal of Service Research*, 14(3), pp. 275–276.

Lipsman, A., Mudd, G., Rich, M., & Bruich, S. (2012). The power of like: How brands reach (and influence) fans through social media marketing. *Journal of Advertising*, 42(1), pp. 40–52.

Litvin, S. W., Goldsmith, R. E., & Pan, B. (2008). Electronic word-of-mouth in hospitality and tourism management. *Tourism Management*, 29(3), pp. 458–468.

Lombard, M., Snyder-Duch, J., & Bracken, C. C. (2010). Practical resources for assessing and reporting intercoder reliability in content analysis research projects. Retrieved 20 January 2012 from http://matthewlombard.com/reliability/#How should researchers calculate intercoder reliability What software is available.

Mayer, R. E. (1997). Multimedia learning: Are we asking the right questions. *Educational Psychologist*, 32, pp. 1–19.

McCarthy, L., Stock, D., & Verma, R. (2010). How travelers use online and social media channels to make hotel-choice decisions. *Cornell Hospitality Reports*, 10(18), pp. 6–18.

Mitropoulou, M., Ninov, I., & Christodoulidou, N. (2015). Social media messages on Facebook: An analysis of five-atar hotels-to-consumer communications. In C. Cobanoglu & S. Ongan (eds.) *Proceedings of the International Interdisciplinary Business-Economics Advancement Conference*, Sarasota-Manatee, FL: University of South Florida, pp. 454–463.

MKG Hospitality Database. (2013). World ranking 2013 of hotel groups and brands. Available at: www.hospitalitynet.org/news/4060119.html [Accessed September 2012].

Munar, A. M., & Jacobsen, J. K. S. (2013). Trust and involvement in tourism social media and web-based travel information sources. *Scandinavian Journal of Hospitality and Tourism*, 13(1), pp. 1–19.

Naylor, R. W., Lamberton, C. P., & West, P. M. (2012). Beyond the "like" button: The impact of mere virtual presence on brand evaluations and purchase intentions in social media settings. *Journal of Marketing*, 76(6), pp. 105–120.

O'Connor, P. (2008). User-generated content and travel: A case study on TripAdvisor.com. In P. O'Connor, W. Höpken, & U. Gretzel (eds.) *Information and Communication Technologies in Tourism 2008*. Vienna, Austria, Springer Verlag, pp. 47–58.

Pan, B., MacLaurin, T., & Crotts, J. C. (2007). Travel blogs and the implications for destination marketing. *Journal of Travel Research*, 46, pp. 35–45.

Sashi, C. M. (2012). Customer engagement, buyer-seller relationships and social media. *Management Decision*, 50(2), pp. 253–272.

Senders, A., Govers, R., & Neuts, B. (2013). Social media affecting tour operators' customer loyalty. *Journal of Travel & Tourism Marketing*, 30(1–2), pp. 41–57.

Sigala, M. (2008). Web 2.0, social marketing strategies and distribution channels for city destinations: Enhancing the participatory role of travelers and exploiting their collective intelligence. In M. Gascó-Hernández & T. Torres-Coronas (eds.) *Information Communication Technologies and City Marketing: Digital Opportunities for Cities around the World*. Hershey, PA: Information Science Reference, pp. 221–245.

Smith, C. (2013). Retailers say social media is having an impact on their bottoms. *Business Insider*, June, p. 21.

Van Doorn, J., Lemon, K. N., Mittal, V., Nass, S., Doreen, P., Pirner, P., & Verhoef, P. C. (2010). Customer engagement behavior: Theoretical foundations and research directions. *Journal of Service Research*, 13(3), pp. 252–266.

Wallace, E., Buil, I., & de Chernatony, L. (2012). Facebook "friendship" and brand advocacy. *Journal of Brand Management*, 20(2), pp. 128–146.

Withiam, G. (2011). Social media and the hospitality industry: Holding the Tiger by the Tail. *2011 Cornell Hospitality Roundtable & Conference Proceedings*, 3(3), pp. 6–15.

Yoo, K.-H., & Gretzel, U. (2008). What motivates consumers to write online travel reviews? *Information Technology & Tourism*, 10(4), pp. 283–295.

Yoo, K.-H., & Gretzel, U. (2010). Web 2.0: New rules for tourism marketing. Proceedings of the 41th Annual Conference of the Travel and Tourism Research Association, San Antonio, TX, June 20–22, 2010. Lake Orion, MI: Travel and Tourism Research Association.

10 Influencer marketing in travel and tourism

Ulrike Gretzel

In the 2012 edition of this book, Volo (2012) describes a new, decentralized communication paradigm based on Web 2.0 that allows tourism marketers to directly and personally connect to customers. While this is still the case, this social media-supported marketer-consumer conversation space has become incredibly crowded. Both marketer and consumer messages might be spread or contested by other consumers or traditional media. In this complex social media-based buzz echoverse (Hewett et al., 2016), it is ever more important for brands to be able to amplify their messages. In addition, platforms like Facebook have developed their display algorithm in a way that makes it increasingly difficult for marketers to organically appear in consumers' social media feeds. At the same time, consumers are adopting ad blocking software at growing rates while also feeling ever more bombarded with information. This fuels a need for information filters and encourages the emergence of a traditional two-step flow of information (Katz, 1957), with opinion leaders pre-processing information and spreading messages to a wider, dedicated audience. These opinion leaders are trusted individuals who offer advice and exercise influence over the opinion of others. In the social media context, these opinion leaders are usually called key opinion leaders (especially in China), or simply influencers.

Influencers are individuals who have the power to affect decisions of others because of their (real or perceived) authority, knowledge, position or relationship (Businessdictionary.com, 2017). Others have defined influencers as individuals who have an active following and can move their followers to take action (MarketingProfs.com, 2016). Keller and Fay (2016) refer to influencers as:

> everyday consumers who are substantially more likely than the average to seek out information and to share ideas, information, and recommendations with other people. They do this both through volunteering their opinions about products and services that they feel passionate about, and by being turned to for their knowledge, advice, and insights.
>
> (p. 1)

Marketers have worked with influencers for a long time. Traditionally, these influencers were celebrities and they were used in advertising to endorse products.

Glover (2009) summarizes the benefits of celebrity endorsements as pertaining to capturing an audience's attention, adding credibility, increasing ad recall, achieving synergies between the product brand and the personal brand of the celebrity, as well as increasing brand recognition. She further stresses their importance for tourism marketing, suggesting that destination image and awareness can be significantly influenced through their endorsements. Indeed, the impact of these traditional celebrity endorsements in tourism advertising has been well documented (McCartney & Pinto, 2014; Van der Veen & Song, 2014; Yen & Teng, 2015).

While celebrities continue to be influential in the social media realm, social media also produced so-called grassroots influencers or micro-celebrities that were able to create a following through their engaging and relevant content. McQuarrie et al. (2013) refer to this ability of regular social media users to amass enough social capital to reach a mass audience as the "mega-phone effect" of social media. In contrast to mainstream celebrities who create celebrity value through exclusiveness, social media micro-celebrities establish their value through authenticity and connectedness (Jerslev, 2016). Hearn and Schoenhoff (2016) describe social media influencers as working "to generate a form of "celebrity" capital by cultivating as much attention as possible and crafting an authentic "personal brand" via social networks, which can subsequently be used by companies and advertisers for consumer outreach" (p. 194). Some of these social media stars end up becoming mainstream celebrities (see for example the Chinese backpacker and blogger T40C described by Shao and Gretzel, 2011). Both celebrities and micro-celebrities are increasingly used by marketers to spread messages to targeted audiences on social media; this practice is referred to as influencer marketing.

Definition of influencer marketing

Carter (2016: 2) describes influencer marketing as "a rapidly growing industry that attempts to promote products or increase brand awareness through content spread by social media users who are considered to be influential". Influencermarketinghub. com (2017a) defines influencer marketing as relying on "technology – and a combination of reach, relevance and resonance – to amplify word-of-mouth, either through organic (unpaid) word-of-mouth, traditionally coming from micro-influencers, . . . [or] 'paid' endorsements, using a combination of macro-influencers, brand advocates, and brand ambassadors" (n.p.). MarketingProfs.com (2016) describes influencer marketing as involving marketers connecting with influencers to build mutually beneficial relationships. Swant (2016) suggests that influencer marketing, rather than relying on household names like traditional advertising, takes advantage of "handheld names", who have developed a sizeable reputation and following on social media. The most important platforms on which marketers employ influencer marketing are: 1) Instagram (used by 89% of marketers engaged in influencer marketing); 2) Facebook and Twitter (both used by 70% of marketers); 3) Youtube (59%); 4) Blogs (48%); and 5) Snapchat (45% of marketers) (Krasniak, 2016).

What influential means on social media and how it can be identified is the 1-Million-Dollar question of influencer marketing. Inkybee (2016) proposes that the most important metrics of influence are: size of audience, how often they post, level of engagement and search engine optimization-based metrics. Specifically looking at bloggers, Solis (2008) lists traffic to the blog, links back to the blog, amount of subscribers to the feed and grasp of the industry as important measures that determine influence. Radey (2015), however, suggests that reach might not be as important as relevance and passion, and that real influence is not a matter of social media followers, as they can easily be amassed or even faked. Similarly, Krasniak (2016) reports that authenticity matters the most, while Hearn and Schoenhoff (2016) stress alignment with the brand. De Veirman et al. (2016) report that high numbers of followers increase popularity perceptions and likeability of an influencer but might also negatively influence perceptions of the product's exclusivity. eMarketer (2015) finds that most influencer marketers select influencers based on their social profile, verified traffic data and demographics and that page rank and search optimization standing are less important selection criteria. What is surprising is that influencers have become almost as important as traditional word-of-mouth from family and friends, with 56% of Twitter users reporting that they rely on recommendations from friends and 49% reporting that they rely on recommendations from influencers (Swant, 2016).

Not all influencers are equal. Marketers generally divide influencers into the following categories: 1) celebrities; 2) industry experts and thought leaders; 3) bloggers and content creators; and 4), micro-influencers (Influencermarketinghub. com, 2017b). Izea (2017a) uses size of the following to distinguish among micro- and macro-influencers, with micro-influencers having 500 to 10,000 followers. Influencermarketinghub.com (2017a) establishes yet another category, namely that of mega-influencers, with audiences of over one million. Current research suggests that while mega-influencers have a lot of reach, micro-influencers make up for their smaller reach through higher relevance and resonance, leading to much higher engagement rates. Morin (2016) advocates that there are also niche influencers that are focused on particular topics like gamers and mom bloggers who are focused on monetizing their social media activities while micro-influencers are often not primarily driven by monetary rewards. Identifying the right influencer for an influencer marketing campaign is therefore absolutely critical to its success.

Influencer marketing is basically marketing to influencers rather than regular consumers but has evolved to encompass specific tactics. Inkybee (2016) describes influencer marketing as involving influencer discovery, influencer outreach, design of influencer campaigns, influencer tracking/measurement and influencer relations. As indicated in the definition above, influencer marketing does not necessarily mean obtaining earned media. Izea (2017a) reports that Kylie Jenner, who has 86.2 million followers on Instagram, receives between $100,000 to $300,000 for a single sponsored Instagram post. Even middle-tiered influencers with 400,000 to 1.5 million followers can currently charge around $5,000 per post (Influencermarketinghub.com, 2017c). However, a recent survey of micro-influencers (less than 5000 followers) shows that they charge on average less than $250 per Instagram post (Nanji, 2017a). It should also be noted that many countries now require influencers to include disclosure statements in their posts if they received money from the brands for which they advocate.

Influencer marketing goes beyond encouraging simple endorsements or message sharing by influencers. Krasniak (2016) lists ongoing brand ambassadorship, product reviews, brand mentions, event coverage, sponsored content and affiliate links as the most important and effective influencer marketing tactics currently used by marketers. These tactics are applied to support various marketing areas. eMarketer (2015) reports that the top three areas for which marketers employ influencers are content promotion, product launch and content creation, followed by other areas such as event management, corporate communications, search engine optimization and crisis management.

Importance of influencer marketing

Recent research suggests that influencer marketing is effective. For instance, one study indicates that 40% of respondents have purchased an item after seeing it used by an influencer on Instagram, Twitter, Vine or YouTube (Swant, 2016). The same research also found that Twitter users reported a 5.2 times increase in purchase intent when exposed to both brand and influencer tweets about the product. In accordance with these findings, MarketingDIVE (Kirkpatrick, 2016) reports that influencer marketing campaigns have the ability to achieve 11 times more return on investment than traditional advertising.

The top five reasons why marketers use influencers in their marketing are 1) improving brand advocacy; 2) expanding brand awareness; 3) reaching new targeted audiences; 4) increasing share of voice (i.e., the percentage of all online content and conversations about the brand in comparison to its competitors); and 5) improving sales conversion (Nanji, 2017b). A report by Social Media Examiner (Krasniak, 2016) adds growing concerns about the rising use of ad blocking as well as ad avoidance by consumers as a main reason.

Various recent studies cement the idea that influencer marketing has become an essential component of social media marketing for a majority of brands. For example, a survey of marketing professionals found that 60% used social influencers as part of their marketing strategies in 2016, mostly to target different or hard to reach audiences (Krasniak, 2016). Morin (2016) indicates that the market value of influencer marketing is between US $10 and $15 billion and will continue to grow over the next few years. Izea (2017b) reports that over a third of marketers now spend over $500,000 a year on influencer marketing. According to Forbes.com (2016a), $255 million are spent per month just for Instagram posts by influencers. Almost half (48%) of recently surveyed marketers expect their influencer marketing budgets to increase in 2017 (Influencermarketinghub.com, 2017a).

Influencer marketing practices

Influencer marketing is still an emerging practice. Nanji (2017b) reports that many marketers are still experimenting with influencer marketing and that only 24%

have ongoing influencer programs while a mere 5% have integrated influencers across all marketing activities. One of the reasons is that measuring the return on investment of an influencer campaign remains difficult. eMarketer (2015) finds that the main challenges of influencer marketing are 1) identifying the right influencers; 2) finding the right engagement tactics; and 3) measuring the performance of an influencer campaign. Identifying the right influencers is often achieved through the use of tools like blog search engines (e.g. blekko.com and socialmention.com), while Klout, Kred and Peer Index are examples of tools that rank social media influencers based on their "social capital" and activity level.

Calculating the "return on influence" is essential for successful influencer marketing. To establish the return of investment of influencer campaigns, influencer marketers currently use QR codes, coupons, promotional codes and trackable links to be able to connect influencer activities with product purchases. They also increasingly rely on tools like Traackr and Snaplytics or content monetization platforms like rewardStyle to provide them with performance measures (Influencermarketinghub.com, 2017a). Performance measures usually implemented include audience reach, impressions, engagement, sentiment, quality of content and various measures of conversion, e.g. traffic to specific landing pages, growth in followers on brand-related social media channels or increased sales.

In practice, influencer marketing takes many forms beyond getting the influencer to spread a marketing message. For instance, marketers can send freebies/samples or invite influencers to events. Instameets are often used by destinations or festivals to encourage influencers to create and share content (Queensland, Australia, 2014). Influencer marketing further involves marketers and influencers co-creating content, marketers featuring influencers in their branded posts, influencers being invited to host contests or giveaways, as well as having influencers take over the brand's social media channels. So-called influencer takeovers not only bring fresh content to the brand's accounts but also allow the brand to be exposed to new audiences (SocialMediaToday, 2016). Establishing ongoing relationships with influencers is often seen as key to the success of influencer marketing as this allows influencers to familiarize themselves with the brand, thus leading to more organic content.

Influencer marketing often involves working with an influencer agency. Niche, Socialyte, Viral Nation, The Amplify, Izea and Mediakix are just a few examples of agencies in this space. Some of them are platform specific (e.g. only for Instagram influencer marketing), while others have a broad portfolio of influencers. These agencies not only connect influencers with marketers or their advertising/PR agencies but also groom interested individuals into successful influencers.

A new development in the influencer marketing field is the emergence of platforms and influencer marketplaces that support both companies/agencies and influencers. Influencer marketplaces like Famebit and Octoly allow brands and agencies to post sponsorship opportunities and support collaboration between brands and creators in making branded video content and reviews (Forbes.com, 2016a). Other platforms not only offer matchmaking services but also post-campaign analytics and use sophisticated machine-learning algorithms to identify and track influencers

(Influencermarketinghub.com, 2017d). Importantly, influencer marketplaces/ platforms allow marketers to scale their influencer marketing efforts by offering central dashboards for running campaigns, tools to manager influencer relation- ships and secure payment functions to support transactions with influencers.

Influencer marketing in travel and tourism

Influencer marketing in travel and tourism builds on the importance of word-of- mouth in the travel context (Litvin et al., 2008). Tourism marketers started working with bloggers early on as blogs quickly became important information sources for travel decision makers and therefore valuable media for marketers (Lin and Huang, 2006). Tourism New Zealand's collaboration with Chinese micro-blogger Yao Chen is a prominent and well-documented example of early influencer marketing in tourism, which allowed the destination to take advantage of Yao Chen's influ- ence on Chinese travellers (Tourism New Zealand, 2012). A more recent example of influencer marketing in travel and tourism is the case of video blogger (vlogger) Jack Harries of JacksGap and Marriott co-creating travel videos, e.g. 24 hours in New Orleans, which has received almost 900,000 views on YouTube (JacksGap, 2015). Marriott has also worked with the comedian Taryn Southern to produce humorous videos that feature influencers in order to promote their Moxy Hotels brand (Influencer Orchestration Network, 2017).

Various lists of important travel influencers exist. For instance, Neoreach (2016) features Jay Alvarrez, an extreme sports enthusiast with over 5 million followers on Instagram and a presence on YouTube and Snapchat as one of the most influential travel social media influencers. Adweek (2016) lists Kate McCully who appears as adventurouskate on Instagram and has 95,000 followers (see Figure 10.1) as an important niche travel blogger and influencer focusing on solo

Figure 10.1 Kate McCulley's Instagram profile

and independent travel for women. Forbes.com (2016b) lists Megan Jerrard, Ann Tran and Scott Eddy as veteran travel social media influencers. Ann Tran, for instance, has over 500,000 Twitter followers and has worked with brands like Marriott and TripAdvisor. Social Media Week (2015) compared travel social media influencers to travel brands and identified eight individuals with more influence than major brands like Kayak, Condé Nast, American Airlines and BB Travel, namely Scott Eddy, Megan Claire, Justin Carmack, Ann Tran, Yasmin, JD Andrews, Paul Jonson and Jeane Beena.

Traackr (2016), a platform offering tools for influencer relationship management, lists various successful travel-related influencer marketing campaigns. For instance, it describes a campaign by TripIt that involves hosting a monthly interactive #TripItChat session on Twitter in which different influencers offer travel tips for a variety of travel topics. Bloglovin' Influence (2016) provides five successful examples of influencer campaigns by travel brands: 1) making travel guides with Airbnb and Aspyn Ovard; 2) finding travel essentials with Proctor & Gamble and Jennifer Chiu; 3) crossing industries with Moët and Chandon and Collage Vintage; 4) Travel reviews with Celebrity Cruises and World of Wanderlust; and, 5) Viral packing guides with Biaggi Luggage and Rachel Grant. All five examples illustrate the way in which travel influencers lend authenticity to travel brands, help create engaging contents and provide access to specific audiences.

Conclusion

In the age of social media, consumers move from being fans to being producers of promotional content for brands, and from occasional endorsers to micro-celebrity-seeking social media influencers (Hearn & Schoenhoff, 2016). Some of these micro- and meso-celebrities have managed to amass a dedicated following that is eager to receive their recommendations. Marketers can take advantage of these influencers and their ability to reach large/targeted audiences with engaging contents by building mutually beneficial relationships with social media influencers that align with their brands. When done right, such influencer marketing strategies can lead to much better returns on investment than the use of branded content or straightforward advertising.

Travel marketers have recognized the great potential of message amplification and targeting afforded by travel social media influencers. The promise of travel perks as well as the ability to associate one's personal brand with desirable travel and tourism brands makes travel and tourism an attractive target industry for influencers. One challenge that both travel marketers and influencers face is how to communicate authenticity when influencers are compensated for their endorsements/contents.

An interesting trend in influencer marketing is the emergence of an influencer marketing industry with increased levels of professionalization among influencers, new forms of intermediaries facilitating exchange processes and new technological tools being developed to support the various aspects of influencer marketing. Both make influencer marketing easier and more trackable. Staying informed of the latest influencer marketing trends thus becomes paramount for travel and tourism marketers.

Despite its prominence and practical significance, there is a lack of research that investigates the travel and tourism influencer marketing phenomenon. Important questions of how to conceptualize influence and how to formulate effective influencer campaigns consequently remain unanswered. How consumers perceive travel and tourism social media influencers and what drives the persuasiveness of influencer messages are additional questions that should be investigated in order to inform the theory and practice of social media marketing.

References

Adweek. (2016). 5 Instagram users who have turned traveling into a lifestyle brand. Available at: www.adweek.com/brand-marketing/5-instagram-users-who-have-turned-traveling-lifestyle-brand-172138/ [Accessed 10 February 2017].

Bloglovin' Influence. (2016). 5 travel brands crushing their influencer marketing game right now. Retrieved from https://influence.bloglovin.com/5-travel-brands-crushing-their-influencer-marketing-game-right-now-554857a2d047#.ld1gay3lk

Businessdictionary.com. (2017). Influencer. Available at: www.businessdictionary.com/definition/influencers.html [Accessed 28 February 2017].

Carter, D. (2016). Hustle and brand: The sociotechnical shaping of influence. *Social Media + Society*, 2(3), pp. 1–12.

De Veirman, M., Cauberghe, V., & Hudders, L. (2016). Marketing through Instagram influencers: Impact of number of followers and product divergence on brand attitude. In *15th International Conference on Research in Advertising (ICORIA)*, June 30–July 2, 2016, Ljubljana, Slovenia. Available at: https://biblio.ugent.be/publication/7223607/file/7223625.pdf [Accessed 20 February 2017].

eMarketer. (2015). Marketers pair up with influencers – and it works: Content creation, promotion the leading tactics for influencer engagement. Available at: www.emarketer.com/Article/Marketers-Pair-Up-with-Influencersand-Works/1012709 [Accessed 20 February 2017].

Forbes.com. (2016a). How influencer marketplace Octoly has generated $8.6 million in earned media value. Available at: www.forbes.com/sites/breebrouwer/2016/10/16/influencer-marketing-octoly-thomas-owadenko/#f19754c6e529 [Accessed 14 February 2017].

Forbes.com. (2016b). How to travel the world as a social media influencer. Available at: www.forbes.com/sites/reneemorad/2016/11/07/how-to-travel-the-world-as-a-social-media-influencer/#7f584a4b1715 [Accessed 10 February 2017].

Glover, P. (2009). Celebrity endorsement in tourism advertising: Effects on destination image. *Journal of Hospitality and Tourism Management*, 16, pp. 16–23. doi:10.1375/jhtm.16.1.16

Hearn, A., & Schoenhoff, S. (2016). From celebrity to influencer. In P. D. Marshall & S. Redmond(eds.) (2015) *A Companion to Celebrity*. West Sussex, UK, John Wiley & Sons/Blackwell, pp. 194–211. Available at: www.blackwellreference.com/subscriber/tocnode.html?id=g9781118475010_chunk_g978111847501015 [Accessed 26 February 2017].

Hewett, K., Rand, W., Rust, R. T., & van Heerde, H. J. (2016). Brand buzz in the echoverse. *Journal of Marketing*, 80(3), pp. 1–24.

Influencermarketinghub.com. (2017a). Why influencer marketing will explode in 2017. Available at: https://influencermarketinghub.com/why-influencer-marketing-will-explode-in-2017/ [Accessed 25 February 2017].

Influencermarketinghub.com. (2017b). What is an influencer? Available at: https://influencermarketinghub.com/what-is-an-influencer/ [Accessed 5 February 2017].

Influencermarketinghub.com. (2017c). Instagram influencer marketing agencies you should know about. Available at: https://influencermarketinghub.com/instagram-influencer-marketing-agencies/ [Accessed 5 February 2017].

Influencermarketinghub.com. (2017d). 8 top influencer marketing platforms. Available at: https://influencermarketinghub.com/8-top-influencer-marketing-platforms/ [Accessed 15 February 2017].

Influencer Orchestration Network. (2017). How hospitality and travel brands make influencer marketing work. Available at: www.ion.co/how-hospitality-and-travel-brands-make-influencer-marketing-work [Accessed 20 February 2017].

Inkybee. (2016). The best practice guide for effective blogger outreach. Available at: www.inkybee.com/blogger-outreach-a-best-practice-guide/#.WKejBzsrKUl [Accessed 10 February 2017].

Izea. (2017a). The power of your everyday influencer is stronger than celebrities. Available at: https://izea.com/2017/02/03/micro-influencers/ [Accessed 3 February 2017].

Izea. (2017b). 2017 state of the creator economy. Available at: https://izea.com/2017/02/10/2017-state-of-the-creator-economy-infographic/ [Accessed 10 February 2017].

JacksGap. (2015). 24 hours in New Orleans. Available at: www.youtube.com/watch?v=pHhW588NiBU [Accessed 10 February 2017].

Jerslev, A. (2016). In the time of the microcelebrity. *International Journal of Communication*, 10, pp. 5233–5251.

Katz, E. (1957). The two-step flow of communication: An up-to-date report on an hypothesis. *Public Opinion Quarterly*, 21(1), pp. 61–78.

Keller, E., & Fay, B. (2016). How to use influencers to drive a word-of-mouth strategy. at: www.kellerfay.com/how-to-use-influencers-to-drive-a-word-of-mouth-strategy/ [Accessed 10 February 2017].

Kirkpatrick, D. (2016). Influencer marketing spurs 11 times the ROI over traditional tactics: Study. Available at: www.marketingdive.com/news/influencer-marketing-spurs-11-times-the-roi-over-traditional-tactics-study/416911/ [Accessed 16 February 2017].

Krasniak, M. (2016). Social influencer marketing on the rise: New research. Available at: www.socialmediaexaminer.com/social-influencer-marketing-on-the-rise-new-research/ [Accessed 1 February 2017].

Lin, Y. S., & Huang, J. Y. (2006). Internet blogs as a tourism marketing medium: A case study. *Journal of Business Research*, 59(10), pp. 1201–1205.

Litvin, S. W., Goldsmith, R. E., & Pan, B. (2008). Electronic word-of-mouth in hospitality and tourism management. *Tourism Management*, 29(3), pp. 458–468.

MarketingProfs.com. (2016). Build social relationships with influencer marketing. Available at: www.marketingprofs.com/chirp/2016/30037/build-social-relationships-with-influencer-marketing-infographic [Accessed 26 August 2016].

McCartney, G., & Pinto, J. F. (2014). Influencing Chinese travel decisions: The impact of celebrity endorsement advertising on the Chinese traveler to Macao. *Journal of Vacation Marketing*, 20(3), pp. 253–266.

McQuarrie, E. F., Miller, J., & Phillips, B. J. (2013). The megaphone effect: Taste and audience in fashion blogging. *Journal of Consumer Research*, 40(1), pp. 136–158.

Morin, R. (2016). The rise of niche and micro-influencers. Available at: https://maximize-socialbusiness.com/the-rise-of-niche-and-micro-influencers-24286/# [Accessed 20 February 2017].

Nanji, A. (2017a). The most popular social network with micro-influencers. at: www.mar-ketingprofs.com/charts/2017/31676/the-most-popular-social-network-with-micro-influencers?adref=nlt030217 [Accessed 2 March 2017].

Nanji, A. (2017b). The state of influencer marketing in 2017. Available at: www.marketing profs.com/charts/2017/31524/the-state-of-influencer-marketing-in-2017?adref= nlt020717 [Accessed 7 February 2017].

Neoreach. (2016). Top 20 travel influencers on Instagram. Available at: https://neoreach. com/top-travel-influencers-instagram/ [Accessed 10 February 2017].

Queensland, Australia. (2014). What is an Instameet? Available at: www.youtube.com/ watch?v=aC0dESsMquk [Accessed 20 February 2017].

Radey, T. (2015). Influencer marketing: Why relevance is more important than vanity met-rics. Available at: www.pr2020.com/blog/influencer-marketing-why-relevance-is-more-important-than-vanity-metrics [Accessed 13 February 2017].

Shao, J., & Gretzel, U. (2011). Social media created the Chinese backpacker star. In W. Frost, G. Croy, J. Laing, & S. Beeton (eds.) *International Tourism and Media Confer-ence, 28–29 November, 2011*. Melbourne, Tourism and Hospitality Research Unit, La Trobe University and Department of Management, Monash University.

SocialMediaToday. (2016). 6 ways to integrate social media and influencer marketing. Available at: www.socialmediatoday.com/marketing/6-ways-integrate-social-media-and-influencer-marketing [Accessed 21 August 2016].

Social Media Week. (2015). 8 people with more social influence than large travel brands. Available at: https://socialmediaweek.org/blog/2015/07/people-with-more-social-influence/ [Accessed 10 February 2017].

Solis, B. (2008). The art and science of blogger relations. Available at: www.scribd.com/ document/3512570/Blogger-Relations-2-0 [Accessed 15 January 2017].

Swant, M. (2016). Twitter says users now trust influencers nearly as much as their friends. Available at: www.adweek.com/digital/twitter-says-users-now-trust-influencers-nearly-much-their-friends-171367/ [Accessed 21 February 2017].

Tourism New Zealand. (2012). Micro-blogging queen Yao Chen the face of campaign shoot. Available at: www.tourismnewzealand.com/news/micro-blogging-queen-yao-chen-the-face-of-campaign-shoot/ [Accessed 20 February 2017].

Traackr. (2016). The best influencer marketing in the travel industry. Available at: www. traackr.com/blog/best-influencer-marketing-travel-industry [Accessed 10 February 2017].

Van der Veen, R., & Song, H. (2014). Impact of the perceived image of celebrity endorsers on tourists' intentions to visit. *Journal of Travel Research*, 53(2), pp. 211–224.

Volo, S. (2012). Blogs: "re-inventing" tourism communication. In M. Sigala, E. Christou, & U. Gretzel (eds.) *Social Media in Travel, Tourism and Hospitality: Theory, Practice and Cases*. Surrey, UK: Ashgate, pp. 149–163.

Yen, C. H., & Teng, H. Y. (2015). Celebrity involvement, perceived value, and behavioral intentions in popular media-induced tourism. *Journal of Hospitality & Tourism Research*, 39(2), pp. 225–244.

Part 3

Social media

Travellers' behavior

Ulrike Gretzel

Users and uses of social media platforms

Recent years have not only seen the emergence of new social media types such as private messaging apps like Whatsapp, WeChat and Snapchat, but have also brought increasing user numbers for established platforms. Facebook continues to be the most successful social media platform worldwide and reports extensive growth from 100 million monthly active users in 2008 to 1.65 billion monthly active users in the first quarter of 2016 (Statista.com, 2016). With more users on social media, fragmentation across platforms is a given; e.g. Pinterest attracts mostly female users (85% female vs. 15% male users) while Snapchat has an extremely young audience (73% of users are millennials) (DMR, 2016a, b). And with both more platforms and more users comes diversification in uses. It is within this complex and dynamic social media landscape that travellers' behaviors have to be conceptualized and understood. While reading and writing online reviews remain an essential component of travellers' social media activities, other aspects of social media use, for instance the taking of travel selfies (Dinhopl & Gretzel, 2016), and their role as e-WOM should not be overlooked.

Another important trend that shapes travellers' use of social media is the rise of mobile technologies and ever greater access to Wi-Fi. While social media use five years ago was still mostly confined to pre- or post-trip stages, travellers can now access social media at any time and almost any place. Although all phases have been addressed in the tourism literature (Leung et al., 2013), very little is still known about during the trip uses and use patterns across the different phases of the tourism experience.

The most recent evolution in the social media context is the emergence of platforms that build on credibility established through bilateral reviews, peer-to-peer exchanges, ease of content generation and the desire for co-creation spurred by social media. Whether termed sharing economy or collaborative consumption, these opportunities for new exchanges among consumers facilitated by Web 2.0 technologies and social media culture have already started to disrupt the tourism industry and are increasingly shaping online and offline behaviors of travellers worldwide. It is against this backdrop that this part of the book investigates travellers' social media-related behaviors.

Overview of part 3

The chapters included in this part of the book speak to the complexity of social media use and illustrate how important it is to understand social media behaviors in the context of travel and tourism. They represent a mix of empirical and conceptual papers that together underscore fundamental shifts in behavior facilitated by Web 2.0 technologies.

In the first chapter, titled *e-WOM engagement: is it worth talking only about posters and lurkers?*, Hammedi and Virlée provide important conceptual foundations for understanding user-generated contents and social media-sharing behaviors. They first define and describe electronic word-of-mouth (e-WOM) and juxtapose it against offline word-of-mouth, highlighting the way social media have transformed how consumers provide other consumers with important information on products and experiences available in the marketplace. Through their critical review of relevant literature, e-WOM emerges as high quality, high credibility information that is available in high volumes, varies in valence and can be directly compared to opinions of others. The chapter also discusses the role of e-WOM in tourism and overviews what antecedents of e-WOM behavior the tourism literature has identified. The core of the paper, however, is the critique of existing literature's assumption that e-WOM is goal-directed, explicit verbal behavior. The authors convincingly argue that on social media, e-WOM can occur in tacit, non-verbal ways (e.g. through liking or sharing pages, products, comments etc.) and can happen without the intent of the consumer to influence others in their purchasing decisions (e.g. through sharing vacation photos). As a result, the chapter challenges researchers to carefully think about classifying consumers simply into posters and lurkers based on whether they provided written comments on a social media site or not. There are clearly more shades to traveller behaviors on social media than is often assumed!

The section continues with another chapter focused on e-WOM behaviors. The chapter *The influence of reviewer identity verification on the online reputation of hotels* by Parra López and Gutiérrez Taño delves into review writing behaviors, seeking to understand whether specific platform policies such as reviewer verification and invitation emails make a difference. They assume that verification leads to more positive evaluations because reviewers feel identified and therefore less free in their evaluations. Also, they assume that invitation emails encourage consumers that have nothing to complain about to still leave a review. Comparing ratings for hotels on TripAdvisor and on Booking, they actually find that the opposite is the case, suggesting that TripAdvisor reviewers are more positive in their evaluations. The authors speculate that the community feel and altruistic undertone of TripAdvisor might be a reason for observed differences. In any case, the chapter suggests that reviewing behaviors are complex and more research is needed to better understand them across different platforms.

The following chapter, *Airbnb as a new disruptive model in tourism: analyzing its competitive potential based on online travel reviews*, also looks at accommodation reviews but compares hotel reviews with sharing economy accommodation offered through Airbnb. Analyzing data from important European and American tourist cities, Díaz Armas, Gutiérrez Taño and García Rodríguez find that the reviews for Airbnb experiences are significantly more positive than hotel accommodation experiences. The chapter therefore illustrates the importance of e-WOM in understanding the disruptive potential of the sharing economy for the accommodation sector and argues that online reviews provide industry and researchers with an important window into consumers' minds.

Also concerned with the sharing economy, the chapter *Collaborative consumption as a feature of Gen-Y consumers: rethinking youth tourism practices in the sharing economy* by Batat and Hammedi establishes that sharing phenomena are intricately linked to Web 2.0 technologies. The authors specifically look into the digital practices of Gen-Y consumers, providing important insights into how connected and digitally immersed this generation is. The chapter identifies Gen-Y as the "Collaboration Generation" and suggests that co-creation and sharing are a way of life for the members of this generation. The chapter then portrays Airbnb as a functional marketplace for Gen-Yers that provides access to resources, Couchsurfing as matching their desires for social experiences, co-creation, involvement and authenticity, and Wwoofing as an opportunity that speaks to Gen-Y values and offers engagement. As such, the chapter shows how social media culture has shaped an entire generation that is now becoming an important travel consumer segment.

Last but not least, Di Pietro et al. in their chapter titled *Have social networks changed travellers' waiting experience? an exploratory study on the airport sector* look at social media use by travellers during a part of the travel experience that is often neglected: the pre-departure airport waiting experience. In their chapter, they overview issues related to waiting experiences and emphasize the importance of managing waiting times. They establish social media as a potentially viable tool to enhance airport experiences as they allow users to virtually connect with others to share their frustration or to psychologically escape the unpleasant experience and reduce perceptions of the length of the waiting time. Their empirical results establish social media use as a distinct alternative to passing time at the airport with, for instance, shopping or eating rather than something that people do in conjunction with other airport activities. However, the interviewees identified the availability of free Wi-Fi as critical to their willingness to engage in social media use. The study also finds that social media use is less prominent among groups of travellers but helps lone travellers starve off boredom and overcome their solitude. As several benefits of social media use at the airport such as reassurance and stress reduction are acknowledged by the interviewees, the chapter concludes that airports need to consider facilitating social media use in order to provide passengers (especially those travelling alone) with better experiences. As such, the chapter draws attention to important functions of social media use during the travel experience and underscores opportunities for experience enhancement.

References

Dinhopl, A., & Gretzel, U. (2016). Selfie-taking as touristic looking. *Annals of Tourism Research*, 57, pp. 126–139.

DMR (2016a). By the numbers: 270 amazing Pinterest statistics (March 2016). Retrieved online June 30, 2016, fromhttp://expandedramblings.com/index.php/pinterest-stats/

DMR (2016b). By the numbers: 80 amazing Snapchat statistics. Retrieved online June 30, 2016, from http://expandedramblings.com/index.php/snapchat-statistics/2/

Leung, D., Law, R., Van Hoof, H., & Buhalis, D. (2013). Social media in tourism and hospitality: A literature review. *Journal of Travel & Tourism Marketing*, 30(1–2), 3–22.

Statista.com. (2016). Number of monthly active Facebook users worldwide as of 1st quarter 2016 (in millions). Retrieved online June 30, 2016, from www.statista.com/statistics/264810/number-of-monthly-active-facebook-users-worldwide/

11 E-WOM engagement

Is it worth talking only about posters and lurkers?

Wafa Hammedi and Justine Virlée

Introduction

The digital revolution has brought foundational changes in marketing, customer relationship and brand management (Kaplan & Haenlein, 2010). Dramatic developments in interactive digital media are revolutionizing marketing, and the rise of social media has catapulted company and consumer contact from the traditional Web 1.0 model to the highly interactive Web 2.0 world in which consumers dictate the nature, extent and context of marketing exchanges. Today, consumers increasingly use digital media not just to search for products or services but also to engage with the companies they buy from and with other consumers who might have valuable insights (Kaplan & Haenlein, 2010, 2011). The development of interactive digital media has fundamentally altered marketing's ecosystem of influence (Malthouse & Hofacker, 2010). The social web is currently reconstituting branding, and dramatic change is under way. We have moved from a world in which the firm/ brand sets the agenda to a world in which consumers decide if and when brands are invited into their virtual environments (Fournier & Avery, 2011; Labrecque et al., 2013). Social media technologies have engendered radically new ways of interacting (Malthouse & Hofacker, 2010). To this end, literally hundreds of different digital platforms exist (e.g. social networks, blogs, discussion groups and podcasts). This new era involves participatory, collaborative, and socially linked behaviors whereby consumers are taking an increasingly active role in co-creating everything from product design to promotional messages (Fournier & Avery, 2011).

Nowadays, consumers are able to share their opinion more easily, more quickly and with a greater number of persons than in an offline context (Dellarocas, 2003). Concretely, this phenomenon of interpersonal influence that takes the form of customer-to-customer interactions in cyberspace is called "e – word-of-mouth" (e-WOM). Hennig-Thurau et al. (2004, p. 39) defined e-WOM as "any positive or negative statement made by potential, actual, or former customers about a product or company, and which is made available to a multitude of people and institutions". Interpersonal influence is particularly powerful in the tourism industry because tourism services are considered "experience goods" in the sense that the quality of the service is unknown before its consumption (Klein, 1998; Murray, 1991). Given the high-involvement nature of the decision for a vacation, customers are increasingly relying on consumers' opinions (Bronner & de Hoog, 2011). Therefore, many consumers consult tourists' reviews shared on dedicated online platforms because this information is perceived as more credible and up to date than the information from the firm (Gretzel & Yoo, 2008; Litvin et al., 2008). Some researchers even consider that interpersonal influence and e-WOM are among the most important sources of information (Litvin et al., 2008).

E-WOM can be beneficial for companies (Litvin et al., 2008). Compete (2007) estimated that e-WOM influences more than US$ 10 billion in online travel purchases every year. Moreover, e-WOM improves consumer awareness of brands, products or services, especially for lesser-known products (Vermeulen & Seegers, 2009). E-WOM also gives companies the opportunity to be aware of what is said by customers about their offerings, and to take these comments into account in order to continually improve their offerings (Litvin et al., 2008). The challenge for tourism providers is to ensure that their customers will share their experience (Van Doorn et al., 2010).

A substantial part of the tourism and hotel decision-making process occurs online. According to a recent survey by TNS-Sofres (2010), 69% of European consumers search for online information while planning their trip; 44% visit official tour-operators' websites before making their purchase, and 68% of Web users prefer to use search engines that provide access to varied sources of information (forums, price comparators, personal blogs, brand communities etc.), the content of which is beyond the direct reach of marketers. Finally, 30% of vacationers seek the advice of other consumers while searching for information, and such recommendations appear to have a deciding influence in 87% of cases.

Despite these huge impacts, many companies do not truly understand how to manage online platforms effectively. As stressed in the Forrester Research report, marketers have many difficulties in evaluating the return on investment (ROI) of spending on digital marketing (Liang et al., 2013; Yang, 2013). In this new business world where people create 500 billion e-WOM impressions a year through digital platforms, the old concept of return on investment (ROI) has been replaced by the new concept known as return on engagement (ROE) (Kumar et al., 2010). In these digital platforms, engagement takes on several forms: customers may become a fan, share, like and reply to/comment on company posts or post their own messages on a company's pages.

An increasing body of research on interactive marketing and online behaviors has emerged. Previous studies have shown that on digital platforms and more precisely peer-to peer platforms, most participants are passive readers rather than active contributors (Bronner & de Hoog, 2011; N'Goala & Morrongiello, 2014). For instance, only 11 to 28% of the travellers share their opinions on the internet after an experience (Bronner & de Hoog, 2011; N'Goala & Morrongiello, 2014). This implies that a large proportion of consumers is influenced by a small segment of consumers who are actively engaged in e-WOM (Moe et al., 2011). Despite their huge contribution to understanding the key drivers of e-WOM, most previous studies have focused on the reader rather than on the reviewer (Bronner & de Hoog, 2011). Most of existing studies focusing on opinion givers devoted attention to the antecedents of e-WOM related to the service experience (e.g. customer satisfaction, service quality, price fairness etc.) (Jeong & Jang, 2011; Liang et al., 2013; Yang, 2013) or focused on the motives for sharing experiences (such as egoism, altruism, exerting power etc.) (Cheung & Lee, 2012; N'Goala & Morrongiello, 2014; Yang, 2013; Yap et al., 2013). However, most of the variance of e-WOM behavior remained unexplained (Liang et al., 2013; N'Goala & Morrongiello, 2014). This suggests that the drivers of e-WOM creation in general and in the tourism sector more specifically may not only be related to the service experience itself. Moreover, most existing research conceptualized consumers' participation in e-WOM as a dichotomous concept (active vs. passive). However, participation in e-WOM is much more complex (Casalo et al., 2010; Malinen, 2015). Indeed, it is considered irrelevant nowadays to talk only about posters vs. lurkers (Malinen, 2015). This typology is very simplistic, as it seems to only value the content posted or created with clear and explicit purpose of influencing others. However recent literature recognizes the potential effect of any type of content posted on the Web 2.0 that can be influential for other consumers even if it was not intended to (Dinhopl & Gretzel, 2016). For instance, it is widely recognized in the psychology field that consumers could influence others without a conscious goal of doing so (Huffman & Houston, 1993).

In this chapter, we firstly clarify the concepts of WOM and e-WOM and show how they relate to each other. Secondly, we overview e-WOM studies in the tourism literature. Finally, we provide a framework that will help to better and more deeply understand the underlying process of e-WOM behaviors. In this chapter we will try to go beyond investigating the traditional typology of posters and lurkers to emphasize a matrix that would help to better classify the participants' behavior relying on goals theory.

Definition of WOM

At the beginning of its conceptualization, WOM was defined by Arndt (1967, p. 295) as an "oral, person-to-person communication between a receiver and a communicator who the receiver perceives as non-commercial, regarding a brand, product or service". Two decades later, Westbrook (1987, p. 261) suggests that WOM includes "all informal communications from consumers directed at other consumers about the ownership, usage, or characteristics of particular goods and services or their sellers". This definition is broader but we notice that in both definitions the key characteristic of WOM is the independence of the source of the message from commercial entities (Litvin et al., 2008).

WOM can be defined by several characteristics. First of all, WOM has a valence and can be positive, negative or neutral (Muntinga et al., 2011). Positive WOM occurs when customers spread positive testimonials about the firm, and negative WOM occurs when testimonials have a negative form (Buttle, 1998). Second, WOM can occur before or after a purchase. In the first case, it is called input WOM while in the second case it is called output WOM (Buttle, 1998). Then, the third characteristic of WOM is related to the solicitation. In some cases, consumers are looking for other consumers' comments while sometimes WOM may be offered without solicitation in the context of a conversation between friends for example (Buttle, 1998). Finally, WOM can occur with or without the intervention of the firm. Indeed, firms are making more and more efforts to stimulate and manage WOM activity (Buttle, 1998).

Finally, the content of WOM communication can be described in terms of cognitive and/or affective characteristics (Yap et al., 2013). The cognitive dimension refers to the rational component of the message and it deals with product attributes such as its performance, or price-value perceptions (Sweeney et al., 2012). By contrast, the affective dimension is more related to the form of the message and addresses the message's depth, intensity, vividness or its level of storytelling (Mazzarol et al., 2007; Sweeney et al., 2012). The way these cognitive and affective dimensions are combined in the message will have a different impact on the attitudes or the behavior of the receiver toward a product or a service (Yap et al., 2013). For example, WOM messages which are high in cognitive content and which are characterized by a higher informational quality are more likely to be more persuasive (Karmarkar & Tormala, 2010).

One can easily understand that WOM has been a widely studied matter given its influence on consumers' attitudes and purchase decisions and its high incidence rate in driving influence (Bone, 1995). It has been suggested that up to 80% of the purchasing decisions are influenced by direct recommendations of other consumers (Voss, 1984). Indeed, a lot of consumers rely on their fellows' recommendations when they have to make a purchase decision in order to reduce uncertainty and perceived risks (Bronner & de Hoog, 2011). Interpersonal influence and WOM are among the most important sources of information when a consumer is willing to try a new product or service (Arndt, 1967; Brown & Reingen, 1987; Reingen & Kernan, 1986; Richins, 1983). Consequently, WOM has a significant role to play in the consumer decision-making process, and thus influences consumers' attitudes and behavior toward products and services (Arndt, 1967; Herr et al., 1991; Von Wangenheim & Bayon, 2007). Moreover, it has been shown that WOM between consumers is more persuasive than a marketing communication from the firm to influence the adoption of a product because this information is perceived as more credible and up to date (Gretzel & Yoo, 2008; Herr et al., 1991; Ryan & Gross, 1943). Indeed, information from the firm is more product-oriented and offers information relative to the product attributes and its technical specifications, whereas consumer reviews are more consumer-oriented and address the product performance from a user's perspective (Bickart & Schindler, 2001). WOM has been studied in many contexts. For example, the effects of WOM have been studied on sales and on product judgments in general (Bone, 1995), but also on sales in specific sectors such as the film (Liu, 2006) or the tourism industry (Cantallops & Salvi, 2014; Litvin et al., 2008; Ye et al., 2011; Zhang et al., 2010), in offline or online contexts. Many researchers also focused on the motivations to engage in positive as well as in negative WOM.

From traditional WOM to e-WOM

With the advent of the internet and the spread of electronic technologies, interactions between consumers have changed their nature to become virtual, and the number of customer-to-customer interactions increased dramatically (Goldsmith & Flynn, 1993). New electronic communication channels such as social networks, blogs, forums and social opinion platforms enable consumers to express their opinion concerning products and services with others more easily and more quickly (Bickart & Schindler, 2001). These interactions between consumers about products or services that occur in the cyberspace are called "e-WOM" (Hennig-Thurau et al., 2004). The internet supports a flow of unconstrained consumer voices (Bronner & de Hoog, 2011), in the sense that everyone can find unbiased information from other consumers about a product or a service, and that everyone can express his/her own consumption-related advice or recommendation (Hennig-Thurau et al., 2004). Many websites gathering consumers' opinions in various fields emerged on the web, including Epinions.com which is an online opinion forum about products and services, or Citysearch, which provides consumers with customers' ratings on restaurants, bars and shops (Lee et al., 2008).

While traditional WOM refers to offline interactions between consumers who share information about a product or a service, e-WOM refers to consumers' comments posted on the internet concerning a product or a service (Hennig-Thurau et al., 2004). In our context, WOM refers for example to a consumer recommending a satisfying airline company to a friend, e-WOM may refer to a rating on a scale of this airline company and to some textual comments about the services on board and the ease of transactions on the website. The big difference between WOM and e-WOM is that in e-WOM, recommendations are directed to multiple individuals, anonymous and available for a long time, if not indefinitely (Bronner & de Hoog, 2011; Hennig-Thurau et al., 2004).

Definition of e-WOM

Hennig-Thurau et al. (2004, p. 39) were the first to focus on e-WOM, who define it as "any positive or negative statement made by potential, actual, or former customers about a product or company, which is made available to a multitude of people and institutions via the Internet". Similarly, based on Westbrook (1987)'s definition of WOM, Litvin et al. (2008, p. 461) defined e-WOM as "all informal communications directed at consumers through Internet-based technology related to the usage or characteristics of particular goods and services, or their sellers".

According to Litvin et al. (2008), e-WOM includes both conversations between firms and customers, and conversations among consumers themselves. E-WOM can be characterized by two dimensions: the communication scope and the level of interactivity (Litvin et al., 2008). It means that e-WOM can take the form of a one-to-one conversation (i.e. emails), a one-to-many (i.e. review sites), or a many-to-many conversation (i.e. virtual communities). Also, e-WOM can be asynchronous, which means that it is characterized by a low level of interactivity (i.e. emails, review sites, blogs); or synchronous, which implies a high level of interactivity (i.e. chatrooms, instant messaging).

Compared to mass communication, one of the most important capabilities of communication on the internet is its bi-directionality (Dellarocas, 2003). It means that we moved from a brand-dictated monologue to a multi-party conversation (Deighton & Kornfeld, 2009; Hennig-Thurau et al., 2010). Some years ago, only firms were able to reach a high number of consumers. Now, consumers have the possibility to make their feelings, opinions and attitudes about products or services available to the global community of internet users (Dellarocas, 2003). Therefore, e-WOM has emerged as a mechanism to promote cooperation among consumers without any real-world social ties by providing each other with recommendations and warnings about products, services or brands (Dellarocas, 2003).

One can think that e-WOM is less personal in the sense that it does not take the form of a face-to-face conversation, but it is likely to be more powerful as it is immediate and it has a significant reach (Hennig-Thurau et al., 2004). Reviews and comments on the internet also benefit from a geographical and temporal freedom, as well as a certain degree of permanence, in the sense they are accessible from anywhere in the world, at any time and almost indefinitely (Gelb & Sundaram, 2002; Kiecker & Cowles, 2001). Moreover, these opinions of consumers on the Internet are instantly accessible to almost everyone connected to the Internet, on a scale that has never been seen in the past (Jansen et al., 2009). The proliferation of e-WOM has already changed consumers' behavior in subtle but important ways (Dellarocas, 2003). For example, more and more consumers are using other consumers' opinions to make decisions about future consumption whereas a few years ago the main sources of information were advertising and personal advice (Dellarocas, 2003). There is no doubt that today's managers need to understand how and why consumers diffuse e-WOM.

The literature has emphasized key characteristics of e-WOM that would influence the receivers' reactions. Table 11.1 summarizes some characteristics that have been empirically tested and have shown a high impact on the online consumers' behaviors with regard to the consumption of e-WOM.

Table 11.1 Overview of the key e-WOM characteristics

	Definition	*References*
Arguments quality or information quality	Translated usually in terms of four concepts: • *Timeliness*: to which extent the message is updated in a timely manner. • *Relevance*: to which extent the message is applicable and useful for decision making • *Accuracy*: to which extent the message is perceived as correct • *Comprehensiveness*: refers to information completeness Another typology talks about: • Persuasive • Emotional • Subjective • Empty messages	Cheung et al. (2009) Lee et al. (2008) Cheung et al. (2008)

	Definition	*References*
Valence of messages	Positive	Chu & Kim (2008)
	Negative	
	Neutral	Cheung et al. (2009)
Source credibility	Expertise	Duhan et al. (1997)
	Trustworthiness	
	Attractiveness	Chu & Kim (2008)
		Choi et al. (2005)
Recommendation consistency	The degree to which the comment/ review/ opinion is consistent with other contributions made by other users	Cheung et al. (2007)
Information volume	Quantity of information shared regarding one product/service or experience	Chen & Xie (2008)
	Number of comments posted	Berger et al. (2010)
		Duan et al. (2008)

E-WOM in the tourism sector

The tourism sector is particularly impacted by e-WOM (Cantallops & Salvi, 2014). Online travellers' reviews influence up to US$ 10 billion in online travel purchases every year (Compete, 2007). In the tourism industry, e-WOM takes the form of online consumer-generated reviews related to travel destinations, hotels, restaurants, airlines or other travel services (Bronner & de Hoog, 2011). These reviews may be posted on a wide range of websites, from fully marketer-generated websites, to fully consumer-generated websites (Bronner & de Hoog, 2011): supplier websites, review sites, online travel agencies' websites (i.e. Booking, Expedia, etc.), travel blogs and forums, and social networks (N'Goala & Morrongiello, 2014). More specifically, the best-known and most powerful review site is TripAdvisor, which is seen as the largest site for unbiased travel reviews (Litvin et al., 2008).

Given e-WOM's potential to strongly affect the performance of firms, especially in the tourism sector, researchers are increasingly studying e-WOM in this context (Cantallops & Salvi, 2014). Table 11.2 below summarizes the results of empirical studies[1] that contributed substantially to understanding e-WOM related behaviors. More precisely, only studies focusing on the antecedents of tourists' behavior on the internet have been selected.

Table 11.2 Key antecedents of e-WOM identified in the tourism literature

Reference	Drivers	Measures of e-WOM
Casalo et al. (2010)	Consumer's attitude, subjective norms (-) consumer's perceived behavioral control, perceived usefulness and identification	Consumer's intention to participate in the online opinion platform
Bronner & de Hoog (2011)	Motives: self-directed, helping other vacationers, social benefits, consumer empowerment and helping companies.	Number of aspects of a vacation mentioned in a post. Valence of the post (positive, negative or neutral) Inclusion of photos in the post
Chu & Kim (2011)	Tie strength, homophily (-), trust, normative influence and informative influence	Opinion seeking, opinion giving and information sharing
Cheung & Lee (2012)	Firm's reputation, sense of belonging to the community and enjoyment of helping.	Consumer's e-WOM intention
Liang et al. (2013)	Subjective norms, tourist's attitude towards e-WOM communication	traveller's adoption of e-WOM traveller's intention to use e-WOM communication media
Yap et al. (2013)	Personal self-enhancement, social benefits, advice seeking, warn other consumers and venting negative feeling	Message with cognitive, neutral or emotional characteristics Positive vs. Negative messages
Kim et al. (2014)	Brand identification, community commitment, Twitter usage frequency, brand trust, community membership intention and the total number of postings	Brand retweet
N'Goala & Morrongiello (2014)	Helping the company, perceived sincerity of the online reviews and confidence in the marketing practices (-) significantly impact tourist's participation in opinion platforms	Tourist's participation in opinion platform
Yen & Tang (2015)	Matching the motivations for posting about hotel experiences with the online media	Altruism and platform assistance motivations are positively correlated with consumer opinion sites

Reference	Drivers	Measures of e-WOM
	Identifying the electronic word-of-mouth (e-WOM) motivations that are affected by hotel attribute performance	Extraversion, social benefits, and dissonance reduction are positively correlated with social network sites
		Hotel attribute performance had a significant effect only on extraversion and dissonance reduction motivations.

In Table 11.2, it can be observed that e-WOM has mainly been measured as participation vs. non-participation or as the overall intention to participate. However, this dichotomous view of participation may result in a loss of information as participation is much more complex and may depend on the activities performed by the platform's members (Casalo et al., 2010; Malinen, 2015). K.-H. Yoo & Gretzel (2011) are the only ones to go beyond this dichotomous conceptualization of participation. They have shown that the creation of content on travel-related reviews, discussion board/forum postings, blogs, comments to a blog, photos and videos is driven by different motivations and impacted by different barriers. Someone who posts on one platform does not necessarily post on any others. Moreover, they have shown that the travellers' personality traits are also impacting the creation of content, leading to a great diversity in content creation behaviors. These results reinforce the necessity to go beyond the traditional dichotomous conceptualization of travellers and to take into account all the types of content beyond the verbal ones. Dinhopl & Gretzel (2016) have also recently suggested that "selfies" taken in the context of tourism consumption do influence others. However, this way of sharing experience might not be driven initially by the goal of influencing others. Indeed, in the social influence literature, it has been emphasized that people are not only influenced by direct and clear communication (such as writing a review on an online platform) but are also influenced by less visible and less goal-directed communication (Cialdini & Goldstein, 2004). Indeed, consumer behaviors are increasingly recognized as influenced by factors unrecognized by the decision makers (Fitzsimons et al., 2002; Lakin et al., 2003). For example, according to Lakin et al. (2003) consumers can imitate their interaction partners' behavior outside of conscious awareness. Consumers can use imitation to create affiliation and this can occur outside of the consciousness. It means that seeing a friend's picture with a monument as background can lead a customer to consider visiting that city in the near future, a way to strengthen the affiliation with that friend. In the meantime that friend, the poster of the picture, might not have any conscious intention to influence others but actually he/she does so.

E-WOM behaviors: a comprehensive framework

Because of its anonymous nature and wide range of contents, the power of e-WOM is expanding. As shown previously there are several critical antecedents of e-WOM effects. Previous literature demonstrated that the direction of e-WOM messages (positive – negative) affects the customer's (reader's) response. For instance, customers are more likely to rely on e-WOM messages if the direction of the messages are all the same. Moreover, consumers can be influenced by content not consciously created to influence them such as selfies or pictures posted on Facebook (Dinhopl & Gretzel, 2016; Lakin et al., 2003). However, given the traditional conceptualization of participation in e-WOM, this type of behavior may not be considered as e-WOM behaviors by the consumers themselves, by researchers and by the marketers. Beyond the nature of the messages shared, this statement demonstrates the extent to which e-WOM is a complex process of social influence. In a recent chapter, the influence of e-WOM was conceptualized as a customer-driven influence process which links the senders to the receivers but also covers important issues, such as deliberate vs. unintentional sender actions, verbal and non-verbal communication, and reflective and impulsive receiver reactions (Blazevic et al., 2013). To better understand the online behaviors of tourists in terms of e-WOM, it is worth breaking down this process and understanding its essential elements. Accordingly, comprehending e-WOM from new perspectives such as goal theory can contribute to better understanding how e-WOM is developed and can also explain further the influence of content on the Web 2.0.

Consumer behavior theory has considered information sharing (sender) and searching (receiver) as goal-oriented behaviors (Huffman & Houston, 1993). The goal-oriented behavior conceptualization has been used in many areas of consumer behavior to understand consumers' preferences (Ratneshwar et al., 2001) and decision-making (Fishbach & Dhar, 2005), loyalty (Wood & Neal, 2009), as well as response to advertising (Pieters & Wedel, 2007). Therefore, it has been shown that investigation of senders' behaviors and their motives that lead to the sharing of experiences should start with the exploration of the goal concepts and the manner in which those goals operate in driving the senders' intentions. Previous literature defined goals as desirable end states that are attainable through action (Kruglanski et al., 2002). Many researchers interested in understanding what drives consumers to share content online focused on motives and barriers (Bronner & de Hoog, 2011; N'Goala & Morrongiello, 2014; Yap et al., 2013; Yen & Tang, 2015; K.-H. Yoo & Gretzel, 2011; K. H. Yoo & Gretzel, 2008). The main motives identified are: helping the service provider (Bronner & de Hoog, 2011; N'Goala & Morrongiello, 2014; K. H. Yoo & Gretzel, 2008) and/or other consumers (Bronner & de Hoog, 2011; Yap et al., 2013; K. H. Yoo & Gretzel, 2008), need for enjoyment/self-enhancement (Yap et al., 2013; K. H. Yoo & Gretzel, 2008), social benefits (Bronner & de Hoog, 2011; Yap et al., 2013; Yen & Tang, 2015), empowerment (Bronner & de Hoog, 2011) and confidence in the marketing practice (N'Goala & Morrongiello, 2014). All these motives are related to one main goal: influencing others. For instance, writing a negative review after a disappointing experience at a hotel might be seen as a way to take revenge on the service provider by spreading negative e-WOM and attempting to influence other travellers. The consumer is then conscious of what s/he is doing and why s/he is doing that (Kruglanski et al., 2002). However, this goal of influencing others may not be activated. Customers might engage in verbal or non-verbal communication without conscious intention to influence others (Bargh et al., 2001).

Current social cognition research proposes that the process of forming an intention to pursue a goal can take place outside awareness (Kruglanski et al., 2002). Bargh et al. (2001) argued that the pursuit of a goal can over time be associated with some features of those situations and lead to the automatic but unconscious activation of those goals. Moreover, Chartrand and Bargh (1996) have shown that non-conscious goal activation leads to the same outcomes as conscious goals activation.

Based on this distinction between conscious vs. non-conscious goal and between verbal vs. non-verbal communication, we developed a framework to better understand tourists' e-WOM behavior (Figure 11.1). Indeed, verbal and non-verbal communication are both important and influential especially with the rising importance of social media (Blazevic et al., 2013). Tourists can use verbal communication such as writing recommendations to share their experience online (Libai et al., 2010). This behavior is always related to a goal but this goal can be pursued consciously or unconsciously (Bargh et al., 2001; Chartrand & Bargh, 1996).

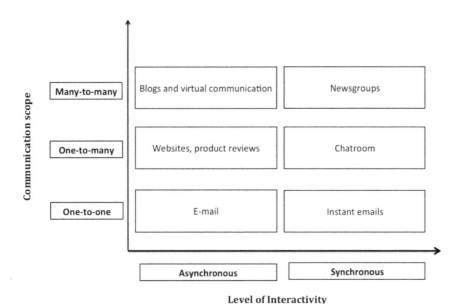

Figure 11.1 A typology of e-WOM media

Source: Litvin et al., 2008

The framework suggests that the conscious vs. unconscious pursuit of a goal will impact how the experience will be shared.

During or after an experience, consumers can communicate in a verbal way about this experience (Blazevic et al., 2013; Libai et al., 2010). This communication can be consciously directed to the goals of influencing others. This is the case of travellers posting a review on an online opinion platform such as TripAdvisor. By sharing his/her opinion, the consumer has the goal to influence other travellers. On the other hand, the travellers can also communicate in a verbal way and influence others while being unconscious of this goal. This is the case when a consumer shares his/her mood on a social network such as Facebook while travelling and using the geographical localization function (example – Figure 11.2).

Customers might also communicate in a non-verbal way after they had a product experience (Libai et al., 2010). Non-verbal communication can also be driven by an activated goal or occur without goal activation. In peer-to peer review platforms, liking others' comments, or rating hotels captures intentional non-verbal communication. Such deliberate non-verbal communication is often motivated by self-presentation goals (Wilcox et al., 2009). Sharing pictures of holidays and tourism experiences, even if it is not verbal, might be done intentionally to attain certain goals. Self-image management (Piwinger & Ebert, 2001), impression management, or social affiliation is among the key goals that are often associated with visible/conspicuous consumption behaviors. Non-verbal communication can also occur when the influencing others goal is not activated. Customers may share knowledge online without a conscious goal but the content may influence others in their network. Selfies are a good example as their sharing is increasingly practiced by tourists (Dinhopl & Gretzel, 2016). By posting a picture of themselves with a monument as the background, tourists may influence other people in their network, even if this was not consciously intentional. According to the literature on social influence, there is a trend actually for social influence processes that are subtle, indirect and outside of awareness (Cialdini & Goldstein, 2004).

Type of digital platform	Message type	Goal activation	
		Activated	**Non-activated**
1. One-to-one platform 2. One-to-many platform 3. Many-to-many platform	**Verbal**	*Intentional* *Proactive or reactive*	*Unintentional* *Proactive or reactive*
	Non-verbal	*Intentional* *Proactive or reactive*	*Unintentional* *Proactive or reactive*

Figure 11.2 A goal activation/message type matrix of e-WOM behaviors

Conclusion

The internet has created a vast multitude of methods for sharing information, communicating with others, and expressing oneself. Identifying and profiling contributors is an important issue for managers, particularly in the context of virtual communities (Wasko & Faraj, 2005). With regard to WOM research, practitioners show increasing interest in stimulating favorable peer-to-peer communication (Kumar et al., 2010). Previous literature has shown that positive e-WOM would generate more demand and profits while negative e-WOM decreases the profit and could bring a lot of damages to the company.

Despite the importance of e-WOM, prior research has largely ignored the specifics and potentially different manifestations of e-WOM communication (Libai et al., 2010). Several studies have focused on the profiling of contributors. Previous literature has emphasized the influential role of the posters and some articles emphasized the need to better understand why consumers post their opinions in order to increase the proportion of opinion givers among tourists (Bronner & de Hoog, 2011; N'Goala & Morrongiello, 2014)

However, classifying contributors in a dichotomous way into posters and lurkers should be questioned and further developed. This perspective assumes that the online behaviors are mainly conscious actions (Huffman & Houston, 1993). As stated earlier, conceptualizing e-WOM as a conscious process could be misleading. Digging into the motivation of behaviors and the exploration of new drivers of e-WOM based on goal theory would contribute to understanding what could be behind these e-WOM behavior profiles. The framework developed in this chapter (Figure 11.1) is based on two dimensions: (1) the type of the messages posted on the online opinion platform that can be verbal (written) or non-verbal (liking a post, rating a hotel or posting photos and videos). The second dimension is intentional vs. unintentional goal activation (Bargh et al., 2001; Chartrand & Bargh, 1996). This framework emphasizes the importance to see e-WOM as a customer behavior that might be driven by the conscious and/or unconscious goal to influence others. According to Bargh et al. (2001), both conscious vs. unconscious goal pursuit leads to the same outcome.

This implies that in some cases, a customer could be unaware of the triggers behind sharing content as there is no purposeful or intentional goal to influence others' attitudes or decisions, but their posting behavior could nevertheless be very influential (Cialdini & Goldstein, 2004). Previous psychology literature has shown that some unconscious processes could trigger some behavioral responses like for instance the tendency to imitate or mimic what others in the same situations are doing or have done (Bargh et al., 2001; Bargh & Morsella, 2008). A good example of this is the recent trend of selfies. The phenomenon became very prominent due to the confluence of front-facing cameras on smartphones and tablets, faster and wider distributions of wireless networks and a cultural proclivity of online self-presentation and representation assisted by the popularity of social networking sites like Facebook and Twitter (Levin, 2014) and in particular the proliferation of self-publishing mobile social media applications – Whatsapp,

Snapchat, Instagram etc. Because of this trend, many individuals are not necessarily conscious that they are influencing others. Many people are taking selfies for fun without any purposeful goal behind and they even are not aware that many people in their networks could be influenced by what is displayed in their pictures. Sharing a happy picture of you in front of your hotel during your holidays may suggest that this could be a good place to consider for those in your network who are planning to visit the same destination. Therefore, these unintentional influences are expected to have an even greater effect on individuals. Accordingly, we think that tourism professionals should benefit from both the intentional and unintentional e-WOM behaviors of the contributors and not only look for ways to turn passive customers to posters but also to see how to create value for the tourism industry and themselves from spontaneous, not necessarily e-WOM-focused behaviors. For instance, selfies have also become increasingly managed by tourists sites (Dinhopl & Gretzel, 2016), for example in the case of the "selfie" billboard on Times Square or the "selfie" stations at the new Beach Mall in Dubai that allows visitors to take and email selfies from the informational boards.

Note

1 Articles were selected among those available on the database "Science direct". To be included in our review, the paper had (1) to focus on opinion giving in (2) in the tourism sector and (3) to be published in a journal.

References

Arndt, J. (1967). Role of product-related conversations in the diffusion of a new product. *Journal of Marketing Research*, 4(3), pp. 291–295. doi:10.2307/3149462

Bargh, J. A., Lee-Chai, A., Barndollar, K., Gollwitzer, P. M., & Trötschel, R. (2001). The automated will: Nonconscious activation and pursuit of behavioral goals. *Journal of Personality and Social Psychology*, 81(6), pp. 1014–1027.

Bargh, J. A., & Morsella, E. (2008). The unconscious mind. *Perspectives on Psychological Science: A Journal of the Association for Psychological Science*, 3(1), pp. 73–79.

Berger, J., Sorensen, A. T., & Rasmussen, S. J. (2010). Positive effects of negative publicity: When negative reviews increase sales. *Marketing Science*, 29(5), 815–827.

Bickart, B., & Schindler, R. M. (2001). Internet forums as influential sources of consumer information. *Journal of Interactive Marketing*, 15(3), pp. 31–40.

Blazevic, V., Hammedi, W., Garnefeld, I., Rust, R. T., Keiningham, T., Andreassen, T. W., . . .Carl, W. (2013). Beyond traditional word-of-mouth: An expanded model of customer-driven influence. *Journal of Service Management*, 24(3), pp. 294–313. doi:10.1108/09564231311327003

Bone, P. F. (1995). Word-of-mouth effects on short-term and long-term product judgments. *Journal of Business Research*, 32(3), pp. 213–223.

Bronner, F., & de Hoog, R. (2011). Vacationers and eWOM: Who posts, and why, where, and what? *Journal of Travel Research*, 50(1), pp. 15–26.

Brown, J. J., & Reingen, P. H. (1987). Social ties and word-of-mouth referral behavior. *Journal of Consumer Research*, 14(December), pp. 350–362.

Buttle, F. A. (1998). Word-of-mouth: Understanding and managing referral marketing. *Journal of Strategic Marketing*, 6, pp. 241–254.

Cantallops, A. S., & Salvi, F. (2014). New consumer behavior: A review of research on eWOM and hotels. *International Journal of Hospitality Management*, 36, pp. 41–51.

Casalo, L., Flavian, C., & Guinaliu, M. (2010). Determinants of the intention to participate in firm-hosted online travel communities and effects on consumer behavioral intentions. *Tourism Management*, 31(6), pp. 898–911.

Chartrand, T. L., & Bargh, J. A. (1996). Automatic activation of impression formation and memorization goals: Nonconscious goal priming reproduces effects of explicit task instructions. *Journal of Personality and Social Psychology*, 71(3), pp. 464–478. doi:10.1037/0022–3514.71.3.464

Chen, Y., & Xie, J. (2008). Online consumer review: Word-of-mouth as a new element of marketing communication mix. *Management Science*, 54(3), 477–491.

Cheung, C. M., Lee, M. K., & Rabjohn, N. (2008). The impact of electronic word-of-mouth: The adoption of online opinions in online customer communities. *Internet research*, 18(3), 229–247.

Cheung, C. M. K., & Lee, M. K. O. (2012). What drives consumers to spread electronic word-of-mouth in online consumer-opinion platforms. *Decision Support Systems*, 53(1), pp. 218–225. doi:http://dx.doi.org/10.1016/j.dss.2012.01.015

Cheung, M. Y., Luo, C., SIA, C. L., & Chen, H. (2007). How do people evaluate electronic word-of-mouth? Informational and normative based determinants of perceived credibility of online consumer recommendations in China. PACIS 2007 Conference, Auckland, NZ, July 4–6, 2007, p. 18. Atlanta, GA: AIS.

Cheung, M. Y., Luo, C., Sia, C. L., & Chen, H. (2009). Credibility of electronic word-of-mouth: Informational and normative determinants of on-line consumer recommendations. *International Journal of Electronic Commerce*, 13(4), 9–38.

Choi, S. M., Lee, W. N., & Kim, H. J. (2005). Lessons from the rich and famous: A cross-cultural comparison of celebrity endorsement in advertising. *Journal of Advertising*, 34(2), 85–98.

Chu, S. C., & Kim, Y. (2011). Determinants of consumer engagement in electronic word-of-mouth (eWOM) in social networking sites. *International Journal of Advertising*, 30(1), 47–75.

Cialdini, R. B., & Goldstein, N. J. (2004). Social influence: Compliance and conformity. *Annual Review of Psychology*, 55(1), pp. 591–621. doi:10.1146/annurev.psych.55.090902.142015

Compete, Inc. (2007). Consumer Generated Content: Learning from Travel Innovators. Available from https://media.competeinc.com/med/uploads/files/traveltrends_consumer_generated_travel_content.html. Accessed on Sept. 8, 2008.

Deighton, J., & Kornfeld, L. (2009). Interactivity's unanticipated consequences for markets and marketing. *Journal of Interactive Marketing*, 23(1), pp. 2–12.

Dellarocas, C. (2003). The digitization of word-of-mouth: Promise and challenges of online feedback mechanisms. *Management Science*, 49(10), pp. 1407–1424.

Dinhopl, A., & Gretzel, U. (2016). Selfie-taking as touristic looking. *Annals of Tourism Research*, 57, pp. 126–139. doi:http://dx.doi.org/10.1016/j.annals.2015.12.015

Duan, W., Gu, B., & Whinston, A. B. (2008). The dynamics of online word-of-mouth and product sales—An empirical investigation of the movie industry. *Journal of Retailing*, 84(2), 233–242.

Duhan, D. F., Johnson, S. D., Wilcox, J. B., & Harrell, G. D. (1997). Influences on consumer use of word-of-mouth recommendation sources. *Journal of the Academy of Marketing Science,* 25(4), 283–295.

Fishbach, A., & Dhar, R. (2005). Goals as excuses or guides: The liberating effect of perceived goal progress on choice. *Journal of Consumer Research*, 32(3), 370–377. doi:10.1086/497548

Fitzsimons, G. J., Hutchinson, J. W., Williams, P., Alba, J. W., Chartrand, T. L., Huber, J., . . .Tavassoli, N. T. (2002). Non-conscious influences on consumer choice. *Marketing Letters*, 13(3), pp. 269–279. doi:10.1023/a:1020313710388

Fournier, S., & Avery, J. (2011). The uninvited brand. *Business Horizons*, 54(3), pp. 193–207. doi:http://dx.doi.org/10.1016/j.bushor.2011.01.001

Gelb, B. D., & Sundaram, S. (2002). Adapting to "word-of-mouse". *Business Horizons*, 45(4), pp. 21–25.

Goldsmith, R. E., & Flynn, L. R. (1993). Opinion leadership for vacation travel services. *Advances in Business Studies*, 1(7–8), pp. 17–29.

Gretzel, U., & Yoo, K. (2008). Use and impact of online travel reviews. In P. O'Connor, W. Hopken, & U. Gretzel (eds.) *Information and Communication Technologies in Tourism*. Wien/New York, Springer-Verlag, pp. 35–46.

Hennig-Thurau, T., Gwinner, K. P., Walsh, G., & Gremler, D. D. (2004). Electronic word-of-mouth via consumer-opinion platforms: What motivates consumers to articulate themselves on the internet? *Journal of Interactive Marketing*, 18(1), pp. 38–52.

Hennig-Thurau, T., Malthouse, E. C., Friege, C., Gensler, S., Lobschat, L., Rangaswamy, A., & Skiera, B. (2010). The impact of new media on customer relationships. *Journal of Service Research*, 13(3), pp. 311–330.

Herr, P. M., Kardes, F. R., & Kim, J. (1991). Effects of word-of-mouth and product-attribute information of persuasion: An accessibility-diagnosticity perspective. *Journal of Consumer Research*, 17(March), pp. 454–462.

Huffman, C., & Houston, M. J. (1993). Goal-oriented experiences and the development of knowledge. *Journal of Consumer Research*, 20(2), pp. 190–207. doi:10.2307/2489269

Jansen, B. J., Zhang, M., Sobel, K., & Chowdury, A. (2009). Twitter power: Tweets as electronic word-of-mouth. *Journal of the American Society for Information Science and Technology*, 60(11), pp. 2169–2188.

Jeong, E., & Jang, S. (2011). Restaurant experiences triggering positive electronic word-of-mouth (eWOM) motivations. *International Journal of Hospitality Management*, 30(2), pp. 356–366. doi:http://dx.doi.org/10.1016/j.ijhm.2010.08.005

Kaplan, A. M., & Haenlein, M. (2010). Users of the world, unite! The challenges and opportunities of social media. *Business Horizons*, 53(1), pp. 59–68. doi:http://dx.doi.org/10.1016/j.bushor.2009.09.003

Kaplan, A. M., & Haenlein, M. (2011). Two hearts in three-quarter time: How to waltz the social media/viral marketing dance. *Business Horizons*, 54(3), pp. 253–263. doi:http://dx.doi.org/10.1016/j.bushor.2011.01.006

Karmarkar, U. R., & Tormala, Z. L. (2010). Believe me, I have no idea what I'm talking about: The effects of source certainty on consumer involvement and persuasion. *Journal of Consumer Research*, 36(6), pp. 1033–1049.

Kiecker, P., & Cowles, D. L. (2001). Interpersonal communication and personal influence on the internet: A framework for examining online word-of-mouth. *Journal of Euromarketing*, 11(2), pp. 71–88.

Kim, E., Sung, Y., & Kang, H. (2014). Brand followers' retweeting behavior on Twitter: How brand relationships influence brand electronic word-of-mouth. *Computers in Human Behavior*, 37, 18–25.

Klein, L. R. (1998). Evaluating the potential of interactive media through a new lens: Search versus experience goods. *Journal of Business Research*, 41(3), pp. 195–203.

Kruglanski, A. W., Shah, J. Y., Fishbach, A., Friedman, R., Woo Young, C., & Sleeth-Keppler, D. (2002). A theory of goal systems. In Zanna, M. (ed.), *Advances in Experimental Social Psychology* (Vol. 34), Cambridge, MA: Academic Press, pp. 331–378.

Kumar, V., Aksoy, L., Donckers, B., Venkatesan, R., Wiesel, T., & Tillmans, S. (2010). Undervaluated and overvalued customers: Capturing total customer engagement value. *Journal of Service Research*, 13(3), pp. 297–310.

Labrecque, L. I., vor dem Esche, J., Mathwick, C., Novak, T. P., & Hofacker, C. F. (2013). Consumer power: Evolution in the digital age. *Journal of Interactive Marketing*, 27(4), pp. 257–269. doi:http://dx.doi.org/10.1016/j.intmar.2013.09.002

Lakin, J. L., Jefferis, V. E., Cheng, C. M., & Chartrand, T. L. (2003). The chameleon effect as social glue: Evidence for the evolutionary significance of nonconscious mimicry. *Journal of Nonverbal Behavior*, 27(3), pp. 145–162. doi:10.1023/a:1025389814290

Lee, J., Park, D., & Han, I. (2008). The effect of negative online consumer reviews on product attitude: An information processing view. *Electronic Commerce Research and Applications*, 7(3), pp. 341–352.

Levin, A. (2014). The Selfie in the Age of Digital Recursion. InVisible Culture, (20). Available at: http://ivc.lib.rochester.edu/category/issues/archives/issue- 20/ [accessed March 1, 2017].

Liang, S. W.-J., Ekinci, Y., Occhiocupo, N., & Whyatt, G. (2013). Antecedents of travelers' electronic word-of-mouth communication. *Journal of Marketing Management*, 29(5–6), pp. 584–606. doi:10.1080/0267257X.2013.771204

Libai, B., Bolton, R., Bügel, M. S., de Ruyter, K., Götz, O., Risselada, H., & Stephen, A. T. (2010). Customer-to-customer interactions: Broadening the scope of word-of-mouth research. *Journal of Service Research*, 13(3), pp. 267–282. doi:10.1177/1094670510375600

Litvin, S. W., Goldsmith, R. E., & Pan, B. (2008). Electronic word-of-mouth in hospitality and tourism management. *Tourism Management*, 29(3), pp. 458–468.

Liu, Y. (2006). Word-of-mouth for movies: Its dynamics and impact on box office revenue. *Journal of Marketing*, 70(3), pp. 74–89.

Malinen, S. (2015). Understanding user participation in online communities: A systematic literature review of empirical studies. *Computers in Human Behavior*, 46, pp. 228–238. doi:10.1016/j.chb.2015.01.004

Malthouse, E., & Hofacker, C. (2010). Looking back and looking forward with interactive marketing. *Journal of Interactive Marketing*, 24(3), pp. 181–184. doi:http://dx.doi.org/10.1016/j.intmar.2010.04.005

Mazzarol, T., Sweeney, J. C., & Soutar, G. N. (2007). Conceptualizing word-of-mouth activity, triggers and conditions: An exploratory study. *European Journal of Marketing*, 41(11–12), pp. 1475–1494.

Moe, W. W., Schweidel, D. A., & Trusov, M. (2011). What influences customers' online comments. *MIT Sloan Management Review*, 53(1), 14–16.

Muntinga, D. G., Moorman, M., & Smit, E. G. (2011). Introducing COBRAs: Exploring motivations for brand-related social media use. *International Journal of Advertising*, 30(1), pp. 13–46.

Murray, K. B. (1991). A test of service marketing theory: Consumer information Acquisition. *Journal of Marketing*, 55(1), pp. 10–15.

N'Goala, G., & Morrongiello, C. (2014). Converting opinion seekers in opinion seekers in the tourism industry: Building trust is critical. *Customer & Service Systems*, 1(1), pp. 77–90.

Pieters, R., & Wedel, M. (2007). Goal control of attention to advertising: The Yarbus implication. *Journal of Consumer Research*, 34(2), pp. 224–233.

Piwinger, M. & Ebert, H. (2001). Impression Management: Wie aus Niemand Jemand wird. In Bentele, G., Piwinger, M., & Schönborn, G. (eds.), *Kommunikationsmanagement: Strategien, Wissen, Lösungen, Art. Nr 1.06*. Neuwied, Germany: Luchterhand.

Ratneshwar, S., Barsalou, L. W., Pechmann, C., & Moore, M. (2001). Goal-derived categories: The role of personal and situational goals in category representations. *Journal of Consumer Psychology*, 10(3), pp. 147–157. doi:http://dx.doi.org/10.1207/s15327663jcp1003_3

Reingen, P. H., & Kernan, J. B. (1986). Analysis of referral networks in marketing: Methods and illustration. *Journal of Marketing Research*, 23(November), pp. 370–378.

Richins, M. L. (1983). Negative word-of-mouth by dissatisfied consumers: A pilot study. *Journal of Marketing*, 47(1), pp. 68–78.

Ryan, B., & Gross, N. C. (1943). The diffusion of hybrid seed corn in two Iowa communities. *Rural Sociology*, 8(March), pp. 15–24.

Sweeney, J. C., Soutar, G. N., & Mazzarol, T. (2012). Word-of-mouth: Measuring the power of individual messages. *European Journal of Marketing*, 46(1–2), pp. 237–257

TNS-Sofres (2010). E-Travel Monitor : Observatoire de notoriété et d'image des e-voyagistes. http://www.tns-sofres.com/publications/e-travel-monitor-observatoire-de-notoriete-et-dimage-des-e-voyagistes. [Accessed online: May 17, 2017]

Van Doorn, J., Lemon, K. E., Mittal, V., Pick, D., & Pirner, P. (2010). Customer engagement behavior: Theoretical foundations and research directions. *Journal of Service Research*, 13(3), pp. 253–266.

Vermeulen, I. E., & Seegers, D. (2009). Tried and tested: The impact of online hotel reviews on consumer consideration. *Tourism Management*, 30(1), pp. 123–127.

Von Wangenheim, F., & Bayon, T. (2007). The chain from customer satisfaction via word-of-mouth referrals to new customer acquisition. *Journal of the Academy of Marketing Science*, 35(2), pp. 233–249.

Voss, P. (1984). Status shifts to peer influence. *Advertising Age*, May 17(M-10).

Wasko, M. M., & Faraj, S. (2005). Why should I share? Examining social capital and knowledge contribution in electronic networks of practice. *MIS Quarterly*, 29(1), pp. 35–57. doi:10.2307/25148667

Westbrook, R. A. (1987). Product/consumption-based affective responses and postpurchase processes. *Journal of Marketing Research*, 24(3), pp. 258–270.

Wilcox, K., Min Kim, H., & Sen, S. (2009). Why do consumers buy counterfeit luxury brands? *Journal of Marketing Research*, 46(2), pp. 247–259. doi:10.1509/jmkr.46.2.247

Wood, W., & Neal, D. T. (2009). The habitual consumer. *Journal of Consumer Psychology*, 19(4), pp. 579–592. doi:http://dx.doi.org/10.1016/j.jcps.2009.08.003

Yang, F. X. (2017). Effects of restaurant satisfaction and knowledge sharing motivation on eWOM intentions: the moderating role of technology acceptance factors. *Journal of Hospitality & Tourism Research*, 41(1), 93–127.

Yap, K. B., Soetarto, B., & Sweeney, J. C. (2013). The relationship between electronic word-of-mouth motivations and message characteristics: The sender's perspective. *Australasian Marketing Journal (AMJ)*, 21(1), pp. 66–74. doi:http://dx.doi.org/10.1016/j.ausmj.2012.09.001

Ye, Q., Law, R., Gu, B., & Chen, W. (2011). The influence of user-generated content on traveler behavior: An empirical investigation on the effects of e-word-of-mouth to hotel online bookings. *Computers in Human Behavior*, 27(2), 634–639.

Yen, C.-L., & Tang, C.-H. (2015). Hotel attribute performance, eWOM motivations, and media choice. *International Journal of Hospitality Management*, 46(0), pp. 79–88. doi:http://dx.doi.org/10.1016/j.ijhm.2015.01.003

Yoo, K.-H., & Gretzel, U. (2008). What motivates consumers to write online travel reviews? *Information Technology & Tourism*, 10(4), pp. 283–295. doi:10.3727/109830508788403114

Yoo, K.-H., & Gretzel, U. (2011). Influence of personality on travel-related consumer-generated media creation. *Computers in Human Behavior*, 27(2), pp. 609–621. doi:http://dx.doi.org/10.1016/j.chb.2010.05.002

Zhang, Z., Ye, Q., Law, R., & Li, Y. (2010). The impact of e-word-of-mouth on the online popularity of restaurants: A comparison of consumer reviews and editor reviews. *International Journal of Hospitality Management*, 29, pp. 694–700.

12 The influence of reviewer identity verification on the online reputation of hotels

Eduardo Parra López and Desiderio Gutiérrez Taño

Introduction

Technological changes and the advance of the internet have caused profound transformations in business and social relationships, especially in the tourism sector where, over the last few years, it has been possible to discern significant changes (Buhalis & Licata, 2002). One of the key developments that has had a notable impact on businesses is the capacity of citizens to participate in and influence a growing number of aspects of the world around them (Parra López et al., 2010; Sigala & Marinidis, 2009).

Websites devoted to publicizing the opinions of customers based on their consumption experiences have developed rapidly. As a result, consumers' opinions and behavior can significantly influence each other (Dichter, 1966) by word-of-mouth (*WOM*) among users and its current equivalent by electronic word-of-mouth (e-WOM) (Litvin et al., 2008). Different studies have demonstrated the great influence that the comments and opinions of hotel customers have on the hotel selection decisions of others (Gutiérrez Taño et al., 2013). This aspect has caused hotel companies to pay attention to the management of the opinions that appear on the web, given the intangible nature of what they are selling and the high risk perceived by their customers (Lewis & Chambers, 2000).

Among the existing opinion platforms in the tourism sector with regard to hotels, there are two types that stand out: one type which accepts the opinion of any customer without checking whether he/she has indeed received the service, and the other type which guarantees that the person giving the opinion has indeed received the service that he/she evaluates. Over the last few years, there has been intense debate in the professional sphere about the fact that TripAdvisor, one of the most influential platforms, accepts opinions without verifying that the users have actually stayed at the establishment, as there is no identity authentication system. However at Booking, there is a system which only allows registered users who have previously made their hotel registration via the Booking website to leave opinions.

In both cases, different studies reveal that both platforms, especially TripAdvisor, have a great impact on the choice of hotels by other customers (Xiang & Gretzel, 2010; Sparks & Browning, 2011).

This study aims to verify whether there are differences in hotel reputation scores between the TripAdvisor and Booking platforms, owing to whether the hotel stay is authenticated or not. Possible explanations for the differences are also discussed, i.e. whether these differences are due to false opinions or to differences in users' behavior when giving their opinions. To carry out the comparative analysis of the effect of the guarantee of authentication of the hotel users' opinions, the reputation scores of a sample of the most representative hotels on each platform have been compared. In addition, an attempt is made to identify the implications that these findings may have on the management of the online reputation of the hotels. In this context, the working hypotheses are as follows:

Hypotheses

The main hypothesis put forward is that the hotel reputation scores obtained from opinions on platforms which verify that customers have really stayed at the establishment are more positive than those obtained on platforms which do not make such verifications. This hypothesis considers that the e-WOM ratings should be more positive when the customers who evaluate the hotels have to identify themselves given that they do not feel as "equally free" as those who are unidentified.

On the basis of this hypothesis, a second explanation would be that the reputation scores of hotels obtained from opinions on platforms which actively invite their clients to contribute opinions are higher than those obtained on platforms which do not encourage ratings/reviews. This suggests that negative experiences and dissatisfaction tend to promote WOM behavior in consumers to a greater degree than positive experiences and satisfaction. For this reason, if consumers are motivated to give their opinions, for example via email, the level of satisfactory responses is greater than when no invitation is issued as in the latter case, the evaluation of negative experiences predominates.

Based on the considerations above, the following hypotheses are proposed:

H1: The "global" reputation scores of hotels obtained from opinions on platforms that verify that customers have actually stayed at the establishments and invite their clients to contribute opinions are more positive than those obtained on platforms, which do not make such verifications.

H2: The "location" ratings of hotels obtained from opinions on platforms which verify that customers have really stayed at the establishments and invite their clients to contribute opinions are more positive than those obtained on platforms which do not make such verifications.

H3: The "value for money" ratings of hotels obtained from opinions on platforms which verify that customers have really stayed at the establishments and invite their clients to contribute opinions are more positive than those obtained on platforms which do not make such verifications.

H4: The "cleanliness" ratings of hotels obtained from opinions on platforms which verify that customers have really stayed at the establishments and invite their clients to contribute opinions are more positive than those obtained on platforms which do not make such verifications.

E-WOM: importance of online opinion sites when choosing a hotel

The importance of word-of-mouth (WOM) for business has been widely discussed and researched, particularly since the worldwide adoption of internet technologies, which have revolutionized the spread and influence of word-of-mouth (Anderson, 1998; Goldenberg et al., 2001; Stokes & Lomax, 2002; Zhu & Zhang, 2010). Several studies reveal the influence of website reviews and ratings on the choice of hotels (Dellarocas, 2003; Vermeulen & Seegers, 2009; Gretzel & Yoo, 2008; Mauri & Minazzi, 2013) while also demonstrating that these reviews can significantly influence other websites (Dichter, 1966).

Stern (1994) underlines that WOM is different from advertising, since it is not influenced or paid for by companies. This increases the perception of its credibility and trustworthiness by customers (Bateson & Hoffman, 1999). Villanueva et al. (2008) and Trusov et al. (2009) found that customers acquired through electronic word-of-mouth (*e-WOM*) added more long-term value to the firm than customers acquired through traditional marketing channels.

By analyzing these definitions, we can identify the main differences between the traditional concept of WOM and the new idea of e-WOM. First, e-WOM is *person-to-person* communication in a digital format, focusing on ratings, recommendations and reviews. E-WOM has gained importance with the increase in the use of technologies and applications based on the internet (Serra & Salvi, 2014; Goldenberg et al., 2001). Moreover, Libai et al. (2010) insist that in the digital age, consumers' e-WOM opinions can be read and seen by millions of users in real time and are available for a long time unlike traditional WOM. Second, and following Buttle (1998) and Mauri and Minazzi (2013), e-WOM is not limited to brands, products or services but can be related to an organization, a destination or product. Third, the credibility (Xia & Bechwati, 2008; Bickart & Schindler, 2005) of reviews on TripAdvisor and Booking web platforms deepens the impact that they have on the online reputation of hotels (Libai et al., 2010). For this reason, TripAdvisor and Booking, as online travel intermediaries, require reviewers to provide personal identifying information (e.g. name, state of residence, gender and date of visit/stay) with the idea to maximize the effect of credibility.

There is clearly a growing trend to share experiences about hotels through specialized websites. However, customers' comments can present biased information, since people who post a comment on the net are generally extremely satisfied or extremely dissatisfied with their stay (Anderson, 1998; Litvin et al., 2008). Therefore, given the importance of these review websites, bad reviews can cause negative images for hotel companies with low scores. By contrast, positive feedback will have a beneficial effect on customers' attitudes towards hotels (Vermeulen & Seegers, 2009). Thus, the importance that e-WOM has in the tourism industry, especially the hotel sector (Gretzel & Yoo, 2008; Litvin et al., 2008; Sparks & Browning, 2011; Stringam & Gerdes Jr., 2010; Serra & Salvi, 2014), is really high. In fact, Öğüt & Onur Tas (2012) suggested that higher customer ratings significantly increased online sales for hotels. Consequently, these reviews should be managed and enhanced (Cheng & Loi, 2014, Liu & Parque, 2015) and regarded as an opportunity to vary service design by analyzing their direction and intensity (Luo & Zhong, 2015).

As Lusky (2012) indicates, 70% of consumers worldwide trust online reviews, while only 47% believe traditional broadcast and print ads. To sum up the potential of online reviews as e-WOM:

- There is greater capacity of dissemination, because while in conventional WOM communication stays within the private sphere, in e-WOM any consumer interested can access the reviews of other consumers about a product or service through the websites.
- Consumers can communicate through different channels, such as websites, blogs, virtual communities, direct messages, emailing, news groups, videos, social networks, reviews websites etc. In addition, anonymity encourages information dissemination.
- Online reviews can be shared by other consumers to create greater credibility than advertising generated by companies.
- E-WOM is perceived positively by the consumer, as something spontaneous, non-commercial and not tampered with by the company.
- E-WOM has the ability to endure over time. While traditional WOM lasts only during a conversation or in consumers' minds for a short period, e-WOM information is stored on the internet and can be accessed at any time and for a long period of time. Therefore, e-WOM can reach thousands of consumers, now and in the future.

Online reputation: anonymous opinions vs. guaranteed opinions

Marketers and academic researchers are exploring new ways of using social networks for communication and online promotion in the current tourism context to achieve competitive advantages through e-WOM (Litvin, Goldsmith, and Pan, 2008). Schmallegger and Carson (2008) suggested the use of communication strategies using "blogs" to communicate, promote or even distribute products. Dellarocas (2003) proposed the use of web aggregators for online information in a bi-directional sense to share the valuations on a wide range of topics such as products, services and events or the creation of a digitized e-WOM network as presented by Henning-Thurau et al. (2004).

The aggregation of all these aspects is what creates the so-called "online reputation" (Dellarocas, 2003; Bolton et al., 2004). The management of this amalgam of sites with their corresponding content requires a multidisciplinary approach that incorporates the ideas of marketing, psychology, economics and the science of decision-making (Malaga, 2001). Therefore, it is possible to argue that the construction of an online reputation is formed through the Web 2.0, as outlined by Inversini et al. (2009), and whose purpose is to attract more tourists, not only to the destination, but also to review websites. Building this online reputation depends on multiple factors, including the decisive presence or absence of a clear target by users. We include at least three factors when characterizing online reputations:

(1) the reviews, comments, photos and other contributions uploaded by users; (2) information generated by other users and accessible through review websites and (3) interactions between companies and users and among users themselves.

Case study: analysis of hotels in TripAdvisor and Booking

To carry out a comparative analysis of the effect of the guarantee of authentication on the opinions of hotel users, the ratings of a sample of hotels on the two most representative platforms of the two models, TripAdvisor and Booking, have been compared. For this purpose, a study has been designed that analyzes the differences between the ratings on TripAdvisor and Booking of two samples: (1) a wide sample of hotels using the Student's *t*-test for two independent samples; (2) a limited sample using the Student's *t*-test for two related or dependent samples, that is to say, for each case (hotel) the score obtained on each of the platforms has been obtained. This analysis aims to verify whether the effect of verification of comments might affect the final reputation score of a hotel.

TripAdvisor represents the model in which the person giving the opinion is not checked as to whether they have actually spent a night at the hotel. It has over 200 million opinions made by customers voluntarily without any automatic action by the hotel provider such as a reminder or incentive. It has been frequently criticized since its creation. Its rating scale is from 1 to 5, offering scores rounded off to the nearest 0.5 points. The system asks the customer for a global score and a rating on a series of items (location, quality of sleep, rooms, service, value for money and cleanliness).

Booking, on the other hand, represents the model in which only registered users who have previously reserved their stay on Booking's website are allowed to leave comments. It has over 40 million opinions from just the last 14 months, which implies that it offers an assessment of the current situation at the hotel. Customers rate the hotels using a scale of four categories (Poor, Fair, Good, Excellent), although the platform transforms them into a scale from 1 to 10 according to the following values: Poor = 2.5; Fair = 5; Good = 7.5; Excellent = 10 (Mellinas et al., 2015). Opinions are requested from the customers after the stay at the accommodation establishment by sending out an email. The customer is asked to rate a series of items (cleanliness, comfort, location, facilities and services, staff and value for money) and a global score is calculated as an arithmetic mean of these ratings. To compare these two different scales, it was necessary to make changes to them. In this paper, Booking's scale has been transformed into a 1 to 5 scale rounded off to the nearest 0.5, taking into account the way that the platform makes the calculation (minimum score 2.5) (Mellinas et al., 2015). The formula used for the transformation is the following: where "x" is the value on the scale of 1 to 10 and "y" is the result of the value on the 1 to 5 scale: $y = (x - 2.5)/7.5 * 4$.

Academic researchers in tourism have used Booking data extensively as they represent an excellent source of information. This website collects millions of opinions about hotels in a rapid, economical and convenient manner. Nevertheless, the majority of the research takes for granted that Booking uses a scoring system on a scale of 1 to 10 (de Albornoz et al., 2011, Bjørkelund et al., 2012; Estárico et al., 2012; Gal-Oz et al., 2010; Grinshpoun et al., 2009; Chaves et al., 2012; Costantino et al., 2012; Filieri & McLeay, 2014; Korfiatis & Poulos, 2013; María-Dolores et al., 2012; Plata-Alf, 2013; Yacouel & Fleischer, 2012; Trenz & Berger, 2013). However, recent studies reveal that in reality Booking uses a scale of 2.5 to 10 (Mellinas et al., 2015; Bjørkelund et al., 2012). This error may cause statistical inaccuracies when this database is used for research without proper transformation. It also tends to inflate the scores at the upper end of the scale.

Independent samples

To obtain the data for a comparative analysis between TripAdvisor and Booking, a wide sample of online ratings of establishments in eight great European and American cities (Barcelona, Berlin, London, Madrid, New York, Paris, San Francisco and Toronto) were compiled. The resulting sample consisted of 7,062 ratings of hotels distributed among the cities and platforms as shown in Table 12.1. Data were obtained in January 2015.

Table 12.1 Structure of the independent samples

	Total	TripAdvisor	Booking
City			
Barcelona	817	519	298
Berlin	966	665	301
London	1368	1067	301
Madrid	756	458	298
New York	746	452	294
Paris	1735	1436	299
San Francisco	409	236	173
Toronto	265	141	124
Total	7062	4974	2088
Category of Hotel			
4 and 5 stars	2813	1702	1111
1, 2 and 3 stars	2966	2157	809
Not classified	1283	1115	168

In Table 12.2, the student's *t*-test results are shown for independent samples of the items. As can be observed, conclusive results are not obtained. For some items, TripAdvisor obtains higher scores than Booking and for others precisely the opposite. Furthermore, there is no constant pattern according to the item and thus the working hypotheses cannot be proven. However, we can confirm that H1, which proposes that the "global" scores of hotels obtained from reviews on platforms that verify that customers have really stayed at the establishments and invite their clients to contribute opinions (Booking) are more positive than those obtained on platforms which do not make such verifications (TripAdvisor). However, hypotheses 2 and 3 contradict this finding given that the "location" and "value for money" ratings of hotels obtained from opinions on platforms which verify that customers have really stayed at the establishments and invite their clients to contribute opinions are less positive than those obtained on platforms which do not make such verifications. Finally, hypothesis 4 is confirmed overall, though there are contradictory results according to the category of hotel. Hypothesis 4 is confirmed for lower category hotels (1, 2 and 3 stars) but not for the higher category ones (4 and 5 stars).

Related samples

To complement the analysis of independent samples, which was not conclusive, an analysis of average differences by means of the Student's *t*-test of related samples was carried out. The related or dependent samples are those in which each item of information from a sample can be univocally associated with another from another group due basically to the fact that the observations of both are carried out on the same sample units. This involves comparing averages when the two samples are related, that is, when a variable is measured under two different conditions. The main advantage of the design of related samples is that they allow bias to be reduced as a result of confounding variables. Furthermore, in this kind of design, each variable serves as its own control. In this way, it is guaranteed that the results obtained are not influenced by other variables such as the size of the hotel, number of opinions, the market in which it operates or type of customers etc.

The study is based on a sample of 100 hotels located in the Canary Islands (Spain), to be more exact on the island of Tenerife, the island which has the largest number of hotels and has the best representation on the platforms analyzed, thus avoiding possible bias due to the type of destination or accommodation. For each hotel, data have been collected from its TripAdvisor and Booking ratings. The data were collected in the second half of 2014. The characteristics of the sample are set out in Table 12.3.

Table 12.2 Student's *t*-test for independent samples from the selected hotels

	Total			4 and 5 stars			1, 2 and 3 stars		
	TripAdvisor	*Booking*	*Sig.*	*TripAdvisor*	*Booking*	*Sig.*	*TripAdvisor*	*Booking*	*Sig.*
Global scores	3.81	4.00	0.00 ***	4.09	4.12	0.12 ns	3.59	3.84	0.00 ***
Location	4.36	4.33	0.07 *	4.53	4.41	0.00 ***	4.23	4.22	0.60 ns
Value for money	3.82	3.68	0.00 ***	3.94	3.70	0.00 ***	3.73	3.65	0.00 ***
Cleanliness	4.10	4.13	0.00 ***	4.37	4.27	0.00 ***	3.88	3.95	0.01 ***

Level of significance: *** p < 0.001;
** p < 0.01;
* p < 0.05; ns non-significant

Table 12.3 Structure of the related samples (island of Tenerife)

	Total	4 and 5 stars	1, 2 and 3 stars
South of Tenerife	67	31	36
Santa Cruz, Tenerife	13	5	8
Puerto de la Cruz, Tenerife	20	9	11
Total	100	45	55

The results of the Student's *t*-test for related samples (Table 12.4) show that for the different items, except for the global score, the ratings given by users are greater on TripAdvisor than on Booking (global scores on Booking are arithmetic means of the different items, while it is a user-indicated score on TripAdvisor).

Therefore, hypotheses 2, 3 and 4 are rejected. Thus, it can be stated that the "location", "value for money" and "cleanliness" ratings of hotels obtained from opinions on platforms which verify that customers have really stayed at the establishments and invite their clients to contribute opinions (Booking) are less positive than those obtained on platforms which do not make such verifications (TripAdvisor) in the hotels analyzed.

Conclusions

As mentioned, the results reveal no support for the hypotheses. These were based on the proposition that reviews on Booking would be more positive than those found on TripAdvisor as they are conditioned by the lack of anonymity. However, the contrary is observed, that is to say the scores of the different subcategory items are generally higher on TripAdvisor than on Booking and therefore cannot be associated with authentication by the platform. Tourists who provide online opinions on TripAdvisor are motivated by both the need to respond to great experiences provided by travel and tour operators and by altruism and hedonistic motivations to contribute to the TripAdvisor community (Yoo & Gretzel, 2008), which could explain the difference in scores.

However, it is worth noting that global scores are higher on Booking (H1), probably because they are calculated as arithmetic means of the different items and do not directly reflect the global perceptions of the guests regarding the hotel. Likewise, Jiang et al. (2010) show, using attribution theory, how negative opinions on specific aspects of hotels do not always imply dissatisfaction. Therefore, the fact that TripAdvisor does not verify that those who give opinions have received the service does not mean that lower ratings have been given; on the contrary, hotels on this platform obtain more positive ratings than, for instance, on Booking, which always verifies that the service has been received. Therefore, the criticism that the hotel sector generally makes about the TripAdvisor platform seems baseless.

Table 12.4 Student's *t*-test for related samples (island of Tenerife)

	Total			4 and 5 stars			1,2 and 3 stars		
	TripAdvisor	*Booking*	*Sig.*	*TripAdvisor*	*Booking*	*Sig.*	*TripAdvisor*	*Booking*	*Sig.*
Global score	3.84	3.89	0.12 ns	4.03	4.06	0.57 ns	3.68	3.75	0.15 ns
Location	4.09	4.03	0.03 **	4.14	4.10	0.29 ns	4.05	3.97	0.04 **
Value for money	3.89	3.82	0.03 **	3.92	3.83	0.03 **	3.87	3.81	0.26 ns
Cleanliness	4.08	3.91	0.00 ***	4.23	4.12	0.01 ***	3.95	3.73	0.00 ***

Note: Level of significance: *** p < 0.001;
** p < 0.01;
*; p < 0.05; ns non-significant

The system to calculate the global reputation score used by Booking does not seem to reflect the real perception of the customer. It seems logical to expect that the weight of each item in the total score to be different. That would explain that while the ratings of individual items are higher on TripAdvisor, the global score is always higher on Booking. These results also reveal that the differences in ratings between Booking and TripAdvisor are not related to the category of hotels. When analyzing the reputation scores by category of hotel, dividing them into hotels of 1, 2 and 3 stars and hotels of 4 and 5 stars, we can see that they approximately follow the same pattern. Moreover, in both types of samples analyzed, hotels with large numbers of ratings were used. Therefore, we cannot say that the variation in average scores is a function of the number of ratings. In summary, the ratings collected from both Booking and TripAdvisor differ regardless of all these factors.

Therefore, as mentioned above, these differences in reputation scores are not due to the fact that e-WOM is more positive when the customers have to identify themselves. Given that the vast majority of the opinions are positive (Melián et al., 2010), consumers feel "equally free" to give ratings on either of the platforms. Another explanation could be the potential for fake reviews by hotel managers who are interested in improving the image of their hotel. However, given the high number of reviews found (average of 566 reviews per hotel on TripAdvisor and 279 on Booking) for the majority of the hotels analyzed in the sample, it would be very difficult for any rise in classification to be caused by such fake reviews. That is to say, positive ratings by hotel managers or negative ones from competitors would not be sufficient to raise or lower the average score of real consumers and their effect on the online reputation to any considerable extent (Cortazar[0] Rodríguez, 2004).

Negative experiences and dissatisfaction tend to promote WOM to a larger extent in customers than positive ones and satisfaction. For this reason, if companies do not obtain a large number of ratings, the predominant nature of them might be more negative than when greater numbers of opinions are expressed. Furthermore, when more opinions are received, there will not only be more negative opinions but there will also be more positive ones and this will also affect the overall online reputation (Melián et al., 2010).

As stated above, the fact that reviewers have to identify themselves or otherwise does not seem to play a significant role in the kind of ratings received on either opinion page. The possible rejection on the part of hotel owners of reviews on opinion sites is due to the fear that these opinions might prejudice the image of their establishments. The ideal outcome for an establishment is to get their most satisfied guests to share their opinions with their personal profile on any social medium or review site. For this purpose, it is of primordial importance to motivate these guests to review the services received on these platforms. Particularly, as many studies show that average scores of the establishments are generally higher as the number of opinions increases (Melián et al., 2010).

The monitoring of e-WOM is important given that for consumers, the opinions of other users generate greater credibility, empathy and more significance than the advertising of the hotel in question. In addition, an increasing number of consumers gain access to these platforms before their holidays with the result that more and more decisions depend on these opinions. Therefore, given the popularity and the influence on consumption decisions of websites offering opinions, hotel management should attempt to obtain as large a number of opinions as possible from their customers. In this way, if there were any negative reviews (unhappy guests are generally more motivated to declare their disagreement in the opinions) or false ones by third parties interested in damaging the image, their significance would be diluted and the average score would better reflect the collective opinion.

Companies need to be very careful with the flow of negative information that might arise from their products or services, since this may affect the perception of people with regard to the products more than if the information is neutral or positive (Herr et al., 1991). As proposed by Beenen et al. (2004), who carried out an experiment in which they managed to increase the contributions of users through rewards, it is possible to achieve greater participation from customers through sending emails specifically requesting their contribution or setting them certain objectives. In this way, through intrinsic motivation, it is possible to achieve greater participation than when the task is simply left to the will of the customer. Therefore, hotel managers should encourage their guests to give opinions emphasizing the importance of their participation and defining a period of time for doing so, either before leaving the hotel at the end of their holidays, or on the bill, or by sending an email with the link to the website, or inviting them to do so on the hotel Wi-Fi, etc. (Parra López et al., 2010). All of these might encourage customers to put their opinions on the websites and help compensate for any negative opinions that might exist, thus improving the online reputation of the hotel.

Limitations

The following limitations and future avenues of research should be considered. The geographical scope of the related sample is based on a single destination. Therefore, future lines of research might be aimed at studying the validity of the conclusions for similar hotels in other locations. In addition, the size of the related sample of 100 hotels could be increased so as to ensure more representative results. Even so, the sample used here is certainly representative of hotels in the Canary Islands.

Moreover, the opinions have been analyzed from two platforms, which, although they are the most representative of the two models, could be extended to other platforms. Another possible line of study is the comparison between the opinions on the platforms given voluntarily by customers vis-à-vis reviews made by a random sample of customers via face-to-face surveys. Finally, it is relevant to investigate whether customers who give their opinions on both platforms have different profiles and motivations that could explain the differences in ratings.

References

Anderson, E. W. (1998). Customer satisfaction and word of mouth. *Journal of Services Research*, 1, 5–17.

Bateson, J. E. G., & Hoffman, K. D. (1999). *Managing services marketing (4thed.).* Chicago: The Dryden Press.

Beenen, G., Ling, K., Wang, X., Chang, K., Frankowski, D., Resnick, P., & Kraut, R. (2004). Using social psychology to motivate contributions to online communities. Proceedings of ACM CSCW 2004 Conference on Computer Supported Cooperative Work, Chicago: 212–221. 6–10 November.

Bjørkelund, E., Burnett, T. H., & Nørvåg, K. (2012). A study of opinion mining and visualization of hotel reviews. In *Proceedings of the 14th International Conference on Information Integration and Web-Based Applications & Services*, New York: ACM. pp. 229–238.

Bolton, G. E., Katok, E., & Ockenfels, A. (2004). How effective are electronic reputation mechanisms? An experimental investigation. *Management science*, 50(11), 1587–1602.

Buhalis, D., & Licata, M. C. (2002). The future e-tourism intermediaries. *Tourism Management*, 23, pp. 207–220.

Buttle, F. A. (1998). Word of mouth: understanding and managing referral marketing. *Journal of strategic marketing*, 6(3), 241–254.

Chaves, M. S.; Gomes, R., & Pedron, C. (2012). Analysing reviews in the Web 2.0: Small and medium hotels in Portugal. *Tourism Management*, 33(5), pp. 1286–1287.

Cheng, V. T. P., & Loi, M. K. (2014). Handling negative online customer reviews: The effects of elaboration likelihood model and distributive justice. *J. Travel & Tourism Marketing*, 31(1), pp. 1–15.

Cortazar Rodríguez, F. J. (2004). Rumores y leyendas urbanas en Internet. Observatorio para la CiberSociedad. Available at: www.cibersociedad.net/archivo/articulo. php?art=194 [Accessed on Jan. 20, 2016].

Costantino, G., Martinelli, F., & Petrocchi, M. (2012). Priorities-based review computation. *AAAI Spring Symposium, 2012 1st Workshop on Intelligent Web Services Meet Social Computing* (Vol. 12), [0]Palo Alto, CA: AAAI, pp. 4.

De Albornoz, J. C., Plaza, L., Gervás, P., & Díaz, A. (2011). A joint model of feature mining and sentiment analysis for product review rating. In P. Clough, C. Foley, C. Gurrin, H. Lee, & G. J. F. Jones (eds.) *Proceedings of the 33rd European Conference on Advances in Information Retrieval (ECIR'11)*, Berlin, Heidelberg, Springer-Verlag, pp. 55–66.

Dellarocas, C. (2003). The digitization of word of mouth: Promise and challenges of online feedback mechanisms. *Management science*, 49(10), 1407–1424.

Dichter, E. (1966). How word-of-mouth advertising works. *Harvard Business Review*, 44(6), pp. 131–144.

Estárico, E. H., Medina, L. F., & Marrero, S. M. (2012). Una aproximación a la reputación en línea de los establecimientos hoteleros españoles. *Papers de Turisme*, 52, pp. 63–88.

Filieri, R., & McLeay, F. (2014). E-WOM and accommodation an analysis of the factors that influence travelers' adoption of information from online reviews. *Journal of Travel Research*, 53(1), pp. 44–57.

Gal-Oz, N., Grinshpoun, T., & Gudes, E. (2010). Sharing reputation across virtual communities. *Journal of Theoretical and Applied Electronic Commerce Research*, 5(2), pp. 1–25.

Gretzel, U., & Yoo, K. H. (2008). Use and impact of online travel reviews. In P. O'Connor, W. Höpken, & U. Gretzel (eds.) *Information and Communication Technologies in Tourism 2008: Proceedings of the International Conference in Innsbruck*. Wien, Austria, Springer-Verlag, pp. 35–46.

Grinshpoun, T., Gal-Oz, N., Meisels, A., & Gudes, E. (2009). CCR: A model for sharing reputation knowledge across virtual communities. In *Proceedings of the 2009 IEEE/WIC/ACM International Joint Conference on Web Intelligence and Intelligent Agent Technology* (Vol. 1), New York: IEEE Computer Society, pp. 34–41.

Gutiérrez Taño, D., Bulchand Gidumal, J., Díaz Armas, R. J., & Parra López, E. (2013). *Antecedentes del uso de los medios sociales por el turista: motivación, oportunidad and capacidad. Cuadernos de Turismo* (Vol. 31), Murcia, Spain: Universidad de Murcia, ISSN 1139–7861.

Hennig-Thurau, T., Gwinner, K. P., Walsh, G., & Gremler, D. D. (2004). Electronic word-of-mouth via consumer-opinion platforms: What motivates consumers to articulate themselves on the Internet? *Journal of Interactive Marketing*, 18(1), pp. 38–52.

Herr, P. M., Kardes, F. R., & Kim, J. (1991). Effects of word-of-mouth and product-attribute information on persuasion: An accessibility-diagnosticity perspective. *Journal of consumer research*, 17(4), 454–462.

Inversini, A., Cantoni, L., & Buhalis, D. (2009). Destinations' information competition and Web reputation. *Information technology & tourism*, 11(3), 221–234.

Jiang, J., Gretzel, U., & Law, R. (2010). Do Negative Experiences Always Lead to Dissatisfaction? – Testing Attribution Theory in the Context of Online Travel Reviews. In Gretzel, U., Law, R. & M. Fuchs (eds.), Information and Communication Technologies in Tourism 2010, Vienna, Austria: Springer Verlag, pp. 297–308.

Korfiatis, N., & Poulos, M. (2013). Using online consumer reviews as a source for demographic recommendations: A case study using online travel reviews. *Expert Systems with Applications*, 40(14), pp. 5507–5515.

Lewis, R. C., & Chambers, R. E. (2000). *Marketing Leadership in Hospitality, Foundations and Practices*, 3rd Edition. New York, John Wiley and Sons.

Libai, B., Bolton, R., Bügel, M. S., De Ruyter, K., Götz, O., Risselada, H., & Stephen, A. T. (2010). Customer-to-customer interactions: broadening the scope of word of mouth research. *Journal of Service Research*, 13(3), 267–282.

Litvin, S. W., Goldsmith, R. E., & Pan, B. (2008). Electronic word-of-mouth in hospitality and tourism management. *Tourism Management*, 29, pp. 458–468.

Luo, Q., & Zhong, D. (2015). Using social network analysis to explain communication characteristics of travel-related electronic word-of-mouth on social networking sites. *Tourism Management*, 46, pp. 274–282.

[0]Lusky, M. (2012). Online reviews, word-of-mouth and recommendations generate the most marketing trust. The Business Journals. http://www.bizjournals.com/bizjournals/how-to/marketing/2012/11/online-reviews-word-of-mouth-and.html Retrieved June, 25, 2013.

Malaga, R. A. (2001). Web-based reputation management systems: Problems and suggested solutions. *Electronic Commerce Research,* 1(4), 403–417.

María-Dolores, S. M., Bernal García, J. J., & Mellinas, J. P. (2012). Los hoteles de la región de Murcia ante las redes sociales and la reputación online. *Revista de Análisis Turístico*, 13, pp. 1–10.

Mauri, A. G., & Minazzi, R. (2013). Web reviews influence on expectations and purchasing intentions of hotel potential customers. *International Journal of Hospitality Management,* 34, 99–107.

Melián González, S., Bulchand Gidumal, J., & González López-Valcárcel, B. (2010). La participación de los clientes en sitios web de valoración de servicios turísticos. El caso de Tripadvisor. Revista de Análisis Turístico 2010 Asociación Española de Expertos Científicos en Turismo (AECIT), www.aecit.org Mirahoteles, 2008. Retrieved from www.mirahoteles.com/fitur2008 Feria Internacional del turismo.

Mellinas, J. P., Martínez, S. M., & Bernal García, J. J. (2015). Booking.com: The unexpected scoring system. *Tourism Management*, 49, pp. 72–74.

Öğüt, H., & Onur Taş, B. K. (2012). The influence of internet customer reviews on the online sales and prices in hotel industry. *The Service Industries Journal*, 32(2), 197–214.

Plata-Alf, D. (2013). Marketing communications in a virtual environment: Opportunities and challenges for companies in the tourism sector. In A. Nalepka & A. Ujwary-Gil (eds.) *Business and Non-Profit Organizations Facing Increased Competition and Growing Customers' Demands*, Nowy Sącz: Wyższa Szkoła Biznesu-National-Louis University, pp. 117–128.

Schmallegger, D., & Carson, D. (2008). Blogs in tourism: Changing approaches to information exchange. *Journal of vacation marketing,* 14(2), 99–110.

Serra Cantallops, A., & Salvi, F. (2014). New consumer behavior: A review of research on eWOM and hotels. *International Journal of Hospitality Management*, 36, pp. 41–51.

Sigala, M., & Marinidis, D. (2009). Exploring the transformation of tourism firms' operations and business models through the use of web map services. European and Mediterranean Conference on Information Systems 2009 (EMCIS 2009). Brunel University, UK. Izmir, Turkey. 13–14 July.

Sparks, B. A., & Browning, V. (2011). The impact of online reviews on hotel booking intentions and perception of trust. *Tourism Management* 32(6), pp. 1310–1323.

Stokes, D., & Lomax, W. (2002). Taking control of word of mouth marketing: the case of an entrepreneurial hotelier. *Journal of Small Business and Enterprise Development*, 9(4), 349–357.

Stern, B. B. (1994). A revised communication model for advertising: Multiple dimensions of the source, the message, and the recipient. *Journal of Advertising,* 23(2), 5–15.

Stringam, B. B., & Gerdes Jr, J. (2010). An analysis of word-of-mouse ratings and guest comments of online hotel distribution sites. *Journal of Hospitality Marketing & Management*, 19(7), 773–796.

Trenz, M., & Berger, B. (2013). Analyzing online customer reviews-an interdisciplinary literature review and research agenda. Proceedings of the 21st European Conference on Information Systems (ECIS). Utrecht, Netherlands. 5–8 June 2013, p. 83.

Trusov, M., Bucklin, R. E., & Pauwels, K. (2009). Effects of word-of-mouth versus traditional marketing: findings from an internet social networking site. *Journal of marketing,* 73(5), 90–102.

Vermeulen, I. E., & Seegers, D. (2009). Tried and tested: The impact of online hotel reviews on consumer consideration. *Tourism Management*, 30, pp. 123–127.

Villanueva, J., Yoo, S., & Hanssens, D. M. (2008). The impact of marketing-induced versus word-of-mouth customer acquisition on customer equity growth. *Journal of marketing Research*, 45(1), 48–59.

Xia, L., & Bechwati, N. N. (2008). Word of mouse: the role of cognitive personalization in online consumer reviews. *Journal of interactive Advertising*, 9(1), 3–13.

Xiang, Z., & Gretzel, U. (2010). Role of social media in online travel information search. *Tourism Management*, 31, pp. 179–188.

Yacouel, N., & Fleischer, A. (2012). The role of cybermediaries in reputation building and price premiums in the online hotel market. *Journal of Travel Research*, 51(2), pp. 219–226.

Yoo, K. H., & Gretzel, U. (2008). What motivates consumers to write online travel reviews? *Information Technology & Tourism*, 10(4), pp. 283–295.

13 Airbnb as a new disruptive model in tourism

Analyzing its competitive potential based on online travel reviews

Ricardo J. Díaz Armas, Desiderio Gutiérrez Taño and Francisco J. García Rodríguez

Introduction

The practice of exchanging accommodation spaces between private citizens has historically taken place between families and friends, albeit informally. The appearance of the internet has prompted a major leap in the scale of this practice (Russo & Quaglieri, 2014). Most recently, due to the emergence of social media platforms that coordinate exchanges and provide reputation mechanisms, it has become one of the central trends for the future of the tourism sector (Pizam, 2014). More specifically, Airbnb is an example of this new paradigm and the best-known case (Pizam, 2014), exemplifying a development which is following the normal pattern of a disruptive innovation (Christensen & Raynor, 2003; Guttentag, 2015) and a P2P business model. One of the classics in the so-called collaborative economy (Rifkin, 2014, Cañigeral, 2012), the Airbnb model is based on a collaborative lifestyle pattern (Botsman & Rogers, 2010), in which private individuals who share an interest and the same philosophy of life make a connection to rent rooms in shared flats or entire apartments, using a "social" system of search and management.

In this context, this chapter will analyze the extent to which the Airbnb business model might be obtaining a competitive advantage over conventional competitors in the hotel sector. For this purpose, the satisfaction levels of tourists staying at Airbnb establishments, compared with those who have selected another kind of accommodation of a more conventional nature, will be evaluated using opinions/reviews from Airbnb and from review platforms (Booking and TripAdvisor) for conventional hotel products. We chose this information because it is the main source of electronic word-of-mouth (e-WOM) directly from user experiences and is therefore an indicator of the extent to which visitors' expectations have been met or exceeded.

We have followed the approach of direct post-consumption evaluation (Zhou et al., 2014). In view of tourists' lack of knowledge about a company's promise of service, online opinions and reviews significantly reduce the uncertainty associated with purchasing the service (Kim et al., 2011; Sparks & Browning, 2011; Arsal et al., 2010). Moreover, this review of the service is free and open to the visitor, and is extremely valuable to the researcher because it is free of bias (Lu & Stepchenkova, 2012).

We begin by carrying out a context analysis of collaborative consumption or the sharing economy and, more specifically, of its importance in the specific case of the holiday accommodation sector, of which the Airbnb business model is the archetype. Then, the increasing importance of tourists' online opinions of accommodation is analyzed as an input to obtain useful satisfaction indicators for comparing tourist satisfaction between the two business models: Airbnb and conventional accommodation (hotels, apartments, Bed and Breakfast) (Luo & Zhong, 2015). Finally, we present the objectives, methodology and main results, concluding with a discussion of the main findings.

Collaborative consumption as a disruptive trend: the case of holiday accommodation and Airbnb

Among the multiple trends which have given rise to disruptive innovations in the current business revolution we are witnessing (Rifkin, 2011) is the so-called "sharing economy", a phenomenon also known as "collaborative consumption". The sharing economy can be defined as a socio-economic system based on the logic of sharing human and material resources; it includes the creation, production, distribution, exchange and consumption of goods and services by different people and organizations (Wikipedia, 2014). It is fundamentally based on a growing international movement anchored in deep-rooted sociological and technological changes and giving priority to sharing rather than to possessing goods (Walsh, 2011). The associated technological revolution is indispensable if we are to understand, survey and define the concept of collaborative consumption. Following Cañigeral (2012, p. 6), collaborative consumption can be defined as "the traditional way of sharing, exchanging, lending, hiring and/or giving redefined through technology and communities". The evolution of technology now makes it possible to boost face-to-face exchanges that used to take place on a much larger scale, thanks to the efficiency of the internet, combined with mechanisms that support the development of trust between strangers (Botsman & Rogers, 2010).

In accordance with Botsman and Rogers (2010), there are three systems in which collaborative consumption could develop:

- Product-service systems, paid for by users, who do not acquire property rights
- Redistribution markets, in which there is a transfer or exchange of used goods
- Collaborative lifestyles, whereby individuals who share the same interests or philosophy of life can connect and exchange intangible resources, such as time, space, skills and money

These types of collaborative consumption have led to different business models that have also evolved over time (Cañigeral, 2012; Tunguz, 2011). Thus, originally, the main business models connected the firm with the consumer (B2C), in that the firm would acquire, maintain and rent out the products. However, a second great wave of business models put consumers or users in contact with each other (P2P), and these were much "more efficient with regard to capital than B2C because they do not require any capital investment to acquire the goods. Of course, they depend on a community to provide those goods, normally in exchange for a certain profit on the transactions" (Cañigeral, 2012, p. 7).

Although these activities within the collaborative economy affect almost all economic sectors, to a greater or lesser extent, in the specific case of tourism, in general, and holiday accommodation in particular, this is one of the most important trends and one that will contribute decisively to shaping the future of the sector (Pizam, 2014). More specifically, in the accommodation sector, Airbnb (www.airbnb.com) is certainly a paradigmatic case. It is the most popular marketplace (Pizam, 2014) and follows the usual pattern of a disruptive innovation (Christensen and Raynor, 2003), which begins with marginal and limited growth to later become explosive – Airbnb has been at this stage for the last few years (Guttentag, 2015).

From the point of view of the typology of Botsman and Rogers (2010), Airbnb follows a P2P business model. More precisely, it corresponds to the collaborative lifestyle pattern, in that private individuals who share interests and a single philosophy of life establish contact in order to rent out rooms in shared flats or entire apartments by means of a "social" system of search and management. Despite its success, the specific characteristics of this "collaborative consumer" of holiday accommodation are not well known, although these consumers generally appear to be

> expert, connected travellers, inclined to responsible consumption, characterised by a high level of trust towards the other members of the community and familiarity with the internet and e-commerce, demanding regarding the quality of their holiday experiences and used to linking their chosen destinations and forms of hospitality with the visits of relatives and friends in the context of more extensive relational environments of a "liquid" and reticular nature (Russo and Quaglieri, 2014, p. 1).

An accommodation service such as Airbnb would in principle suffer from significant disadvantages when competing with other more traditional accommodation alternatives that are available to tourists when selecting their accommodation, in terms of quality of service, friendliness and availability of staff, brand reputation and safety (Chu & Choi, 2000; Guttentag, 2015). For this reason, following Guttentag (2015), the Airbnb business model is based on a cost advantage: the host's fixed costs are covered a priori (supplies, community costs), labor costs are minimal or non-existent and most importantly, there are no fiscal charges. Guests also benefit from accommodation in a private residence: the feeling of a home away from a home, unlike a hotel; advice from the host about local lifestyle; the chance to get involved as a resident rather than as a visitor; and access to home amenities (kitchen, washing-machine, hair dryer etc.).

Online opinions as a reference of holidaymaker satisfaction with the accommodation

New social technology has simplified communication between people and users, allowing for total transparency of comments and product evaluation (Toh et al., 2011; Jun et al., 2010; Verma, 2010; Wen, 2009). These opinions are perceived by the market as exact; they are modifying consumer behavior and redefining the role of the influencer during the purchasing process, generating impartial information and supplying more realistic expectations. Highly accessible online consumer opinions help consumers discover costs and benefits perceived by other users who have commented on and evaluated their consumption experiences. As a result, others can make decisions with a certain degree of confidence, despite never having purchased that service before, thereby notably reducing the perceived risk (Wen, 2009).

In this case, the success of emerging business models resulting from the collaborative economy is clearly linked to opinions expressed online. In fact, in these models, negative reviews will exclude that service, thereby ensuring the continuation of services more in line with user expectations, provided that all comments and assessments are freely given. For this reason, product and service reviews are considered an opportunity to regulate supply (Luo & Zhong, 2015).

The tourist industry, and the accommodation sector in particular, is currently very much influenced by electronic word-of-mouth (e-WOM) (Serra-Cantallops & Salvi, 2014). There is an abundance of literature on online reputation deriving from e-WOM (Lee et al., 2011; Xie et al., 2011; Yacouel & Fleischer, 2011; Arsal et al., 2010; Black & Kelley, 2009; Litvin et al., 2008). Authors such as Yoon and Uysal (2005), or more recently Cheng and Loi (2014), state clearly that e-WOM is the most-used information source by people interested in travel. More and more tourists are publishing and sharing their opinions in real time (Gretzel, 2006; Gretzel & Yoo, 2008; Pan et al., 2007), making it increasingly easy to find the opinions and personal experiences of others when searching for tourism products online (Xiang & Gretzel, 2010). Tourism businesses must therefore manage and encourage these comments to achieve competitive advantages (Cheng & Loi, 2014).

E-WOM allows people to make inferences about the promise made by accommodation providers in their communications and the service that they really offer. Consequently, e-WOM has greater impact on accommodation and reputation and therefore on results and business performance (Xie et al., 2014). It should not be forgotten that, in tourism, apart from drastically changing the way in which tourists search for information and take decisions on purchasing or reservations (Yoo & Gretzel, 2008; Xiang & Gretzel, 2010), the internet and social media also exert considerable influence on the trip itself and on the reflection when it is over (Li & Wang, 2011; Wu & Pearce, 2014).

Importantly, online comments from tourists represent a rich vein of impartial and unbiased information, which may contribute to the study and analysis of satisfaction in the accommodation sector (Kim & Hardin, 2010; Lu & Stepchenkova, 2012). According to Zhou et al. (2014), one of the approaches that can be used to measure satisfaction with a hotel service is by directly valuing the service at the post-consumption stage. Thus, expectations are not taken into consideration and only specific aspects of the accommodation are evaluated, as well as the overall experience. This approach has seen a resurgence since the appearance of social media, due to the great quantity of user-generated information now available on hotel and online travel agency websites and on hotel review platforms, resulting in a highly suitable way of analyzing satisfaction (Kozak, 2000).

According to Mauri and Minazzi (2013), this information is valuable because it helps understand customer satisfaction and the extent to which the customer is more or less satisfied post-consumption. One drawback involves concerns for data reliability and the representativeness of those who publish the information (Kozinets, 2010). Nevertheless, Yoo and Gretzel (2008) emphasize that online consumer reviews arise from the desire to altruistically help others in their choice, and Zehrer et al. (2011) argue that the data are generally reliable. Similarly, as O'Connor (2010) indicates, unlike the information obtained through a survey, online users are free to write about what they believe is relevant to a certain experience. It is bias-free information and is useful for understanding emerging market trends and new tourist activities (Wu & Pearce, 2014). Furthermore, it constitutes a cheap and efficient source of information (Gerdes & Stringam, 2008), which is increasingly used in the academic sphere (Banyai & Glover, 2012; Gerdes & Stringam, 2008; Magnini et al., 2011; O'Connor, 2010; Pekar & Ou, 2008; Mkono, 2012).

Empirical work

Objective

This chapter analyzes the extent to which the disruptive innovation of Airbnb, currently in an explosive growth phase, may be gaining a competitive advantage on conventional competitors in the hotel sector. This research aimed to evaluate the satisfaction levels of tourists staying in Airbnb, compared with those who chose a more conventional establishment, based on the opinions or reviews arising from the respective user experiences.

Methodology

To obtain data for the comparative analysis of the satisfaction levels of tourists staying at Airbnb establishments, compared with those who chose other, more conventional accommodation, we extracted a wide range of online evaluations on establishments in eight important European and American cities (Barcelona, Berlin, London, Madrid, New York, Paris, San Francisco and Toronto). Evaluations of traditional accommodation options were obtained from TripAdvisor and Booking, two of the most influential platforms for online hotel reviews, with two different approaches.

TripAdvisor has over 200 million opinions which are volunteered by customers with no reminder or incentive. The reviews were gathered over the lifetime of the platform, and the evaluation scale is from 1 to 5, offering data rounded off to the nearest 0.5 points. The system asks the customer to give an overall review and an evaluation of series of items (location, sleep quality, rooms, service, value for money and cleanliness).

Booking has over 40 million opinions from the last 14 months, which implies that it offers an evaluation of the current situation of the hotel. Customers rate the individual aspects of the establishments according to four categories (bad, ordinary, good, excellent). Customers are then asked to evaluate a series of items (cleanliness, comfort, location, facilities and services, staff and value for money). The overall evaluation is calculated as an arithmetic average of these evaluations and presented on a scale from 1 to 10. Opinions are requested by email from guests after their stay at the establishment.

Airbnb sends an email after the stay requesting a customer evaluation of the hosts and a host evaluation of the guests; results are only published when both evaluations have been given. Airbnb uses the same scale as TripAdvisor from 1 to 5, offering data rounded off to 0.5 points. The platform requests an overall review and also an evaluation of a series of items (precision, communication, cleanliness, location, arrival, value).

The dependent variable used in the analysis is the average of the overall evaluations across all establishments sampled at a particular destination, taken from online user evaluations, which are measured on a scale of 1 to 5, on all three platforms. This makes it possible to determine the differences in perceived quality and, therefore, the competitive potential of these new business models. Booking's scale has been transformed into a scale from 1 to 5, rounded off to the nearest 0.5, taking into account the way in which the platform carries out its calculation (minimum score 2.5) (Mellinas et al., 2015).

The extraction was done by web scraping, a technique that uses ad hoc software programs that gather information from websites. These programs simulate the browsing behavior of a human on the internet, using http protocol. The resulting sample was 25,652 evaluations of accommodation establishments, distributed by city and platform, as shown in Table 13.1.

Table 13.1 Size of sample by platform and city

	TripAdvisor	*Booking*	*Airbnb*	*Total*
Barcelona	815	842	1,666	3,323
Berlin	843	656	1,748	3,247
London	1,586	803	1,797	4,186
Madrid	692	807	1,571	3,070
New York	549	423	2,326	3,298
Paris	1,566	523	2,170	4,259
San Francisco	305	207	1,727	2,239
Toronto	261	221	1,548	2,030
Total	6,617	4,482	14,553	25,652

Establishment categories according to each platform are Bed and Breakfast (B&B)/Hostel and Hotels, for TripAdvisor; Apartments, Hostel and Hotels, for Booking; and Shared room, Private room and The Entire property, for Airbnb. The resulting sample by category is given in Table 13.2.

For the sample from TripAdvisor and Booking platforms, the distribution by establishment category is shown in Table 13.3.

Results

To discover the differences between evaluations by customers of traditional establishments compared with the new channels (Airbnb, which represents a disruptive business model, compared with TripAdvisor and Booking, which represent traditional accommodation business models), a Student's *t*-test was carried out using type of platform as an independent variable and evaluation average as a dependent variable. Figures 13.1 and 13.2 give a representation of the averages of overall evaluations and of items of the establishments for the three platforms, where the average Airbnb scores are greater than those of TripAdvisor and Booking in all cases.

Table 13.2 Distribution of the sample by establishment category according to platform

	TripAdvisor	*Booking*	*Airbnb*
Apartment		1,378	
B&B/Hostel	1,643	1,016	
Hotel	4,974	2,088	
Shared room			2,011
Private room			6,231
The Entire property			6,311
Total	6,617	4,482	14,553

Table 13.3 Distribution of the sample by category according to the platform

Category (Stars)	*TripAdvisor*	*Booking*
1	106	138
2	793	493
3	1,834	802
4	1,273	1,074
5	274	252
Total	4,280	2,759

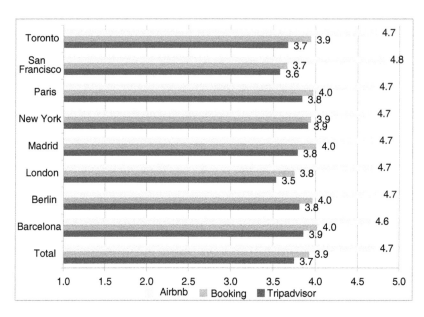

Figure 13.1 Average of accommodation establishment evaluations by destination and platform

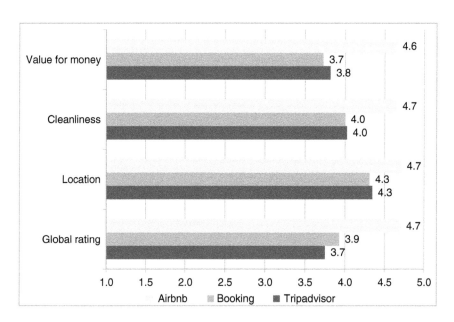

Figure 13.2 Average of accommodation establishment item evaluations by platform

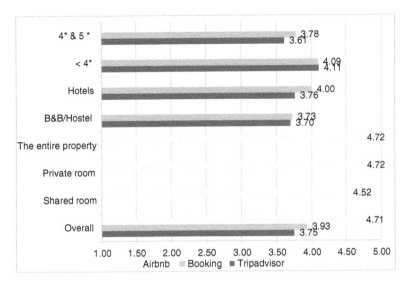

Figure 13.3 Average of accommodation establishment evaluations according to category/
type and by platform

Figure 13.3 gives the averages of the platform evaluations by hotel category and accommodation type studied. The evaluations are higher for Airbnb than for TripAdvisor and Booking in all cases.

Table 13.4 gives the aggregate results of the Student's *t*-test analysis of averages in order to discover whether these differences in averages are significant. According to the Student's *t*-test analysis of averages between Airbnb and traditional platforms, the difference in averages is significant in the overall sample and in all the cities. The evaluations given by Airbnb customers are also more favorable in all type of accommodation cases than those of TripAdvisor and Booking. Likewise, the difference between the most favorable evaluations of TripAdvisor and Booking (4- and 5-star hotels) and the least favorable of Airbnb (shared room) continues to show a favorable average for Airbnb, with significant differences.

Table 13.5 also shows significant differences between the scores of the Airbnb establishments according to type of accommodation. Thus, it is clear that private rooms are more satisfactory to guests because scores are significantly better than for shared rooms. However, the averages of private rooms and entire property types on Airbnb are the same.

Table 13.6 gives the result of the Student's *t*-test analysis of averages for the different evaluation items that can be compared, showing that there are significant differences between the scores of Airbnb establishments and those of TripAdvisor and Booking.

Table 13.4 Overall student's *t*-test results

	Airbnb	TripAdvisor	Significance Airbnb-TripAdvisor	Booking	Significance Airbnb-Booking
TOTAL	4.71	3.75	0.000	3.93	0.000
Barcelona	4.65	3.86	0.000	4.02	0.000
Berlin	4.74	3.81	0.000	3.96	0.000
London	4.67	3.53	0.000	3.75	0.000
Madrid	4.69	3.79	0.000	4.01	0.000
New York	4.67	3.91	0.000	3.94	0.000
Paris	4.69	3.84	0.000	3.97	0.000
San Francisco	4.82	3.58	0.000	3.66	0.000
Toronto	4.72	3.67	0.000	3.95	0.000
B&B/Hostel	4.71	3.70	0.000	3.73	0.000
Hotels	4.71	3.76	0.000	4.00	0.000
< 4*	4.71	4.11	0.000	4.09	0.000
4 and 5 *	4.71	3.61	0.000	3.78	0.000
Airbnb shared vs TripAdvisor/ Booking	4.52	3.75	0.000	3.93	0.000

Table 13.5 Student's *t*-test results for Airbnb shared vs. private rooms

	Shared room	Private room	Significance
Airbnb	4.52	4.72	0.000
	Private room	Entire property	
Airbnb	4.72	4.72	0.964

Table 13.6 Student's *t*-test results for items of evaluation

	Airbnb	TripAdvisor	Significance Airbnb-TripAdvisor	Booking	Significance Airbnb-Booking
Overall evaluation	4.71	3.75	0.000	3.93	0.000
Location	4.71	4.34	0.000	4.31	0.000
Cleanliness	4.65	4.03	0.000	4.00	0.000
Value	4.65	3.82	0.000	3.73	0.000

Conclusions

In the context of the trend known as the "collaborative or sharing economy", a great variety of business models have been developed in different sectors and for different activities (Cañigeral, 2012; Tunguz, 2011). In the accommodation sector, Airbnb (www.airbnb.com), is a prominent case in point (Pizam, 2014). Airbnb should, in principle, have significant disadvantages when competing with other more traditional alternatives available to tourists when selecting accommodation, especially in terms of quality of service, friendliness and availability of staff, brand reputation and security (Chu & Choi, 2000; Guttentag, 2015). However, the results of this research suggest that the segment of customers who use the accommodation services supplied by the platform satisfy their expectations to a greater extent than those using traditional services. These travellers are distinguished by a high level of trust towards other members of the community, as well as familiarity with the internet and online commerce (Russo & Quaglieri, 2014, p. 1), and apparently obtain greater satisfaction from accommodation experiences. Therefore, the supposed disadvantages of an accommodation service like Airbnb appear to have been overcome by the benefits for guests who stay in a private residence: a feeling of home away from home, unlike a hotel; advice from the host about local lifestyle; the chance to get involved as a resident rather than as a visitor; and access to home amenities (Guttentag, 2015).

According to Mauri and Minazzi (2013), this information is valuable as it helps understand customer satisfaction and the extent to which the customer is more or less satisfied post-consumption. Russo and Quaglieri (2014) suggest that, in comparison with tourists who stay at hotels, those who hire Airbnb holiday rentals are not undemanding. According to these authors, these tourists are quite particular and their greater satisfaction with the accommodation experience lies in the fact that their expectations as consumers are better met.

Other reasons why Airbnb hosts might obtain better indicators is that they consider the model to be centered exclusively on avoiding bad experiences and on attracting the best visitors because visitors are evaluated at Airbnb. Also, by way of contrast with traditional accommodation models, at Airbnb, owners center all their efforts on the relationship with the visitor – personal attention, empathy – and may be much more motivated because their aim is to avoid negative comments. Owners realize that negative comments could affect demand. Conversely, employees at a traditional accommodation option have other objectives, which are not always aligned with reducing negative comments or generating positive ones.

The differences recorded in post-consumption satisfaction between the two business models in accommodation in favor of Airbnb will probably continue or even grow unless adjustments are made by the hotel industry regarding value propositions and the perceived value for money, leading to differences in the volume of sales (Öğüt and Onur Taş, 2012). This cumulative dynamic might be facilitated by online opinions, encouraging increasing numbers of visitors to value and comment on their experiences, thus acting as a natural market regulator (Luo & Zhong, 2015).

All this is a clear indication of the great competitive potential of these new collaborative economy business models, specifically in the holiday accommodation sector. These results are extendable to the main urban destinations of European and American cities and to all hotel categories. However, certain specificities have been detected in the Airbnb business model in relation to the different products marketed, and shared accommodation services obtain lower scores and recommendations than those for private rooms or the entire property. This implies that aspects such as reputation and security might be affected by bad experiences in this type of truly shared accommodation.

As in all studies of this nature that focus on such an emergent and complex phenomenon as the collaborative consumption of holiday accommodation, there are certain limitations. In order to measure satisfaction, we followed the direct evaluation approach, one of three approaches mentioned in the literature, together with improving on expectations and comparative evaluation (Zhou et al., 2014). We used TripAdvisor and Booking for hotel accommodation evaluations made voluntarily by users and in an altruistic fashion. We did not sample the total population but chose those who volunteered to evaluate and give an opinion; the information gathered might therefore involve a certain bias. Nevertheless, insofar as the central objective was to analyze the suitability in terms of satisfaction of the Airbnb business model in comparison with the traditional accommodation model, this bias is limited because both populations are similar. Furthermore, authors such as Mauri and Minazzi (2013) and Zehrer et al. (2011) assure us of the importance and reliability of these evaluations.

Finally, this work could be enhanced if the qualitative evaluations on the platforms were considered complementary to the quantitative scores, since the analysis could contribute explanatory factors of the differences recorded in this chapter, thereby clarifying the benefits and costs that signal the differences between both accommodation models.

References

Arsal, I., Woosnam, K. M., Baldwin, E. D., & Backman, S. J. (2010). Residents as travel destination information providers: An online community perspective. *Journal of Travel Research.*, 49(4), pp. 400–413.

Banyai, M., & Glover, T. D. (2012). Evaluating research methods on travel blogs. *Journal of Travel Research*, 51(3), pp. 267–277.

Bauwens, M., Lacomella, F., Mendoza, N., Burke, J., Pinchen, C., Léonard, A., & Mootoosamy, E. (2012). *A Synthetic Overview of the Collaborative Economy*, P2P Foundation.

Black, H. G., & Kelley, S. W. (2009). A storytelling perspective on online customer reviews reporting service failure and recovery. *Journal of Travel and Tourism Marketing*, 26(2), 169–179.

Botsman, R., & Rogers, R. (2010). *What's Mine Is Yours: The Rise of Collaborative Consumption*, New York, Harper Business.

Cañigeral, A. (2012). Innovación en modelos socio-económicos. Introducción al Consumo Colaborativo. Ver. Retrieved from www.scribd.com/fullscreen/58880914?access_key= key-2fi003avv1spqak6f6pv

Cheng, V. T. P., & Loi, M. K. (2014). Handling negative online customer reviews: The effects of elaboration likelihood model and distributive justice. *Journal of Travel and Tourism Marketing*, 31(1), p. 1–15.

Christensen, C. M., & Raynor, M. E. (2003). *The Innovator's Solution: Creating and Sustaining Successful Growth.* Boston, MA: Harvard Business School Press.

Chu, R. K., & Choi, T. (2000). An importance-performance analysis of hotel selection factors in the Hong Kong hotel industry: A comparison of business and leisure travellers. *Tourism Management*, 21(4), pp. 363–377.

Gerdes Jr., J., and Stringam, B. B. (2008). Addressing researchers' quest for hospitality data: Mechanism for collecting data from web resources. *Tourism Analysis*, 13(3), pp. 309–315.

Gretzel, U. (2006). Consumer generated content trends and implications for branding. *E-Review of Tourism Research*, 4(3), pp. 9–11.

Gretzel, U., & Yoo, K. (2008). Use and impact of online travel reviews. In P. O'Connor, W. Höpken, & U. Gretzel (eds.) *Information and Communication Technologies in Tourism* (Vol. 2), Wien/New York, Springer-Verlag, pp. 35–46.

Guttentag, D. (2015). Airbnb: disruptive innovation and the rise of an informal tourism accommodation sector. *Current Issues in Tourism*, 18(12), pp. 1192–1217.

Jun, S. H., Vogt, C. A., & MacKay, K. J. (2010). Online information search strategies: a focus on flights and accommodation. *Journal of Travel and Tourism Marketing.*, 27, pp. 579–595.

Kim, E. E. K., Mattila, A. S., & Baloglu, S. (2011). Effects of gender and expertise on consumer´s motivation to read online hotel reviews. *Cornell Hospitality Quarterly*, 52(4), pp. 399–406.

Kim, J. S., & Hardin, A. (2010). The impact of virtual worlds on word-of-mouth: Improving social networking and service scape in the hospitality industry. *Journal of Hospitality Marketing & Management*, 19(7), pp. 735–753.

Kozak, M. (2000). Comparative assessment of tourist satisfaction with destinations across two nationalities. *Tourism Management*, 22(4), pp. 391–401.

Lee, H. A., Law, R., & Murphy, J. (2011). Helpful reviewers in TripAdvisor, an online travel community. *Journal of Travel and Tourism Marketing*, 28(7), pp. 675–688.

Li, X., & Wang, Y. (2011). China in the eyes of western travelers as represented in travel-blogs. *Journal of Travel and Tourism Marketing*, 28(7), pp. 689–719.

Litvin, S. W., Goldsmith, R. E., & Pan, B. (2008). Electronic word-of-mouth in hospitality and tourism management. *Tourism management*, 29(3), 458–468.

Lu, W., & Stepchenkova, S. (2012). Ecotourism experiences reported online: Classification of satisfaction attributes. *Tourism Management*, 33(3), pp. 702–712.

Luo, Q., & Zhong, D. (2015). Using social network analysis to explain communication characteristics of travel-related electronic word-of-mouth on social networking sites. *Tourism Management*, 46, pp. 274–282. Available Online.

Magnini, V. P., Crotts, J. C., & Zehrer, A. (2011). Understanding customer delight: An application of travel blog analysis. *Journal of Travel Research*, 50(5), pp. 535–545.

Mauri, A. G., & Minazzi, R. (2013). Web reviews influence on expectations and purchasing intentions of hotel potential customers. *International Journal of Hospitality Management*, 34(1), pp. 99–107.

Mellinas, J. P., Martínez, S.-M., & Bernal García, J. J. (2015). Booking.com: The unexpected scoring system. *Tourism Management*, 49(2015), pp. 72–74.

Mkono, M. (2012). A netnographic examination of constructive authenticity in Victoria Falls tourist (restaurant) experiences. *International Journal of Hospitality Management*, 31(2), pp. 387–394.

O'Connor, P. (2010). Managing a hotel's image on TripAdvisor. *Journal of Hospitality Marketing and Management*, 19(7), pp. 754–772.

Öğüt, H., & Onur Taş, B. K. (2012). The influence of internet customer reviews on the online sales and prices in hotel industry. *The Service Industries Journal*, 32(2), 197–214.

Pan, B., MacLaurin, T., & Crotts, J. C. (2007). Travel blogs and the implications for destination marketing. *Journal of Travel Research*, 46, pp. 35–45.

Pekar, V., & Ou, S. (2008). Discovery of subjective evaluations of product features in hotel reviews. *Journal of Vacation Marketing*, 14(2), pp. 145–156.

Pizam, A. (2014). Peer-to-peer travel: Blessing or blight?. *International Journal of Hospitality Management*, 38(2014), pp. 118–119.

Rifkin, J. (2011). *La Tercera Revolución Industrial*, Barcelona, Ed. Paidós.

Rifkin, J. (2014). *La sociedad de coste marginal cero: El Internet de las cosas, el procomún colaborativo y el eclipse del capitalismo*, Barcelona, Ed. Paidós.

Russo, A. P., & Quaglieri, A. (2014). La lógica espacial del intercambio de casas: una aproximación a las nuevas geografías de lo cotidiano en el turismo contemporáneo. *Scripta Nova Revista Electrónica de Geografía y Ciencias Sociales*, 17(483). Retrieved from www.ub.es/geocrit/sn/sn-483.htm

Serra-Cantallops, A., & Salvi, F. (2014). New consumer behavior: A review of research on eWOM and hotels. *International Journal of Hospitality Management*, 36, pp. 41–51.

Sparks, B. A., & Browning, V. (2011). The impact of online reviews on hotel booking intentions and perception of trust. *Tourism Management*, 32, pp. 1310–1323.

Toh, R. S., DeKay, C. F., & Raven, P. (2011). Travel planning: Searching for and booking hotels on the internet. *Cornell Hospitality Q*, 52(4), pp. 388–398.

Tunguz, T. (2011). The new market places: Peer to peer collaborative consumption. *MIT Entrepreneurship Review*. Retrieved October 14, 2014 from http://miter.mit.edu/articlenew-market-places-peer-peer-collaborative-consumption/

Verma, R. (2010). Customer choice modeling in hospitality services: A review of past research and discussion of some new applications. *Cornell Hospitality Q*, 51(4), 470–478.

Walsh, B. (2011). Today's smart choice: Don't own share. *Time Magazine Special Issue: 10 Ideas That Will Change the World*. Accessed online (May 19, 2017) at http://content.time.com/time/specials/packages/article/0,28804,2059521_2059717_2059710,00.html

Wen, I. (2009). Factors affecting the online travel buying decision: A review. *International Journal of Contemporary Hospitality Management*, 21(6), pp. 752–765.

Wikipedia. (2014). Sharing economy. Retrieved October 14, 2014 from www.wikipedia.org/wiki/Sharing economy

Wu, M. Y., & Pearce, P. L. (2014). Appraising netnography: towards insights about new markets in the digital tourist era. *Current Issues in Tourism*, 17(5), 463-474.

Xiang, Z., & Gretzel, U. (2010). Role of social media in online travel information search. *Tourism Management*, 31(2), pp. 179–188.

Xie, H. J., Miao, L., Kuo, P., & Lee, B. (2011). Consumers' responses to ambivalent online hotel reviews: The role of perceived source credibility and pre-decisional disposition. *IJHM*, 30, pp. 178–183.

Xie, K., Zhangb, Z., & Zhangb, Z. (2014). The business value of online consumer reviews and management response to hotel performance. *International Journal of Hospitality Management*, 43, pp. 1–12.

Yacouel, N., & Fleischer, A. (2011). The role of cybermediaries in reputation building and price premiums in the online hotel market. *Journal of Travel Research.*, 50(1), pp. 1–8.

Yoo, K. H., & Gretzel, U. (2008). What motivates consumers to write online travel reviews? *Information Technology & Tourism*, 10, pp. 283–295.

Yoon, Y., & Uysal, M. (2005). An examination of the effects of motivation and satisfaction on destination loyalty: A structural model. *Tourism Management*, 26(1), pp. 45–56.

Zehrer, A., Crotts, J. C., & Magnini, V. P. (2011). The perceived usefulness of blog postings: An extension of the expectancy-disconfirmation paradigm. *Tourism Management*, 32(1), pp. 106–113.

Zhou, L., Yea, S., Pearce, P. L., & Wua, M.-Y. (2014). Refreshing hotel satisfaction studies by reconfiguring customer review data. *International Journal of Hospitality Management*, 38, pp. 1–10.

14 Collaborative consumption as a feature of Gen-Y consumers

Rethinking youth tourism practices in the sharing economy

Wided Batat and Wafa Hammedi

Introduction

Sharing is not a new phenomenon, while collaborative consumption (Belk, 2014) has emerged thanks to technological innovations such as Web 2.0 and mobile apps; it was also facilitated by the economic recession in 2008, which had huge consequences in terms of economic insecurity, unemployment – especially for generation Y youth, along with the emergence of green consumption practices and a vision of a "new economy" that focuses on a more sustainable logic and collaborative practices enabled by connected and resilient communities. This "new economy" promises equal and high satisfaction, promotes sustainable and ecofriendly behaviors among communities, and empowers consumers through shifting the power from producers to consumers. Thus, "collaborative consumption" as introduced in the literature by Botsman and Rogers (2010) is the translation of connected consumption that creates a "new sharing economy" based on the idea of accessibility, second-hand goods, recycling, swapping etc. as an alternative way to owning goods beyond the traditional notion of private ownership. Internet-related collaborative consumption has transformed mobility, consumption practices and shopping, service provisions, work practices, travel and tourism experiences etc. This has led to the rise of alternative business models based on sharing services, goods and best practices in numerous consumption domains such as Freecycle, Skillshare, Zipcar, RelayRides and Citizen Space. In the tourism sector, connected consumption initiatives occur across sectors such as travel, accommodations, destinations, tours and experiences, food and catering.

Amongst the most popular connected tourism initiatives among Gen-Y consumers are: Airbnb, Couchsurfing, Wwoofing, HowToSwapCities, Vayable, Guidehop, and GrandTourGo. It is assumed that Gen-Y consumers are changing their consumption and tourism behaviors by becoming more collaboration-oriented since they realize that the old system is broken, and no longer holds the answer to all their consumption expectations. These Gen Y'ers are defined as digital natives (Tapscott, 2009; Palfrey and Gasser, 2008). They are born between 1981 and 2002. They are perceived as a unique generation with atypical consumption patterns that make them different from their predecessors, the Baby Boomers and Generation X. While Gen Y is the dominant and the largest living generation of consumers

(Pendergast, 2010), there is a lack of studies exploring Gen-Y internet-related collaborative consumption, especially in the field of tourism.

The objective of this chapter is thus to provide a comprehensive overview of Gen-Y collaborative consumption practices in tourism by introducing three main examples of connected consumption initiatives: Airbnb, Couchsurfing, and Wwoofing in order to explore the significance of these three modes of collaborative consumption, specifically focusing on the following dimensions: engagement, sharing, expertise and efficacy. This chapter first presents the existing literature on collaborative consumption. It then addresses the particularities of Gen-Y consumers living within a digital context and using technology and specifically the internet within their collaborative consumption experiences. Details regarding the analysis of the three connected collaborative consumption initiatives (Airbnb, Couchsurfing, and Wwoofing) are presented in this part. The last part of this chapter expands on collaborative consumption research by integrating Gen-Y practices and discussing the dark side of the sharing economy. This provides a useful guide to understanding Gen-Y collaborative consumption particularities and offers insights for tourism and marketing researchers as well as the tourism industry.

Collaborative consumption: towards a "new sharing economy"?

In recent years, a transition from ownership towards accessibility can be observed across a wide variety of markets. In contrast to a conventional situation where consumers would buy products and become the owners, in an accessibility-based system consumers pay for temporary access-rights to a product. Clearly this idea of commerce has already been dominant for many decades (probably even centuries for some goods and services), in the form of house or car renting services in B2C markets. Several initiatives based on access-business models have emerged and have introduced this business model as an alternative economy to the property economy. Different terminologies are used to refer to the phenomenon, such as sharing economy, collaborative consumption or access-based economy.

The rising interest in these initiatives is driven by several macroeconomic factors. One major factor is the decreasing consumer trust in the corporate world as a result of the financial and economic crisis. In addition, unemployment rates have risen and the purchasing power of consumers has dropped. Therefore, people are in need of new ways to earn or save money, which is why consumers are currently more receptive to peer-to-peer business models centered on consumer needs both as a potential supplier and buyer. Furthermore, the required technology for hosting an online peer-to-peer market has, in recent years, become available at more reasonable cost. There is also an environmental argument which has contributed to the emergence of the sharing economy. Indeed, environmental issues emphasize the coming out of a new consumer who believes that the more he/she shares consumption items and services, the fewer earth resources will be consumed. This allows more efficient and sustainable modes of consumption. The Internet has made the sharing enormously simpler and for the consumer, it seems to hold the potential to unite cost reduction, benefit augmentation, convenience and environ-mental consciousness in one mode of consumption.

As a result, the potential of the sharing economy is significant. While estimates for the current size of the nascent market vary, some studies have estimated that by 2025 the five main sectors of the sharing economy could represent $335 billion (Pricewaterhouse Coopers, 2015). The speed of growth with which sharing sys-tems have spread would suggest also that this new trend might represent an impor-tant threat to established industries.

Sharing economy, collaborative consumption, and access-based models

Moving from a traditional ownership model to a shared consumption model requires a deeper understanding of what differentiates these consumption modes. Traditionally, consumers are motivated to own products and services as they are considered as a way to confirm, extend or even modify their self-identification throughout their purchase and consumption. Therefore, owning things has always been considered as an identification act (Belk, 1988). The consumer-objects rela-tionship is therefore considered to be strong, long-term, and symbolic. The new emerging consumption trend refers to sharing as anything to which access is enabled through pooling of resources, products or services (Bardhi & Eckhardt, 2012). In contrast to the long-term possession model, sharing is supposed to be temporary and a circumstantial consumption context (Chen, 2009).

While the traditional ownership model has been extensively explored in various disciplines, the sharing model and its underlying processes, governance modes and consumer motives remain not well understood in the literature. Many terms are often used interchangeably in the literature and also by companies when establish-ing systems that take their roots from the sharing economy and may look similar but fundamentally they are not. In the tourism sector, multiple initiatives refer to different types of collaborative consumption. Thus, the question that came to our mind is to understand how and to which extent tourism initiatives such as Airbnb, Couchsurfing, and Wwoofing would be considered sharing initiatives among Gen-Y consumers. Defining clearly the concepts of sharing, collaborative con-sumption, and access-based consumption could help us to better differentiate shar-ing initiatives from mainstream consumption practices and analyze them more deeply within Gen-Y tourism practices.

Sharing involves the act and process of distributing what is ours to others for their use and or the act and process of receiving or taking something from others for our use (Belk, 2007). Some authors even define sharing as "nonreciprocal pro-social" behavior (Benkler, 2004). Two reasons seem to be behind such behavior; either functional reasons such as survival or mainly altruism. Prior studies high-lighted that sharing is more likely to occur within family, close kin and friends than among strangers, which might also be referred to as "sharing in" as defined by Belk (2014). When sharing involves exchanging something between strangers, it is then called "sharing out" (Schor & Fitzmaurice, 2015).

The second term used in sharing studies is *collaborative consumption*. This concept was originally defined as one or more persons consuming economic goods or services in the course of engaging in joint activities with one or more others (Felson & Speath, 1978). Despite its focus on the joint-activity, the definition remains broad since it does not focus enough on the acquisition and distribution of any resource(s). This definition mainly emphasizes the coordination of consumption at a particular time and place, but the consumption act could be subject to a transaction/market exchange. Therefore, the recent contribution of Belk by defining collaborative consumption as "people coordinating the acquisition and distribution of a resource for a fee or other compensation" (Belk, 2014, p. 1597) appears to be more accurate and complete and helps to better differentiate the concept "collaborative consumption" from "sharing" and "access-based models". The presence of compensation (either monetary or non-monetary) makes collaborative consumption slightly different from sharing. Therefore, bartering, trading and swapping could also be considered as collaborative consumption activities.

The third term used in sharing studies is *Access-based models (or internet-facilitated sharing)*. Since common access is similar to sharing, it does not require a transfer of ownership (Bardhi and Eckhart, 2012). Yet, access may differ from sharing in that access is not necessarily altruistic or prosocial and requires the presence of either an economic exchange or reciprocity. The existing literature emphasizes the important shift in the property regimes to more access-based regimes characterized by short-term limited use of assets controlled by networks of suppliers. Access-based models have also existed in other forms of sharing mainly in non-profit or public sectors like borrowing books, or consuming art by museum visitors (Chen, 2009) and are derived from traditional rental forms in the marketplace like car or apartment rentals.

Yet, very little attention has been paid to access as a mode of consumption. Indeed, through accessibility-based systems, consumers are increasingly paying for temporary access-rights to a product or a service. Within these accessibility-based business models, there is a trend towards peer-to-peer platforms that enable consumers to access consumer-owned property or competencies. For instance the peer-to-peer car sharing company Getaround that allows people to borrow cars from others in the US, or the platform called Fon that enables people to share some of their home Wi-Fi network in exchange for getting free Wi-Fi from anyone of the 7 million people in Fon's network, are good examples of this emerging trend. Companies can facilitate peer-to-peer markets for nearly all assets or services owned by peers. Thus, the role of companies has shifted from value provider towards creating a match between a peer owning a certain resource and a peer in need of that resource, at the right time and against reasonable transaction costs.

Since today's consumer society is characterized by the sharing economy enabled by a digital context where most consumers are young and digital natives, it is important to explore the intersection of collaborative consumption with the practices among youth consumers, namely Gen-Y consumers who have been defined as a "collaborative generation" which is very comfortable in using sharing platforms in the process of their consumption experiences and especially during travel activities.

Exploring the intersection of collaborative consumption and Gen-Y digital practices

Gen-Y youth are considered as a "collaborative generation" since their consumption behaviors are based on sharing information, products and services among their peer community and with other consumers. Digital equipment, the internet and social media are part of today's Gen-Y consumption culture, and allow collaborative behaviors in various consumption fields such as tourism and hospitality. In this section, we first define the generational approach and the main consumption characteristics of Gen-Y consumers. Then, Gen-Y use of technology and digital equipment for collaborative practices is introduced. This leads us to a deeper understanding of the co-creation process that is at the heart of collaborative consumption.

Gen-Y tourists: a generational approach

The logic of "generation" or "generation gap" is not a new idea; the first publication is dated from the 1950s in the work of Karl Mannheim (1952) in sociology through his revolutionary concept of "Generational Theory" (GT). The notion of "generation" is a multi-dimensional concept defined by different stakeholders: demographers, media and journalists, popular culture, marketers, consumer researchers and the members of the generation themselves (Fields et al., 2008; Pendergast, 2007). Despite the number of competing versions legitimate for theorizing using the GT framework (Pendergast, 2010), Mannheim's generational theory is still popular and supported within recent research on the "generational effect" in the humanities (Donnison, 2007; Huntley, 2006). The sociological approach of Mannheim's GT, as recalled by Namer (2006), emphasizes the link that constructs a generation (born within the same generation) and the generation unit, which is composed of elements that structured this link. Mannheim underlines the acceleration of the process related to the emergence of new generations due to the succession of increasingly rapid changes that characterize the contemporary era.

The main objective of the GT is to understand and characterize cohorts of people according to their membership within a generation, which might be objectively identified through the year of birth. The features of a generation are defined according to a dynamic approach derived from a socio-cultural theoretical framework encompassing a large and a collective perspective rather than an individual focus. This approach goes beyond individuals as it allows shaping patterns, cultural tendencies and consumption practices across the whole generational group. In the most thorough examination of generations within the multidisciplinary literature to date, Attias-Donfut (1991) argued that the concept of generation refers to four dimensions:

- A demographical dimension which includes all individuals within the same age range/group;
- A genealogical and familial dimension (parents/children);

- A historical dimension (the average time for a person to get old enough to be autonomous and get involved within the adult society);
- A sociological dimension, which represents a generational cohort or a group of individuals sharing a set of certain practices and representations as they have approximately the same age and consequently have lived at the same time.

Pendergast (2010) identifies six main living generations within today's consumer society according to the birth year and the age range in 2011: GI Generation, Silent Generation, Baby Boomer, Gen X, Generation Y, and Generation Z. Based on Howe and Strauss's (2000) updated definition of generational theory, Pendergast (2009) classified the three principal living generations according to various elements in order to establish the key features of each generation:

- The Baby Boomer generation is identified as an idealist generation (e.g. Civil Rights movement) entering elderhood. The members of this generation are policy makers and dominate many leadership positions, both in private and public sectors. Their work and life philosophy are based on a strong work ethic, respect of authority and waiting for their turn for promotion, which is traditionally based on experience and seniority;
- The X Generation members who are in the midlife phase of their life cycle follow the Baby Boomers. In contrast to the members of the Baby Boomer Generation who are optimistic, Gen X members are regarded as pessimistic and depressed compared to the energy and the enthusiasm of the idealist generation of Baby Boomers. As Gen X members enter the power phase in their work, they have more responsibilities and leadership positions. Their work philosophy differs from Baby Boomers, as they prefer cooperative leadership and team spirit within their workplace;
- Following Gen X, Generation Y members or "Gen Y'ers" are the next living generation in the life cycle. They are the dominant and the largest current generation within the marketplace and society since the Baby Boomers (Sweeney, 2005). In 2009, Gen Y'ers represented about 25% of the total of the American population (Mature Market Institute, 2009) and will comprise 34% of the American population by 2015, being far more diverse than their parents were before them. Generation Y members are defined as a hero generation with civic pride, and are featured as conventional and committed.

Besides, Gen-Y youth are generally considered as team-oriented with a focus on their feelings within their workplace and life experiences. They are empowered and digital experts because of the characteristics of the digital society in which they live. Gen-Y members use their new knowledge to improve their work experience and their social life. Thus, Generation Y is recognized as a producer of influential international business leaders (e.g. Facebook founder Mark Zuckerberg). These hero leaders are *collaborative* and *interactive* which fits with the Gen-Y profile and makes them unique in terms of social behaviors and consumption practices.

The emergence of this generation of young consumers raises questions about the continuity and the rupture of consumption and tourism practices, leisure activities, and lifestyle. Gen Y'ers are believed to have unique characteristics that make them different from preceding generations (Wolburg & Pokrywczynski, 2001). This makes understanding the behaviors, perceptions and aspirations of Gen-Y consumers important, particularly in the tourism field since it is the first generation immersed within a digital context where Gen-Y tourists are more eager to engage in multitasking and using collaborative and interactive modes of consumption enabled by social media (Bardhi et al., 2010).

Gen-Y tourists' collaborative consumption in a digital society

Gen-Y tourists are the first generation who has been immersed within a high tech landscape where the internet and social media represent an integral part of their practices and are used for different purposes such as posting pictures and comments, socializing, fun, sharing tourism experiences and exchanging information about products, tourism destinations and services etc. Authors such as Prensky (2001) refer to Gen Y'ers as digital natives and Gen X'ers as digital immigrants. For Prensky (2006) Gen-Y youth are native speakers of the "digital language" of computers, the internet, social media and video games. While Gen Xers are considered overall as very techno-savvy, Gen Y'ers have been intertwined with the internet and mobile phones (Simões & Gouveia, 2008). These digital natives adapt faster to computer and internet services because they have always had them (Batat, 2008). The internet gives them more freedom and independence. It is also practical in terms of searching information, as they expect speed, convenience, flexibility and power provided by digital devices (Sweeney, 2005).

Furthermore, the internet has had a profound influence on their views of consumption and communication as they have become accustomed to the instant and immediate nature of the Web (Sweeney, 2005). Having used these technologies since childhood, Gen-Y tourists/consumers develop typical behaviors such as multitasking, which is a way of life within this generation. Gen-Y youth develop coping mechanisms to deal with their impatience and accelerate their learning, thus permitting them to accomplish more than one task at the same time (Sweeney, 2005). Being efficient in an abundant society means that Gen Y'ers have to search for new opportunities to update their knowledge and avoid missing information (Pew Research Center, 2007). Thus, Gen Y consumers make considerable efforts to regain control by generating new and creative knowledge that might be a source of value and a competitive advantage for companies. Vargo and Lusch (2008) refer to this mechanism as a co-creation of value based on the participation of the consumer who is supposed to be active, competent and empowered (Bonnemaizon & Batat, 2011).

Considering Gen-Y tourists/consumers as co-producers or co-creators of value has changed the marketing way of thinking from top-down to bottom-up. Generation Y is considered as a "Collaboration Generation" (Sweeney, 2005). Indeed, Gen Y'ers are active producers of user-generated content that can contribute to the co-creation of value by activating their digital skills and knowledge to shape the company's offers (Cermak et al., 1994). With the democratization of digital products and the easy access to the internet on mobile devices such as smartphones, new behaviors in terms of creation, collaboration, and sharing information on touristic consumption practices and tourism destinations have emerged among online-connected communities. Gen-Y consumers who are co-producers of content have become more influential and are often seen as valuable and authentic sources of information for industries and consumers. It is then important to understand the main characteristics of Gen-Y collaborative consumption and the use of the internet within youth consumption and tourism experiences. The next section will focus on the analysis of three popular collaborative consumption initiatives among Gen-Y tourists: Airbnb, Couchsurfing, and Wwoofing in order to explore the meanings of collaborative consumption and the dimensions of engagement, sharing, expertise and efficacy in Gen-Y collaborative consumption in tourism.

Gen-Y and tourism-related sharing initiatives

Travel and hospitality involve an inherently social experience that is temporary by nature. Thus, it lends itself perfectly to either access-based models or peer-to-peer (P2P) economy models where people interact (in)-directly with each other to get temporary access to assets instead of owning them. For instance, travel is an industry that has taken a big opportunity to rethink the way travel happens. Accommodation (e.g. Airbnb, Couchsurfing, etc.) and transportation services (Zipcar, Blablacar etc.) have done extremely well in this new sharing consumption model. New businesses have emerged and contributed to reshaping parts of how the travel and tourism industry operate within a youth marketplace characterized by sharing principles and enabled by advances in mobile technologies and an increasing trust in the internet and online payments. As a consequence, the tourism and hospitality sector has been the arena of sharing practices, especially for Gen-Y tourists who use sharing tourism platforms in order to organize their trip, book their room, socialize etc. without getting in touch with tourism professionals and thus escaping the mainstream economy of tourism. The following tourism sharing platforms depict some examples of sharing initiatives that are very popular among Gen-Y consumers and cover the most important part within tourism experiences, namely accommodation. Finding accommodation can be accomplished in different ways by Gen-Y tourists through the three sharing tourism platforms selected in this study: Airbnb, Couchsurfing and Wwoofing.

In this section, we mainly focus on the analysis of the top three popular sharing initiatives among the Generation Y in the tourism sector. Their underlying mechanisms and dimensions will be explained in order to gain a better understanding of their positioning regarding tourism-sharing typologies. Through these three sharing examples, we will introduce the main dimensions of collaborative consumption and sharing activities associated with each accommodation sharing platform: market mediation, consumer involvement, anonymity and temporality.

Airbnb as a functional tool for collaborative consumption among Gen-Y tourists

Airbnb is a community marketplace where guests can book accommodations from a list of verified hosts. Membership to the site is completely free and there is no cost to post a listing. Using a targeted user interface designed to narrow down travelling preferences, Airbnb offers an attractive, cost-saving alternative to traditional hotel bookings and vacation home rentals. Upon finding a desired listing, guests are prompted to sign up for membership, which provides access to contact the host directly as well as to payment information for a request. Only once the host accepts the transaction and the guest checks in is the credit card charged, along with a 6–12% transaction fee from Airbnb.

The process is similarly simple for hosts, who receive a notification once a guest indicates interest in a particular listing and who have the option to approve or deny the transaction. Once the listing is booked, the host receives the payment, and Airbnb takes a 3% transaction fee. In this sense, Airbnb could be classified as an access-based system which is fully market-mediated, targeting functional needs. Its success relies on the social access and the extensive involvement of its members, especially Gen-Y tourists looking for cheap opportunities by escaping the mainstream tourism accommodation offers. For hosts, Airbnb is a source of benefit since it allows the owners to share and/or rent out their property.

The Airbnb marketplace includes a reputation system to build trust and reliability among market participants. In particular, the longstanding review system lets renters read about hosts before submitting a reservation request. Similarly, hosts can read about renters before accepting. Among the dimensions of this collaborative consumption system, Airbnb reflects the dimension of "market mediation" that underlines that sharing access is mainly for profit. In so doing, Gen-Y tourists try to optimize their purchase process and get an economic benefit through the use of Airbnb, which is considered as no more than a website allowing for the booking of other interesting economical options. This practice emphasizes the functional dimension related to the use of Airbnb among Gen-Y consumers who are always looking for bargains, or even free accommodation. Moreover, getting more economical accommodation on Airbnb allows them to arrange long travel that may cost a lot compared to their accommodation. This sharing activity leads Gen-Y tourists to travel for longer and stay longer without getting in touch with tourism professionals.

Another dimension that shapes sharing activities on Airbnb is "anonymity". This dimension shapes the relationship with and behavior toward other consumers. Anonymous access does not need any interactions with other consumers accessing the same object before or after them. The traditional hotel hosting system relies on sharing infrastructure by the tourists but no interaction before or after the holidays is necessary. By booking a hotel room, consumers gain exclusive access to the accommodation but do not need or want to have interactions with other tourists accessing the same hotel. Instead, sharing services such as Airbnb require more social access where interactions with other online consumers to get their feedback about the accommodation they have already experienced is more important and interactions happen with the host during and sometimes even after the experience.

Couchsurfing as part of Gen-Y tourism social experiences

Couchsurfing is the practice of sleeping overnight on a couch in the houses of friends or fellow members of a social network. This trend illustrates the sharing initative which is supposed to be a non-market-mediated system since it relies on the high involvement of consumers and requires social access before and after the experience. The stage "after the experience" is very important to assess the experience, which might be positive or negative. Indeed, couchsurfers have to learn to adjust to being in someone else's space, learn trusting, being less fearful and more open and relaxed as if they are with long-time friends or even family. Although there is no monetary exchange and the couchsurfing experience is technology-mediated through the platform, the cost is minimal and exchanges can be beneficial for both the couchsurfer and the host. For example, spending some of the money saved on food to share or bringing a gift from home.

The dimension of consumer involvement is another compoment of collaborative consumption and represents an integral part of Couchsurfing, which usually involves a high level of interactions with the host. For instance, the traditional rental models represent a good example of sharing services characterized by low consumer involvement. Couchsurfing does require extensive involvement because it is based on shared values, social interactions, socialization, shared center of interests etc. The dimension of "consumer involvement" in Couchsurfing sharing accommodations is expected to affect the experience in a positive way. With this form of sharing economy, the interest of Gen-Y young tourists goes beyond economical aspects of their travel; it is indeed based on the willingness to engage in authentic friendship and to socialize, get together with locals, discover the destination through the eyes of locals and developing new friendships around the world. The focus is then on new human experience, social interactions and authentic discovery of the destination.

Wwoofing as a form of collaborative consumption among responsible Gen-Y tourists

Originally called "Working Weekends on Organic Farms", there are a number of new sharing economy companies offering lodging in exchange for volunteer work. WWOOF is a farm volunteering and hosting system based on exchange of labor for food/accommodation. The presence of compensation here, even if non-monetary, makes this a "market-mediated initiative" and illustrates a collaborative consumption model rather than a sharing model. The role of the Wwoofing platform is to connect people who want to volunteer on organic farms with people who are seeking volunteer help. Volunteers work for free and in return, hosts provide food, lodging and learning opportunities about organic farming. Since Wwoofing does not require reciprocity, this makes this practice more representative of collaborative consumption rather than of sharing. Beyond the dimension of market mediation, Wwoofing is also considered as an ethical and engaged way of travel. The motivations of Gen-Y tourists to wwoof mainly emerge from their system of values and pro-environmental behaviors. Wwoofing allows them to learn more about sustainable agriculture practices and other food cultures.

To sum up, these three examples of popular accommodation sharing platforms among Gen-Y tourists highlighted different collaborative and sharing dimensions but they all have one dimension in common: "temporality". This dimension captures the long-term/short-term access and interaction with the object. Access can be longitudinal where a membership in a community or a club is required (e.g. Zipcar) or short-term characterized by a one-time transaction like renting a car or a hotel. The second aspect related to the usage could vary from a long-term usage to hourly usage. In tourism the traditional holiday timeshare is to some extent a good example of encompassing long-term or short-term sharing initiatives depending on tourists' motivations. Table 14.1 shows the differences between these three sharing platforms and the motivations of Gen-Y tourists in terms of collaborative consumption and sharing activities.

Towards collaborative tourism for Gen-Y: managerial implications

Applications based on collaborative consumption enabled by technology, the internet, and social media are having major impacts on tourism. The shift from old business models to collaborative and creative ways of ownership, participating and coproducing constitutes a new reality that tourism professionals and marketers should consider when targeting the "collaborative generation" of Gen-Y tourists. This generation will always consider new and creative ways to get items and travel for free/low cost. Besides, this "free generation" is also considered to be engaged, responsible, ethical and in search of tourism destinations, products and services that fit with its own value system. Therefore, tourism professionals and marketers who are charging Generation Y tourists for items and services that these consumers with some effort may get for free are losing value because they fail to capture this segment of the market.

According to PhoCusWright (2014), the huge interest of Generation Y in the collaborative initiatives – around 25% of Gen-Y travellers will use collaborative platforms for their travels compared to only 8% of Gen X – refocuses the debate about what is highly valued by consumers and what service companies should offer. This segment seems to be very interested in the basic service (e.g. transportation, lodging) and not in sophisticated service which explains their acceptance of amateur service providers as they devote more attention to the social aspect of their service consumption. Professionals might therefore take advantage of this trend by rethinking and redesigning their offerings to make them less sophisticated and invest more in enhancing the social and interactive aspects of their business.

Table 14.1 Collaborative consumption and sharing tourism website usages among Gen-Y
tourists

Sharing platforms	Airbnb	Couchsurfing	Wwoofing
Collaborative dimensions	Market mediation Anonymity Temporality (short stay)	Consumer involvement Temporality (short stay)	Market mediation Temporality (short stay)
Gen-Y motivations	Functional needs Economic benefit Travel optimization	Social needs Shared experiences Authenticity Socialization	Values Engagement and ethics Pro-environmental behaviors
Typology of sharing practices	Access-based model	Collaborative consumption Co-creating experiences	Collaborative consumption Sharing ideologies and workforce

Conclusion

Social technologies radically disrupted consumer behavior and therefore require changes in marketing. Thanks to digital tools consumers are increasingly empowered and tend to make optimal use of the various digital platforms to not just share their activities and opinions but also products and services. We are therefore experiencing early indicators of the important shift toward a more collaborative economy, which is expected to impact every sector of society and business. Sharing is quickly spreading; customers have access to rooms, cars and bikes, ad hoc taxi services (e.g. Uber). Despite the advantages offered by these emergent business models to their users, these initiatives could raise several problems to the existing traditional–based businesses operating in those markets. These alternative consumption models could threaten the existing businesses, as they might be disintermediated very rapidly. The increasing powerful crowd is expected to facilitate peer-to peer transactions by allowing a monetization of consumers' assets and purchase from each other directly at lower costs and sometimes in more convenient ways. This flexibility and cost reduction offered by these alternative models will compete directly with the existing corporations that might perceive collaborative-based businesses as illegal and unfair. In some countries, sharing initiatives are considered as illegal and even have been deemed as criminal behavior. The case of ride-sharing Uber in several countries (e.g. France, Netherlands and Spain) illustrates the conflict with existing companies in the transport sector. The taxi service providers had objections against what is considered as unethical and unfair competition by the ride-sharing service company. Uber encountered heavy fines and legal threats in many countries and was even banned and considered as illegal activity in many of them.

Traditional corporations are also complaining about the lack of regulation of these emerging businesses. Accordingly, this problem of regulation seems to be strongly linked to other issues like safety and service quality control, which are prevalent in the service industry. For instance, the European trade association of hotels, restaurants and cafés (www.hotrec.eu), in their recent report of priority actions for EU tourism 2015, has emphasized that these issues, which were qualified as priority problems for European tourism professionals, need to be solved. The tourism professionals go even further to qualify some of the sharing initiatives as representative of the so-called shadow tourism economy.

References

Attias-Donfut, C. (1991). *Générations et Ages de la Vie*, Paris: PUF.

Bardhi, F., & Eckhardt, G. (2012). Access-based xonsumption: The case of car sharing. *Journal of Consumer Research*, 39, pp. 881–898.

Bardhi, F., Rohm, A. J., & Sultan, F. (2010). Tuning in and tuning out: Media multitasking among young consumers. *Journal of Consumer Behaviour*, 9(4), pp. 316–332.

Batat, W. (2008). Exploring adolescent development skills through internet usage: A study of French 11–15 year olds. *International Journal of Consumer Studies*, 32(4), pp. 379–381.

Belk, R. (1988). Possessions and the extended self. *Journal of Consumer Research*, 15(September), pp. 139–168.

Belk, R. (2007). Why not share rather than own? *Annals of the American Academy of Political and Social Science*, 611(1), 126–140.

Belk, R. (2014). You are what you can access: Sharing and collaborative consumption online. *Journal of Business Research*, 67(8), pp. 1595–1600.

Benkler, Y. (2004). Sharing nicely: On shareable goods and the emergence of sharing as a modality of economic production. *Yale Law Journal*, 114, pp. 273–358.

Bonnemaizon, A., & Batat, W. (2011). How competent are consumers? The case of the energy sector in France. *International Journal of Consumer Studies*, 5(34), pp. 348–358.

Botsman, R., & Rogers, R. (2010). *What's Mine Is Yours: The Rise of Collaborative Consumption*, New York, Harper Collins.

Cermak, D., File, K. M., & Prince, R. A. (1994). Customer participation in service specification and delivery. *Journal of Applied Business Research*, 10(2), pp. 90–98.

Chen, Y. (2009). Possession and access: Consumer desires and value perceptions regarding contemporary art collection and exhibit visits. *Journal of Consumer Research*, 35(April), 925–940.

Donnison, S. (2007). Unpacking the millennial's: A cautionary tale for teacher education. *Australian Journal of Teacher Education*, 32(3), pp. 1–13.

Felson, M., & Speath, J. (1978). Community structure and collaborative consumption. *American Behavioral Scientist*, 41, pp. 614–624.

Fields, B., Wilder, S., Bunch, J., & Newbold, R. (2008). *Millennial Leaders: Success Stories from Today's Most Brilliant Generation Y Leaders*, Australia, Ingram Publishing Services.

Howe, N., & Strauss, W. (2000). *Millennial's Rising: The Next Great Generation*, New York, Vintage Books.

Huntley, R. (2006). *The World According to Y*, Crows Nest, Australia, Allen & Unwin.

Mannheim, K. (1952). *Essays on the Sociology of Knowledge*, London, Routledge & Kegan Paul.

Mature Market Institute. (2009). Demographic profile America's Gen Y. Retrieved from www.metlife.com/assets/cao/mmi/publications/Profiles/mmi-gen-y-demographic-profile.pdf

Namer, G. (2006). *Karl Mannheim, Sociologue de la Connaissance: La Synthèse Humaniste ou le Chaos de l'Absolu*, Paris, L'Harmattan.

Palfrey, J., & Gasser, U. (2008). *Born Digital: Understanding the First Generation of Digital Natives*, New York, Basic Books.

Pendergast, D. (2007). The MilGen and society. In N. Bahr & D. Pendergast (eds.) *The Millennial Adolescent*. Camberwell, Victoria, Australian Council for Educational Research, pp. 23–40.

Pendergast, D. (2009). Generational theory and home economics: Future proofing the profession. *Family and Consumer Sciences Research Journal*, 37(4), pp. 504–522.

Pendergast, D. (2010). Getting to know the Y Generation. In P. Benckendorff, G. Moscardo, & D. Pendergast (eds.) *Tourism and Generation Y*. Australia, CABI Publisher, pp. 1–16.

Pew Research Centre. (2007). Teens and Social Media. Retrieved from www.pewinternet. org/PPF/r/230/report_display.asp

PhoCusWright. (2014). Share this! Private accommodation & the rise of the new gen renter. Retrieved from http://veilletourisme.ca/2014/11/12/comportement-en-ligne-des-voyageurs-dairbnb/

Prensky, M. (2001). *Digital Natives, Digital Immigrants*, Australia: Horizon MCB University Press.

Prensky, M. (2006). Listen to the natives. *Educational Leadership*, 63(4), pp. 8–13.

Pricewaterhouse Coopers. (2015). The sharing economy. Retrieved from http://download. pwc.com/ie/pubs/2015-pwc-cis-sharing-economy.pdf

Schor, J. B., & Fitzmaurice, C. (2015). Collaborating and connecting: The emergence of a sharing economy. In L. Reisch & J. Thogersen (eds.) *Handbook on Research on Sustainable Consumption*. Cheltenham, UK, Edward Elgar, pp. 410–425.

Simões, L., & Gouveia, L. B. (2008). Consumer behaviour of the millennial generation. Paper presented at the 3rd Conference III Jornadas de Publicidade e Comunicação. A Publicidade para o consumidor do Séc. XXI, UFP, Porto.

Sweeney, R. (2005). Reinventing library buildings and services for the millennial generation. *Library Administration and Management*, 19, pp. 165–176.

Tapscott, D. (2009). *Grown Up Digital: How the Net Generation is Changing Your World*, New York, NY: McGraw Hill.

Vargo, S. L., & Lusch, R. F. (2008). Service-dominant logic: Continuing the Evolution. *Journal of the Academy of Marketing Science*, 36(1), pp. 1–10.

Wolburg, J. M., & Pokrywczynski, J. (2001). A psychographic analysis of Generation Y college students. *Journal of Advertising Research*, 41(5), pp. 33–53.

15 Have social networks changed travellers' waiting experience?

An exploratory study on the airport sector

Laura Di Pietro, Roberta Guglielmetti Mugion, Maria Francesca Renzi, Martina Toni and Marianna Sigala

Introduction

As recognized by Watson et al. (2002), because of the need – from both companies' and consumers' points of view – for ubiquitous, universal and simultaneous access to information/services and their personalized exchange (Di Pietro et. al., 2015), the increasing use of Social Networks (SNs) by travellers seems to be an interesting topic to investigate. Indeed, SNs represent an additional way besides the traditional opportunities/possibilities to generally occupy or fill free time, leisure time and/or idle time. Specifically, during the travel experience, travellers have several moments' time in which they have to wait for some operations necessary for their trip; they have waiting, idle and spare times.

Because of the lack of studies focused on whether and how SNs are changing waiting time during the travel experience, the present chapter is aimed at studying the above relation by focusing on airport travellers. Airports represent a complex context, rich in explanatory power for studying travellers' motivation. Our study proposes a qualitative approach in order to investigate travellers' insights in using SNs during waiting times at the airport, aiming to uncover additional opportunities for researchers and practitioners. Hence, we conducted qualitative interviews focused on airport travellers, analyzing how and why they use SNs during their waiting times at the airport. In the present study, we detected insights and constructs that embody motivations while passengers are waiting. Indeed, to acquire knowledge on these aspects represents a focal point to develop innovative services, simultaneously generating benefits for both companies and travellers. This chapter is organized as follows. The first part contains a theoretical background on the waiting times at the airport and as a psychological and social experience of individuals. A methodology is presented in the second part, followed by a section on the results. The final parts of the paper contain a discussion, conclusions and ideas for future research.

The evolution of the waiting times experience

As a main premise, the waiting time can be defined as the time from which a customer is ready to receive a service until the time the service commences (Taylor, 1994), and it is a common aspect of many service experiences; for this reason, waiting experience should be seen as part of the overall service package (Jones & Hwang, 2005). Thus, waiting time, including processing time, crowding and the availability of passenger amenities for comfort and convenience are measures of service-level components (Brunetta et al., 1999). As highlighted by many authors, waiting time can be considered frustrating, stressful and expensive (Jones & Hwang, 2005; Van Riel et al., 2006). As confirmed by Martín-Cejas, (2006), the average waiting time is a relevant aspect of the quality perception of tourists when arriving at their destination. This factor is difficult to measure; thus, it can be evaluated in a subjective manner. In the case of waiting, subjective time refers to how individuals perceive and feel about the length of a time period (Baker & Cameron, 1996). From a subjective perspective, customers frequently overestimate the amount of time they spend waiting (Hornik, 1984; Katz et al., 1991), and as the perception of waiting time increases, customer satisfaction tends to decrease (Katz et al., 1991). Past studies have enhanced the relevance of the gap between actual and perceived waiting times, highlighting the importance of reducing the latter rather than the former. As many authors stated, this gap is important not only for fulfilling operational efficiency (Hall, 1991; Canel & Kadipasaoglu, 2002; Ittig, 2002; Mantel & Kellaris, 2003; Sheu et al., 2003; Luo et al., 2004), but also from the customer satisfaction perspective (Smidts & Pruyn, 1994; Hornik & Zakay, 1996; Davis & Heineke, 1998; Antonides et al., 2002; Luo et al., 2004) because the perceived waiting time is a more accurate predictor of customer satisfaction (Nie, 2000) and extended waiting and delays are considered to be relevant sources of customer dissatisfaction (Dubé et al., 1991; Maister, 1985; Taylor, 1994; Taylor & Claxton, 1994; Murdick et al., 1990). For this reason, many companies in the airline industries have included waiting time as a measure of service quality (Sheu & Babbar, 1996).

As highlighted by Jones and Hwang (2005), perceptions of waiting time can be influenced by variables such as the length of a queue (Nie, 2000; Rafaeli et al., 2002; Baker & Cameron, 1996), the number of people behind a person in the queue (Zhou & Soman, 2003), the level of interest in the activity designed to occupy time (Nie, 2000), the rate of queue movement (Nie, 2000; Baker & Cameron, 1996), spatial layout (Baker & Cameron, 1996), social interactions (Baker & Cameron, 1996) and the level of comfort while waiting, as uncomfortable waits feel longer than comfortable waits (Davis & Heineke, 1998). The perception could depend on the mood, and individuals in negative moods pay more attention to the passage of time, while the contrary effect is found among people in positive moods, who enjoy the experience (Hornik, 1984). Moreover, a study by Jones and Hwang (2005) demonstrated that as a wait time becomes longer, the perceived time increase varies depending on the context.

However, the level of overestimation may be reduced if a person's time is occupied while waiting (Groth & Gilliland, 2001; Luo et al., 2004). Time perception may be influenced by internal states such as affect, that is, reactions to external stimuli in the physical environment (Poynter, 1989). As indicated by Baker and Cameron's study (1996), affect mediates the influence of the service environment on the perception of waiting time indirectly through the degree of filled time. The degree of filled time is a construct based on the cognitive timer model that states that empty time with no distractions will seem longer than time filled doing something, on the basis of the principle of "keeping people occupied" because filled time passes more quickly than empty time (McGrath & Kelly, 1986). The waiting experience can be improved by keeping people busy and distracted while waiting (Maister, 1985). Taylor (1994, 1995) examined the link between the attribution and degree of filled time and the perception of wait time. Two ways to fill the time for waiting consumers are social interaction and distraction (Baker & Cameron, 1996), and researchers have explored various ways of influencing customers' perceived waiting time, including changing the service environment (Katz et al., 1991), engaging customers during the wait (Dubé & Schmitt, 1996) and providing feedback about expected waiting time (Hui & Zhou, 1996).

Katz et al. (1991) found that distractions during waiting experiences tend to make waiting more enjoyable and reduce dissatisfaction with waiting (Kumar et al., 1997). Technologies such as the internet possess interactive, social and informational dimensions that can engage users during waiting times. Social media illustrate specific motives related to waiting times identified by several authors (Schutz, 1958; Flaherty et al., 1998): interpersonal/communication needs such as escape, relaxation and pleasure; needs traditionally fulfilled by media such as social interaction, passing time, habit, information and entertainment; and other needs such as time shifting and meeting people.

Currently, consumers have more freedom to use social media wherever and whenever they want due to the ubiquity of the internet; concerning the use of social media, Matthew and Soumitra (2008) suggested two groups of motives: rational motives that are connected with career striving, sharing knowledge and information and the irrational motives that include the need for social relations, acceptance and being a part of social communities. In the specific case of the travel experience, SNs can bring several benefits to passengers. At first, SNs can engage users during the wait, given that empty time with no distraction seems longer than time filled with something interesting (Baker & Cameron, 1996) and that the more someone pays attention to the passage of time, the slower it seems to pass (Hornik, 1984). However, at the same time, the presence of other people in a service setting can be intrusive and can generate negative affect (Baker & Cameron, 1996); thus, the internet is a functional alternative for people who do not find face-to-face communication rewarding (Papacharissi & Rubin, 2000). Hence, SNs can represent a suitable solution for reducing the perceived time because they engage users and allow them go "elsewhere" online if there is an uncomfortable situation due to crowded space. People look for social interaction, and regardless of whether users are accompanied, the internet and social media can allow people waiting in line to interact by discussing the wait, sharing frustration and finding consolation (Baker & Cameron, 1996) with their online network. The possibility of interaction with other people in a positive way allows people to fill the time in distracting and entertaining ways (Baker & Cameron, 1996), and group waiting increases customers' tolerance for waiting time because it distracts people from paying attention to the time (Maister, 1985).

Indeed, other studies noted that people feel more comfortable in group waiting rather than waiting alone because, as Maister (1985) stated, group waiting distracts people from paying attention to the time. Hence, the psychological and social perspectives are crucial aspects to be investigated (Durrande-Moreau, 1999; Nie, 2000). An interesting contribution from the tourism sector that we take into consideration in interpreting our qualitative results is a study by Parra-Lopez et al. (2012) that proposed an investigation of the intention to use social media during vacation trips. They adopted the MOA model first proposed by MacInnis and Jaworski (1989) that was focused on the motivation, opportunities and abilities to understate the main factors that affect the intention to use SNs in waiting situations.

SNs and waiting times for airport travellers

In this study we focus on travel experiences in the airport, analyzing if and how passengers' waiting time is affected by the emerging role of SNs, focusing on passengers' attitudes. Travellers that have to fly to reach their destinations have to implement complex procedures and activities, with the involvement of different places/areas in which they have to spend their spare time during the wait between two operations.

The airports of departure and arrival represent the first and last points of contact of a trip. Their structures represent spaces in which passengers have to transit and spend several hours waiting for their flights in which they can decide to undertake a purchase experience or conduct other leisure activities. In many cases, the check-in desk represents the first operational process that passengers meet during the customer journey, even if it represents only a limited area of the overall airport context. Therefore, the desk check-in process represents the first step in which passengers have to wait during queuing times and the waiting time before their flights. Many people who fly take waiting times at check-in into account, generally preferring to use the web channel if possible. People anticipate queues by arriving two or three hours before the departure of their flights. Thus, passengers usually have a considerable amount of time to spend at the airport before getting to their desired destinations (check-in counter, departure lounge, gate, concessions, services etc.) and after arriving to their airport of destination (luggage delivery, passport control etc.) before exiting the airport terminal.

Consequently, waiting time can be considered an experience inside the travel experience specifically in a complex context such as the airport. Moreover, in the travel sector, SNs are increasingly adopted by travellers in order to gather information, to plan their trips and to share their experiences with others (Buhalis & Law, 2008; Cox et al., 2009; Yoo & Gretzel, 2008, 2012; Mauri & Minazzi, 2013). Therefore, travellers currently have many other possibilities to fill in their idle and spare time not only with tangible experiences but also using the main opportunities offered by mobile technologies (i.e. social networks). Indeed, mobile technologies can enhance the experience of waiting times, allowing people to conduct self-determined activities that turn idle and spare time into fruitful moments.

In this context, it seems to be relevant to emphasize the crucial role of airport management companies because they have to manage, check and coordinate the passenger experience during waiting times inside airport spaces before and after flights. Airports propose different kinds of travel services (check in, luggage delivery etc.) and other services and facilities (restaurants, shops, parking etc.) in order to fill waiting times and reduce passenger inconvenience (Brunetta et al., 1999). Therefore, in order to create value, the offered additional services should be managed/executed efficiently by the airport companies, proposing attractive possibilities to passengers to spend their spare time in the commercial areas of the airport (Martín-Cejas, 2006).

Methodology

In order to understand users' motivations related to the usage of SNs during waiting times, qualitative interviews were conducted. The in-depth interview technique was chosen because it represents the most powerful means of deeply understanding the experiences (Thompson et al., 1989; Kvale, 1983). We adopted a purposive sampling strategy, consistent with the objectives of the research. Forty interviews were carried out involving both Italian (n = 20) and international individuals who spoke English (n = 20). The target was composed of users of mobile technology and SNs, including youth and young adults of different nationalities who travel approximately three times per year for leisure or for business. The individuals were able to use smartphones and were generally oriented with the use of technology and near-field communication (NFC) services. Considering the results of previous studies (Parasuraman & Colby, 2015; Liébana-Cabanillas et al., 2014), the choice of the target is due to the need to capture key relevant aspects from people oriented towards the use of ICT and SNs and who own a large number of electronic devices (laptops, smartphones, tablets etc.) (Di Pietro et al., 2015). The interviews addressed issues related to personal information, habits and ICT use during waiting times; in particular, as already explained, the context under examination is the waiting time at the airport after the due operations (waiting time after check-in, at the gate, in security control, in luggage delivery etc.). The interviews were conducted face-to-face (using Skype in the case of foreign people) in order to catch all details and to transcribe each interview verbatim, following the recording process suggested by Glaser and Strauss (1967). The consecutive content analysis was composed of four phases (Mayan, 2009; Thompson, 1997; Spiggle, 1994): coding, categorizing, thematizing and integrating. Text analysis software (MAXQDA11) was utilized for the interpretation and to facilitate the extraction and classification of concepts.

In the coding phase, the units of analysis were identified through a code and, on the basis of the objectives, the topics consistent with the research were detected ("on-topic"), whereas the "off-topic" subjects were not considered. Once the codes were named, on the basis of analogies and similarities, they were assigned to a given category, and each category abides by the principles of internal homogeneity and external heterogeneity. Additionally, the categories were combined in order to agglomerate them into themes; in this way, it was possible to understand the connections between the categories. In the last phase of integration, the themes were compared and discussed.

Results

The sample was composed of 46 individuals divided into males (60%) and females (40%), of which 48% were foreign people (who spoke English) and the others were Italian citizens (52%). The sample belonged to the 18–29 (51%), 30–39 (24%), 40–49 (15%) and over 50 (10%) age categories. It involved people who flew approximately three times per year, for leisure (60%) or for business purposes (40%). All the respondents usually use SNs at the airport when they travel. Regarding the sample composition, the predominance of young people and young adults favors youth because these people are typical users of technological services (Liébana-Cabanillas et al., 2014; Parasuraman and Colby, 2015; Anne Coussement & Teague, 2013; Howcroft et al., 2002; Karjaluoto et al., 2002). The whole sample indicated using Facebook, and the majority of them also use Twitter, Instagram and LinkedIn. The main activities carried out include posting pictures, checking flight information and keeping in contact with family and friends.

Eighteen "on-topic" subjects were selected from the interviews: business/leisure trips, group/lone passenger, being in contact, flight information check, customized information, unlimited activities; idle time, passing time, Wi-Fi presence, availability of Wi-Fi free of charge (related to Social Media usage), solitude, laziness, boredom, relaxing, anti-stress, consolation, alienation and the perception of time.

In Figure 15.1 the processes of categorizing, thematizing and integrating are shown.

Interpreting the interviews, the main categories that summarize the use of SNs during waiting times are *Trip condition, Reassurance, Self-determined activities, Accessibility, Mood and Comfortable effects.* Accordingly, *Trip condition* is separated into business/leisure reasons and groups/lone passengers; *Reassurance* includes the possibility of being in contact with family and checking flight information; *Self-determined activities* are characterized by the possibility to obtain customized information and to conduct unlimited activities; Social Network usage during waiting times can be due to *Accessibility* (idle time, passing time, Wi-Fi provision, availability of Wi-Fi free of charge) and *Mood*, which concerns the fact of being alone (solitude), lazy and bored; finally, SN usage provides *Comfortable effects* against tiredness and stress, also enhancing alienation and waiting consolation by sharing the experience and making the time pass quickly.

Proceeding with the categories' agglomeration through interpretation, the main themes that arose are *"Functional aspects", "Freedom of choice", "Disposition"* and *"Leisure"*. In particular, the usage of SNs during waiting time can be useful (*"Functional aspects"*) on the basis of the trip condition (business/leisure trip and group/lone passenger), the possibility of conducting self-determined activities and for reassurance aims towards the trip itself (checking flight information) and the family (transmit trip information).

SN use further enables "*Freedom of choice*" that embodies self-determined activities and accessibility aspects; this theme refers to the possibility (self-determined

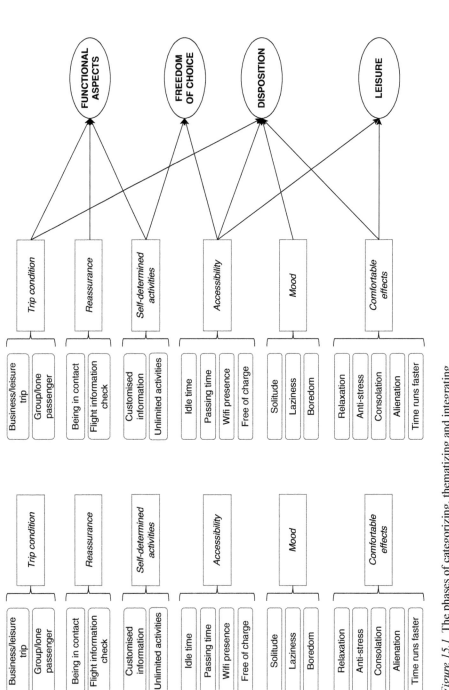

Figure 15.1 The phases of categorizing, thematizing and integrating

activities) and the opportunity (accessibility) to use SNs. There are several aspects that allow the chance to use Social Media, which thus prepares the ground for "*Disposition*", such as accessibility, mood, comfortable effects and trip condition. The fourth theme is "*Leisure*", which represents all the comfortable effects given by Social Media usage described above.

Discussion

In this research in particular, people were interviewed about the experience of waiting time and their usage of social media in that context. At first, it emerged that a given mood of solitude, laziness and boredom encourages social media use. The aspects related to accessibility cover a key role, and they represent opportunities and enablers of using a social network; these aspects include Wi-Fi provision, availability of Wi-Fi free of charge, the availability of residual time for leisure activities (passing time) and additional time after having visited shops and duty free (idle time). The interviews show that activities on social networks are alternative rather than simultaneous, and they deprive time from other shopping and leisure activities arranged onsite; indeed, some people shop and use social networks during idle time, whereas others instead of buying products, prefer surfing on social networks because it is an activity that can be done free of charge. Moreover, being with company is still the best form of entertainment during the waiting time on a trip, given that most of the interviewees argued that when people travel in a group, they usually do not care much about entertaining themselves with social media. On the contrary, entertainment is a key point for lone passengers, given that waiting is source of stress. The case of lone passengers' perception of the airport experience depends on how much an airport is able to create an enjoyable experience through the activities provided. Certainly, airports' offerings in terms of entertainment are often basic and limited, including duty free, coffee shops, common spaces and luxury shops. However, an airport cannot cover all the needs of passengers, and for this reason, any inconvenience cannot be completely compensated by entertainment offerings.

Although people use the airport's website and SNs to determine detailed information about the flight, they do not use them to leave feedback on the airport's service. Wi-Fi provision and the consequent SN access during waiting time can improve the experience of both business and leisure passengers, making the waiting time experience pleasant without perceiving inconveniences. Indeed, Wi-Fi allows people to look for customized information and to carry out unlimited activities that they prefer more than the airport offerings. Providing Wi-Fi solutions, the passengers can entertain themselves without entailing a change of airport offerings. Hence, Wi-Fi provision is one of the requirements that an airport should provide besides shops and duty free in order to enlarge its offerings, including all the unlimited activities of the internet and virtual world. The possibility to spend time in this way allows users to avoid perceiving delays through the sense of alienation, meaning distancing themselves from the experience, that makes waiting more relaxing, short and enjoyable.

Conclusion and future perspectives

On the basis of our results, SNs represent one of the alternatives that the airport can offer to improve the waiting experience. The increasing use of SNs inside the airport represents a clear and prominent phenomenon that needs to be managed by airports. Indeed, in order to take advantage of this emerging issue, airports need to invest in Wi-Fi technology, with the goal of enabling easy, satisfactory and free accessibility. Functional access to Wi-Fi and the availability of time allow people to use social networks for the main purposes indicated: checking up-to-date information, reassuring themselves and being in contact with family and friends.

Because people do not use SNs often when they travel in a group and lone passengers seem to use more social networks because they are looking for company and share experiences through a virtual community, SNs represent a tool to substitute the group and engage people. Because unfilled waiting makes people, especially lone passengers, tired and stressed, social networks represent a solution to compensate the inconvenient passing of the time and to allow passengers to console themselves by sharing experiences and being in contact with other people.

This exploratory study is the first part of a wider investigation. Further studies should investigate the phenomenon in a quantitative way through the validation of a theoretical model inspired by the MOA model (Parra-Lopez et al., 2012; MacInnis and Jaworski, 1989), proposing new predictors of the motivation construct.

References

Antonides, G., Verhoef, P., & Van Aalst, M. (2002). Consumer perception and evaluation of waiting time: a field experiment, *Journal of Consumer Psychology*, 12(3), pp. 193–202.

Baker, J., & Cameron, M. (1996). The effects of the service environment on affect and consumer perception of waiting time: An integrative review and research propositions. *Journal of the Academy of Marketing Science*, 24(4), pp. 338–349.

Brunetta, L., Righi, L., & Andreatta, G. (1999). An operations research model for the evaluation of an airport terminal: SLAM (simple landside aggregate model). *Journal of Air Transport Management*, 5(3), pp. 161–175.

Buhalis, D., & Law, R. (2008). Progress in information technology and tourism management: 20 years on and 10 years after the Internet The state of eTourism research. *Tourism Management*, 29(4), pp. 609–623.

Canel, C., & Kadipasaoglu, S. (2002). An efficiency study for a student health center. *International Journal of Health Care Quality Assurance*, 15(4), pp. 159–167.

Coussement, M. A., & Teague, T. J. (2013). The new customer-facing technology: mobile and the constantly-connected consumer. *Journal of Hospitality and Tourism Technology*, 4(2), pp. 177–187.

Cox, C., Burgess, S., Sellito, C., & Buultjens, J. (2009). The role of user generated content in tourists' travel planning behaviour. *Journal of Hospitality Marketing and Management*, 18(8), pp. 743–764.

Davis, M. M., & Heineke, J. (1998). How disconfirmation, perception and actual waiting times impact customer satisfaction, International. *Journal of Service Industry Management*, 9(1), pp. 64–73.

Di Pietro, L., Mugion, R. G., Mattia, G., Renzi, M. F., & Toni, M. (2015). The integrated model on mobile payment acceptance (IMMPA): An empirical application to public transport. *Transportation Research Part C: Emerging Technologies*, 56, pp. 463–479.

Dubé, L., & Schmitt, B. H. (1996). The temporal dimension of social episodes: Position effect in time judgments of unfilled intervals. *Journal of Applied Social Psychology*, 26(20), pp. 1816–1826.

Dubé, L., Schmitt, B. H., & Leclerc, F. (1991). Consumers' affective response to delays at different phases of a service delivery. *Journal of Applied Social Psychology*, 21(10), pp. 810–820.

Durrande-Moreau, A. (1999). Waiting for service: Ten years of empirical research. *International Journal of Service Industry Management*, 10(2), pp. 171–194.

Flaherty, L. M., Pearce, K., & Rubin, R. B. (1998). Internet and face-to-face communication: Not functional alternatives. *Communication Quarterly*, 46, pp. 250–268.

Glaser, B., & Strauss, A. (1967). The discovery grounded theory: Strategies for qualitative inquiry. Aldin, Chicago.

Groth, M., & Gilliland, S. W. (2001). The role of procedural justice in the delivery of services: a study of customers' reactions to waiting. *Journal of Quality Management*, 6, pp. 77–97.

Hall, R. W. (1991). Queuing methods for service and manufacturing Prentice Hall, Englewood Cliffs, NJ.

Hornik, J. (1984). Subjective vs. Objective time measures: A note on the perception of time in consumer behavior. *Journal of Consumer Research*, 11(June), pp. 615–618_9.

Hornik, J., & Zakay, D. (1996). Psychological time: The case of time and consumer behaviour. *Time and Society*, 5(3), pp. 385–397.

Howcroft, B., Hamilton, R., & Hewer, P. (2002). Consumer attitude and the usage and adoption of home-based banking in the United Kingdom. International journal of bank marketing, 20(3), pp. 111–121.

Hui, M. K., & Zhou, L. (1996). How does waiting duration information influence customers' reactions to waiting for services? 1. *Journal of Applied Social Psychology*, 26(19), pp. 1702–1717.

Ittig, P. T. (2002). The real cost of making customers wait, international. *Journal of Service Industry Management*, 13(3), pp. 231–241.

Jones, P., & Hwang, J. L. (2005). Perceptions of waiting time in different service queues, Working Paper, University of Surrey. Accessed online (October 16, 2016) at: http://epubs.surrey.ac.uk/2205/

Karjaluoto, H., Mattila, M., & Pento, T. (2002). Factors underlying attitude formation towards online banking in Finland. International. *Journal of Bank Marketing*, 20(6), pp. 261–272.

Katz, K. L., Larson, B. M., & Larson, R. C. (1991). Prescription for the waiting-in-line blues: entertain, enlighten, and engage. *Sloan Management Review*, 32(2), p. 44.

Kumar, P., Kalwani, M. U., & Dada, M. (1997). The impact of waiting time guarantees on customers' waiting experiences. *Marketing Science*, 16(4), pp. 295–314.

Kvale, S. (1983). The qualitative research interview: A phenomenological and a hermeneutic mode of understanding. *Journal of Phenomenological Psychology*, 14, pp. 171–196.

Liébana-Cabanillas, F., Sánchez-Fernández, J., & Muñoz-Leiva, F. (2014). Antecedents of the adoption of the new mobile payment systems: The moderating effect of age. *Computers in Human Behavior*, 35, pp. 464–478.

Luo, W., Liberatore, M., Nydick, R. L., Chung, Q. B., & Sloane, E. (2004). Impact of process change on customer perception of waiting time: A field study, Omega: The international. *Journal of Management Science*, 32(1), pp. 77–83.

MacInnis, D. J., & Jaworski, B. J. (1989). Information processing from advertisements: Toward an integrative framework. *The Journal of Marketing*, 53(4), pp. 1–23.

Maister, D. (1985). The psychology of waiting lines. In J. A. Czepiel, M. R. Solomon, & C. F. Surprenant (eds.) *The Service Encounter*. Lexington, MA, Lexington Books, pp. 113–123.

Mantel, S. P., & Kellaris, J. J. (2003). Cognitive determinants of consumers' time preceptions: The impact of resources required and available. *Journal of Consumer Research*, 29(4), pp. 531–538.

Martín-Cejas, R. R. (2006). Tourism service quality begins at the airport. *Tourism Management*, 27(5), pp. 874–877.

Matthew F., Soumitra D. (2008). *Throwing Sheep in the Boardroom: How Online Social Networking Will Transform Your Life, Work and World*. Hoboken, NJ, Wiley.

Mauri, A. G., Minazzi, R. (2013). Web reviews influence on expectations and purchasing intentions of hotel potential customers. International. *Journal of Hospitality Management*, 34, pp. 99–107.

Mayan, M. J. (2009). *Essentials of Qualitative Inquiry*, Walnut Creek, CA, Leaf Coast Press.

McGrath, J. E., & Kelly, J. R. (1986). *Time and Human Interaction: Toward a Social Psychology of Time*. New York: Guilford Press.

Murdick, R. G, Render, B., & Russell, R. S. (1990). *Service Operations Management*. Boston, MA, Allyn and Bacon.

Nie, W. (2000). Waiting: Integrating social and psychological perspectives in operations management, Omega: The International. *Journal of Management Science*, 28, pp. 611–629.

Papacharissi, Z., & Rubin, A. M. (2000). Predictors of internet use. *Journal of Broadcasting and Electronic Media*, 44(2), pp. 175–196.

Parasuraman, A., & Colby, C. L. (2015). An updated and streamlined technology readiness index TRI 2.0. *Journal of Service Research*, 18(1), pp. 59–74.

Parra-Lopez, E., Gutierrez-Tano, D., Diaz-Armas, R. J., & Bulchand-Gidumal, J. (2012). Travellers 2.0: motivation, opportunity and ability to use social media. In M. Sigala, E. Christou, & U. Gretzel(eds.) *Social Media in Travel, Tourism and Hospitality: Theory, Practice and Cases*, Surrey, UK: Ashgate, pp. 171–187.

Poynter, D. (1989). Judging the duration of time intervals: A process of remembering segments of experience. *Advances in Psychology*, 59 (Special Issue on Time and Human Cognition: A Life-Span Perspective), pp. 305–331.

Rafaeli, A., Barron, G., & Harber, K. (2002). The effect of queue structure on attitudes. *Journal of Service Research*, 5(2), pp. 125–139.

Schutz, W. C. (1958). *FIRO: A three-dimensional theory of interpersonal behavior*. New York: Holt, Rinehart & Winston.

Sheu, C., & Babbar, S. (1996). A managerial assessment of the waiting time performance for alternative service process designs. *Omega*, 24(6), pp. 689–703.

Sheu, C., McHaney, R., & Babbar, S. (2003). Service process design flexibility and customer waiting time. *International Journal of Operations and Production Management*, 23(8), pp. 901–917.

Smidts, A., & Pruyn, A. (1994). How waiting affects customer satisfaction with the service: The role of subjective variables. In *Management of Services: a multidisciplinary approach, (3rd conference)*, Aix-en-Provence, France: Institut d'Administration des Entreprises, Universite d'Aix-Marseille III, pp. 677–696.

Spiggle, S. (1994). Analysis and interpretation of qualitative data in consumer research. *Journal of Consumer Research*, 21(3), pp. 491–503.

Taylor, S. (1994). Waiting for service: The relationship between delays and evaluations of service. *Journal of Marketing*, 58(2), pp. 56–69.

Taylor, S. (1995). The effects of filled waiting time and service provider control over the delay on service evaluations of service. *Journal of the Academy of Marketing Science*, 23(1), pp. 38–48.

Taylor, S., & Claxton, J. D. (1994). Delays and the dynamics of service evaluations. *Journal of the Academy of Marketing Science*, 22(3), pp. 254–264.

Thompson, C. J. (1997). Interpreting consumers: A hermeneutical framework for deriving marketing insights from the texts of consumers' consumption stories. *Journal of Marketing Research*, 34(4), pp. 438–455.

Thompson, C. J., Locander, W. B., & Pollio, H. R. (1989). Putting consumer experience back into consumer research: The philosophy and method of existential-phenomenology. *Journal of consumer research*, 16(2), pp. 133–146.

Van Riel, A. C., Semeijn, J., Ribbink, D., & Peters, Y. (2006). Managing the Waiting Experience at Checkout. In Proceedings 17th Annual Conference of POMS. Boston: Production and Operations Management Society.

Watson, R. T., Pitt, L. F., Berthon, P., & Zinkhan, G. M. (2002). U-commerce: Expanding the universe of marketing. *Journal of the Academy of Marketing Science,* 30(4), pp. 333–347.

Yoo, K. H., & Gretzel, U. (2008). Use and impact of online travel reviews. In P. O'Connor, W. Ho"pken, & U. Gretzel (eds.) *Information and communication technologies in tourism*, Vienna, Austria: Springer Verlag, pp. 35–46.

Yoo, K.H., & Gretzel, U. (2012). Use and Creation of Social Media by Travelers. In Sigala, M., Christou, E., & Gretzel, U. (eds.), *Social Media in Travel, Tourism and Hospitality*, Surrey, UK: Ashgate, pp. 189–206.

Zhou, R., & Soman, D. (2003). Looking back: Exploring the psychology of queuing and the effect of the number of people behind. *Journal of Consumer Research*, 29(4), pp. 517–530.

Part 4

Social media, knowledge management, market research, business intelligence, social media analytics

Marianna Sigala

Social media, market intelligence and the evolution of smart tourism

The explosive growth of social media channels, the devices to access them and the software applications developed provide firms with unprecedented opportunities to collect and leverage a vast amount of data for creating business and customer value. The rise of customers' social media usage also yields new ways to generate customer data (such as social media profiles, online activities and conversations) in an ever-increasing volume and variety. Indeed, social media advances and usage are fuelling big data trends. Data has been characterized as the "oil" of the digital economy that will be traded, owned and developed as a production resource that can enable firms to boost their innovation and creativity and so, achieve a differentiated and competitive advantage. By accessing data located outside of the firms' boundaries and integrating them with internal data, firms can enrich transactional data and develop a 360 degree holistic view of their customers by understanding not only what and when customers purchase, but also why and how they buy and consume offerings, how the consumption experience is evaluated and what it means to them (Sigala, in press). Indeed, social media data enables firms to collect customer insights allowing them to better understand not only current customer needs, but also the reasons behind these needs and how these change over time (Wieneke & Lehrer, 2016). Table 4.1 summarizes some of the major differences and qualities of social media data that further empower firms in relation to traditional marketing data.

Data trends generate new forms of data-driven marketing such as recommendations, geo-fencing, search marketing, social Customer Relationship Marketing (CRM), market segmentation, personalization and marketing-mix optimization

Table Part 4.1 Traditional marketing data vs. social media data

Traditional marketing data	Social media data
Transactional data	Data about the social and contextual factors of transactions and consumption experiences
Aggregate data of market segments	Individual – personalized demand data
Old data	Real time and streaming data
Poor data	Multimedia data

(Wedel & Kannan, 2016; Sigala, in press). Big data has been identified as one of the most important resources for developing smart tourism (Gretzel et al., 2015), and recent studies increasingly show how big data analytics can enrich decision-making and market research in tourism in various areas such as predicting tourism demand, measuring tourists' satisfaction and designing personalized tourism experiences (Xiang & Fesenmaier, 2017; Liu et al., 2017).

Consequently, marketing analytics and knowledge management have come to play a central role in these developments (Sigala & Chalkiti, 2015), and so, there is an urgent demand for new, more powerful metrics and analytical methods that can make data-driven marketing practices more efficient and effective. Firms have already started investing in data capture and storage, but not enough in data analytics, while research has paid too much attention on debating the role of data as a source of competitive advantage and there is a lack of research on how to capitalize on it (Weineke & Lehrer, 2016; Wedel & Kannan, 2016). Thus, it is yet not sufficiently clear which types of metrics and which types of analytics can work for which types of problems and data, and what new methods are needed for analyzing new types of data. Little is also known about how companies and their management should evolve to develop and implement skills and procedures to compete in this new environment. Data exploitation and leverage requires transforming data into meaningful knowledge that is subsequently disseminated throughout the firm and acted upon. This in turn implies that firms need to develop human skills to interpret and understand the data as well as the organizational structures and processes to share and use the generated insights within the organization. Research, however, has failed to unravel the organizational capabilities that firms need to develop for utilizing social media data for generating and exploiting customer and market insights. For example, what organizational resources, structures and cultures firms should adopt and what type of education and training firms should use for developing the big data skills of their staff has yet to be determined.

Big data is often characterized by the four "Vs" namely volume, velocity, variety and veracity. The first two characteristics are important from a computing standpoint, while the second two are important from an analytics standpoint. However, what is missing is a business and customer perspective representing the ability of firms to leverage big data for creating customer and business value. Hence, it might be appropriate to add a fifth "V" referring to value in order to highlight the equally important issue of recognizing the need to ensure that firms have the necessary capabilities to leverage big data for generating value as well as the tools and methodologies to assess how well and/or badly they are achieving this. In this vein, future research is required for investigating the capabilities, resources, management practices and methodologies that firms need to develop for profiting from the big data revolution.

Overview of part 4

The last part of the book is devoted to discuss several of the issues raised related to how tourism and hospitality firms can harness social media data for generating value. It includes five chapters providing theoretical underpinnings and practical examples of: the type of social media data that can be used; the business problem that data can solve; and, the data analytic methodology used for analyzing and interpreting the data.

The first chapter titled *Sentiment analysis: a review* is written by Jing Ge, Marisol Alonso Vazquez and Ulrike Gretzel and provides an overview of the analytical methods available for conducting sentiment analysis, which represents one of the important pillars of social media analytics. The chapter first identifies sentiment analysis as an increasingly important and ever widely applied approach to social media monitoring and then offers an overview of different sentiment analysis techniques. It further discusses examples of how sentiment analysis has been applied in tourism and hospitality research. Importantly, it ends with a critical discussion of the limitations of sentiment analysis and outlines challenges that future research on sentiment analysis will have to overcome in order to continuously provide value to tourism researchers and marketing practitioners.

In the chapter titled "*Social media analysis from a communication perspective. The case of the argumentative analysis of online travel reviews*", Silvia De Ascaniis and Lorenzo Cantoni adopt a communication perspective for developing a method to analyze and interpret online travel reviews. Social media content is considered as a *communicative artefact* created and received in a specific context, according to the goals of a producer, in view of a receiver, using a code for conveying the meaning and a channel for its physical transmission. This perspective on communication relies, mainly, on the notion of *speech acts*, and takes into consideration especially verbal communication. The chapter also shows that the method can be applied to the different types of mediated communication artefacts, supported by different media and using different codes. The chapter also identifies and discusses the implications of the method. For example, information system developers can generate indications for helping online users in the process of information seeking and selection or develop algorithms both to rank reviews in terms of their argumentative quality, and to filter them according to their potential usefulness to consumers.

Social media data from online review websites is also the type of data that is examined in the chapter titled "*Measuring visitor satisfaction with a cultural heritage site: social media data vs. onsite surveys*" and written by Laura Di Pietro,

Roberta Guglielmetti Mugion, Maria Francesca Renzi and Martina Toni. The specific business problem that the researchers aim to explore relates to the reliability of online tourists' reviews and the credibility of such data in relation to data collected via traditional onsite customer surveys. To achieve that, the study used content analysis and descriptive statistics for data analysis in order to investigate the credibility and usefulness of online reviews for managing quality and understanding tourists' experiences at a cultural site.

In their chapter titled "*Business intelligence for destinations: creating knowledge from social media*", Matthias Fuchs, Wolfram Höpken and Maria Lexhagen also study the business value of online tourism reviews, but they focus on proposing and describing a methodology that destination management organizations can use for extracting and analyzing such information. To achieve this, the chapter discusses how to apply machine-learning methods and a dictionary-based approach for extracting and analyzing user-generated content from the social media platforms TripAdvisor.com and Booking.com. Practical examples and implications are further developed by applying this data analytical framework for developing a Business Intelligence-based knowledge infrastructure for Åre (a leading Swedish mountain tourism destination). The chapter illustrates how the Destination Management Information system Åre (DMIS-Åre) supports knowledge creation as a precondition for destination development and competitiveness by supporting the storage of customer-based data (i.e. UGC) at the level of the destination and applying techniques of Business Intelligence (BI) to gain new and valuable social media knowledge.

In their chapter titled "*Community characteristics in tourism Twitter accounts of European countries*", Kostas Zafiropoulos, Konstantinos Antoniadis and Vasiliki Vrana use and analyze data from Twitter user profiles for investigating whether Twitter users form communities. The social media metrics used for answering this business problem include mentions/replies (m/r) networks of 37 national DMOs in Europe, while clustering coefficient, degree-skewness, average shortest path and assortativity are used as data analytics techniques and frameworks for exploring whether the properties of small-world formation, i.e. scale-free networks and homophily, are present or not. The findings of the study provide numerous implications for grouping and segmenting Twitter users based on their Twitter usage and relating their community characteristics with Twitter performance metrics. In this vein, the study provides an interesting theoretical framework and data analytics process for identifying, developing and managing social media communities on Twitter and nurturing user online engagement.

Social media analytics, metrics and knowledge management is a huge area requiring multidisciplinary approaches and frameworks. Of course, five chapters are not enough to capture the plurality and the diversity of the metrics, the analytical methods, theoretical lenses and concepts that need to be developed for collecting, analyzing, interpreting and using social media data in innovative and creative ways for solving business problems. However, the chapters do provide very useful insights regarding how tourism and hospitality firms can develop an appropriate methodology for identifying, matching and using robust metrics, techniques and theory-based thinking for developing data-driven strategies and extracting value from social media metrics.

References

Gretzel, U., Sigala, M., Xiang, Z., & Koo, C. (2015). Smart tourism: Foundations and developments. *Electronic Markets*, 25(3), pp. 179–188.

Knuz, W., Aksoy, L., Bart, Y., Heinonen, K., Kabadayi, S., Ordenes, F. V., Sigala, M., Diaz, D., & Theodoulidis, B. (2017). Customer engagement in a big data world. *Journal of Services Marketing*, 31(2), pp. 161–171.

Liu, Y., Teichert, T., Rossi, M., Li, H., & Hu, F. (2017). Big data for big insights: Investigating language-specific drivers of hotel satisfaction with 412,784 user-generated reviews. *Tourism Management*, 59, pp. 554–563.

Sigala, M. (in press). Social Customer Relationship Management: Approaches, applications and implications in tourism and hospitality. *International Journal of Contemporary Hospitality Management*.

Sigala, M., & Chalkiti, K. (2015). Knowledge management, social media and employee creativity. *International Journal of Hospitality Management*, 45, pp. 44–58.

Wedel, M., & Kannan, P. K. (2016). Marketing analytics for data-rich environments. *Journal of Marketing*, 80, pp. 97–121.

Wieneke, A., & Lehrer, C. (2016). Generating and exploiting customer insights from social media data. *Electronic Markets*, 18, pp. 1–24.

Xiang, Z., & Fesenmaier, D. R. (2017). Big data analytics, tourism design and smart tourism. In Xiang, Z., & Fesenmaier, D. R. (eds.) *Analytics in Smart Tourism Design*, Springer International Publishing, pp. 299–307.

16 Sentiment analysis

A review

*Jing Ge, Marisol Alonso Vazquez
and Ulrike Gretzel*

Introduction

Today, tourism and hospitality consumers are not isolated anymore when making purchase decisions. Social media represent support networks that allow these consumers to tap into a vast universe of peer opinions, critiques, feedback, recommendations or warnings about specific tourism and hospitality products or services (Benckendorff et al., 2014; Hvass & Munar, 2012; Miguéns et al., 2008; Milano et al., 2011; Munar & Jacobsen, 2014; Sigala et al., 2012; Thevenot, 2007; Xiang & Gretzel, 2010; Zeng & Gerritsen, 2014). This subjective and experience-based information can be expressed and published in diverse social media platforms such as forums, discussion groups, review platforms, personal blogs, public opinion blogs, microblogs and social networking sites but also visual platforms like YouTube, Flickr, Instagram and Pinterest. Such social media content published by consumers is known as *user-generated content* in the current literature (Gretzel, 2015; Krumm et al., 2008). It has been considered by academics and practitioners as valuable information that can inform the emergence of new trends in markets, changes in the reputation of companies or destinations, consumer behaviors, processes of decision making and satisfaction/dissatisfaction with specific products/ services (Liu, 2010; McGarrity, 2016).

While some of the consumer-generated content comes in the form of numerical values (e.g. in the case of review or rating scores), the bulk of information posted on social media is in the form of text. Such text not only contains factual information but also subjective evaluations, expressing so-called sentiment. This consumer sentiment is of particular value for tourism and hospitality marketers aiming to gather market intelligence but also for consumers who need to gain a quick overview of the collective opinion about a destination, provider or product/service/ experience. Due to the sheer amount of consumer-generated content available, extracting sentiment manually has become impractical, spurring a whole field of inquiry commonly referred to as sentiment analysis.

Academic literature has highlighted increasing interest in and value of sentiment analysis in academia and practice (Leung et al., 2013). There are also a growing number of software companies that are offering sentiment analysis tools (Liu, 2010). However, some authors have voiced concerns regarding the high cost of text mining tools and issues related to uncertainty on the return of the investment (Akehurst, 2009; Schuckert et al., 2015). Also, while tremendous progress has been made in sentiment analysis due to advances in natural language processing (NLP),[1] current approaches are still far from reaching human-like abilities to discern specific sentiments. And even humans are not that great at determining sentiment, as it is inherently subjective (Tsvetovat et al., 2012). As a result, sentiment analysis remains a hotbed of research and development for academia and industry. This chapter seeks to provide a general introduction to the field and aims at highlighting some of the challenges that remain in advancing current approaches.

Overview and definitions

Sentiment

Sentiment can be defined as an attitude, thought or judgment prompted by feelings or a specific view or opinion (Merriam-Webster, 2016). Similarly, the Cambridge English Dictionary (2016) defines sentiment as a general feeling about something. The word's most common synonyms are emotion or feelings; in fact, according to the Oxford English Dictionary (2016), its roots come from the Latin word *'sentire'*, which means to feel. In current computer science literature three main streams of sentiment definitions can be found. The first stream of research defines sentiment as opinion. Examples of definitions that illustrate this stream are the following: sentiment is defined as (1) opinions people express towards a subject (i.e. a topic of interest or a feature of the topic), and it is manifested through the polarity of the opinion, including positive and negative polarity (Yi et al., 2003); (2) a positive or negative emotion, evaluation or stance (Wilson et al., 2009); and (3) textual expressions that indicate positive (favorable) or negative (unfavorable) opinions toward the subject (Nasukawa and Yi, 2003). The second stream of research defines sentiment through focusing on feelings as illustrated in the following definitions: sentiment is defined as a personal positive or negative feeling (Go et al., 2009). The third stream of research defines sentiment through focusing on both feeling and opinion, as Liu (2015) suggests: sentiment can be seen as the underlying feeling, attitude, evaluation, or emotion associated with an opinion. In contrast, Pang and Lee (2008) define it as a settled opinion reflective of one's feelings.

On a basic level, sentiment has two components: an opinion and a target at which it is directed. A more complex opinion, however, according to Liu's (2010, 2012, 2015) perspective, involves five components of relevance for understanding the sentiment. These are: (1) the target entity it relates to; (2) the specific target entity aspect to which the opinion refers; (3) the opinion holder; (4) the time when the opinion is expressed; and, (5) the polarity of the opinion in relation to the target entity aspect. For example, a hotel review posted on September 1, 2015 says: "as a business traveller, I found the hotel's location to be great," encompasses the (1) target entity *"hotel"*, (2) the aspect *"location"*, (3) the opinion holder *"I"*, who travels for business, (4) the opinion posting time *"September 1, 2015"*, and (5) the sentiment *"great"*, which reflects a positive polarity. It is important to note that not all opinions have these five components. It is also important to point out that sentiment can be expressed in implicit ways. For instance, the review could have said "*convenient*", which is a word that then has to be translated in terms of sentiment polarity. The aspect could also be implicitly described, e.g. when the review says the hotel was "*near the main attractions*", the specific aspect implicitly described is the hotel's location. Further, sentiment can be expressed in comparative terms, e.g. when saying "*this hotel is better than most hotels in Rome*". Finally, in the case of sarcasm, statements communicate the opposite sentiment of what they explicitly say. All of these characteristics make sentiment linguistically complex and therefore difficult to analyze.

Two aspects of sentiment are of primary concern: sentiment orientation and sentiment intensity. Sentiment orientation is also called polarity or semantic orientation – the former mainly focuses on regular opinions whereas the latter is also concerned with comparative and implicit sentiment (Liu, 2015). While positive and negative orientations indicate people's subjective opinions and feelings, neutral usually means the absence of sentiment (Liu, 2012). In practice, consumers may express a variety of positive and negative sentiments that reflect emotions such as disappointment, satisfaction, anger, surprise, gratification etc. (Jiang et al., 2010; Liu, 2012). However, consumers may also ask questions, provide factual information or make general statements, all of which usually contain no sentiment (i.e. they are neutral) (Jansen et al., 2009). Notably, opinions can involve both positive and negative orientations, in which case they are referred to as mixed sentiment (Stieglitz & Dang-Xuan, 2013). For instance, consumers may praise the hotel room size but complain about the high price.

Sentiment intensity shows sentiment orientations have different levels of strength, which can be identified through sentiment words with varied strength or words indicating intensifiers and diminishers (Liu, 2015). For example, *fine* is clearly weaker than *superb*. The use of intensifiers increases the degree of positivity or negativity, whereas using a diminisher decreases the degree of intensity. For instance, some of the common English intensifiers are *very*, *absolutely*, *extremely* and *really*, and diminishers are *slightly*, *a bit*, and *somewhat*.

Sentiment words

Sentiment words are instrumental to identifying sentiment orientations and intensity (Liu, 2012; 2015). There are two types of individual words: base-type words are used to look at regular sentiment and comparative words are used to identify semantically more complex sentiment (Liu, 2015). The base-type individual words consist of adjectives, adverbs, nouns and verbs (Hu & Liu, 2004; Nasukawa & Yi, 2003). Adjectives are the most common words used to determine positive (e.g. nice, wonderful) and negative sentiment (e.g. bad, poor). An adverb is used to denote the sentiment towards the verb it modifies, such as in "*worked beautifully*". In contrast, verbs are more complex as they can be used in either direct or indirect ways (Hu & Liu, 2004; Wiebe et al., 2004). One can express the sentiment in a straightforward manner. For instance, "*We hated the food.*" On the other hand, the sentiment expressions denoted in verbs may depend on the relationships with their arguments (Hu & Liu, 2004). For example, "*Airbnb beats the traditional hotel industry*" implies a positive sentiment directed towards the subject but negative sentiment towards the object of the sentence. Apart from base-type sentiment words, comparative words along with superlative ones, such as better, worse, and so on, are used to express opinions (Liu, 2015). Sentiment can also be embedded in phrases such as "*the bee's knees*", which means excellent. Sentiment can further be expressed through emphatic spelling such as "*sooooooo good*" or punctuation, as in "*that was so bad!!!!!!!!!*". Of particular concern is negation, as it changes the polarity of sentiment words, e.g. "*not bad!*". Importantly, different languages express sentiment in different ways. Identifying sentiment words automatically is particularly difficult in languages that do not parse words, such as Chinese. Further, sentiment words and expressions can differ across topic domains.

Sentiment analysis

Xiang et al. (2015, p. 121) define sentiment analysis as "a special type of text mining with the focus on identification of subjective statements and contained opinions and sentiments, particularly in consumer-generated content on the Internet". Rather than trying to detect topics, sentiment analysis focuses on identifying positive and negative opinions, emotions and evaluations expressed in natural language (Wilson et al., 2009). The literature offers various descriptions of sentiment analysis:

*   Sentiment analysis, or opinion mining, aims at capturing users' attitudes by investigating, analyzing and extracting subjective texts involving users' opinions, preferences and sentiment (Nanli et al., 2012).
*   Sentiment analysis is concerned with the identification of expressions of opinions, their polarity and strength of expression, as well as their relationship to the subject (Nasukawa & Yi, 2003).
*   Sentiment analysis is the task of identifying positive and negative opinions, emotions, and evaluations (Bermingham & Smeaton, 2010).
*   Sentiment analysis refers to the field of study that analyzes people's opinions, appraisals, attitudes, and emotions toward entities expressed in written text. The entities can be products, services, organizations, individuals, events, issues, or topics (Liu, 2012; 2015).
*   Sentiment analysis aims at the judgment of the sentiment expressed in a subjective text, which is capable of distinguishing positive, negative, or even more subtle sentiment, such as anger, grief or joy. It largely involves two subsequent tasks: identification of subjective/objective information, and the sentiment classification of subjective information (Nanli et al., 2012). Sentiment classification involves both polarity and strength.

Sentiment analysis provides a methodology to computationally process unstructured data (Piryani et al., 2017). The text analyzed can be an entire document, a sentence or part of a sentence, with or without embedded metadata (Thelwall,

2017). Sentiment analysis typically involves pre-processing the text using linguistic tools such as stemming, tokenization, speech tagging, entity extraction and relation extraction (Feldman, 2013), followed by a series of steps as outlined by Thelwall (2017): (1) subjectivity/opinion detection; (2) polarity detection; (3) sentiment strength detection; (4) specific emotion detection; and, (5) aspect-sentiment detection. The quality of sentiment analysis outcomes is usually evaluated by comparing the results with the work of human coders or by comparing the results of multiple methods (Ribeiro et al., 2016).

Sentiment analysis approaches

There are essentially two approaches to sentiment analysis: lexicon-based approaches and machine-learning approaches. Lexicon-based approaches require the availability or a priori construction of a suitable lexicon while machine-learning approaches automatically classify text but usually require training datasets derived through human coding (Paltoglou & Thelwall, 2017).

Approaches to compiling sentiment lexicons

There are three main existing approaches to compiling a list of sentiment words or a so-called sentiment lexicon: manual approach, lexical approach and corpus-based approach (Liu, 2015).

1   Manual approach: The manual approach involves human coding and is therefore labor-intensive and time-consuming. However, it ensures capturing nuances and domain-specific meanings.
2   Lexical approach: Pre-existing resources are used to identify the sentiment words. A lexicon is a stock of terms that belong to a particular subject or language. The lexicon could be manually compiled, such as in the case of the General Inquirer (Stone et al., 1966), a resource often used in sentiment analysis (Wilson et al., 2009). Dictionaries not only list but also define and describe words. Dictionaries used for sentiment analysis (e.g. WordNet; Miller et al., 1990) provide synonyms and antonyms for each word. The advantage of dictionary-based approaches is that one can easily and quickly find a large number of sentiment words with their orientations. However, the sentiment orientations of words collected this way are general or domain and context independent (Liu, 2015). This is a problem as oftentimes, also in the tourism domain, sentiment is embedded in domain-specific phrases and meanings.
3   Corpus-based approach: This approach has mainly been applied in two ways: (1) given a seed list of known sentiment words, discovering other sentiment words and their orientations from a domain corpus, and (2) adapting a list of known sentiment words to a new one using a domain corpus (Liu, 2015). More specifically, the first way is to exploit the linguistic rules or conventions on connectives to simultaneously identify sentiment words and to

determine their orientations in a given corpus (Kanayama & Nasukawa, 2006). The second way is to use syntactic relations of opinions and targets to extract sentiment words (Hu & Liu, 2004). Corpus-based approaches are useful to identify domain-specific words and their sentiment orientations (Liu, 2015). Nevertheless, the approaches are limited in terms of identifying contextual subjectivities and sentiments at the phrase or expression level. Contextual sentiment means although a word or phrase in a lexicon is marked as positive or negative, in the context of the sentence expression it may have no sentiment or have the opposite sentiment (Wilson et al., 2009).

Analytical techniques

Researchers mainly use machine-learning approaches and lexicon-based approaches, both of which have advantages and limitations. Hybrid approaches are also possible and are used to overcome the shortcomings of the individual techniques.

1   Lexicon-based approaches: Lexicon-based approaches use a sentiment lexicon with information about which words and phrases are positive and which ones are negative (Nanli et al., 2012). Researchers first create a sentiment lexicon through compiling sentiment word lists (see the different ways of accomplishing this described above) and then determine the degree of subjectivity of a text unit based on the positive and negative indicators identified by the lexicon (Pang & Lee, 2004). As previous discussion suggests, one can use manual approaches, lexical approaches and corpus-based approaches to create a sentiment lexicon (Liu, 2015). The key advantage of the lexicon-based approach is its domain independence, which means that it can be applied to any domain. Moreover, it can easily be extended and improved – if an error occurs, one can correct some existing rules and/or add new rules to the system's rule base (Liu, 2015). On the other hand, a text is often considered as a collection of words without considering any of the relations between individual words (Boiy & Moens, 2009), which is limited to identify semantic or comparative sentiment. Besides, it also needs a heavy investment in time and effort to build the initial knowledge base of lexicon, patterns, and rules (Liu, 2012).

2   Machine-learning approaches are used to construct algorithms and build a model by feature selection and by learning from labeled training datasets (Hu & Liu, 2006; Pang et al., 2002). Well-known methods include the support vector machine (SVM), Naïve Bayes, and the N-gram model, all of which have been used for sentiment classification of online travel reviews (Ye, Zhang, & Law, 2009). Machine-learning approaches are credited for their capability to model many features and their adaptability to adjusting input (Boiy & Moens, 2009). In other words, learning algorithms can automatically learn from all kinds of features for classification through

optimization (Liu, 2015). However, machine-learning techniques require manual annotation of sufficient and representative training data, which is often very costly and time-consuming (Turney, 2002). Some of the research uses rule-based methods to automate the process of training data annotation (Wiebe & Riloff, 2005), but these do not consider the context of terms and thus might not produce the reliable and high-quality training data necessary for machine-learning (Liu, 2015). As machine-learning approaches rely on the training data, a sentiment classifier trained from the labeled data in one domain often does not work in another domain (Liu, 2012). To tackle this problem, lexicon-based approaches are recommended.

Levels of analysis

Approaches can also be distinguished based on the level of analysis they involve:

1   Document-level analysis aims to identify and classify sentiment orientations or polarities within a whole opinion document (Pang et al., 2002). It has been largely applied to determine the overall positive or negative sentiment of text in question-answering systems, forum discussions, blogs and online reviews and has proven useful for companies, recommender systems, and editorial sites to create summaries of people's experiences and opinions (Liu, 2012; Pang & Lee, 2004). For example, given an online travel review, the system determines whether the review expresses an overall positive or negative opinion about hotel services. As document-level analysis is useful to classify the overall opinion about the text (Yi et al., 2003), it is considered as the simplest sentiment analysis and therefore draws attention to the limitations of performing fine-grained tasks (Liu, 2015).

Document-level analysis restrictively focuses on opinions on a single topic (e.g. a single product) and therefore is not applicable to a document or even a portion of a document which evaluates or compares multiple topics (Yi et al., 2003). For companies, this means they cannot capture the complete information that matters to them. This limitation poses a critical challenge of conducting sentiment analysis in tourism. On social media, tourists post and share their travel-related comments, opinions, and personal experiences (Xiang & Gretzel, 2010). It has been found that they are interested in many aspects of the accommodation or the destination and mention multiple topics in the online posts such as transportation, restaurants, night life, shopping and prices (Kasper & Vela, 2011; Miguéns et al., 2008). For example, though tourists could be generally happy about a hotel service, they might be dissatisfied by the limited availability of dining options in the area. For companies, these individual weaknesses and strengths are as important as the overall satisfaction level of customers, as they permit them to improve their service quality in specific areas.

   Other drawbacks of document-level analysis are concerned with the neglect of neutral sentiment and the context. Most document-level sentiment classification ignores the neutral class mainly because it is more difficult to perform three-class classification (i.e. positive, neutral, negative) accurately (Liu, 2015). On social media, however, consumers often ask questions and exchange information, and such text likely only contains neutral sentiment (Jansen et al., 2009). In tourism, it has also been found that tourists tend to publish purely descriptive posts that do not carry positive or negative evaluation (Kasper & Vela, 2011), such as *"we spent three hours in the museum"*. Given that document-level analysis is too coarse to perform in-depth natural language analysis that is beyond text classification (Liu, 2015), other types of analysis are typically adopted.

2   The goal of sentence-level analysis is to determine sentiment polarities within a given sentence (Liu, 2015). It has been widely applied to determine the sentiment of online reviews and microblogging posts (Go et al., 2009; McDonald et al., 2007). Sentence-level analysis focuses on subjectivity classification, which distinguishes sentences (i.e. objective sentences) that express factual information from sentences that express subjective views and opinions (i.e. subjective sentences) (Liu, 2012). This means that unlike document-level analysis that often ignores the neutral class, the neutral class cannot be ignored in sentence-level classification because a document may contain many sentences that express neither positive nor negative sentiment. Moreover, sentence-level analysis goes further than document-level classification as it moves closer to opinion targets and sentiments about the targets (Liu, 2015). Despite of these merits, sentence-level analysis has a few limitations that restrict its application on social media.

Sentence-level analysis can only identify regular opinions conveyed in simple sentences and is not applicable when determining semantic opinions expressed in compound and complex sentences (Liu, 2012). For instance, *"we should visit Australia in December, because then the weather in Korea is bad"* and *"this hotel is doing very well in this poor economy"*. Sentence-level classification also cannot deal with opinions or sentiment in comparative sentences (Liu, 2012). For example, *"the seafood tastes better than the pasta in this restaurant"*. Although these sentences clearly convey sentiment, one cannot simply identify the sentence as being positive, negative or neutral. The reason is that they have different semantic meanings from regular opinions (Liu, 2015). This limitation raises a problem for determining the intricate consumer sentiment on social media. It has been found that tourists are in favor of online travel reviews that contain a balance of pros and cons; moreover, the major motivations for writing reviews include helping others by sharing positive experiences, saving others from negative experiences and warning others of bad services (Gretzel et al., 2007). It is very likely that these opinions are expressed through evaluations, comparisons and explanations, which are not regular opinions.

What is more, sentence-level analysis is not capable of identifying sentiment in the following three cases: (1) no predetermined corresponding sentiment pattern is available; (2) the sentence is not complete; and (3) parser failure due to missing punctuation or wrong spelling (Yi et al., 2003). The first limitation raises two problems for conducting sentiment analysis on social media given the magnitude of data available and the language model. With the existence of an API, it is very easy to collect a massive amount of posts. However, using such massive amounts of cases for manual annotation of sufficient and representative data and training the algorithms is very costly and time-consuming (Turney, 2002). In reality, therefore, it is usually the case that tests only consist of a thousand training items to determine the sentiment pattern (Go et al., 2009).

Moreover, it is well recognized that the use of dialect, slang and emoticons on social media is much higher than in other domains (Zappavigna, 2012). There-fore, it is very likely that the predetermined sentiment patterns derived from training the limited items are not able to identify the huge amount of data retrieved on social media and the sentiment expressed through peculiar social media language. The second and third limitations pose challenges for conducting sentiment analysis on social media given the distinctive characteristics of social media posts. While larger pieces of text such as online reviews represent sum-marized thoughts of authors, some social media posts are shorter and more casual and they are posted from many different media such as mobile phones (Go et al., 2009). Therefore, it is common that these posts are delivered through a few words and emotions and contain misspellings and missing punctuations (Zappavigna, 2012).

3   Phrase-level analysis aims to identify sentiment polarities based on certain phrases in each sentence of a text (Morinaga et al., 2002). Although it is viewed as a useful method in performing fine-grained tasks (Wilson et al., 2009), it also has considerable limitations. Phrase-level analysis does not consider the word's contextual polarity – the polarity of the expression is the expression in which a word appears and the word's contextual polarity puts the context of the sentence into consideration (Wilson et al., 2009). Words usually have the same prior and contextual polarity; however, very often a word's prior and contextual polarities differ (Liu, 2012). In other words, there are many factors within the sentence which constrain the capability of using prior polarity of the words and phrases for sentiment analysis. Certain phrases that contain negation words intensify rather than change polarity (Wilson et al., 2009). For example, *"this place is not only good but amazing"*. Moreover, a positive or negative sentiment word may have opposite orientations in dif-ferent application domains (Liu, 2012). For example, *"cool"* usually indicates positive sentiment, e.g. *"the decoration of this café is so cool"* but it can also imply negative sentiment, e.g. *"Without central heat, this café is too cool"*. Moreover, a sentence containing sentiment words may not express any senti-ment, which often occurs in interrogative and conditional sentences (Liu, 2015). For example, *"can you tell me which local restaurant is good?"* and *"if I can find a good restaurant on my way back, I will have dinner there."* Both sentences contain the sentiment word *"good,"* but neither expresses a positive or negative opinion on any specific restaurant.

Phrase-level analysis is also limited in terms of identifying the sentiment without the use of sentiment words, as many of these sentences are actually objective sentences that are used to express some factual information in addition to sentiment (Liu, 2012). For example, the sentence "*I waited for a long time to be served in this restaurant*" implies a negative sentiment about the service since it indicates this customer is not happy about having to wait. Another important aspect of contextual polarity is the perspective of the person who is expressing the sentiment (Wilson et al., 2009). For example, consider the phrase "*did not make it*" in the sentence "*there are too many people visiting this park. All tickets are sold out; I didn't make it*". From a firm's perspective, this could be positive because they did a good job promoting the park. From a customer's perspective, this is negative. Therefore, the contextual polarity of this phrase ultimately depends on the perspective of the person who is expressing the sentiment.

4   Aspect-based analysis, also known as feature-based, topic-based, entity-based and target-based analysis, aims to identify sentiment targets and assign sentiments to the targets (Hu & Liu, 2006). Instead of looking at language constructs (i.e. documents, paragraphs, sentences, clauses, phrases), aspect-level analysis directly looks at the opinion itself. According to Liu (2012, 2015), aspect-based analysis consists of the following core components. First, entity extraction and categorization is concerned with the sentiment domain such as the specific product. Second, aspect extraction and categorization aims to identify all the topics involved in the entity, such as the color and price of the product. Third, aspect-sentiment classification aims to determine whether an opinion on an aspect is positive, negative or neutral. Other components mentioned in aspect-based analysis are time extraction and standardization, opinion holder identification and opinion quintuple generation. The following example presents details the opinion quintuple generation.

Example: An online review published by Big Robbin on March 22:

I don't enjoy my stay at this hotel because the room service is bad. But my wife has a pleasant stay because she really loves the food.

Classification: (1) entity: hotel; (2) aspect: room service and food; (3) opinion holder: big Robbin, big Robbin's wife; (4) aspect-sentiment: room service is negative; food is positive; (5) the identification of the time when the review was published: March 22; (6) generating the following two opinion quintuples: (hotel, room service, negative, big Robbin, March-22); (hotel, food, positive, big Robbin's wife, March-22).

As opposed to document-level, sentence-level and phrase-level analysis, aspect-level analysis is credited for its capability of performing fine-grained analysis because it discovers what exactly consumers like and dislike (Liu, 2015). As the definition suggests, it permits researchers to identify a sentiment target, which helps one to understand the sentiment analysis problems identified in the aforementioned three levels of analysis. For instance, though the sentence *"although the service is not that great, I still love the atmosphere of this restaurant"* clearly includes a positive sentiment, one cannot say that this sentence is entirely positive. Moreover, aspect-level analysis is able to identify two types of sentiment, i.e. regular and comparative opinions (Liu, 2012). A regular opinion expresses a sentiment only on a particular aspect or topic, e.g. *"the seafood in this restaurant tastes very good,"* which expresses a positive sentiment on the aspect *taste* of seafood. A comparative opinion compares multiple aspects based on some of their shared topics, e.g. *"the seafood tastes better than the pasta in this restaurant"*, which compares seafood and pasta based on their tastes and expresses a preference for seafood. On the other hand, aspect-level analysis also has limitations that pose challenges for conducting sentiment analysis on social media.

The problem of aspect-level analysis is to extract and categorize aspect expressions – aspect relates to an actual word or phrase that appears in the text which is presented in different ways and sometimes is implicit. For example, Motorola may be written as Mot, Moto, and Motorola (Liu, 2015). Therefore, researchers need to recognize they all refer to the same item (i.e. mobile phone). On social media, users may use different expressions to refer to the same thing. First, communication on social media is characterized by brevity, especially on microblogs; therefore, it is common that users deploy abbreviations to say the topic or aspect. Moreover, communication on social media occurs without geographic boundaries; thus, the same aspect could be expressed differently by users from different regions or countries. Finally, users can also use slang, sarcasm and metonymy as implicit expressions, given the popularity of this type of language on social media (Zappavigna, 2012). This is typically a problem for tourism because tourists from all over the world share their experiences on social media platforms (Leung et al., 2013).

Aspect-level analysis is also limited in identifying consumer sentiment expressed in a highly networked social media space. Communication on social media occurs in an interconnected and multidirectional online space, allowing for one-to-many interactions (Hennig-Thurau et al., 2013). This means that consumers may express different types of sentiment to firms and their peers through commenting and reposting/tagging simultaneously. Therefore, researchers not only need to identify the target of sentiment, but also to whom customers express their sentiment. For example: *"This local event is very interesting. I am sad that we didn't go because you were sick @user"*. Clearly, this consumer expresses positive sentiment towards a firm but negative sentiment toward his or her friend being tagged. For business organizations, it is important to acknowledge customer sentiment that is of relevance to them. By doing so, they can better allocate their resources and adjust the marketing strategies in a more effective way. This is typically the case for tourism. Social media have been widely adopted by travellers to share their travel stories and experiences with organizations, families and friends before, during and after the trip (Leung et al., 2013). This means that they are more likely to express different sentiments in relation to different targets, which may or may not be relevant to companies.

5   Emotion-level analysis attempts to detect expressions of different types of emotion, e.g. anger or joy (Thelwall, 2017). This type of analysis goes beyond simple polarity detection and requires a much more fine-grained technique, often reliant on lexicon-based approaches.

Challenges for sentiment analysis

The growth in the quantity of subjective, opinionated information (Balahur & Jacquet, 2015) and the distinctive means through which it is delivered on social media have brought about crucial challenges to sentiment analysis. The first one is concerned with social media-afforded multimodal communication – users can publish text, videos, pictures and emoticons. While video per se is a single modality, the analysis needs to decompose it into two modalities: audio and visual. The former includes vocal expressions such as prosody and laughter, and the latter consists of facial expressions and physical gestures (Wollmer et al., 2013). These aspects complicate the dimensions and process of sentiment analysis. One must consider the differences in person-to-person communication patterns – some people express themselves more vocally while others more visually (Morency et al., 2011). This means that prior to identifying and classifying sentiment orientations, one needs to decode and interpret these audio and visual dimensions. This is also the case for analyzing static pictures.

The other challenge concerning multimodal communication is identifying sentiment expressed through emoticons and graphic icons. Apart from using emoticons to convey facial expressions, the advanced technological basis of social media provides users with a large array of emoticons manifesting kinetic gestures and graphic icons delivering informative, symbolic and referential content. Particularly, referential icons represent specific referents and convey semantic contents (Marcoccia et al., 2008). Researchers need to extract the semantic meaning and sentiment indicated in these emoticons and icons and then build a lexicon or train the algorithms that are flexible and comprehensive enough to determine sentiment orientations. Moreover, these context or culture-specific icons require researchers to have not only proficient analytical skills, but also an intrinsic understanding of the cultural and social context of the social media texts.

The identification of sentiment delivered through intertextual text is also challenging. Intertextuality, i.e. the shaping of a text's meaning by another text, creating relationality, interconnectedness and interdependence between texts (Allen, 2011), can be found in all types of social media platforms, such as Facebook, microblogging sites and online review sites (Vásquez, 2015). Intertextual forms of text encompass: (1) hyperlinks leading to another website (i.e. hyperlinking); (2) publishing a post through editing a previous message; (3) reposting and repetition of the previous posts; and, (4) publishing a post with combined textual and image components (Allen, 2011; Vásquez, 2015). All of them play a large role in the meaning-making process, and such meaning does not exist in a single text, but rather each text derives its meaning as a result of its embeddedness in multiple layers of texts (Vásquez, 2015). This means that the analysis of intertextual text is far beyond analysis that treats sentiment expression as isolated documents, sentences, phrases or specific aspects.

Another challenge is concerned with determining sentiment in a highly interconnected and multidirectional social media space (Hennig-Thurau et al., 2013). Social media allow consumers to verbally interact with firms and other users simultaneously through tagging. In other words, when responding to firm-initiated posts, they can also tag other users. Thus, in addition to identifying a person who expresses sentiment (i.e. opinion holder) and sentiment text (Liu, 2015), it is also critical to look at the target of the consumer sentiment, which might or might not be relevant to firms. Thus, social media-afforded actions like tagging need to be considered in conjunction with sentiment expressions.

Consumers' social networks on social media are extended to world-systems levels (Yoo & Gretzel, 2010), indicating that people from different countries share their opinions on social media. This poses another challenge – creating linguistic resources for multilingual sentiment analysis (Osimo & Mureddu, 2012). The current lexicons containing sentiment-related words, as well as annotated corpora are mainly created for English (Balahur & Jacquet, 2015). Manual annotation of a massive amount of data on social media is a cumbersome process (Liu, 2015). Therefore, to fulfill the need to create lexicons for sentiment in languages other than English, researchers use machine translation systems to automatically obtain resources for other languages (Balahur & Jacquet, 2015). This might not be a commendable approach given the peculiarities of language on social media and the fundamentally different cross-language structures. First, it is challenging to deal with the variability of the abbreviations, acronyms, graphic symbols such as emoticons and non-standard orthography and the pervasive use of irony and sarcasm on social media (Balahur & Jacquet, 2015). Further, it is also a challenge to tackle the unique linguistic characteristics of other languages, such as those from Asian countries. For instance, Chinese, one of the major language used by a large portion of the world's population as well as internet users, differs entirely from English in terms of phonetic aspects, syntactic dependency and a variety of semantic word senses (Zhang et al., 2009).

Other equally important challenges include cross-platform sentiment analysis, real-time sentiment analysis (Osimo & Mureddu, 2012), dealing with spam opinion (Liu, 2015; Seerat & Azam, 2012) and editability afforded by social media. Social media encompass a myriad of platforms that perform different functions and entail specific modes of communications (Gretzel & Yoo, 2013), including recreational, informational, transformational and relational modes (Kozinets, 1999). This leads to the creation of social media platform-specific cultures (Gretzel & Yoo, 2013). Therefore, the sentiment measurement might not be consistent across platforms and different approaches may consequently be required. Moreover, social media afford real-time communication – posts are presented in a reverse chronological format based on the time of publication. This provokes a challenge in terms of identifying how consumer sentiments change along with the specific event (e.g. sales promotion campaign) or if consumers change their opinion about a product over time (Seerat & Azam, 2012).

Third, spam opinions or fake opinions are becoming more and more sophisticated, as opinions in social media are increasingly used in practice. It is very hard to recognize fake opinions by manually reading them. This makes it difficult to find gold-standard data to help design and evaluate detection algorithms (Liu, 2015). Finally, editability refers to the ability of users to modify or revise content they have already posted, including revising and deleting the content (Treem & Leonardi, 2012). This is a challenge for researchers to ensure the reliability of the analysis; because consumers control the posts after the original display, they can either change the sentiment content from positive to negative or vice versa or delete the post.

Applications of sentiment analysis in tourism and hospitality

Sentiment analysis is widely used in tourism and hospitality to understand the social media comments of travellers. In tourism destination research, sentiment analysis has been proposed as a tool to monitor brands' reputation (Choi, Lehto & Oleary, 2007; Marchiori & Cantoni, 2011; Sigala et al., 2012). Sentiment analysis applied to comments on online reviews of hotels and restaurants has been identified as essential for creating appropriate strategies for customer service management (Levy et al., 2013; Pantelidis, 2010). The faster the managers respond to costumers' complaints and needs, the faster they can mitigate issues that can have a direct impact on their companies' revenue (Noone et al., 2011). Automated sentiment analysis is therefore critical. However, O'Connor's (2010) study of managing a hotel's image via conducting sentiment analysis on social media data found few hotels take this task seriously. According to this authors' perspective, the lack of credibility of travellers' reviews contributes to this disinterest from some hotel managers.

Another topic of interest in current tourism and hospitality research is the relationship between travel reviews' ratings and sentiment. There are empirical findings that proclaim that travellers' ratings and sentiments are congruent, while other findings suggest discrepancies (e.g. high rating and negative sentiment). These results suggest a disconnect between the description of the experience and the actual overall satisfaction rating given and emphasizes the importance of sentiment analysis to complement the simple monitoring of review ratings.

Conclusion

This chapter provided an overview of the current state of sentiment analysis, which is developing very fast due to increased computing power, access to data and advances in machine-learning. Sentiment analysis is especially important in tourism, where the analysis of rapidly growing amounts of unstructured data published on social media has many academic and practical applications. The need for ever more efficient and reliable sentiment analysis approaches has led to a dramatic increase in availability of analysis tools. However, Feldman (2013) points out that many of the commercial sentiment analysis tools use very simplistic approaches and leave a lot to be desired. Ribeiro et al. (2016) also warn of using off-the-shelf tools and suggest that researchers need to perform experiments with different methods before applying them to particular datasets as different sentiment methods can lead to very different interpretations. The many challenges to correctly identifying sentiments and their targets discussed in this chapter clearly hint at an ongoing need for more research in this area. They also identify tourism and hospitality not only as a very important application domain but as especially complex and therefore difficult for sentiment analysis.

Note

1 A branch of artificial intelligence that deals with analyzing, understanding and generating the languages that humans use naturally in order to interface with computers in both written and spoken contexts using natural human languages instead of computer languages ("Webopedia," 2016)

References

Akehurst, G. (2009). User generated content: The use of blogs for tourism organisations and tourism consumers. *Service Business*, 3(1), pp. 51–61.

Allen, G. (2011). *Intertextuality*. New York, Routledge.

Balahur, A., & Jacquet, G. (2015). Sentiment analysis meets social media: Challenges and solutions of the field in view of the current information sharing context. *Information Processing & Management*, 51(4), pp. 428–432.

Benckendorff, P. J., Sheldon, P. J., & Fesenmaier, D. R. (2014). Social media and tourism. *Tourism information technology*, 2nd Edition. Wallingford, UK, CABI, pp. 120–147.

Bermingham, A., & Smeaton, A. F. (2010). Classifying sentiment in microblogs: Is brevity an advantage? In *Proceedings of the 19th ACM International Conference on Information and Knowledge Management*. ACM, pp. 1833–1836.

Boiy, E., & Moens, M. F. (2009). A machine learning approach to sentiment analysis in multilingual Web texts. *Information retrieval*, 12(5), pp. 526–558.

Cambridge English Dictionary. (2016). Sentiment. Retrieved online December 5, 2016, from: http://dictionary.cambridge.org/us/dictionary/english/sentiment.

Choi, S., Lehto, X. Y., & Oleary, J. T. (2007). What does the consumer want from a DMO website? A study of US and Canadian tourists' perspectives. *International Journal of Tourism Research*, 9(2), pp. 59–72.

Feldman, R. (2013). Techniques and applications for sentiment analysis. *Communications of the ACM*, 56(4), pp. 82–89.

Go, A., Bhayani, R., & Huang, L. (2009). Twitter sentiment classification using distant supervision. *CS224N Project Report, Stanford*, 1, pp. 12.

Gretzel, U. (2015). Web 2.0 and 3.0. In L. Cantoni & J. A. Danowski (eds.) *Communication and Technology*, Handbooks of Communication Science (HOCS) series, Berlin, De Gruyter Mouton, pp. 181–192.

Gretzel, U., & Yoo, K. H. (2013). Premises and promises of social media marketing in tourism. In S. McCabe (ed.) *The Routledge Handbook of Tourism Marketing*, New York, Routledge, pp. 491–504.

Gretzel, U., Yoo, K. H., & Purifoy, M. (2007). *Online Travel Reviews Study*. College Station, TX, Laboratory for Intelligent Systems in Tourism.

Hennig-Thurau, T., Hofacker, C. F., & Bloching, B. (2013). Marketing the pinball way: Understanding how social media change the generation of value for consumers and companies. *Journal of Interactive Marketing*, 27(4), pp. 237–241.

Hu, M., & Liu, B. (2004). Mining opinion features in customer reviews. *AAAI*, 4, pp. 755–760.

Hu, M., & Liu, B. (2006). Opinion extraction and summarization on the web. Retrieved online December 3, 2016, From: www.aaai.org/Papers/AAAI/2006/AAAI06-265.pdf.

Hvass, K. A., & Munar, A. M. (2012). The takeoff of social media in tourism. *Journal of Vacation Marketing*, 18(2), pp. 93–103.

Jansen, B. J., Zhang, M., Sobel, K., & Chowdury, A. (2009). Twitter power: Tweets as electronic word of mouth. *Journal of the American Society for Information Science and Technology*, 60(11), pp. 2169–2188.

Jiang, J., Gretzel, U., & Law, R. (2010). Do negative experiences always lead to dissatisfaction?: Testing attribution theory in the context of online travel reviews. In U. Gretzel, R. Law, & M. Fuchs (eds.) *Information and Communication Technologies in Tourism 2010*. Vienna, Austria, Springer Verlag, pp. 297–308.

Kanayama, H., & Nasukawa, T. (2006, July). Fully automatic lexicon expansion for domain-oriented sentiment analysis. In *Proceedings of the 2006 Conference on Empirical Methods in Natural Language Processing*. Association for Computational Linguistics, pp. 355–363.

Kasper, W., & Vela, M. (2011, October). Sentiment analysis for hotel reviews. *Computational Linguistics-Applications Conference*, Vol. 231527, pp. 45–52.

Kozinets, R. V. (1999). E-tribalized marketing?: The strategic implications of virtual communities of consumption. *European management journal*, 17(3), pp. 252–264.

Krumm, J., Davies, N., & Narayanaswami, C. (2008). User-generated content. *IEEE Pervasive Computing* 4, pp. 10–11.

Leung, D., Law, R., Van Hoof, H., & Buhalis, D. (2013). Social media in tourism and hospitality: A literature review. *Journal of Travel & Tourism Marketing*, 30(1–2), pp. 3–22.

Levy, S. E., Duan, W., & Boo, S. (2013). An analysis of one-star online reviews and responses in the Washington, DC, lodging market. *Cornell Hospitality Quarterly*, 54(1), pp. 49–63.

Liu, B. (2010). Sentiment analysis and subjectivity. In N. Indurkhya & F. J. Damerau (eds.) *Handbook of Natural Language Processing*, 2nd Edition. Boca Raton, FL, Chapman and Hall/CRC, pp. 627–666.

Liu, B. (2012). *Sentiment analysis and opinion mining*. Williston, VT, Morgan & Claypool Publishers.

Liu, B. (2015). *Sentiment Analysis: Mining Opinions, Sentiments, and Emotions*, Cambridge: UK, Cambridge University Press.

Marchiori, E., & Cantoni, L. (2011). The online reputation construct: Does it matter for the tourism domain? A literature review on destinations' online reputation. *Information Technology & Tourism*, 13(3), pp. 139–159.

Marcoccia, M., Atifi, H., & Gauducheau, N. (2008). Text-centered versus multimodal analysis of instant messaging conversation. *Language@ internet*, 5(7), pp. 1–20.

McDonald, R., Hannan, K., Neylon, T., Wells, M., & Reynar, J. (2007, June). Structured models for fine-to-coarse sentiment analysis. *Annual Meeting-Association for Computational Linguistics*, 45(1), p. 432.

McGarrity, L. (2016). What sentiment analysis can do for you? Marketingprofs. Retrieved online November 20, 2016, from www.marketingprofs.com/opinions/2016/29673/what-sentiment-analysis-can-do-for-your-brand?adref=nl040516.

Merriam-Webster. (2016). Sentiment. Retrieved online December 1, 2016, from www.merriam-webster.com/dictionary/sentiment.

Miguéns, J., Baggio, R., & Costa, C. (2008). Social media and tourism destinations: TripAdvisor case study. Paper presented at the Advances in Tourism Research 2008 Conference, Aveiro, Portugal, May. 26–28, 2008.

Milano, R., Baggio, R., & Piattelli, R. (2011). The effects of online social media on tourism websites. In R. Law, M. Fuchs, & F. Ricci (Eds.) *Information and Communication Technologies in Tourism 2011*. Vienna, Austria, Springer Verlag, pp. 471–483.

Miller, G. A., Beckwith, R., Fellbaum, C., Gross, D., & Miller, K. J. (1990). Introduction to WordNet: An on-line lexical database. *International journal of lexicography*, 3(4), pp. 235–244.

Morency, L.- P., Mihalcea, R., & Doshi, P. (2011). Towards multimodal sentiment analysis: Harvesting opinions from the web. In *Proceedings of the 13th International Conference on Multimodal Interfaces*. ACM, pp. 169–176.

Morinaga, S., Yamanishi, K., Tateishi, K., & Fukushima, T. (2002, July). Mining product reputations on the web. In *Proceedings of the eighth ACM SIGKDD international conference on Knowledge discovery and data mining,* ACM, pp. 341–349.

Munar, A. M., & Jacobsen, J. K. S. (2014). Motivations for sharing tourism experiences through social media. *Tourism management*, 43, pp. 46–54.

Nanli, Z., Ping, Z., Weiguo, L., & Meng, C. (2012). Sentiment analysis: A literature review. *Proceedings of the International Symposium on Management of Technology (ISMOT)*, Hangzhou, IEEE, pp. 572–576.

Nasukawa, T., & Yi, J. (2003). Sentiment analysis: Capturing favorability using natural language processing. In *Proceedings of the 2nd International Conference on Knowledge Capture*. ACM, pp. 70–77.

Noone, B. M., McGuire, K. A., & Rohlfs, K. V. (2011). Social media meets hotel revenue management: Opportunities, issues and unanswered questions. *Journal of Revenue & Pricing Management*, 10(4), pp. 293–305.

O'Connor, P. (2010). Managing a hotel's image on TripAdvisor. *Journal of Hospitality Marketing & Management*, 19(7), pp. 754–772.

Osimo, D., & Mureddu, F. (2012). Research challenge on opinion mining and sentiment analysis. Research Report. Universite de Paris-Sud, Laboratoire LIMSI-CNRS, Bâtiment, 508. Retrieved online December 6, 2016, from www.w3.org/2012/06/pmod/opinionmining.pdf.

Oxford English Dictionary. (2016). Sentiment. Retrieved online December 1, 2016, from https://en.oxforddictionaries.com/definition/sentiment.

Paltoglou, G., & Thelwall, M. (2017). Sensing social media: A range of approaches for sentiment analysis. In *Cyberemotions*. Springer International Publishing, pp. 97–117.

Pang, B., & Lee, L. (2004, July). A sentimental education: Sentiment analysis using subjectivity summarization based on minimum cuts. In *Proceedings of the 42nd Annual Meeting on Association for Computational Linguistics*. Association for Computational Linguistics, p. 271.

Pang, B., & Lee, L. (2008). Opinion mining and sentiment analysis. *Foundations and Trends in Information Retrieval*, 2(1–2), pp. 1–135.

Pang, B., Lee, L., & Vaithyanathan, S. (2002, July). Thumbs up?: Sentiment classification using machine learning techniques. In *Proceedings of the ACL-02 Conference on Empirical Methods in Natural Language Processing-Volume 10*. Association for Computational Linguistics, pp. 79–86.

Pantelidis, I. S. (2010). Electronic meal experience: A content analysis of online restaurant comments. *Cornell Hospitality Quarterly*, 51(4), pp. 483–491.

Piryani, R., Madhavi, D., & Singh, V. K. (2017). Analytical mapping of opinion mining and sentiment analysis research during 2000–2015. *Information Processing & Management*, 53(1), pp. 122–150.

Ribeiro, F. N., Araújo, M., Gonçalves, P., Gonçalves, M. A., & Benevenuto, F. (2016). SentiBench-a benchmark comparison of state-of-the-practice sentiment analysis methods. *EPJ Data Science*, 5(1), pp. 1–29.

Schuckert, M., Liu, X., & Law, R. (2015). Hospitality and tourism online reviews: Recent trends and future directions. *Journal of Travel & Tourism Marketing*, 32(5), pp. 608–621.

Seerat, B., & Azam, F. (2012). Opinion mining: Issues and challenges (a survey). *International Journal of Computer Applications*, 49(9).

Sigala, M., Christou, E., & Gretzel, U. (2012). *Social media in travel, tourism and hospitality: Theory, practice and cases*. Surrey, UK, Ashgate Publishing, Ltd.

Stieglitz, S., & Dang-Xuan, L. (2013). Emotions and information diffusion in social media: Sentiment of microblogs and sharing behavior. *Journal of Management Information Systems*, 29(4), pp. 217–248.

Stone, P. J., Dunphy, D., Smith, M. S., & Ogilvie, D. M. (1966). *General Inquirer: A Computer Approach to Content Analysis*. Cambridge, MA, MIT Press.

Thelwall, M. (2017). Sentiment analysis for small and big data. In N. G. Fielding, R. M. Lee,. & G. Blank (eds.) *The Sage Handbook of Online Research Methods*. Los Angeles, CA: Sage, pp. 344–360.

Thevenot, G. (2007). Blogging as a social media. *Tourism and Hospitality Research*, 7(3–4), pp. 287–289.

Treem, J. W., & Leonardi, P. M. (2012). Social media use in organizations: Exploring the affordances of visibility, editability, persistence, and association. *Communication yearbook*, 36, pp. 143–189.

Tsvetovat, M., Kazil, J., & Kouznetsov, A. (2012). Implicit sentiment mining-New approach overcomes inherent problems while exploring media bias and electoral sentiment. *OR/MS Today*, 39(6), p. 20.

Turney, P. D. (2002). Thumbs up or thumbs down? semantic orientation applied to unsupervised classification of reviews. In *Proceedings of the 40th Annual Meeting of the Association for Computational Linguistics*, Philadelphia.

Vásquez, C. (2015). Intertextuality and interdiscursivity in online consumer reviews. In R. H Jones, A. Chik, & C. A. Hafner (eds.) *Discourse and Digital Practices: Doing Discourse Analysis in the Digital Age*. New York, Routledge, pp. 66–80.

Wiebe, J., & Riloff, E. (2005, February). Creating subjective and objective sentence classifiers from unannotated texts. In *International Conference on Intelligent Text Processing and Computational Linguistics*. Springer Berlin Heidelberg, pp. 486–497.

Wiebe, J., Wilson, T., Bruce, R., Bell, M., & Martin, M. (2004). Learning subjective language. *Computational linguistics*, 30(3), pp. 277–308.

Wilson, T., Wiebe, J., & Hoffmann, P. (2009). Recognizing contextual polarity: An exploration of features for phrase-level sentiment analysis. *Computational Linguistics*, 35(3), pp. 399–433.

Wollmer, M., Weninger, F., Knaup, T., Schuller, B., Sun, C., Sagae, K., & Morency, L.- P. (2013). Youtube movie reviews: Sentiment analysis in an audio-visual context. *Intelligent Systems, IEEE*, 28(3), pp. 46–53.

Xiang, Z., & Gretzel, U. (2010). Role of social media in online travel information search. *Tourism Management*, 31(2), pp. 179–188.

Xiang, Z., Schwartz, Z., Gerdes, J. H., & Uysal, M. (2015). What can big data and text analytics tell us about hotel guest experience and satisfaction?. *International Journal of Hospitality Management*, 44, pp. 120–130.

Ye, Q., Zhang, Z., & Law, R. (2009). Sentiment classification of online reviews to travel destinations by supervised machine learning approaches. *Expert Systems with Applications*, 36(3), pp. 6527–6535.

Yi, J., Nasukawa, T., Bunescu, R., & Niblack, W. (2003). Sentiment analyzer: Extracting sentiments about a given topic using natural language processing techniques. In *ICDM 2003: Third IEEE International Conference on Data Mining*. IEEE, pp. 427–434.

Yoo, K. H., & Gretzel, U. (2010, June). Web 2.0: New rules for tourism marketing. In *Proceedings of the 41th Annual Conference of the Travel and Tourism Research Association*.

Zappavigna, M. (2012). *Discourse of twitter and social media: How we use language to create affiliation on the web*. London, Continuum International Publishing Group.

Zeng, B., & Gerritsen, R. (2014). What do we know about social media in tourism? A review. *Tourism Management Perspectives*, 10, pp. 27–36.

Zhang, C., Zeng, D., Li, J., Wang, F. Y., & Zuo, W. (2009). Sentiment analysis of Chinese documents: From sentence to document level. *Journal of the American Society for Information Science and Technology*, 60(12), pp. 2474–2487.

17 Social media analysis from a communication perspective

The case of the argumentative analysis of online travel reviews

Silvia De Ascaniis and Lorenzo Cantoni

A communication perspective to study social media content

This chapter proposes a method to study social media content, which is based on a *communication perspective*. This means that social media content is considered as a *communicative artefact* created and received in a specific context, according to the goals of a producer, in view of a receiver, using a code for conveying the meaning and a channel for its physical transmission (Jakobson, 1960). In particular, the perspective on communication that is adopted considers language as a *social action* and texts as artefacts conceived with a *purpose*, that is for producing an effect on the social reality shared by the producer and the receiver. According to such perspective, if one wants to understand the meaning of a text, she needs to go beyond what is literally said and consider all the other elements of the communicative event. The *meaning* of a text corresponds to the overall intended change the text has been conceived to bring in the inter-subjectivity of the receivers. This means that, after a text has been uttered, things are no longer the same for the receivers, and the meaning of that text corresponds to the change it brought to them. This perspective on communication relies, mainly, on the notion of *speech act*, and takes into consideration especially verbal communication; it can be applied, though, to the different types of mediated communication artefacts, supported by different media and using different codes, thus also to social media.

The notion of speech acts was elaborated by the philosopher J. L. Austin in the essay *How to do things with words* (1962), which was influenced by the works of Gottlob Frege, Karl Bühler and Émile Benveniste. The notion of speech act had a deep influence, in the last century, in the way communication was intended: it promoted the shift from a notion of communication as a mechanic process where a message is codified by a sender and de-codified by a receiver, to a notion where the speaker's communicative intentions represent the core of the communicative event. It promoted, as well, the idea that communication is made possible by the interactions among participants (Sbisà, 2007). In his work, Austin aimed at setting a relation between language and action that is between to speak and to do. He developed a proper *theory of speech acts*, with the aim of explaining in which sense and under which conditions "to speak is to do". This theory was later reformulated and systematized by the philosopher of language John Searle (1969), who investigated what people actually do when they speak. According to Searle, a theory of language is part of a theory of action, because "speaking a language is performing speech acts, acts such as making statements, giving commands, asking questions, making promises, and so on" (Searle, 1969, p. 16).

From a psychological and behavioral point of view, the effect the speaker intends to achieve performing a speech act – i.e. his/her communicative goal – can be characterized with the notion of *habit change* which has been mainly elaborated by C. S. Peirce (1955). Peirce explains that a habit change is "a modification of a person tendencies toward action, resulting from previous experiences or from previous exertions of his will or acts, or from a complexus of both kinds of cause" (p. 476).

When it comes to mediated communication artefacts – thus, also, to social media content, their communicative goal is particularly influenced by the *medium*. The purpose of a post published on a travel forum, for instance, does not only depend on the communicative intentions of the author, but also on the general objectives of travel forums that are to provide information and logistic recommendations to people travelling. In the case of pictures posted on the Facebook page of a DMO, their goal is likely to show aspects of the destination and attract visitors. If a family picture of the DMO manager is posted, it results in an "out of place" effect.

Approaching social media content from the perspective of communicative acts within a discursive system means defining them as *textual genres*, that is, as communicative artefacts defined by a goal and implemented through specific strategies. A prospective tourist searching the web in need for recommendations, for instance, is usually able to recognize a text she comes upon as a forum post or as a travel review, and expects that text to be of help for satisfying her needs exactly because it is a post or a review. This "spontaneous" knowledge is knowledge of textual (and speech) genres, which people use in everyday life to classify the communicative events they are involved in, and to give congruent feed-backs. We use genres, in fact, "to package our speech and make of it a recognizable response to the exigencies of the situation" (Berkenkotter & Huckin, 1995, p. 7). Genre analysis has a long-established tradition in literary studies, and genre approaches are having, since the last decade, a considerable impact on the way discourse is understood. Most of them build upon the concept of genre developed by Bakhtin (1986, p. 60), who posited that: "language is realized in the form of concrete utterances (oral or written) by participants in the various areas of human activity. (. . .) Each separate utterance is individual, of course, but each sphere in which language is used develops its own relatively stable types of these utterances. These we may call speech genres." These considerations should be extended, again, beyond verbal communication to be applied to the different types of mediated communication artefacts. Bakhtin's words could be rephrased to include in the definition of a textual genre different "relatively stable types" of communication strategies developed through a variety of media using a number of often combined codes.

In this chapter, a specific textual genre is considered: Online Travel Reviews (OTR). It emerged in the field of travel and tourism with the advent of social media, and has become an established and recognized source of recommendation.

The communicative goal and characteristics of OTR are first defined, and then a method to study them is proposed.

Online travel reviews as a new textual genre

The communicative goal of an OTR is to provide a travel advice in order to help the reader to make an informed decision about her prospective travel experience. This goal is made explicit also by review platforms in the guidelines for authors. The primary commitment usually imposed to reviewers by online platforms is 'to be helpful', which might correspond to the personal goal of the reviewer, or might be just an accepted and contemplated outcome if the reviewer pursues other goals, like venting or bragging. It is a different matter in the case of spam, which are created to promote a product or service, despite any personal experience or opinion. De Ascaniis (2013) conducted an extensive study to define destination OTR as a proper textual genre and to determine its characteristics. She combined an analysis of the medium where they are published and an analysis of a sample of OTR about a notorious destination. The analysis showed that some types of utterances are relatively stable or "compulsory", in the sense that they constitute common communicative strategies used by reviewers to make their recommendations, while others are "optional", because they serve different contingent purposes. A destination OTR can be defined as:

> A travel recommendation about a destination, in the form of a direct or indirect visit recommendation, given by expressing an opinion on the destination. A constellation of arguments is put forward to support the opinion, which is based on a personal previous travel experience. Those aspects of the experience or of the destination itself that are considered most relevant are described, and suggestions are provided to help the reader to get the most from her trip. Narratives of the personal travel story and trip details, constitute additional elements, which contribute shaping prospective tourists' expectations.
>
> (De Ascaniis, 2013, p. 150)

The definition points out three essential components of OTR: they are *recommendations* relying upon *opinions* that are justified with *arguments* based on personal experiences. People writing OTR, indeed, propose a *reasoning chain*, to support the recommendation they make. OTR, thus, can be seen as "invitations to reason in a certain way", to lead the reader forming an opinion about a tourism product or service and, hence, make a travel decision. Other types of online travel-related textual genres are much less rich in opinions, because they pursue different communicative goals. Posts on travel forums, for instance, are short dialogical moves aimed, mostly, at giving quick and precise pieces of information to share place-related knowledge. Travel blogs and diaries, for their part, are longer monographic texts usually addressing – even if implicitly – a specific audience that are people who share the same interests in the case of blogs, or relatives and friends who are this way updated about the traveller's adventures in the case of diaries.

However, since prospective tourists must deliberate about their journey, they are primarily interested in the reasons why it is or it is not worthwhile to visit a certain destination, engage in certain activities or select one or the other accommodation (De Ascaniis & Greco Morasso, 2011). In fact, among the different forms in which User Generated Content is created online, OTR are the prevalent form in the field of tourism, and in the last few years a number of studies have investigated them under different respects (Gretzel et al., 2007; Yoo & Gretzel, 2008; Smith et al., 2005; De Ascaniis & Gretzel, 2013; Dickinger, 2011).

In order to understand how OTR contribute to and inform travel decision-making, the *reasoning texture* interweaving the text must be considered. This means going "inside" the reviews, and looking at the logic and pragmatic aspects which constitute them as a specific type of communicative act, taking place in a quite defined mediated context. Understanding tourists' reasoning paths, then, might be much more revealing than just trying to catch the dominant opinion expressed online, and offers to tourism operators a powerful tool for understanding consumers' needs and enhance reciprocal understanding. In fact, aggregated data made available by online platforms such as ratings, top-pictures, top-discussed topics, keywords association, easily allow one to get the main sentiment about a travel product/ service, but when one selects a text and goes through it, how does this text inform and mold her opinion? How and why does it influence her decision? Having access to the reasons given by tourists when commenting on their travel experiences, and being able to study them – that is to make an *argumentative analysis* of OTR – carries a lot of implications at the practical level. As a prime factor, it means understanding which features of a certain tourism product are appreciated the most, and why; then, on this basis, it means to enhance their promotion and to identify areas or aspects of improvement.

In the following section, the main characteristics of argumentation as a specific type of communication activity are presented, to explain, then, how to do an argumentative analysis of OTR.

Argumentation in online travel reviews

"Argumentation is a verbal and social activity of reason aimed at increasing (or decreasing) the acceptability of a controversial standpoint for the listener or reader, by putting forward a constellation of propositions (i.e. arguments) intended to justify (or refute) the standpoint before a rational judge" (Van Eemeren et al., 1996, p. 5).

In the case of OTR, the *standpoint* is constituted by a travel advice about a destination, which can be expressed with a directive of this kind: "I advice/recommend you to visit x". With this standpoint, the reviewer advises the reader to engage or not engage in a course of action, for the reader's benefit. The *argument* directly supporting the standpoint is the reviewer's overall opinion about the destination or her 'final verdict' about her travel experience at the destination. Thus, the main argumentative move of OTR can be generically expressed in these terms: "I advise/ recommend you to visit x, because my opinion of x is y". This argument works, in

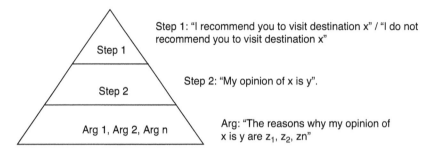

Figure 17.1 Argumentative structure of destination OTR

turn, as standpoint for other arguments ("constellation of propositions") that are the data used by the reviewer to support her opinion. Data can be, for instance, descriptions of attraction or reports of travel events. Some of these arguments may have their own argumentative structure, like suggestions about behaviors to have or logistic decisions, which are put forward with local pragmatic standpoints.

For the sake of clarity, we will call the main standpoint *stdp 1*, and the standpoint working as argument for it *stdp 2*. Stdp 2 is always explicit in OTR, even if it has not always been a verbal modality in the text. In fact, reviewers are asked by the platform to give a rate to the object they are reviewing, before publishing it; rating represents a summary statement of the reviewer's opinion. It usually adopts different semiotic codes than the linguistic one, like stars, ordinal numbers, bullets. Ratings often precede the main review text, and catch readers' eyes thanks to their color and design, contributing this way to create a first impression of the object of interest, well before the review text itself.

The argumentative structure of OTR can represented with the generic schema in Figure 17.1.

The argumentative analysis of online opinions in OTR

The first step when doing an argumentative analysis of a text is to identify the precise standpoint advanced by the speaker/writer, the arguments used to support it and to make explicit their inferential structure. In the reconstruction process, some parts of the text might be removed, because they are irrelevant for the inferential pattern, while some others might be added, because they are important for the inferential pattern but were left implicit in the text. Also, ambiguous formulation might be replaced with clearer ones, and some parts of the text might be rearranged in order to highlight their relevance for the justification of the opinion at stake (van Eemeren & Grootendorst, 2004). The argumentative reconstruction helps to systematically account for every passage in a text, which contributes to the "final verdict".

Figure 17.2 is an example of an online review retrieved from TripAdvisor.com, concerning destination Rome, while Figure 17.3 represents its argumentative reconstruction.

❝ One of the best places to visit ❞

Rome

DawnLouiseAustralia
Australia

Rome was a fantastic place. I heard from some that it was a dirty city but I did not find it to be so. It is very old but that is part of the attraction. The Roman Ruins are definately a must see and doing it with a tour is also recommended. But be warned that it is best to prebook your entry into such sites as it can be quite crowed when queing for a ticket.

The food is great and the people are very friendly. The shopping is also an enjoyable experience. I could not fault it.

Figure 17.2 Example of OTR on destination Rome

The standpoint is pointed out immediately in the title, where the reviewer gives her travel advice: "Rome is one of the best places to visit". The argument directly supporting the standpoint is expressed in the opening sentence, and is an overall evaluation of the city: "Rome is a fantastic place". The reviewer anticipates, right after, a possible counter-argument, but she also denies it according to her experience: someone would question the attractiveness of Rome saying that it is dirty, but this does not correspond to what she saw. The reviewer lists the reasons why, instead, Rome has to be considered a fantastic city, in the rest of the review: it has many old sights to be seen, the food is great, people are friendly and it offers interesting shopping opportunities. Since all these arguments independently support the standpoint, they are called *multiple arguments* (Snoeck Henkemans, 2001). The warning that there might be found queues at the Roman Ruins, so that to avoid them it is better to pre-book the ticket, can be reconstructed as a counter-argument for visiting the Ruins, which is rebutted suggesting a means to enjoy the visit anyway. The argument according to which Rome is fantastic because it is old, is reinforced by indicating one best "representative" of antique sights worth visiting, that are the Roman Ruins; the reviewer adds a suggestion, that is to take a guided tour to visit the Ruins, which is bound to the implicit argument that it is possible to make the visit to the Ruins even more interesting. These three arguments all together cooperate to support the reviewer's opinion about Rome, and together constitute an argument of the same weight of the previous ones; they are called *coordinate arguments* (Snoeck Henkemans, 2001). In the case of coordinate arguments, premises must cooperate in order to avoid possible *objections*. Objections to the argument that Rome is attractive because is an ancient city may be something like "Ancient cities are poor in interesting attractions" or "Historic sites

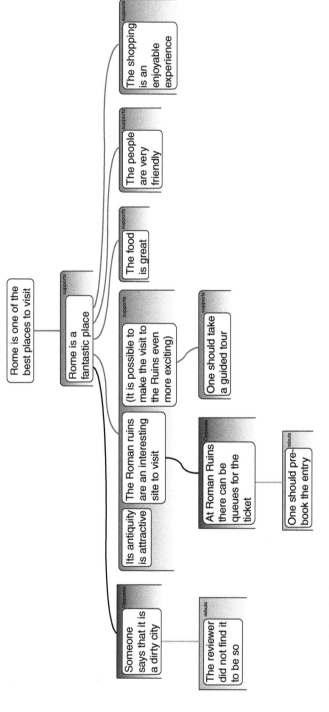

Figure 17.3 Standpoint-argument configuration of the OTR "One of the best places to visit"

in ancient cities cannot be really enjoyed because it is difficult to understand what they represent". Objections depend on the values the tourist ascribes to different aspects of the destination (such as historical sites), and on the type of travel she has in mind. Objections are here anticipated and avoided by the reviewer providing a rebuttal, in the form of coordinate premises: Roman Ruins *are* an interesting attraction exactly for their antiquity, and it is possible to have a fruitful visit relying on guided tours.

In the case of longer and more complex OTR, the argumentative reconstruction helps to systematize all the arguments used by the reviewer, allowing this way to grasp the "invitation to reason" the reviewer makes to the reader. A second example is now discussed.

The standpoint specifies the audience that is addressed, that are people interested in 'cultural destinations', at the same time highlighting the main reasons why Rome should be considered worth a visit, that are for its richness in history, art, architecture and the good cuisine. Two other coordinate arguments refer, respectively, to a particular activity that is promenading around the city at night, and to a specific attraction, that is the Angelus prayer on Sunday morning in St. Peter's Square, each one allowing the experience to be even more exciting. It is interesting

❝ A late comer to the Eternal City ❞

Rome

⊙⊙⊙⊙◯
Rozmic
Bedfordshire

At 60 I have just experienced my first visit to Rome.
For anybody who has an interest in History, Art, Architecture and good cuisine (all of which apply to me) a trip to the Eternal City comes highly recommended. Try to stay in the city instead of having to travel in and thereby have the opportunity of promenading around the city at night (when the lights are on!). The Trevi Fountain is best experienced at night. It's not cheap but Italy has never been that kind of destination. Also, you can encounter the inevitable rip-off merchants at the main tourist spots (eg Colloseum) but we found them to be a low-level irritation. Just say no.
A vist to st. Peter's Square on Sunday morning is a must (whether or not you are catholic) but take an umbrella against the sun; there's no shade!
One niggle: Unless you stop at one of the many restaurants, cafes or bars (and hence will be expected to buy a drink!) there is virtually no-where to sit down for a break. Apart from three benches located in the jewish quarter we found none anywhere else!

Rozmic - June 2011

Figure 17.4 Example of OTR on destination Rome

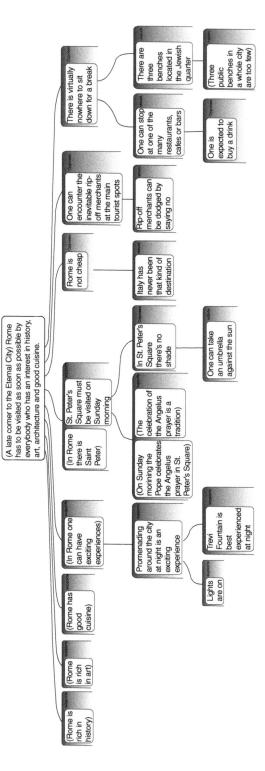

Figure 17.5 Standpoint-argument configuration of the OTR "A late comer to the eternal city"

to note that the argument about the Angelus prayer is for the most part implicit: the reviewer only suggests to visit St. Peter's Square on Sunday morning, while she takes for granted that the reader knows what usually happens on the Square on Sunday morning. Though, she provides a cue, saying that even if one is not Catholic, she should go there: here, the reviewer relies upon a shared knowledge within the community of interlocutors. Three counter-arguments are finally put forward to show negative aspects of the destination, but two of them are defeated through rebuttals.

The evaluation of arguments

Reconstructing the inferential relations between standpoints and arguments allows evaluation of the strength of the arguments, which means if they are reasonable enough and adequate to justify the standpoint. To evaluate arguments it needs, first, to consider what is exactly said in the standpoint. In the majority of OTR, the advice of visiting/not visiting a destination is directed towards a varied audience, but the reviewer might give indications about circumstances that restrict the scope of the standpoint. It makes a difference, in fact, whether a visitor suggests a destination for a short visit or for a longer-term holiday, for a family trip, a honeymoon or a study stay: some or other aspects of the destination become prominent accordingly. The "limits" imposed on the scope of the standpoint determine which arguments are appropriate and which ones should be avoided.

A good, persuasive argument does not depend only on logical force, but also on the choice of the right cultural and contextual – often implicit – premises and on its capacity to appeal to the audience. Aristotle in the "Rhetoric", emphasizes that an argument to be convincing needs to achieve a balance between *logos*, *ethos* and *pathos*. These are called *persuasive proofs*, that are the means through which argumentation is realized in a discourse.

The dimension of *logos* refers to the rules of reasons related to the construction of arguments. The argumentative reconstruction that we have presented above, aims at making explicit such rules.

Ethos refers to the extent to which people are inclined to go along with an argument because of who expresses it. A speech may convince the interlocutor because it "is spoken in such a way as to make the speaker worthy of credence; for we believe fair-minded people to a greater extent and more quickly on all subjects in general and especially where there is not exact knowledge but room for doubt" (I.2.4). Trust represents, for Aristotle, almost the strongest form of argument, the most authoritative form of persuasion, because it relates to the social nature of persuasion that is on the dependence that we generally place on each other for what we believe and value. Trust, however, cannot be compelled; it must be given. A speaker cannot make an audience trust her but can create the conditions for that trust to develop, and knowledge of things is one basic required condition (Tindale, 2004). The authority of any reviewer, indeed, comes from her direct experience, from her actual knowledge of the things and from her mainly altruistic goal: she is reckoned a reliable testimony. Some platforms for travel review, as TripAdvisor, even assign particular "authoritative" role to some reviewers; these are the so called "destination experts", who are granted the status of expert because they are residents or have relevant previous experiences in a given destination. Trusting fellow travellers as reliable testimonies is, indeed, the key to understand UGC in tourism. Like word-of-mouth recommendations, in fact, UGC are supposedly unbiased, differently from official reviews.

Aristotle identifies a third means to persuasively argue in front of an audience that is to lead it through the speech to feel *emotions* (I.2.5). Since the whole person is addressed when speech aims at persuasion, emotions must be given their own place. Our judgments, in fact, change according to our emotional state. This means or rhetorical proof is called *pathos*, and refers to the set of feelings, emotions, intuitions, sympathies and prejudices that people bring to decision. Aristotle describes emotions (*pathê*) as "those things through which, by undergoing change, people come to differ about their judgments and which are accompanied by pain and pleasure, for example, anger, pity, fear, and such things as their opposites" (II.1.8). In OTR, pathos is reached through linguistic choice, register, use of rhetorical figures, and is particularly emphasized in the destination overall evaluation and in visit recommendations. Reviewers try to describe the emotions they felt in their travel experience, which they keep in their memory and importantly contribute to shape their travel opinion, this way driving readers "to taste" their same emotions, to create expectations and, in the end, to take the proposed course of action (i.e. visit or not visit the destination).

A case is now presented, of an analysis – i.e. identification, reconstruction and evaluation – of the arguments given by reviewers when recommending/not recommending a visit to a destination.

A case: reviewers' arguments to recommend a visit to Rome

The sample of analysis

The corpus of analysis consists of a random selection of all the reviews posted on TripAdvisor about destination Rome, in English, German and Italian. Twenty reviews per year were randomly selected starting from the first publication year that was 2007, up to the first eight months of 2015. Among the many platforms for travel reviews, TripAdvisor was chosen because it is the most popular, it provides the largest amount of content, and has the highest ranking in search engines. Destination reviews are listed by TripAdvisor in the Travel Guide section (www.tripadvisor.com/AllReviews-g187791-Rome_Lazio.html). A manual filtering of the initial sample comprising 180 OTR excluded those about specific tourism services or attractions. The final sample of analysis comprised 158 OTR, distributed as follows: 67 in English, 49 in German, 42 in Italian.

The analytical procedure

The analysis followed three steps:

(1) first, the arguments supporting the generic evaluative standpoint – i.e. *stdp 2* "My opinion of destination x is y" – were identified and classified into categories. This analytical step was supported by *UAM Corpus Tool*, a software for text annotation and analysis, which allows one to explore linguistic patterns and linguistic features in a text that cannot be explored with simple concordances, and that cannot be automatically tagged because they pertain to the semantic or pragmatic level;[1]

(2) second, each review was analytically reconstructed, to point out the types of argumentative structures – i.e. multiple arguments or coordinate arguments – most frequently used when advancing different categories of argument. This analytical step was supported by *Rationale*, a tool for argument diagramming, which allows one to represent argumentative structures by distinguishing among subordinate, coordinate and multiple arguments;[2]

(3) third, in order to evaluate the strength of the different categories of arguments, the restrictions imposed to the recommendation standpoint were considered, that is the type of visitor addressed, the length of stay recommended, the type of tourism experience desired.

Results

Arguments were first distinguished in positive and negative, and then classified into categories following a bottom-up approach until the saturation level, that is until no new category was found in the texts, but the existent categories were enough to categorize the types of arguments encountered. No unclassified residuals were left. If the same argument was repeated in the review, it was counted only once in the coding procedure. Table 17.1 reports the distribution of positive

Table 17.1 Types and distribution of positive arguments

Positive argument type	Example	Frequency
History, art, culture	"You could walk hand in hand to all the monuments"	84
Food	"And the food and wine well – fabulous"	39
Attractions	"Each time we go we have found something new to explore"	43
Activities opportunities (e.g. events, shopping)	"There is something for everyone"	29
Special places	"A visit to St. Peter's Square on Sunday morning is a must."	29
Tourism orientation (= tourism services, transportation means, safety, cost of life, walkability)	"We both love walking during our holidays . . . well Rome is the best place to do it" "The city felt pretty safe with a quite strong police presence"	25
Atmosphere	"Rome has to be the most romantic place on earth"	23
Local people	"people everywhere are generally kind and helpful"	15

arguments (N = 287) into categories, providing an example for each one of them (examples are taken from English OTR).

The reasons given by reviewers to support a visit to Rome confirm its fame that is one of a city rich in art, whose culture has been shaped by the legacy of a glorious past. Heritage is not only represented by works of art, but also by the gastronomic tradition, in fact, food-related experiences and the many sites deserving a visit are among the most frequent arguments. As for the biggest cities, Rome has a lot to offer in terms of activities that can be performed apart from sightseeing. Among the sites that make the city unique and particularly worth a visit, are Saint Peter, the Trevi fountain, the Spanish stairs and the many centuries' old churches. Among the aspects helping the visitor to have a nice experience, the walkability of the city center is highly appreciated. Finally, the romantic atmosphere and the friendliness of the local people also represent good reasons to recommend a visit.

Table 17.2 reports the distribution of negative arguments (N = 73) into categories with respective examples.

Among the arguments advanced by reviewers to discourage a visit to Rome, the massive presence of pickpockets and people trying to take advantage of tourists is the most frequent, together with insufficient tourism and public services. Traffic and chaos, dirty streets and graffiti on public walls, can also make the visit a negative experience. It is interesting to note, that positive arguments are four times more than negative arguments: it is a matter of fact, indeed, that they are usually posted more positive than negative reviews, and it has been proved that people writing OTR are driven mostly by the wish to reciprocate great experiences and by altruistic reasons, than by complaining or venting reasons (Gretzel et al., 2007).

The analysis of the argumentative structure of OTR showed that most of them have a linear non-complex reasoning structure: visually, it develops mostly horizontally, meaning that numerous multiple arguments and (some) counter-arguments are provided to support or reject the standpoint. Reviewers often provide a list of the city aspects that were of relevance for them or that impressed them the most; each single aspect (i.e. argument) would likely not be enough to justify a

Table 17.2 Types and distribution of negative arguments

Negative argument type	Example	Frequency
Thieves and cheats	"Beware of touts and cheats or pickpockets as most tourist sites are crowded."	23
Tourism orientation (= tourism services, public services, transportation means, cost of life)	"There is also a lack of anywhere to sit down in public benches, (. . .) and there is very little green."	20
Traffic and chaos	"One thing that stands out about Rome is how absolutely frenetic it is. (. . .) Traffic is absolute chaos."	16
Dirt	"Shame about the graffiti everywhere."	9
Local people	"Not to mention the ignorance of the people."	5

visit – unless that for specific audiences, like the food argument for an audience fond of gastronomic traditions – but each new argument makes the argumentation stronger.

As for the types of standpoint, two aspects emerged from the sample that may "restrict" the visit recommendation. First, even though many reviewers stated that they visited Rome for one day only, often as a stop within an organized trip, and many others declared that they are loyal visitors of the eternal city, there is an overall agreement that Rome is a destination to be visited for a minimum of three days. A second type of standpoint is bound to specific travel motivations: Rome is a must for a romantic holiday and for history and art lovers. The multiple arguments provided prove to be more or less persuasive according to the specific standpoint.

Discussion

The method proposed in this chapter for the analysis of social media content and, specifically, for the analysis of Online Travel Reviews, has implications at several levels. The formalization of OTR in terms of a textual genre provides information systems developers with indications for helping online users in the process of information seeking and selection. It may, in fact, direct the development of algorithms both to rank reviews in terms of their argumentative quality, and to filter them according to their potential usefulness to consumers. The reconstruction of the arguments used to report about a travel experience at a specific destination, then, allows one to let emerge the dominant perceived touristic value of that destination. The touristic value can be exploited to better promote it on the market, as well as to train people working at different levels with the destination about its most appreciated – and, conversely, its most complained about – aspects. Eventually, the evaluation of arguments based on the authority of the arguer as well as the adequacy of the arguments to the audience addressed and to the specific visit recommendation, represent critical elements to be considered when making travel decisions.

Notes

1 The software can be freely downloaded from the website: www.wagsoft.com/CorpusTool/. It has been developed and is constantly improved by Mick O'Donnel (2008).
2 *Rationale* is the last version of *Reason!Able*, a software developed at the University of Melbourne and Austhink (the "Australian Thinking Institute") by Tim van Gelder and Andy Bulka, within the *Reason!* Project.

References

Austin, J. L. (1962). *How to Do Things With Words*. Oxford, Clarendon Press.
Bakhtin, M. (1986). The problem of speech acts. In C. Emerson & M. Holquist (eds.) *Speech Genres and Other Late Essays*, pp. 60–102. Austin: University of Texas Press.
Berkenkotter, C., & Huckin, T. (1995). *Genre Knowledge in Disciplinary Communication*. Hillsdale, NJ, Lawrence Erlbaum.

De Ascaniis, S. (2013). *Destination Online Travel Reviews: An Argumentative and Textual Genre Perspective*. Unpublished doctoral dissertation. Università della Svizzera italiana, Lugano, Switzerland.

De Ascaniis, S., & Greco Morasso, S. (2011). When tourists give their reasons on the web: The argumentative significance of tourism related UGC. In R. Law, M. Fuchs, & F. Ricci (eds.) *Information and Communication Technologies in Tourism 2011*. Wien/New York, Springer, pp. 125–137.

De Ascaniis, S., & Gretzel, U. (2013). Communicative functions of online travel review titles: A pragmatic and linguistic investigation of destination and attraction OTR titles. *Studies in Communication Sciences*, 13, pp. 156–165.

Dickinger, A. (2011). The trustworthiness of online channels for experience- and goal-directed search tasks. *Journal of Travel Research*, 50(4), pp. 378–391.

Eemeren, van F. H., & Grootendorst, R. (2004). *A systematic theory of argumentation: The pragma-dialectical approach*. Cambridge: Cambridge University Press.

Eemeren, van F. H., Grootendorst, R., Snoeck Henkemans, A. F., Blair, J. A., Johnson, R. H., Krabbe, E. C. W., Plantin, Chr., Walton, D. N., Willard, Ch. A., Woods, J., & Zarefsky, D. (1996). *Fundamentals of Argumentation Theory*. Mahwah, NJ, Erlbaum.

Gretzel, U., Yoo K. H., & Purifoy, M. (2007). Online travel review study: Role and impact of online travel reviews. Laboratory for Intelligent Systems in Tourism, Texas A&M University.

Jakobson, R. O. (1960). Linguistics and poetics. In T. A. Sebeok (ed.) *Style in Language*, Cambridge, MA, MIT Press.

O'Donnell, M. 2008. "Demonstration of the UAM CorpusTool for text and image annotation". Proceedings of the ACL-08: HLT Demo Session (CompanionVolume), Columbus, Ohio, June 2008. Association for Computational Linguistics. pp. 13–16.

Peirce, C. S. (1955). Logic as semiotic: The theory of signs. In J. Buchler (ed.) *The Philosophical Writings of Peirce*. New York, Dover Press.

Sbisà, M. (2007). How to read Austin. *Pragmatics*, 17(3), pp. 461–473.

Searle, J. R. (1969). *Speech Acts*. Cambridge, Cambridge University Press.

Smith, D., Menon, S., & Sivakumar, K. (2005). Online peer and editorial recommendations, trust, and choice in virtual markets. *Journal of interactive marketing, 19*(3), 15–37.

Snoeck Henkemans, F. (2001). Argumentation structures. In F. H. van Eemeren (ed.) *Crucial Concepts in Argumentation Theory*. Amsterdam, Amsterdam University Press, pp. 101–134.

Tindale, C. W. (2004). *Rhetorical Argumentation*. Thousand Oaks, CA, Sage Publications.

Yoo, K. H., & Gretzel, U. (2008). What motivates consumers to write online travel reviews? *Information Technology and Tourism*, 10(4), pp. 283–295.

18 Measuring visitor satisfaction with a cultural heritage site

Social media data vs. onsite surveys

Laura Di Pietro, Roberta Guglielmetti Mugion, Maria Francesca Renzi and Martina Toni

Introduction

As recognized by Zeng and Gerritsen (2014), in recent years, the role of Social Media (SM) in the tourism sector has been growing strongly, affecting various factors, such as information search and decision-making behaviors (Fotis, 2012), tourism promotion and best practices for interacting with consumers. In addition, the role of SM for cultural attractions in the tourism sector is expanding. Indeed, many cultural sites are reviewed, evaluated and discussed daily by users through general and specific online platforms (i.e. social networks, blogs, communities and forums). As argued by Kozinets et al. (2014), organizations are increasingly using SM platforms to develop strong relations with their users and to interact directly and systematically with them. This SM usage is also an emerging phenomenon for the tourism and cultural heritage sector. Hence, SM represents a rich platform offering data related to customers' knowledge and interrelations with others. For researchers and practitioners, this implies the need to study SM's ability to attract new cultural tourist flows through electronic word-of-mouth (e-WOM) and improve the level of the services provided through the effective management of online reviews.

Currently, the comments on SM have become an important information source (Gretzel et al., 2011; Yoo & Gretzel, 2008) because, as posited by Ye et al. (2011), consumers are able to obtain sufficient information from SM sources, reducing the level of perceived uncertainty (Liu & Park, 2015). Hence, e-WOM contributes significantly to the reputation of tourist attractions and affects the entire travel cycle: before, during and after travel (Zeng & Gerritsen, 2014). Thus, the reliability of online reviews represents a crucial factor for fostering both powerful e-WOM and effective service improvement. However, the credibility of this kind of data is one of the main concerns encountered. Therefore, this study is focused on comparing online and onsite evaluations by cultural tourists to detect differences between the data collected through traditional surveys and the online reviews provided by customers on SM.

To achieve this goal, we propose empirically studying a young and successful Italian cultural site that embeds innovative technological implementations; our study will compare the results of a qualitative study conducted on a specific social network (TripAdvisor) with the results of a traditional survey conducted onsite. The comparison's objective is to determine whether there is consistency between the two methods of collecting data and to verify the credibility of the SM evaluations. We use qualitative analysis and descriptive statistics for data analysis, investigating the credibility and potentiality of the information available on a specific SM for a successful and innovative cultural site.

Literature review

Social media and customer satisfaction management

Understanding and investigating customer needs, expectations and perceptions requires considering the different service provision channels (Di Pietro et al., 2014) and new communication methods supported through SM. Recently, a growth in the diffusion of social media has been observed. The majority of current social networks (SN) (e.g. TripAdvisor, Airbnb, Facebook, Twitter, LinkedIn, YouTube and Flickr) enable users to create a public or partially public profile and to establish several types of connections with other people (Boyd & Ellison, 2007). In general, it must be emphasized that interactive technologies have an increasingly strong social impact (Chung & Buhalis, 2008). As highlighted by Huang and Behara (2007), online communities facilitate the manifestation of individual subjectivity, allowing online users to expand and strengthen personal SN and reduce communication barriers. Moreover, social interactions are a source of creativity and innovation (Chiu et al., 2006), and they enhance collaboration, learning and the creation and sharing of knowledge (Garrigos, Alcamì & Ribera, 2012). Chalkiti & Sigala (2008) revealed that, because of the knowledge creation capability and affordability of online networking platforms, online networking positively contributes to the information sharing, knowledge creation and idea generation capabilities of peer-to-peer virtual communities (Zeng & Gerritsen, 2014). Consequently, SM platforms are full of information regarding the customers' (written) beliefs and their evaluations of different aspects. This is particularly true for the tourism sector, in which there is an increased use of SM by tourists to share information and evaluate the trip experience. Consequently, in this context, e-WOM is becoming increasingly essential for the choice of destinations, sites, hotels and museums during trip planning. At the same time, to confront users' increasing use of information from websites in making travel-related decisions and to shape perceptions and images regarding destinations and travel offerings (Fotis et al., 2011; Cox et al., 2009), many hospitality and tourism companies have been integrating SM into their online business strategies. Indeed, the possibility for consumers to share opinions, past experiences and tips with the online community also plays a strategic role for companies providing new possibilities to better understand audience opinions mainly because of the written means of expression, which encourages the development of new studies on social customer feedback tools. Thus, SM are becoming essential tools for managers to improve the decision-making process and integrate the available knowledge on customer satisfaction gathered through traditional channels with new data originating from the internet. This is confirmed by the fact that companies are integrating their customer relationship management systems with social customer feedback tools (Greenberg, 2010).

Consequently, social channels are creating new perspectives both for customers, in terms of their means of expressing their evaluations through SM, and for companies, regarding the managerial practices used to collect and manage information on customer satisfaction from multiple perspectives. The tourism and hospitality sector is particularly rich in information and explanatory power to illuminate this phenomenon.

Social media, WOM and e-WOM

WOM has been acknowledged as a major influence on what people know, feel and do, affecting awareness, expectations, perceptions, attitudes and behavior (Buttle, 1998). The shift from WOM to e-WOM is occurring more readily than was previously imagined, given the increasing development of the internet (Buhalis & Law, 2008). An interesting definition of e-WOM was proposed by Hennig-Thurau (2004, p. 39): "any positive or negative statement made by potential, actual or former customers about a product or company, which is made available to a multitude of people via the Internet". E-WOM is more voluminous (Chatterjee, 2001), persistent and accessible because the text-based information presented on the internet is archived and available for an indefinite period of time (Hennig-Thurau et. al., 2004; Park and Lee, 2009). E-WOM can be conveyed in different ways, including reading comments, sharing experiences and leaving feedback across online channels such as blogs, review platforms, virtual communities and SNs (Phelps et al., 2004; Dwyer, 2007) where people can interact about places, experiences, products, and services (Brown et al., 2007; Cheung et al., 2009; Kaplan & Haenlein, 2010). Consequently, e-WOM communication has become a major component of consumer interaction (Brown et al., 2005).

As argued by Litvin et al. (2008), e-WOM and interpersonal influence are important drivers of purchasing decisions, particularly in the hospitality and tourism industry, mainly because of the intangibility, seasonality and perishability of these services. In the tourism context, SM seems to be a main source of information for travel planning and decision-making (Xiang & Gretzel, 2010); thus, tourists seek e-WOM sources to obtain information and reviews about the attractions, accommodations and dining options of a given destination (Arsal et al., 2010; Litvin et al., 2008; Xiang & Gretzel, 2010).

The aim of both WOM and e-WOM is the same: disclosure of information in order to support other consumers to make the correct/conscious decisions (Allsop et al., 2007). Several studies present e-WOM as having the same high levels of influence as WOM (Lee & Youn, 2009; Cheung, Lee, & Rabjohn, 2008; Litvin et al., 2008; Hennig-Thurau & Walsh, 2003), differentiating them only by the channel (Litvin et al., 2008); however, several important distinctions arise from the literature. The feedback available online is accessible to a wide audience (Cheung et al., 2009), which can utilize the information when needed. Moreover, customers have the potential to reach a global audience quickly and easily (Chu & Choi, 2011) and to exchange opinions widely, leading to information democracy (Sawhney & Kotler, 2001). Hence, it is clear that the WOM and e-WOM do not share the same level of credibility because there is not a direct relationship between the source of information and the receiver (Brown et al., 2007; Lee & Youn, 2009; Park & Lee, 2009); indeed, within SM, there is a lack of knowledge about who is providing or reviewing the information and what are their motivations (Kietzmann et al., 2011). Thus, credibility becomes a pillar of the e-WOM, as many authors state that it is a precursor to the acceptance of information received and an antecedent to influence a decision/choice (Hilligoss & Rieh, 2008). In addition to depending on the source of information, credibility also relies on contents and channels (Tham et al., 2013). In addition, Brown et al. (2007) showed that the credibility of e-WOM is influenced by the environment in which it is created and propagated, highlighting the importance of factors such as the density of the social network, rational and emotional components of the message, level of message negativity, efficiency of the exchange and the characteristics of the message (Allsop et al., 2007). Nevertheless, the presence of a larger community of members enhances the reliability of the reviews by facilitating the emergence of more diverse views (Smith et al., 2007; Sun et al., 2006).

From companies' perspectives, e-WOM has more benefits than traditional WOM and may represent a useful tool for managing customer complaints, improving products/services and achieving customer satisfaction. Because of its quantity and accessibility at any time, e-WOM is also more measurable than traditional WOM (Park & Kim, 2008). However, issues related to credibility are pertinent. For this reason, we present a comparison of the results gathered by a quantitative survey with those related to an analysis of the comments available on SM in order to study the credibility of online users' evaluation.

Methodological approach

Our study proposes a comparison between the online and offline customer feedback released after a visit to a cultural site located in Rome, Italy. At this site, it is possible to visit recently discovered, ancient ruins (Roman Domus) from the Roman Empire, which are enhanced by the use of new technologies, specifically augmented reality. The visit itinerary and the technological installations strongly overlap and it is not possible to access the site without being guided by technology. Indeed, the augmented reality guides visitors throughout the entire cultural experience. In a short time, this site has become one of the more visited cultural attractions in Rome, and it has been ranked first on "Things to do in Rome" on TripAdvisor.com. The museum organizes 19 tours per day (15 in Italian, three in English and one in French); each tour includes approximately 15 visitors, and there is an average of approximately 300 visits per day. Therefore, we selected this case for our empirical study to answer our research questions. First, a qualitative analysis has been conducted to implement a netnographic approach applied to the evaluations released by the customers on the SM platform TripAdvisor.com. We select this SM because it represents the best example of successful consumer sharing, and "TripAdvisor branded sites make up the largest travel community in the world, reaching 350 million unique monthly visitors and 320 million reviews and opinions covering more than 6.2 million accommodations, restaurants and attractions. The sites operate in 47 countries worldwide" (tripadvisor.com, 2016). However, as argued by Ayeh et al. (2013), the main concern about this SM involves the credibility of its information.

As stated by Kozinets (2002), "Netnography" is a methodology to conduct qualitative research, adapting ethnographic techniques to study communities based on computer-mediated communications. Hence, through this methodology, the reviews available on the SM page of the cultural site have been analyzed, interpreted and coded to classify comments and grades, identifying the key issues that characterize visitors' perceptions. Moreover, as emphasized by several authors (i.e., Sherry, 1991; Thompson, 1997), the most useful interpretations of such information "take advantage of its contextual richness and come as a result of penetrating metaphoric and symbolic interpretation (Levy, 1959, Sherry, 1991, Thompson, 1997), rather than meticulous classification" (Kozinets, 2015, pp. 245–246). Specifically, the community investigated in this study is the TripAdvisor community for the specific museum website, in which the users are mainly "tourists" who, based on Kozinetz's definition, are the kind of users who lack strong social ties but have deep interest in the activity. This online community is chosen because of its suitability for the investigation. The phases of conducting a Netnographic analysis are based on Kozinets's (2002) suggestion: initially, the community is chosen on the basis of the topic (customer reviews and ratings concerning tourism attractions) and on the traffic; then, the information embedded within the website is selected and classified. As grounded theory suggests (Glaser & Strauss, 1967), data collection should end when there are no new insights on the topic. The data analysis was developed through the Maxqda 11 software. For each evaluation, we defined a key word to classify the most recurrent issues (tangible aspects, booking services, personnel, technological support and customer feelings) to analyze the frequencies of these issues. We focused on both positive and negative elements highlighted by customers.

To generalize the results, we compare the online with onsite feedback and e-WOM with WOM, respectively; thereafter, a survey was planned and conducted onsite by "triangulating" the data obtained through the administration of a questionnaire to an audience following a cultural visit. The questionnaire used for the survey is divided into five sections: (1) socio-demographic information; (2) general information (how the customer became aware of the museum, with whom the customer visited the museum, and where the ticket was purchased); (3) waiting time before the visit; (4) perception concerning the visit to the museum (overall satisfaction, tangible factors, reservation services, staff, spaces and technological support); and (5) post-visit factors (suggestions, ratings and comments regarding the visit). In particular, in the last section of the questionnaire, we introduce a question for investigating the overall perception of the visit, reproducing the same scale used on TripAdvisor.com. For the other questions, a Likert scale from 1 to 6

(1 = "strongly disagree" and 6 = "completely agree") was adopted. A total of 280 questionnaires were collected according to a finite population sample. At the end of the survey period, a comparison between the results of the two analyses was conducted to verify the reliability and coherence of the two different typologies of collected data. After checking the qualitative data's consistency, the outcome of the studies was interpreted to address the research questions.

Results

First, we present the results of the qualitative analysis conducted using the netnography method applied to the TripAdvisor community. Then, we introduce the results detected through the survey administered onsite at the end of the visit. Hence, a comparative analysis between the two analyses is developed with the objective of showing differences and similarities between the two studies.

Qualitative results

Of a total of 2,223 reviews available on the website, a sample of 1,500 were extracted (70%), respecting the original distribution of the rating among the categories (1,222 "*Excellent*", 210 "*Very good*", 50 "*Average*", 8 "*Poor*", and 10 "*Terrible*"). The sample of 1,500 customer evaluations on TripAdvisor was drawn from 49% females and 51% males. Each review was analyzed to detect the frequently recurring and more relevant key issues identified directly and spontaneously by visitors on TripAdvisor. We generated two maps that show the positive (Fig. 18.1) and negative (Fig. 18.2) key elements (and their frequencies) that characterize the online comments about the cultural and technological visits.

The reviews of the museum available on social media are mainly positive and, as shown in Figure 18.1, the main and more recurrent comments are about the technological applications at the cultural site. Studying the visitors' online feedback shows that the virtual reconstruction generated by the augmented reality stimulates positive feelings (identification with the past, 446; unmissable, 329; interesting, 190; touching, 164; fascinating, 85; worthwhile, 79; instructive/educational 72; amazing, 69; and fun, 46) that make the experiences valuable and overwhelming. On the other site, a minor number of negative factors have also been detected through the netnography. More specifically, certain critical issues are concerned with the personnel, the lack of advertising of the cultural site, the e-ticketing process and factors associated with functional elements (i.e. waiting time, cost, informative material etc.).

Quantitative results

The survey conducted onsite comprised answers from 280 visitors, 57% female and 43% male. The ages of the respondents were structured as follows: 30–49 (40%), 50–65 (30%) and 18–29 (22%). Of the questionnaires, 63% were completed in Italian and 37% were completed in English. The surveyed visit was the

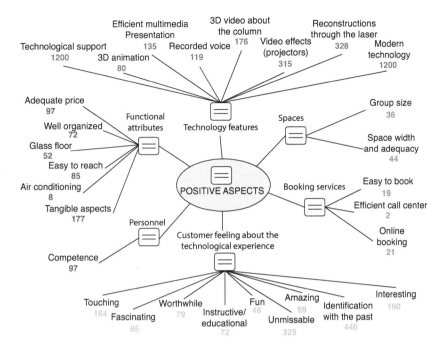

Figure 18.1 Key positive elements gathered via the online reviews
Source: Elaboration using MaxQDA 11

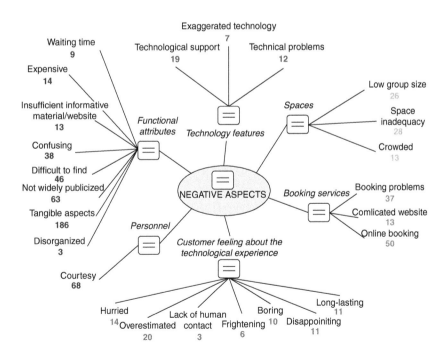

Figure 18.2 Key negative elements gathered from online reviews

first to the site for 90% of the respondents, whereas 10% of the respondents asserted they had previously visited the site. An analysis of the sources that encourage customers to visit the cultural site shows that the most important factors are WOM (52.22%) and e-WOM on the internet and social media (38.89%). Of the respondents, 96% show a high level of overall satisfaction, with a mean value of 5.65. Moreover, 98% of the visitors were willing to recommend visiting this cultural site (with 81% of the respondents giving the exhibition 6 points and 17% of the respondents giving the exhibition 5 points), producing an important level of WOM and e-WOM. The high level of satisfaction appears to be a consequence of the strong positive impact that the technological implementation has on the visitors' perceptions. Indeed, 97% of the respondents assert a very high level of satisfaction concerning the technological experience (77% of the respondents giving the technology installation 6 points and 20% giving it 5 points). More specifically, the respondents assert that the technological application greatly increases their level of involvement during the visit, and the respondents recognize the technology's utility in simplifying learning through entertainment (Table 18.1).

In addition to indicating many positive factors, the quantitative survey showed certain critical elements that concern the "functional" factors. Of the respondents, only 38% stated that it is easy to navigate the cultural site, with a mean value of approximately 4.78 (Table 18.2); in addition, 27% of the sample affirmed that the informative material is not appropriate (mean= 3.88). In addition, the reservation system presents certain issues, as confirmed by the low mean values shown in Table 18.2.

Concerning the last question, reproducing the overall review scale used on TripAdvisor, the respondents solely expressed positive opinions: 64% *Excellent*, 35% *Very good* and 1% *Average* (no one asserted a *Poor* or *Terrible* opinion). This evaluation confirms the high level of satisfaction visitors have with the technological cultural visit.

Table 18.1 Mean value concerning the evaluation of the technological visit

Items referring to the technological application	Mean
I am satisfied with the technology used in the museum	5.73
Technological support makes the visit more engaging	5.82
The available technology enhances learning	5.77
The technological equipment of the museum is useful	5.69
The technological equipment of the museum is fun	5.06
The technological equipment of the museum is surprising	5.57
The technology isolates me from other people during the visit	4.14
The technology standardizes the visit	3.71
Technological support is adequate	5.44
The technology provides orientation in the museum	5.26
The technology provides direct substantial information	5.39

Table 18.2 Mean values of the more critical items

Critical items	Mean
It's easy to orient oneself in the museum	4.78
The museum provides appropriate informational material (maps, brochures, etc.)	3.88
The booking service is satisfactory	4.43
The reservation channels are adequate	4.28
The methods of buying tickets are clear	4.40

Table 18.3 Comparison between online and onsite evaluations

Evaluation	TripAdvisor	Survey
Excellent	81.5%	64%
Very Good	14%	35%
Average	3.3%	1%
Poor	0.53%	0
Terrible	0.67%	0

Discussion

This study shows that there is consistency between the results of a traditional survey and the reviews available on SM, supporting the credibility of SM as a tool for collecting information on customers. Indeed, both the qualitative and quantitative results show a high level of visitor satisfaction, emphasizing the strong and positive impact that the technological application has on visitor perception. More specifically, the implementation of the augmented reality at the cultural site represents the dominant element included in the *Excellent* and *Very good* reviews on TripAdvisor.com, accompanied by adjectives such as "amazing", "useful", "interesting" and "funny". In other words, the technological experience generates positive sensations in the visitors, inducing them to provide positive reviews online on SM, thereby generating important e-WOM. Similarly, the onsite survey reflects a high level of appreciation for the technological feature, particularly regarding the high level of engagement it generates. Moreover, the onsite survey shows that the two main channels of information that influenced the audience to visit this cultural site were WOM and e-WOM. Indeed, the high quality of the visit and the site's strong presence on SM allowed this cultural site to overcome the lack of an advertising campaign.

Furthermore, comparing the overall evaluations on TripAdvisor with the evaluations at the end of the questionnaire, it is possible to notice the same positive trend in visitor perceptions (Table 18.3). The sole marginal difference involves the difference in the distribution of the *Excellent* and *Very good* evaluations: for TripAdvisor, there are more *Excellent* evaluations than *Very good* evaluations. Conversely, for the onsite survey, there are slightly fewer *Excellent* evaluations, whereas there are more *Very good* assessments.

Conclusion

As recognized by Zeng and Gerritsen (2014), research on the role of SM in tourism remains in its infancy. Our study is focused on the identification of shared factors and differences between the traditional methods used to collect data through quantitative surveys and the new methods used to gather information through the netnographic analysis of customer reviews (i.e. comments and ratings) on SM. Moreover, the most relevant consequence in terms of CS related to the use of SM is the virality stimulated by the written form, which has had an increasing impact on WOM and e-WOM. We developed a two-fold analysis on an Italian cultural site that allowed us to compare the results obtained from a netnographic study conducted on customer reviews available on a social network (TripAdvisor) and the data gathered by a traditional survey (a face-to-face questionnaire) conducted onsite. The comparison's objective is to understand the reliability of the two methods to collect data and verify the credibility of the results gathered by the netnographic analysis on SM reviews. Netnographic analysis is a fairly new technique and is suitable for the study of customers' behavior and culture and the relationships that are established between them.

Our study shows that the large and active use of SM by customers during their cultural visits emphasizes new opportunities in the field of customer satisfaction management for the tourism and cultural heritage sector. Specifically, it is important to integrate Netnography into SM analysis, in addition to using the traditional methodologies and tools for studying CS. This integration allows for a better understanding of what customers truly believe, their expectations and their desires to generate a new level of quality and new offers.

References

Allsop, D. T., Bassett, B. R., & Hoskins, J. A. (2007). Word of mouth research: Principles and applications. *Journal of Advertising Research*, 47(4), pp. 398–411.

Arsal, I., Woosnam, K. M., & Baldwin, E. D. (2010). Residents as travel destination information providers: An online community perspective. *Journal of Travel Research*, 49(4), pp. 400–413.

Ayeh, J., Au, N., & Law, R. (2013). Towards an understanding of online travellers' acceptance of consumer-generated media for travel planning: Integrating technology acceptance and source credibility factors. In L. Cantoni & Z. Xiang (eds.) *Information and Communication Technologies in Tourism*. Heidelberg, Springer, pp. 254–267.

Boyd, D. M., & Ellison, N. B. (2007). Social network sites: Definition, history, and scholarship, *Journal of Computer-Mediated Communication*, 13(1), pp. 210–230.

Brown, T. J., Barry, T. E., Dacin, P. A., & Gunstet, R. F. (2005). Spreading the word: Investigating antecedents of consumers' positive word-of-mouth intentions and behaviors in a retailing context. *Journal of the Academy of Marketing Science*, 3(2), pp. 123–138.

Brown, T. J., Broderick, A. J., & Lee, N. (2007). Word of mouth communication within online communities: Conceptualizing the online social network. *Journal of Interactive Marketing*, 21(3), pp. 2–20.

Buhalis, D., & Law, R. (2008). Progress in information technology and tourism management: 20 years on and 10 years after the Internet: The state of eTourism research. *Tourism Management*, 29(4), pp. 609–623.

Buttle, F. A. (1998). Word-of-mouth: Understanding and managing referral Marketing. *Journal of Strategic Marketing*, 6, pp. 241–254.

Chalkiti, K., & Sigala, M. (2008). Information sharing and knowledge creation in online forums: The case of the Greek online forum 'DIALOGOI'. *Current Issues in Tourism*, 11(5), pp. 381–406.

Chatterjee, P. (2001). Online reviews: Do consumers use them? In M. C. Gilly & J. Myers-Levy (eds.) *Advances in Consumer Research*. Provo, UT, Association for Consumer Research, pp. 129–134.

Cheung, C. M., Lee, M. K., & Rabjohn, N. (2008). The impact of electronic word-of-mouth: The adoption of online opinions in online customer communities. Internet research, 18(3), 229-247.

Cheung, M., Luo, C., Sia, C., & Chen, H. (2009). Credibility of electronic word-of-mouth: Informational and normative determinants of on-line consumer recommendations. *International Journal of Electronic Commerce*, 13(4), p. 9.

Chiu, C.-M., Hsu, M.-H., & Wang, E. T. G. (2006). Understanding knowledge sharing in virtual communities: An integration of social capital and social cognitive theories. *Decision Support Systems*, 42, pp. 1872–1888.

Chu, S., & Choi, S. M. (2011). Electronic word of mouth in social networking sites: A cross cultural study of the United States and China. *Journal of Global Marketing*, 24(3), pp. 263–281.

Chung, J. Y., & Buhalis, D. (2008). A study of online travel community: Factors affecting participation and attitude. In *ENTER 2008 Proceedings*. Innsbruck, Springer-Verlag, Wien, ISBN:9783211772799, pp. 267–278.

Cox, C., Burgess, S., Sellitto, C., & Buultjens, J. (2009). The role of user-generated content in tourists' travel planning behavior. *Journal of Hospitality Marketing & Management*, 18(8), pp. 743–764.

Di Pietro, L., Guglielmetti Mugion, R., Renzi, M. F., & Toni, M. (2014). An audience-centric approach for museums sustainability. *Sustainability*, 6(9), pp. 5745–5762. doi:10.3390/su6095745.

Dwyer, P. (2007). Measuring the value of electronic word of mouth and its impact in consumer communities. *Journal of Interactive Marketing*, 21(2), pp. 63–79.

Fotis, J. (2012). Discussion of the impacts of social media in leisure tourism: The impact of social media on consumer behaviour: Focus on leisure travel. Available at: http://johnfotis.blogspot.com.au/p/projects.html [Accessed 30 September 2015].

Fotis, J., Buhalis, D., & Rossides, N. (2011). Social media impact on holiday travel: The case of the Russian and the FSU markets. *International Journal of Online Marketing*, 1(4), pp. 1–19.

Garrigos, F. J., Alcamì, R. L., & Ribera, T. B. (2012). Social networks and Web 3.0: Their impact on the management and marketing of organizations. *Management Decision*, 50(10), pp. 1880–1890.

Glaser, B. G., & Strauss, A. L. (1967). *The Discovery of Grounded Theory: Strategies for Qualitative Research*. Chicago, Aldine Pub. Co.

Goldenberg, J., Libai, B., & Muller, E. (2001). Talk of the network: A complex systems look at the underlying process of word-of-mouth. *Marketing Letters*, 12(3), pp. 211–223.

Greenberg, P. (2010). *CRM at the Speed of Light: Social CRM 2.0 Strategies, Tools, and Techniques for Engaging Your Customers*, 4th Edition. London, UK: McGraw-Hill Osborne.

Gretzel, U., Fesenmaier, D. R., Lee, Y. J., & Tussyadiah, I. (2011). Narrating travel experiences: the role of new media. In R. Sharpley & P. Stone (eds.) *Tourist Experiences: Contemporary Perspectives*. New York, Routledge, pp. 71–182.

Hennig-Thurau, T. (2004). Customer orientation of service employees: Its impact on customer satisfaction, commitment, and retention. *International Journal of Service Industry Management,* 15(5), 460–478.

Hennig-Thurau, T., Gwinner, K. P., Walsh, G., & Gremler, D. D. (2004). Electronic word-of-mouth via consumer-opinion platforms: What motivates consumers to articulate themselves on the internet? *Journal of Interactive Marketing*, 18(1), pp. 38–52.

Hennig-Thurau, T., Walsh, G., & Walsh, G. (2003). Electronic word-of-mouth: Motives for and consequences of reading customer articulations on the Internet. *International journal of electronic commerce*, 8(2), 51–74.

Hilligoss, B., & Rieh, S. Y. (2008). Developing a unifying framework of credibility assessment: Construct, heuristics and interaction in context. *Information Processing and Management*, 44, pp. 1467–1484.

Huang, C. D., & Behara, R. S. (2007). Outcome-driven experiential learning with Web 2.0. *Journal of Information Systems Education*, 18(3), pp. 329.

Kaplan, A. M. & Haenlein, M. (2010). Users of the world, unite! The challenges and opportunities of social media. *Business Horizons*, 53(1), pp. 59–68.

Kietzmann, J. H., Hermkens, K., McCarthy, I. P., & Silvestre, B. S. (2011). Social media? Get serious! Understanding the functional building blocks of social media. *Business Horizons*, 54(1), pp. 241–251.

Kozinets, R. (2002). The field behind the screen: Using netnography for marketing research in online communities. *Journal of Marketing Research*, XXXIX, pp. 61–72.

Kozinets, R. (2015). *Netnography: Redefined*, 2nd Edition. London, Sage Publications Ltd.

Kozinets, R., Dolbec, P. Y., & Earley, A. (2014). Netnographic analysis: Understanding culture through social media data analysis. In U. Flick (ed.) *The SAGE handbook of qualitative data analysis*, London, Sage, pp. 262–277.

Lee, M., & Youn, S. (2009). Electronic word of mouth (eWOM): How eWOM platforms influence consumer product judgement. *International Journal of Advertising*, 28(3), pp. 473–499.

Levy, S. J. (1959). Symbols for sale. *Harvard Business Review*, 37 (July–August), pp. 117–124.

Litvin, S. W., Goldsmith, R. E., & Pan, B. (2008). Electronic word-of-mouth in hospitality and tourism management. *Tourism Management*, 29(3), pp. 458–468.

Liu, Z., & Park, S. (2015). What makes a useful online review? Implication for travel product websites. *Tourism Management*, 47(April), pp. 140–151.

Park, C., & Lee, T. (2009). Information direction, website reputation and eWOM effect: A moderating role of product type. *Journal of Business Research*, 62(1), pp. 61–67.

Park, D. H., & Kim, S. (2008). The effects of consumer knowledge on message processing of electronic word-of-mouth via online consumer reviews. *Electronic Commerce Research and Applications*, 7(4), pp. 399–410.

Phelps, J. E., Lewis, R., Mobilio, L, Perry, D., & Raman, N. (2004). Viral marketing or electronic word-of-mouth advertising: Examining consumer responses and motivations to pass along email. *J Advert Res*, 44(4), pp. 333–348.

Sawhney, M. S., & Kotler, P. (2001). The age of information democracy. In D. Iacobucci (ed.) *Kellogg on Marketing*. New York, John Wiley and Sons, pp. 386–408.

Sherry, J. F, Jr. (1991). Postmodern alternatives: The interpretive turn in consumer research. In H. H. Kassarjian & T. Robertson (eds.) *Handbook of Consumer Research*, Englewood Cliffs, NJ, Prentice Hall, pp. 548–591.

Smith, T., Coyle, J. R., Lightfoot, E., & Scottet A. (2007). Reconsidering models of influence: The relationship between consumer social networks and word of mouth effectiveness. *Journal of Advertising Research*, 47(4), pp. 387–397.

Sun, T., Young, S., Wu, G., & Kuntaraporn, M. (2006). Online word-of-mouth (or mouse): An exploration of its antecedents and consequences. *Journal of Computer-Mediated Communication*, 11(4), pp. 1104–1127.

Tham, A., Croy, G., & Mair, J. (2013). Social media in destination choice: Distinctive electronic word-of-mouth dimensions. *Journal of Travel & Tourism Marketing*, 30(1–2), pp. 141–152.

Thompson, C. J. (1997). Interpreting consumers: A hermeneutical framework for deriving marketing insights from the texts of consumers' consumption stories, *Journal of Marketing Research*, 34(November), pp. 438–455.

Xiang, Z., & Gretzel, U. (2010). Role of social media in online travel information search. *Tourism Management*, 31(2), pp. 179–188.

Ye, Q., Law, R., Gu, B., & Chen, W. (2011). The influence of user-generated content on traveler behavior: An empirical investigation on the effects of e-word-of-mouth to hotel online bookings. *Computers in Human Behavior*, 27, pp. 634–639.

Yoo, K. H., & Gretzel, U. (2008). What motivates consumers to write online travel reviews? *Information Technology & Tourism*, 10, pp. 283–295.

Zeng, B., & Gerritsen, R. (2014). What do we know about social media in tourism? A review. *Tourism Management Perspectives*, 10, pp. 27–36.

19 Business intelligence for destinations

Creating knowledge from social media

Matthias Fuchs, Wolfram Höpken
and Maria Lexhagen

Introduction

User generated content (UGC) shows a huge potential to reduce information asymmetries in travel and tourism markets (Leung et al., 2013). Today, product rating and feedback functionality is offered to customers on most online travel platforms, leading to a dramatic increase of available UGC (Xiang & Gretzel, 2010; Schmunk et al., 2014, p. 254). Product reviews constitute a highly relevant information source for customers, supporting travel planning and decision making (Cox et al., 2009; Sidali et al., 2012; Sparks et al., 2013). Similarly, UGC represents a valuable knowledge source for tourism suppliers to learn from customers how to enhance service quality (Sigala, 2011; Lexhagen et al., 2012). More than 65% of users use review sites when making travel decisions and more than 95% of users consider review sites as credible, thus, stressing the importance of UGC also for tourism managers (Kensik & Wachowiak, 2011). However, the arising challenge for tourism, and especially destination managers is to identify relevant reviews and efficiently analyze them, which necessitates an automatic extraction of decision relevant knowledge from UGC with sufficient quality and reliability (Pan et al., 2007). Although review sites offer scalar ratings, such ratings do not provide any information on specific product characteristics that customers like or don't like (Schmunk et al., 2014, p. 254). Rather, such information is typically contained within textual reviews and can only be extracted by techniques from the areas of opinion mining and sentiment analysis (Liu, 2011).

This chapter presents a Business Intelligence-based knowledge infrastructure recently developed as a genuine novelty at the leading Swedish mountain tourism destination Åre (Fuchs et al., 2014; Höpken et al., 2015). The prototypically implemented Destination Management Information system Åre (DMIS-Åre) supports knowledge creation as a precondition for destination development and competitiveness (Pyo et al., 2002). Despite that a huge amount of customer-based data (i.e. customer transactions, behavior and feedback, respectively) is available at destinations, this valuable knowledge source typically remains unused (Fuchs et al., 2010). Thus, with a special focus on UGC, this chapter highlights how DMIS-Åre stores customer-based data (i.e. UGC) at the level of the destination and applies techniques of Business Intelligence (BI)[1] to gain new and valuable social media knowledge. The chapter is structured as follows: While the second section introduces the knowledge destination framework, the third section highlights the features of the DMIS-Åre prototype. In the fourth section, a BI-based framework for UGC-extraction and -analysis, which has recently been validated by the authors on the basis of UGC data from TripAdvisor.com and Booking.com (Schmunk et al., 2014), is discussed. The fifth Section shows examples of social media knowledge creation through DMIS-Åre based on extracted UGC. The conclusion summarizes study findings and sketches future research.

The knowledge destination framework

Knowledge creation at destinations can be significantly enhanced by applying BI methods. However, the literature only recently emphasizes BI for knowledge creation in the travel and tourism domain (Magnini et al., 2003; Wong et al., 2006; Fuchs & Höpken, 2009). So far, there is only a few BI studies at the level of destinations (Pyo et al., 2002; Fuchs et al., 2013; Höpken et al., 2014). Following the knowledge destination framework (Höpken et al., 2011), knowledge activities deal with extracting information from various customer and supplier-based sources and with the generation of knowledge to be applied in the form of intelligent services for customers (Jannach et al., 2013) or destination stakeholders (Fuchs et al., 2015). Thus, the knowledge destination framework distinguishes between a *knowledge generation* and a *knowledge application layer*:

> The *knowledge generation layer*, through methods of information gathering, extraction and storage, makes knowledge sources accessible to stakeholders. For instance, on the customer side, knowledge can be generated through data from feedback mechanisms, like surveys and social media platforms. Similarly, tourists' information traces (e.g. web search) can be made explicit through web-mining (Pitman et al., 2010). Furthermore, knowledge about tourists' buying behavior can be generated through mining transaction data (Höpken et al., 2014), while tourists' mobility behavior can be traced by GPS/WLAN-based position tracking (Zanker et al., 2010). On the supply side, knowledge about products can be extracted from web-sites, for instance, in the form of availability information and product profiles.
>
> The *knowledge application layer* offers e-services that inform about supply elements and tourists' activities. For instance, on the customer side, intelligent location-based services adaptive to the user can guide tourists to attractive destination spots (Höpken et al., 2010; Rasinger et al., 2009). On the supply side, BI-based management information systems (*MIS*) enable the de-centralized provision of knowledge relevant to destination management organisations and private/public destination suppliers.
>
> (Fuchs et al., 2011)

The *architectural framework* illustrates the technical components for the knowledge generation and application layer. The former comprises the various sources

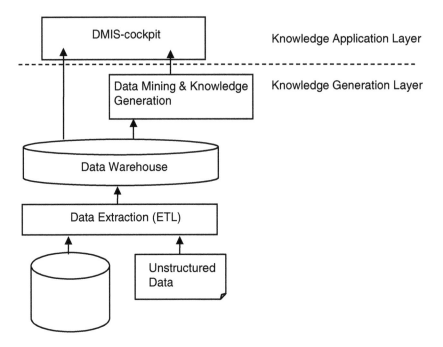

Figure 19.1 The knowledge destination framework architecture

Source: adapted from Höpken et al., 2011, p. 420

of *customer*-based data (web search, booking and feedback data), technical components for data extraction, transformation and loading (ETL), a centralized data warehouse, and data mining (Liu, 2011; Höpken et al., 2011). Finally, the decentralized presentation and ad hoc visualization of data mining models and underlying data rests on the knowledge application layer, the *DMIS-Åre cockpit* (Fig. 19.1)

The business intelligence-based destination management information system Åre

Knowledge relevant in a destination context subsumes knowledge about market cultivation and for destination management and development (Bornhorst et al., 2010). Especially *customer-based knowledge* can be gained through techniques, such as customer segmentation and service performance evaluation. Thus, knowledge sources considered by DMIS-Åre reflect tourists' web navigation, booking and feedback behavior, respectively (Fuchs et al., 2015). Data extracted, stored, analyzed and visualized by DMIS-Åre include customers' information search and product consumption patterns as well as demographic and psychographic characteristics, buying motives and destination brand perceptions. Based on the literature (Dwyer & Kim, 2003; Fuchs & Weiermair, 2004; Gretzel & Fesenmaier, 2004;

Chekalina et al., 2014) and input from destination stakeholders, a comprehensive set of DMIS indicators reflecting the destination performance was defined (Fuchs et al., 2015):

- *Economic performance indicators* comprise bookings, overnights, prices, occupancy, sales etc.
- *Customer behavior indicators* comprise website navigation and search (page views, search terms etc.), booking patterns (booking channels, cancellations etc.), customer profiles (country of origin, age, gender etc.), tourists' travel and consumption behavior (destination activities, purpose of visit etc.).
- *Customer perception and experience indicators* comprise destination brand awareness, tourists' judgment of destination value-areas (winter/summer activities, attractions, destination services etc.), value-for-money, customer satisfaction (functional and emotional, total satisfaction), and loyalty (Chekalina et al., 2014).

Through a business process-oriented multi-dimensional data modelling approach, these indicators are assigned to *sequential* processes, namely "*"Web-Navigation"*, *"Booking"* and *"Feedback"* (Höpken et al., 2013; Fuchs et al., 2015). Each process is composed by the main variable(s) of analysis and their context (*dimensions*). By identifying common (i.e. *conformed*) dimensions across different business processes, this allows DMIS to provide analyses *across* processes, and thus, to join so far disconnected knowledge areas (Kimball et al., 2008; Höpken et al., 2013).

Data extraction, transformation and loading (ETL) is based on the *Rapid Analytics BI®* server, while the DMIS cockpit is developed as an *html*-based web application. DMIS-Åre is technically validated and prototypically implemented at the destination Åre (Fuchs et al., 2014; Höpken et al., 2015). In its present form DMIS provides instant reports (*dashboards*) and OLAP analyses, thus, grants destination stakeholders real-time access to data stored in the data warehouse. The most relevant business process in DMIS, *"Feedback"*, embraces the most comprehensive data input, including (1) destination brand equity surveys for recent winter and summer seasons (Chekalina et al., 2014), (2) real-time feedback from Åre guests during their stay provided by an e-customer registration and survey tool (e-CRST) accessible via Quick Response codes (Höpken et al., 2012), (3) User Generated Content (UGC) (Gräbner et al., 2012), and (4) customer feedback based on surveys conducted by destination suppliers, such as the accommodation providers Copperhill Mountain-Lodge and Tott-Hotel Åre.

4. A framework for UGC extraction and analysis

As mentioned, after introducing the knowledge destination framework (Höpken et al., 2011) and a brief discussion about the features of the BI-based DMIS-Åre (Fuchs et al., 2014; Höpken et al., 2015), a description of the framework for UGC extraction and analysis, which is integrated in DMIS-Åre, will now follow. Online reviews regarding Åre are gained from the social media platforms TripAdvisor.

com and Booking.com and text-processing techniques are applied to automatically extract single statements from each of the reviews. Subsequently, by using machine-learning techniques and a dictionary-based approach, these statements are classified as either "positive" experiences, "negative" experiences or "neutral" (Liu, 2011). Moreover, the statements are classified into product areas, like "Food-Breakfast", "Rooms", and "Service-Personnel". From the proportion of classified positive and classified negative statements, an average feedback value (normalized between 0–1) is computed. More precisely, by following Hippner and Rentzmann (2006) the presented framework for UGC extraction and analysis comprises five steps discussed next (Schmunk et al., 2014):

- *Document selection*: relevant review sites are identified as input to the mining procedure of the sentiment analysis regarding hotels in the destination. The review sites Booking.com (10 hotels and 248 reviews) and TripAdvisor.com (17 hotels and 1,193 reviews) were selected for the case of Åre. To collect relevant pages from review sites, a web crawler was used, fetching *html* pages and following contained links based on regular expressions specified for each site (Schmunk et al., 2014, p. 256).
- *Document (pre-)processing*: The pre-processing of collected *html* documents includes four sub-steps: (1) extraction of relevant opinion texts from *html*-code based on regular expressions, (2) removal of empty reviews, (3) filtering of English texts, since sentiment analysis is language dependent (e.g. word lists in the case of the dictionary-based approach or stop word removal and stemming in the case of machine-learning approaches),[2] and (4) generation of single statements based on sentences end characters as delimiters (Schmunk et al., 2014, p. 257). Pre-processing of TripAdvisor.com, finally, delivers 127 reviews and 1,296 usable single statements, while from Booking.com 81 reviews and 220 statements are gained (total number of reviews = 208; total number of usable statements = 1,516).
- *Mining* includes the sub-tasks recognition of properties, subjectivity, and sentiments, respectively. For machine-learning methods training data were created for all classification tasks (i.e. properties, subjectivity and sentiments). Sentences are tokenized, stop words removed, words reduced to their stem, and finally, a word vector is created based on TF-IDF scores. Subsequently, the machine-learning methods Naïve Bayes, Support Vector Machines (SVM) and k-nearest neighbour (k-NN) are applied (Liu, 2011). For the dictionary-based approach, a word list for each class (i.e. property, subjectivity and sentiment) is employed. In this case, the class of a sentence is directly deduced by the word list for which the majority of contained words belong to (Schmunk et al., 2014, p. 258).
- *Evaluation:* A 10-fold cross-validation is used to evaluate the machine-learning models, while the dictionary-based approach is evaluated by comparing the results with pre-classified test data (Liu, 2011). For the recognition of properties SVM gained the highest accuracy (i.e. percentage of correctly classified statements within test data) of 72.35%. Interestingly, the highest

accuracy of 82.63% for subjectivity recognition was achieved by the dictionary-based method. Finally, the best result for sentiment recognition is gained again by the SVM method, showing an accuracy of 76.80% (Schmunk et al., 2014, p. 260).

- *Usage:* The outcome of the sentiment analysis provides valuable information on customer reviews and opinions in a structured format (Schmunk et al., 2014, p. 262). This UGC-based data is, thus, stored in the multi-dimensional destination data warehouse of DMIS-Åre (Höpken et al., 2013). Besides data extracted from the review sites (e.g. review date, hotel name, demographic data of reviewer and the review text itself), the analysis outcome provides the product properties to which the opinion is linked and its orientation (sentiment). Thus, social media knowledge is made available for powerful OLAP analyses and cross-process analyses as discussed in the next section.

Creation of social media knowledge through DMIS-Åre

The DMIS-Åre *dashboard* in Figure 19.2 displays the customers' (i.e. guest) profile directly deduced from social media content, such as travel purpose, travel companies, number of UGC-based statements by origin countries etc.

A further dashboard functionality summarizes parts of additional information directly extracted from social media sites, such as the date of the review, review site, hotel name and the full customer review (Fig. 19.3).

The DMIS-Åre *dashboard* in Figure 19.4 displays the "average feedback" value, extracted and calculated from UGC as described in the previous section, grouped by hotel "product areas" and major hotels in Åre. Hotel and destination managers can, thus, monitor the performance in terms of customer feedback (UGC) in total or grouped by hotel product area. Moreover, UGC-based performance metrics can be benchmarked among various accommodation suppliers (Fuchs and Weiermair, 2004).

The *OLAP* functionality additionally offered by DMIS-Åre provides hotel and destination managers with a multitude of opportunities to gain knowledge from social media content through grouping the indicator variable ("average feedback value") by the various dimensional variables. For instance, the OLAP in Figure 19.5 displays the indicator variable grouped by the dimension *date* (→ attribute "DateYear"). Interestingly, the finding reveals that, in tendency, more recent online reviews are less positive.

A similar UGC-based OLAP analysis grouping the indicator variable by the *date* dimension (→ attribute "DateSeason") reveals that most satisfied customers can be found in Åre during the "High Winter" and "Summer Season", respectively (Figure 19.6).

Interestingly, with regard to the dimensions *customer profile* (→ attribute "CusProTravelGroup") and *vacation purpose* (→ attribute "TraProTravelPurposeVacation"), the social media-based feedback value is most positive for families (Figure 19.7) and vacation travellers (Figure 19.8), respectively.

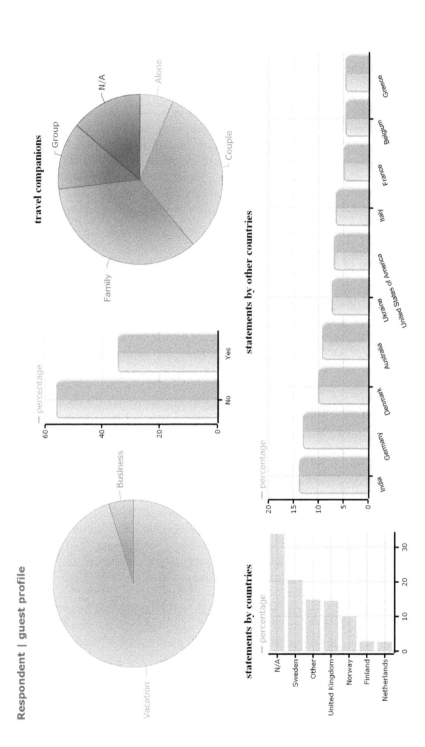

Figure 19.2 DMIS-Åre dashboard: guest profile extracted from social media sites

			`select` ▾
April, 2013	booking.com	Åre Continental Inn	Golven i rummen som var utslitna och 'kladdiga'. Badrummet med vattenskadat golv kring golvbrunnen. Hade önskat t ex en tavla i rummet eller något annat så det kändes lite mer 'mysigt', nu var det så strerilt rummetAtt allt var i samma hus. Snygg poolanläggning och snygg matsal. Frukosten var OK.
April, 2013	booking.com	Tott Hotell	För oerfaren personal i restaurangen.Tott har ett suveränt läge. ski in- ski out.
April, 2013	booking.com	Holiday Club Hotell	The kitchen is terrible. I recommend visitors to have the breakfast which was good but eat lunch and dinner elsewhere.The spa / pool / sauna area is fantastic! This alone makes the stay an excellent bargain.
April, 2013	booking.com	Holiday Club Hotell	Frukosten var under all kritik, kaffet odrickbart, nara två val av frukt som dessutom låg framme utan kylning. Av 100-tals hotell i denna prisklass var frukosten det sämsta jag upplevt. När vi kom på kvällen var receptionen obemannad och vi hänvisades till en kiosk där personalen var helt ointresserad av att informera oss om frukosttider, i vilken riktning, våning vi skulle ta oss. Vi kände oss som boskap på väg in i en fålla.Närhet till tågstation och liftar. Trevlig reception, när den hålls öppen. Städning bra, rum var ok men inte den standard man förväntar sig för ett pris på 2.200 kr/natt.
April, 2013	booking.com	Karolinen Hotell	The walls were pretty thin, and our bedroom happened to be next to the tv of the neighbours. Problem was easily solved by moving the beds to the living room though.Very kind staff, good food, and okay beds. Close to Åre Bjørnen where we could jump right on the ski bus towards the ski elevators. Not too close to the centre, so it's quiet and peaceful in the evenings.

Figure 19.3 List of reviews

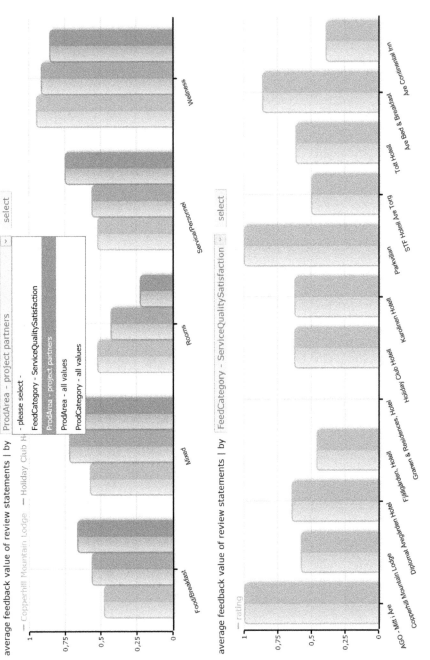

Figure 19.4 DMIS-Åre dashboard: UGC-based feedback value grouped by Åre hotels and product area

average feedback value of review statements | by [ProdArea - all values] [select]

items	Copperhill Mountain Lodge	Diplomat Åregården Hotel	Fjällgården, Hotell	Holiday Club Hotell	Karolinen Hotell	STF Hotell Åre Torg	Hotell Tott	Åre Bed & Breakfast	Åre Continental Inn	Granen & Residences, Hotel
Food/Breakfast	0.478	0.704	1	0.565	0	0.500	0.667	0.667	1	?
Location	0.841	0.938	0.556	0.772	1	0.909	0.933	1	0.667	0
Mixed	0.576	0.633	0.667	0.722	1	0.625	0.895	1	0.625	0
Rooms	0.524	0.500	0	0.429	0.333	0.333	0.227	?	0.111	?
Service/Personnel	0.522	0.750	0	0.562	?	0.500	0.750	1	1	?
Wellness	0.950	0.778	?	0.917	?	?	0.857	?	1	?

Figure 19.4 (Continued)

indicators

number of indicators: ○ 0 ● 1 ○ 2 ○ 3 ※ total amount of classified, non-neutral statements

FdbFeedbackValue ⋮ average

---

grouping

select the characteristics the final result should be grouped by:

Date ⋮ DateYear ⋮ add

DateYear||

---

execute

query database   reset

DateYear	average_of_FdbFeedbackValue	Total
2013	0.516	281
2012	0.642	464
2011	0.620	171
2010	0.555	128
2009	0.647	17
2008	0.800	15
2007	0.900	10

Figure 19.5 DMIS-Åre OLAP: UGC-based feedback value grouped by year

DateSeason	average_of_FdbFeedbackValue	Total
HighWinter	0.620	647
Summer	0.601	218
LowWinter	0.545	154
Fall	0.537	67

Figure 19.6 DMIS-Åre OLAP: UGC-based feedback value grouped by season

CusProTravelGroup	average_of_FdbFeedbackValue	Total
Family	0.603	451
Couple	0.599	441
TravelGroup	0.593	108
Alone	0.450	40

Figure 19.7 DMIS-Åre OLAP: UGC-based feedback value grouped by travel group

TraProTravelPurposeVacation	average_of_FdbFeedbackValue	Total
No	0.739	46
Yes	0.594	1040

Figure 19.8 DMIS-Åre OLAP: UGC-based feedback value grouped by travel purpose

The "sorting function" offered by DMIS-Åre's OLAP functionality allows hotel and destination managers to quickly recognize that the *product areas* (→ attribute "ProdArea") "location" and "wellness" gained the highest average feedback score values, while "rooms" and "food/breakfast" are gaining only medium average score-values (Figure 19.9).

OLAP analyses are considered as especially powerful when grouping an indicator variable by multiple dimensions (Larose, 2005, p. 59; Kimball et al., 2008). An example of a multi-dimensional OLAP analysis is provided in Figure 19.10. The dimensional variables *customer profile* (→ attribute "CustomerProfileTravel-Group") and *product* (→ attribute "ProductArea") are jointly utilized to group the indicator variable "AverageFeedbackValue". Due to space limitations, the figure only displays OLAP findings with the relatively largest number of statements (no. of statements > 23). Interestingly, it can be shown that couples are comparatively more satisfied with the service personnel than families.

Further findings gained through multi-dimensional OLAP analyses are displayed in Figure 19.11. The three dimensional variables *date* (→ attribute "Date-Season"), *customer* (→ attribute "CustomerCountry") and *product* (→ attribute "ProductArea") are simultaneously considered to group the indicator variable. Again, only the findings showing more than 12 statements are displayed. Interestingly, domestic tourists visiting the destination during the "High Winter" season are especially dissatisfied with hotel "Rooms". By contrast, British guests visiting Åre in the "High Winter" season are especially satisfied with the "Food/breakfast" offers.

The analysis goal of the multi-dimensional OLAP displayed in Figure 19.12 is to list the accommodation supplier, the social media platform where the feedback was posted, the product area and the feedback value of each single statement. Thus, the indicator variable is again the overall "feedback value" which is grouped by the four dimensional variables *statement text* (i.e. "VariableFeedback") (→ attribute "VarFeed"), *travel profile* (→ attribute "TraProLodgingSupplier"), *product* (→

ProdArea	average_of_FdbFeedbackValue	Total
Wellness	0.904	73
Location	0.830	182
Mixed	0.679	193
Service/Personnel	0.589	56
Food/Breakfast	0.581	148
Rooms	0.406	160

Figure 19.9 DMIS-Åre OLAP: UGC-based feedback value grouped by product area

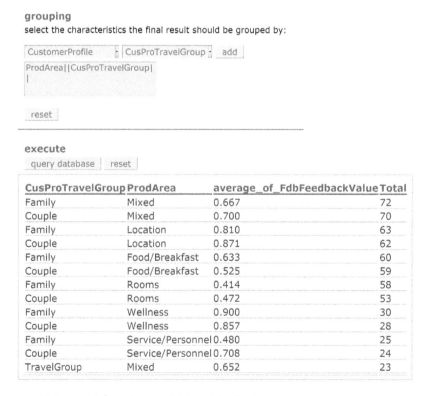

CusProTravelGroup	ProdArea	average_of_FdbFeedbackValue	Total
Family	Mixed	0.667	72
Couple	Mixed	0.700	70
Family	Location	0.810	63
Couple	Location	0.871	62
Family	Food/Breakfast	0.633	60
Couple	Food/Breakfast	0.525	59
Family	Rooms	0.414	58
Couple	Rooms	0.472	53
Family	Wellness	0.900	30
Couple	Wellness	0.857	28
Family	Service/Personnel	0.480	25
Couple	Service/Personnel	0.708	24
TravelGroup	Mixed	0.652	23

Figure 19.10 DMIS-Åre OLAP: UGC-based feedback value grouped by travel group and product area

DateSeason	CusCountry	ProdArea	average_of_FdbFeedbackValue	Total
HighWinter	Sweden	Rooms	0.321	28
HighWinter	Sweden	Location	0.708	24
HighWinter	United Kingdom	Food/Breakfast	0.750	24
HighWinter	Sweden	Mixed	0.739	23
HighWinter	Sweden	Food/Breakfast	0.471	17
HighWinter	United Kingdom	Mixed	0.824	17
HighWinter	United Kingdom	Location	0.846	13
HighWinter	United Kingdom	Rooms	0.500	12
HighWinter	Norway	Rooms	0.444	9
Summer	Norway	Rooms	0.444	9
HighWinter	Finland	Mixed	0.625	8
HighWinter	Sweden	Wellness	1	8
LowWinter	Norway	Rooms	0.250	8

Figure 19.11 DMIS-Åre OLAP: UGC-based feedback value grouped by season, country and product area

attribute "ProdArea"), and *social media platform* (i.e. "Channel") ($\rightarrow$ attribute: "ChaName"). This final example especially demonstrates the extensive flexibility of the OLAP approach applied by DMIS-Åre (Höpken et al., 2015; Fuchs et al., 2015).

As outlined in previously, a final powerful feature of DMIS-Åre is to join so far disconnected and separately filed knowledge areas through common (i.e. *conformed*) dimensions across different business processes (Kimball et al., 2008; Höpken et al., 2013). This condition, namely to relate customer feedback to web navigation and booking behavior is considered as crucial for enhanced organizational learning and creativity processes in destinations (Fuchs et al., 2014, p. 201). More concretely, this procedure allows DMIS-Åre to provide analyses *across* the three implemented processes *Web Navigation* (site clicks, unique sessions), *Booking* (total bookings, booking price, numbers of persons/booking, average time between booking and arrival, average stay duration/booking) and *Feedback* (total feedback answers, average feedback value) (Höpken et al., 2015). As mentioned in earlier, the average feedback value is generated not only through UGC extracted from various social media platforms (Schmunk et al., 2014). Rather, the multidimensional structures of the DMIS-Åre data warehouse (Höpken et al., 2013) are populated also by feedback data from destination brand equity surveys (Chekalina et al., 2014), real-time feedback from Åre guests during their stay provided by an electronic customer registration and survey tool (e-CRST) accessible via Quick-Response codes (Höpken et al., 2012), and, finally, data from customer surveys conducted by various destination suppliers (i.e. the accommodation providers Copperhill Mountain-Lodge and Tott-Hotel Åre).

Thus, the following cross-process analyses link customer feedback from different sources with data from the web navigation and booking process, respectively. For instance, for each country of customer origin, Figure 19.13 lists key

TraProLodgingSupplier	ChaName	ProdArea	VarFeed	average_of_FdbFeedbackValue
AGO - Mitt i Åre	booking.com	Mixed	I have never stayed at a hotel anywhere in the world that required the guest to clean the room Great location easy booking and arrival	1
AGO - Mitt i Åre	booking.com	N/A	Unclear policy toward check out cleanliness	0
AGO - Mitt i Åre	booking.com	Rooms	How can I be charged for allegedly not cleaning the room when I felt the room was cleaned and the fact that it is a hotel	?
Copperhill Mountain Lodge	booking.com	Food/Breakfast	Breakfast was ok more juice pressers needed and waffels was not a good thing because of the smell of grease in a low seeling area	0
Copperhill Mountain Lodge	booking.com	Food/Breakfast	Good food	1
Copperhill Mountain Lodge	booking.com	Food/Breakfast	The chef is a poor cook we found better food at even the simplest cafes in Björnen	0

Figure 19.12 DMIS-Åre OLAP: UGC-based feedback value grouped by supplier, channel, product area and statement text

Group by attribute	Total bookings	Total clicks	Total feedback, answers	Total sessions	Average booking price in SEK	Average number of persons per booking	Average time between booking and arrival in days	Average stay duration per booking	Average time spent on single webpage in seconds	Average visit time on websites in seconds	Average pages visited on websites	Average feedback value
Australia	33	165	156	56	4029.485	2.606	49.100	4.818	20.826	73.226	2.946	0.859
Belgium	33	1207	130	361	5355.424	2.970	112	5.364	20.692	85.960	3.344	0.702
China	14	456	71	230	3087.250	3.500	164.500	8.786	6.685	35.707	1.983	0.859
Denmark	1830	2392	107	521	6235.034	4.527	115.609	6.144	17.057	89.379	4.591	0.778
Estonia	1080	161	16	53	4837.395	5.292	85.108	5.838	24.085	94.556	3.038	0.784
Finland	3155	4543	1039	893	7852.046	4.386	95.536	6.160	16.915	100.814	5.087	0.812
France	25	2923	12	739	4616	3.040	38.318	5.042	19.187	82.978	3.955	0.715
Germany	105	3268	150	665	5307.040	3.155	124.425	6.644	13.377	82.701	4.914	0.837
Netherlands	279	2168	150	490	7894.760	3.802	104.493	6.588	13.741	87.556	4.425	0.750
Norway	10625	27636	9093	5889	3901.213	4.911	71.890	3.297	16.439	87.700	4.693	0.767
Sweden	56073	162942	36880	39139	5023.956	3.860	83.014	5.498	17.407	84.981	4.163	0.773
United Kingdom	1042	48513	303	12843	4929.136	3.009	59.399	6.786	17.259	76.811	3.777	0.765

Figure 19.13 Key performance indicators (KPIs) gained through DMIS-Åre's Cross Process Analysis

performance indicators (KPIs) across the booking process, the web navigation process and the feedback process (Schmunk et al., 2014, p. 262). For instance and interestingly enough, the cross-process analysis reveals that Finnish tourists show a relatively high average feedback value (i.e. 0.812), pay a relatively high average booking price per overnight (7,852 SEK) and are characterized by a relatively long average duration of stay (i.e. 6.16 days). In contrast, tourists from Belgium show a relatively low average feedback value (i.e. 0.702), pay a comparatively lower booking price per overnight (i.e. 5,355 SEK) and show a relatively short average duration of stay (i.e. 5.36 days).

Conclusions and future research

The presented research conducted in collaboration with stakeholders of the leading Swedish mountain destination Åre, addressed the generation of customer-based knowledge to provide an all-stakeholder encompassing *Destination Management Information System* (DMIS-Åre). Major critical concepts, like the elicitation of knowledge needs, data extraction, data warehousing and user-interfaces have been conducted, technically validated and prototypically implemented as a genuine novelty in Åre (Fuchs et al., 2014; 2015; Höpken et al., 2014; 2015). Customer data sources are provided by major destination stakeholders and constantly imported through a semi-automated process which is extracting, loading and transforming customer-based data into the homogenous and centralized destination data warehouse (Höpken et al., 2013; Fuchs et al., 2015). The prototype, in its present version, comprises the processes *Web-Navigation, Booking and Feedback*.

The focus of this chapter was on a BI-based framework for UGC extraction and analysis validated on the basis of data from TripAdvisor.com and Booking.com (Schmunk et al., 2014). By utilizing this framework, various examples of use-cases for knowledge application through DMIS-Åre based on social media knowledge are shown and discussed. More precisely, the mining task of the conducted sentiment analysis has been divided into the recognition of the property, the recognition of the subjectivity and the recognition of the sentiment (Schmunk et al., 2014, p. 263). Each of these tasks has been successfully implemented by utilizing a dictionary-based approach and the machine-learning methods Naïve Bayes, Support Vector Machines (SVM) and k-nearest neighbour (k-NN) (Liu, 2011). For the detection of properties, SVM achieved the best accuracy (i.e. 72.38%), while the recognition of subjectivity of a statement performed best by the dictionary-based approach (i.e. accuracy of 82.63%). Finally, for the classification of sentences into positives and negatives, the SVM method achieved the best accuracy amounting to 76.80% (Schmunk et al., 2014, p. 264). Thus, the gained social media knowledge can be considered as a valuable input to BI-based decision support in destinations, either on its own, or related to other business indicators as part of the destination data warehouse of the BI-based DMIS-Åre (Höpken et al., 2015). The practicality and usefulness of this input for social media knowledge generation has been approved through various DMIS features, namely dashboards (Figures 19.2–19.4), one-dimensional

(Figures 19.5–19.9) and multi-dimensional OLAP analyses (Figures 19.10–19.12), and, finally, a cross-process analysis (Figure 19.13).

To conclude, the agenda for future research regarding the BI-based framework for UGC extraction and analysis comprises the extension of word lists (i.e. especially for infrequent features), the use of larger sets of training data for machine-learning techniques and, finally, the use of web services in order to automatically retrieve online reviews from the various social media platforms in tourism (Schmunk et al., 2014, p. 264). A further future research activity relates to the extension of the presented framework for UGC analysis. More precisely, beyond the most accurate recognition of both the property, the sentiment and subjectivity, the framework will be extended to also recognize destination brand equity-based feedback categories, like brand awareness, tangible and intangible destination resources, value-in-use, value-for-money and brand loyalty (Chekalina et al., 2014). Moreover, in the course of future research, the DMIS cockpit, beyond dashboard and OLAP functionalities, will also provide visualizations for data mining processes, like classification, clustering or prediction (Mayer et al., 2015). Finally, it is envisaged to extract and integrate social media content in a real-time context, ideally from ubiquitous data sources, such as mobile apps utilized by tourists during destination stay (Kolas et al., 2015).

Acknowledgements

This research was financed by KK-Foundation project 'Engineering the Knowledge Destination' (no. 20100260; Stockholm, Sweden). The authors would like to thank the managers Lars-Börje Eriksson (Åre Destination AB), Niclas Sjögren-Berg and Anna Wersén (Ski Star Åre), Peter Nilsson and Hans Ericsson (Tott-Hotel Åre), and Pernilla Gravenfors (Copperhill Mountain-Lodge Åre) for their excellent cooperation.

Notes

1 BI is an umbrella term comprising a) *data identification and preparation*, b) *database modelling* and *data warehousing*, and c) the application of *Online Analytical Processing* (OLAP) and *data mining* (DM) techniques (Larose, 2005). DM comprises *classification* (e.g. artificial neural networks [ANN], decision tree analysis, K-nearest neighbor techniques, etc.), *estimation* and *prediction, clustering* (e.g. Kohonen Networks) and *association rules* (particularly for market basket analyses) (Fuchs et al., 2015, p. 162).
2 To filter English texts, supervised learning was used and a Naïve Bayes classifier was trained, based on a small sample of texts for each relevant language as training data reaching an accuracy of 100% (Liu, 2011; Schmunk et al., 2014).

References

Bornhorst, T., Ritchie, J. R., & Sheehan, L. (2010). Determinants for DMO and destination success: An empirical examination. *Tourism Management*, 31(2), pp. 572–589.
Chekalina, T., Fuchs, M., & Lexhagen, M. (2014). A-value creation perspective on the customer-based brand equity model for tourism destinations. *Finnish Journal of Tourism Research*, 10(1), pp. 7–23.

Cox, C., Burgess, S., Sellitto, C., & Buultjens, J. (2009). The role of user-generated content in tourists' travel planning behavior. *Journal of Hospitality Marketing & Management*, 18(8), pp. 743–764.

Dwyer, L., & Kim, C. (2003). Destination competitiveness: Determinants and indicators. *Current Issues in Tourism Research*, 6(5), pp. 369–417.

Fuchs, M., Abadzhiev, A., Svensson, B, Höpken, W., & Lexhagen, M. (2013). A knowledge destination framework for tourism sustainability: A business intelligence application from Sweden. *Tourism: An Interdisciplinary Journal*, 61(2), pp. 121–148.

Fuchs, M., Eybl, A., & Höpken, W. (2011). Successfully selling accommodation packages at online auctions: The case of eBay Austria. *Tourism Management*, 32(5), pp. 1166–1175.

Fuchs, M., Höpken, W., Föger, A., & Kunz, M. (2010). E-Business readiness, intensity, and impact: An Austrian DMO Study. *Journal of Travel Research*, 49(2), pp. 165–178.

Fuchs, M., Höpken, W., & Lexhagen, M. (2014). Big data analytics for knowledge generation in tourism destinations: A case from Sweden. *Journal of Destination Marketing and Management*, 3(4), pp. 198–209.

Fuchs, M., Höpken, W., & Lexhagen, M. (2015). Applying business intelligence for knowledge generation in tourism destinations: A case from Sweden. In: H. Pechlaner & E. Smeral (eds.) *Tourism and Leisure: Current Issues and Perspectives of Development in Research and Business*. New York, Springer, pp. 161–174.

Fuchs, M., & Höpken, W. (2009). Data mining in tourism (In German: Data Mining im Tourismus'). *Praxis der Wirtschaftsinformatik*, 270(12), pp. 73–81.

Fuchs, M., & Weiermair, K. (2004). Destination benchmarking: An indicator system's potential for exploring guest satisfaction. *Journal of Travel Research*, 42(3), pp. 212–225.

Gräbner, D., Zanker, M., Fliedl, G., & Fuchs, M. (2012). Classification of customer reviews based on sentiment analysis: The case of TripAdvisor. In M. Fuchs, F. Ricci, & L. Cantoni (eds.) *Information and Communication Technologies in Tourism*. New York, Springer, pp. 460–470.

Gretzel, U., & Fesenmaier, D. (2004). Implementing a knowledge-based tourism marketing information system. *Journal of Information Technology & Tourism*, 6(2), pp. 245–255.

Hippner, H., & Rentzmann, R. (2006). *Text Mining*. Ingolstadt, Springer.

Höpken, W., Deubele, Ph, Höll, G., Kuppe, J., Schorpp, D., Licones, R., & Fuchs, M. (2012). Digitalizing loyalty cards in tourism. In M. Fuchs, F. Ricci, & L. Cantoni (eds.) *Information and Communication Technologies in Tourism*. New York, Springer, pp. 272–283.

Höpken, W., Fuchs, M., Höll, G. Keil, D., & Lexhagen, M. (2013). Multi-dimensional data modeling for a destination data warehouse. In L. Cantoni & Ph. Xiang (eds.) *Information and Communication Technologies in Tourism*. New York, Springer, pp. 157–169.

Höpken, W., Fuchs, M., Keil, D., & Lexhagen, M. (2011). The knowledge destination: A customer information-based destination management information system. In R. Law, M. Fuchs & F. Ricci (eds.) *Information and Communication Technologies in Tourism*, New York, Springer, pp. 417–429.

Höpken, W., Fuchs, M., Keil, D., & Lexhagen, M. (2015). Business intelligence for cross-process knowledge extraction at tourism destination, *Information Technology and Tourism*. 15(2), pp. 101–130.

Höpken, W., Fuchs, M., & Lexhagen, M. (2014). The knowledge destination: Applying methods of business intelligence to tourism. In J. Wang (ed.) *Encyclopedia of Business Analytics and Optimization*, Pennsylvania, IGI Global, pp. 307–321.

Höpken, W., Fuchs, M., Zanker, M., & Beer, Th. (2010). Context-based adaptation of mobile applications in tourism. *Information Technology and Tourism*, 12(2), pp. 175–195.

Jannach, D., Zanker, M., & Fuchs, M. (2013). Multi-criteria customer-feedback for improved recommender systems in tourism. *Journal of Information Technology and Tourism*, 14(2), pp. 119–149.

Kensik, J., & Wachowiak, H. (2011). *Untersuchung der Bedeutung und Glaubwürdigkeit von Bewertungen auf Internetportalen*. Bonn, Gabler Verlag.

Kimball, R., Ross, M., Thronthwaite, W., Mundy, J., & Becker, B. (2008). *The Data Warehouse Lifecycle Toolkit*, 2nd Edition. Indianapolis, Wiley & Sons.

Kolas, N., Höpken, W., Fuchs, M., & Lexhagen, M. (2015). Information gathering by ubiquitous services for CRM in tourism destinations: An explorative study from Sweden. In I. Tussyadiah & A. Inversini (eds.) *Information and Communication Technologies in Tourism*. New York, Springer, pp. 73–85.

Larose, D. (2005). *Discovering Knowledge in Data*. New Jersey, John Wiley & Sons.

Leung, D., Law, R., van Hoof, H., & Buhalis, D. (2013). Social media in tourism and hospitality: A literature review. *Journal of Travel & Tourism Marketing*, 30(1), pp. 3–22.

Lexhagen, M., Kuttainen, C., Fuchs, M., & Höpken, W. (2012). Destination talk in social media: a content analysis for innovation. In Advances in hospitality and tourism marketing & management conference, 31st May–3rd of June 2012, Corfu, Greece.

Liu, B. (2011). *Web Data Mining: Exploring Hyperlinks, Contents and Usage Data*. 2nd Edition. Chicago, Springer.

Magnini, V., Honeycutt, E., & Hodge, S. (2003). Data mining for hotel firms: Use and limitations. *Cornell Hotel and Restaurant Administration Quarterly*, 44(December), pp. 94–105.

Mayer, V., Höpken, W., & Fuchs, M. (2015). Integration of data mining results into multidimensional data models. In I. Tussyadiah, & A. Inversini (eds.) *Information and Communication Technologies in Tourism*. New York, Springer, pp. 155–166.

Pan, B., MacLaurin, T., & Crotts, J. (2007). Travel blogs and the implications for destination marketing. *Journal of Travel Research*, 46(1), pp. 35–45.

Pitman, A., Zanker, M., Fuchs, M., & Lexhagen, M. (2010). Web-usage mining in tourism. In U. Gretzel, R. Law, & M. Fuchs (eds.) *Information and Communication Technologies in Tourism*. New York, Springer, pp. 393–403.

Pyo, S., Uysal, M., & Chang, H. (2002). Knowledge discovery in databases for tourist destinations. *Journal of Travel Research*, 40(4), pp. 396–403.

Rasinger, J., Fuchs, M., Höpken, W., & Beer, Th. (2009). Building a mobile tourist guide based on tourists' on-site information needs. *Tourism Analysis*, 14(4), pp. 483–502.

Schmunk, S., Höpken, W., Fuchs, M., & Lexhagen, M. (2014). Sentiment analysis: Implementation and evaluation of methods for sentiment analysis with Rapid-Miner®. In Ph. Xiang & I. Tussyadiah (eds.) *Information and Communication Technologies in Tourism*. New York, Springer pp. 253–265.

Sidali, K., Fuchs, M., & Spiller, A. (2012). The effect of e-Reviews on consumer behavior. In M. Sigala, U. Gretzel & Christou, E. (eds.) *Web 2.0 in Travel, Tourism and Hospitality: Theory, Practices and Cases*, Surrey, Ashgate Publishing, pp. 239–253.

Sigala, M. (2011). Social media and crisis management in tourism: Applications and implications for research. *Information Technology & Tourism*, 13(4), pp. 269–283.

Sparks, B., Perkins, H., & Buckley, R. (2013). Online travel reviews as persuasive communication. *Tourism Management*, 39(1), 1–19.

Xiang, Z., & Gretzel, U. (2010). Role of social media in online travel information search. *Tourism Management*, 31(2), pp. 179–188.

Wong J., Chen, H., Chung, P., & Kao, N. (2006). Identifying valuable travelers and their next foreign destination by applying data mining techniques. *Asia Pacific Journal of Tourism Research*, www.informaworld.com/smpp/title~content=t713694199~db=all~ta b=issueslist~branches=11 – v1111(4), pp. 355–373.

Zanker, M, Jessenitschnig, M., & Fuchs, M. (2010). Automated semantic annotation of tourism resources based on geo-spatial data. *Information Technology and Tourism*, 11(4), pp. 341–354.

20 Community characteristics in tourism Twitter accounts of European countries

Kostas Zafiropoulos, Konstantinos Antoniadis, and Vasiliki Vrana

Nowadays, internet and social media have opened new possibilities for marketing and branding countries, for creating a unique and competitive identity and image (Vrana & Zafiropoulos, 2011) for segmenting audiences and for promoting differentiated brand propositions to different targeted segments (Blumrodt & Palmer, 2014). Destination Marketing Organizations (DMOs) are the main vehicle for countries to compete and attract visitors (Pike & Page, 2014). The increasing use of social media has forced DMOs to adopt and integrate them into their strategic programs in order to enhance their visibility on the market, strengthen their competitiveness and create new markets and new competitive advantages (Dwyer & Kim, 2003; Katsoni & Venetsanopoulou, 2013; Milwood et al., 2013). DMOs may also use social media to better communicate with online target audiences, to take feedback from tourists, to interact with them and allow them to share their views and experiences, travel advices, suggestions and recommendations (Sotiriadis & van Zyl, 2013; Xiang & Gretzel, 2010). Kavoura and Stavianea (2015) claimed that people search for information on social media in order to seek what other people think for planning a journey. Moreover, people who interact with social media over a long period of time, have a "sense of belonging" in a community, trust the opinions of other users and take them into consideration when making a purchase decision or decide to visit a travel destination (Kavoura & Stavianea, 2014; Kozinets, 2002).

Twitter was officially launched in October 2006 (Krishnamurthy et al., 2008) and it now is the most popular microblogging site with about one billion registered users. On July 2015 Twitter has 316 million monthly active users who post about 500 million tweets a day (Digital Marketing, 2015). Tweets are short messages, less than 140 characters with an average 11 words per message (O'Connor et al., 2010) that answers the "What's happening". Chu et al. (2010) claimed that Twitter now is an information publishing venue. Indeed a percentage of 63% of Twitter users say that it is a source for news for them (Digital Marketing, 2015). This growing use of Twitter implies that DMOs may use Twitter to disseminate information about the country, provide access to tourism services, connect with tourists and potential visitors and listen to their voice.

Research on social media and especially on Twitter use by DMOs is limited. Hamill et al. (2010) investigated social media adoption levels by National DMOs in Europe. They found that 21 out of the 25 DMOs under investigation were using Twitter and that leading national DMOs were not fully engaged with social media. Nguyen and Wang (2012) studied "Sweden" and "VisitSweden", the most active Twitter accounts for Sweden. They claimed that DMOs need to emphasize online marketing and social media activities to achieve benefits and to integrate them with traditional marketing activities. DMOs' attitude towards using social media in Egypt was examined by Hassan (2013). Despite the fact that DMOs believe that social media are an important marketing tool, they are not fully using them. Stepchenkova et al. (2013) investigated how Florida is viewed as a destination by visitors and residents by analyzing content of tweets. Bayram and Arici (2013) also used content analysis to explore the usage of social media among the DMOs of Balkan countries and how social media is being used to enhance their brands and to reach potential visitors. They found that the most used social media tools were Facebook and Twitter and proposed that DMOs should use more social networking sites to communicate with their potential customers and give them the ability to broadcast their opinions. Milwood et al. (2013) identified the differences in the adoption and management of social media tools in the US and Switzerland. US DMOs are at different stages in their adoption of social media and need to strategically organize their web marketing efforts in order to maximize efficient use of them. Sevin (2013) investigated how Twitter is utilized by five prominent American destinations. The findings indicate that DMOs tend to use Twitter mainly to share information about events – such as festivals, concerts and fairs and do not necessarily make use of interpersonal communication and networking capabilities offered by Twitter. Antoniadis et al. (2014) investigated the performance of 37 European countries' Twitter accounts using indexes of Twitter performance such as number of followers of each account and indexes of followers' community involvement. An overall performance index is constructed. European countries are then ranked according to their Twitter accounts' performance. They found that Twitter use is in accordance with countries' tourism performance and that Twitter, as a medium of eBusiness, does not fail to provide information and to promote countries' Destination Image. In a recent study Antoniadis et al. (2015) investigated DMOs the mentions/replies (m/r) network of the followers for 37 European countries' Twitter accounts. The findings reveal that m/r networks of followers do not constitute communities, rather people use tourism organizations' Twitter accounts as announcement boards or as one more channel for one-way communication with the public.

This study explores further the potentiality of community formation among followers of National DMOs Twitter accounts of 37 European countries, by measuring social networking and Twitter performance indexes. It records the mentions/replies (m/r) networks of the followers and measures properties of small-world, scale-free networks and homophily. These properties apply to many social media networks which form communities within them, and it is interesting to see if they also apply to the specific context. Next, these indexes are used to create clusters of accounts regarding community characteristics. It is of interest to explore the degree to which communities of followers really exist for tourism Twitter accounts, and to see how accounts differentiate from each other according to community formation of their followers.

Twitter and social networks

With the rise of internet and social media, new online social networks have emerged as users interact with their acquaintances, friends and people sharing common interests (Anagnostopoulos et al., 2008; Vrana et al., 2013). Musiał & Kazienko (2013, p. 31) defined internet-based social networks as a "set of human beings or rather their digital representations that refer to the registered users who are linked by relationships extracted from the data about their activities, common communication or direct links gathered in the internet – based systems".

Twitter users follow, retweet, reply and mention one another and thus social networks and communities are formed and discussion is promoted. When user "A" follows another user "B" then user "A" subscribes to the "B" user's tweets as a follower. User's "B" updates will then appear in "A" user's Home tab (Marwick & Boyd, 2010). This act of following is not mutual (Hargittai & Litt, 2012) in the vein that user "B" need not follow back user "A" (Kwak et al.,2010). Highly skewed distributions have been recorded both at followings' and followers' action (Bakshy et al., 2011; Boyd et al., 2010; Huberman et al., 2009; Kwak et al., 2010).

A reply is a response to another user's tweet. If user "A" replies to user "B" then user "A" writes a tweet that begins with the @username of user "B". The @replies only show up in a user's "C" timeline if user "C" follows both the sender of the original Tweet, user "A" and the recipient of the @reply to that tweet, user "B".

Mentioning is another way that followers can get information in Twitter and directly interact with another user. However, a mention is not necessarily a direct response to another user. If user "A" mentions user "B", then user "A" writes a tweet that contains "B" user's @username anywhere in the body of the tweet.

A retweet is a reposting of someone else's tweet. If user "A" retweets a tweet of user "B" then he/she quickly shares that tweet with all of his/her followers. Retweeting allows user "A" to add his/hers own comments and questions and a better chance that the original tweeter will notice his/hers retweet. Rudat and Buder (2015) claimed that retweeting makes spreading news quick and easy; Boyd et al. (2010) claimed that it is not only a form of information diffusion, but also a mean of participating in a diffuse conversation.

Properties of social networks

A social network can be represented as a finite set of nodes (members) and edges (ties – connections) that link the nodes (Musiał & Kazienko, 2013). Social Network Analysis (SNA) is used for mapping and quantifying of relationships, flows and interaction between the members of a network (Krackhardt, 1996) and reveal the interesting properties that social networks have (Staab, 2005).

A subject of scientific fascination of social networks is the small-world phenomenon (Easley & Kleinberg, 2010), that was first undertaken by Milgram (1967).

Travers and Milgram (1969) suggested that we live in a "small world" where people are connected by "six degrees of separation" in the vein that any two people in the world are connected with about six intermediate acquaintances. The small-world phenomenon applies to many other networks for realistic situations than networks of friends (Newman, 2000). To define the small-world phenomenon, two ingredients are used. The average shortest path length in the network, that it is significantly smaller than the average shortest path length in a random graph of the same size, so the most nodes in the network could be reached by any other node in a small number of steps (Watts & Strogatz, 1998) and the relatively large clustering coefficient, indicating that the nodes connected to a given node are also likely to be connected to one another (Barrat & Weigt, 2000).

Apart from the small-world property, scale-free property has also been discovered in many natural and artificial complex networks (Wang & Chen, 2003). A scale-free network is a network with no typical number of connections per node; rather the distribution of the number of connections per node follows a power law and is independent of the network scale (Barabasi, 2002). This implies there are many nodes with few connections and a small but significant number of nodes with many connections (Van Noort et al., 2004). Scale-free networks tend to expand continuously by the addition of new nodes. These new nodes are attached preferentially to nodes that are already well connected (Choromański et al., 2013).

Another pervasive property of social networks is "homophily". Homophily is defined as the tendency of individuals to associate and bond with similar others (McPherson et al., 2001, p. 416). Homophily applies to many types of social interaction, along with many dimensions of similarity such as gender, age, race, profession, religion etc. In a social network connections tend to be more frequent among similar nodes than among dissimilar ones (Currarini & Vega Redondo, 2013), for example a high similarity between friends is observed (Zafarani et al., 2014). Assortativity index is used to measure homophily in social networks and denotes the degree-similarities between neighboring nodes (Vrana et al., 1014).

Methodology

In this study 37 European countries' tourism Twitter accounts were recorded in a survey during 8–10 October 2013. These accounts are: Spain, VisitBritain, VisitNorway, VisitScotland, Italy_it, VisitHolland, VisitGreecegr, DiscoverIreland, HungaryTourism, VisitPortugal, GermanyTourism, MySwitzerland_en, GoVisitDenmark, VisitMonaco, OurFinland, Belgiuminfo, Austriatourism, Visit_Poland, VisitCyprus, CzechTourism, Croatia_hr, VisitSweden, UK_Franceguide, SloveniaInfo, RomaniaTourism, Visit_Russia, VisitMontenegro, VisitMalta, Visit_Turkey, VisitEstonia, Luxembourginfo, ExplorMacedonia, VisitLithuania, VisitIceland, Travel_Latvia, VisitSlovakia, Andorraworld_en. In two cases, France and Lithuania (UK_FranceGuide and Lithuania UK), central tourism websites did not link to Twitter accounts so other tourism Twitter accounts were used through search on the internet.

Followers, following, number of tweets, Topsy score and Total Effective Reach were recorded for the 37 accounts. These serve as Twitter performance indexes of the accounts. Although number of followers describes how many users have subscribed to an account, not all the followers really read the tweets; let alone they do not engage in discussing them. Number of tweets is a direct indication of an account activity and an indirect indication of how old an account is since established accounts might post more tweets. For an account, Topsy score (Topsy.com) takes into account the retweets and mentions than matter and it is a measure of users' community involvement for this account. Total Effective Reach (http://twtr-land.com) is the total amount of people who are exposed to a tweet or its retweets, for the 10 most popular tweets of an account. Topsy score and Total Effective Reach give some evidence of the followers involvement in getting and spreading the information originally provided by the 37 accounts (Antoniadis et al., 2014, Antoniadis et al., 2015).

Next, the mentions/replies (m/r) networks or the way that followers of each account mention or reply to each other gives a description of the actual involvement within a potential community context. In this study the users who prove their involvement by mentioning and replying to tweets are studied, not those who just happened to follow an account. The 37 m/r networks (one for each account along with its followers) were recorded for the latest tweet using NodeXL for Windows. Then the 37 networks were analyzed using Social Networking Analysis with an interest to explore if they display "small-world", "scale-free" and homophily characteristics. These characteristics regard community features and in this research they were measured using Assortativity, Clustering coefficient, degree-Skewness and Average shortest path of each network, using the igraph package in R. Clustering coefficient is an index ranging from zero to one. Large values indicate small-world properties. Average shortest path is an average value of how far a follower is from another follower. When the average shortest path is small, this is evidence that friends are only a few steps away, so this could be taken to display a community characteristic. If a network has a degree distribution with a very large Skewness, that is, only few users post the most while the large proportion of followers post a little, the network possibly fits with a power-law degree distribution. Networks with power-law degree distributions (scale-free networks) are assumed to provide evidence that these networks constitute small-worlds. Degree Assortativity measures the property that highly connected nodes link with other highly connected nodes (positive assortativity ranging up to 1) or the reverse where highly connected nodes are more likely to link to less connected nodes (negative assortativity ranging up to -1). Statistics of these indexes are reported in the findings section.

Next, correlation analysis and Principal Component Analysis summarize the associations between the four community indexes. Two-step Cluster Analysis is use to locate groups of accounts regarding their community characteristics. Finally, the association of community indexes with Twitter performance indexes are reported and discussed.

Findings

The m/r networks refer to the followers of the tourism accounts and their followers. For each tourism account, such an m/r network contains all the m/r connections that contain within them the mentions and replies made by the tourism accounts followers. It is a network consisting of the mentions and replies made by the followers that are directly connected to the tourism accounts, plus these followers; followers. In this way it is expected that the total set of followers who could provoke discussions is included in the analysis.

The average shortest path is really small and this may be a sign of small-world formation (mean 1.0855, st. dev. 0.1630). However, Skewness being small (mean 3.9958, st. dev. 2.8422), and clustering coefficient being nearly equal to zero (mean 0.0256, st. dev. 0.1235) contradict the hypothesis of small-worlds formation. Further, assortativity is negative (mean -0.5666, st. dev. 0.1444), meaning that less active users connect to highly active ones. These findings reveal that on average small-world characteristics are hardly identified. Although mean average shortest path is small and Skewness is fairly high, it is the negative assortativity and the nearly zero clustering coefficients that contradict the conclusion of community formation.

Next, the correlation coefficients of the four indexes are calculated. The greater the Clustering coefficient the greater the assortativity ($r = 0.548$, $p < 0.05$). This means that accounts presenting homophily characteristics to a higher degree tend to partially have small-world properties regarding transitivity. On the other hand, however, there is a reverse association between average shortest path and assortativity. The larger the assortativity, the larger the average shortest path is. Thus, regarding shortest paths, there is hardly evidence that networks characterized by homophily are associated small-worlds. Indexes do not converge, but there is only partial evidence that the main indexes of the study are associated (Table 20.1).

To portrait the big picture of the intercorrelations among the four community indexes, a Principal Components Analysis (PCA) with Varimax rotation is done. Two Principal Components (PC) are produced explaining 85% of the total initial variance. Skewness and Clustering coefficient load highly to the first PC, low Skewness is associated with high Clustering coefficient, vice versa high Skewness is associated with low clustering coefficient. Skewed networks are not transitive: a few accounts produce most of the information, while the rest mention or reply to them only a little. The second PC loads highly to Average shortest path and

Table 20.1 Correlation coefficients between small-world and homophily indexes

	Assortativity	Clustering coefficient	Skewness
Clustering coefficient	0.548*		
Skewnness	−0.376	−0.281	
Average shortest path	0.704**	0.108	0.117

(*: $p < 0.05$,
**: $p < 0.01$)

Assortativity: low average shortest path is associated with high assortativity (Table 20.2). The combination of all these associations hardly offers evidence that small-worlds are constructed.

The two PC are used to further cluster the Twitter accounts with regards to their values on the small word and homophily indexes. Two-step cluster analysis produces two clusters. The average values of the indexes for the two groups of accounts are reported in Table 20.3. Group 1 consists of five accounts: Spain, Italy_it, MySwitzerland_en, OurFinland and VisitMalta. This group has on average, greater assortativity, larger clustering coefficient, Skewnness nearly equal to the one of the second group and larger shortest path. For these accounts the properties of small worlds and homophily are more evident. Further, from Table 20.4 it is obvious that these accounts are also the most active in Twitter regarding the five performance indexes. They do worse only regarding the total number of tweets they post. These countries could be considered to excel regarding their Twitter appearance and to have more active and involved communities of followers.

Table 20.2 PCA with Varimax rotation component matrix

	PC 1 Percentage of explained variance 43%	PC 2 Percentage of explained variance 42%
Skewness	−.880	.049
Clustering coefficient	.835	.222
Average shortest path	−.106	.966
Assortativity	.482	.835

Table 20.3 Mean values of small-world and homophily indexes for clusters of accounts

	Assortativity	Clustering coefficient	Skewness	Average shortest path
Group 1(N = 5)	−.373	.135	4.768	1.395
Group 2 (N = 14)	−.635	.004	5.253	1.007
Total (N = 19)	−.566	.039	5.126	1.109

Table 20.4 Mean values of performance indexes for clusters of accounts

	Followers	Following	Number of Tweets	Topsy score	Effective reach total (based on 10 most popular tweets)
Group 1(N = 5)	33,150	5,733	4,306	2,218	76,805
Group 2 (N = 14)	19,078	1,672	8,924	897	64,412
Total (N = 19)	22,781	2,741	7,709	1,245	67,673

Conclusions

In this chapter we explored whether followers of tourism Twitter accounts form communities discussing or retransmitting tweets. To do that, we recorded the mentions/replies networks of the followers of European countries' central tourism organizations along with their followers. These networks represent active followers' connections and not only connections among people who just happen to follow each other and/or the central tourism organizations' accounts.

Community characteristics include small-world properties and homophily. The first are generally measured through the use of clustering coefficients, average shortest paths, Skewness and Assortativity. Generally, Skewness is low to medium, assortativity is negative, and clustering coefficient is close to zero, thus providing evidence of small-worlds formation. On the contrary, average shortest path is small. This offers little evidence that followers constitute communities discussing the information produced by the central accounts.

From the analysis it is obvious only indexes were calculated for only 19 of the 37 accounts. This happens because the m/r networks cannot be formed since the accounts have only few followers.

It is a general property that community indexes have small standard deviations. Tourism Twitter accounts do not differentiate significantly regarding community characteristics. However, there is a small group of accounts which have index values that are closer to the standards of small-worlds communities. For these accounts homophily and small-world properties are more evident. These accounts generally have better Twitter performance indexes as well.

It is a more general characteristic of Twitter accounts with a national or international appeal that they mostly serve as announcement boards and not as potential for a discussion among their followers. Followers of these accounts are only interested in reading tweets to get fast and short information and they generally are not involved in discussing and mentioning the original tweets. Although generally tourists are actively involved in spreading information from tourism Twitter accounts (for example @TripAdvisor), this is not a habit or a need when referring to national tourism Twitter accounts. Further, it is known from the authors' experience and communications that when Twitter is used as a local-level administration medium, the involvement of citizens is bigger. It remains to be studied if this also happens in tourism Twitter accounts that address to a local-level followers' audience, such as Twitter accounts of specific regions, popular islands, cities, museums etc.

References

Anagnostopoulos, A., Kumar, R., & Mahdian, M. (2008). Influence and correlation in social networks. In *KDD '08*. Las Vegas, Nevada, USA, August 24–27, pp. 7 – 15.

Antoniadis, K., Vrana, V., & Zafiropoulos, K., 2014. Promoting European countries destination image through twitter. *European Journal of Tourism, Hospitality and Recreation*, 5(1), pp. 85–103.

Antoniadis, K., Zafiropoulos, K., & Vrana, V. (2015). Communities of followers in tourism twitter accounts of European Countries. *European Journal of Tourism, Hospitality and Recreation*, 6(1), pp. 11–26.

Bakshy, E., Hofman, J., Mason, W., & Watts D. (2011). Identifying 'Influencers' on Twitter. *WSDM 2011*. Hong Kong, February 9–12.

Barabasi, A. L. (2002). *Linked: The New Science of Networks*, Cambridge, MA, Perseus Books Group.

Barrat, A., & Weigt, M. (2000). On the properties of small-world network models. *The European Physical Journal*, 13, pp. 547–560.

Bayram, M., & Arici, S. (2013). Destination marketing organizations' social media usage: A research on Balkan countries. *International Conference on Economic and Social Studies (ICESoS'13)*. Sarajevo, May 10–11.

Blumrodt, J., & Palmer, A. (2014). On-line destination branding: An investigation into the divergence between brand goals and on-line implementation. *The Journal of Applied Business Research*, 30(6), pp. 1597–1606.

boyd, d., Golder, S., & Lotan, G. (2010). Tweet, tweet, retweet: Conversational aspects of retweeting on twitter. In *HICSS-43.*, Kauai, HI, January 6, IEEE, pp. 1–10.

Choromański, K., Matuszak, M., & MięKisz, J. (2013). Scale-free graph with preferential attachment and evolving internal vertex structure. *Journal of Statistical Physics*, 151(6), pp. 1175–1183.

Chu, Z., Gianvecchio, S., Wang, H., & Jajodia, S. (2010). Who is tweeting on twitter: Human, bot, or cyborg? *ACSAC '10*. Austin, Texas USA, December 6–10, pp. 21–30.

Currarini, S., & Vega Redondo, F. (2013). A Simple Model of Homophily in Social Networks. University Ca' Foscari of Venice, Dept. of Economics Research Paper Series No. 24 .Retrieved from http://papers.ssrn.com/sol3/papers.cfm?abstract_id=1697503 [Accessed 22 August 2015].

Digital Marketing. (2015). By the numbers: 150+ Amazing Twitter statistics. Retrieved from http://expandedramblings.com/index.php/march-2013-by-the-numbers-a-few amazing-twitter-stats/ [Accessed 4 August 2015].

Dwyer, L., & Kim, C. (2003). Destination competitiveness: Determinants and indicators. *Current Issues in Tourism*, 6(5), pp. 369–414.

Easley, D., & Kleinberg, J. (2010). *Networks, Crowds, and Markets: Reasoning about a Highly Connected World*, New York, Cambridge University Press.

Hamill, J., Stevenson, A., & Attard, D. (2010). National DMOs and Web 2.0. In M. Sigala, E. Christou, & U. Gretzel (eds.) *Social Media in Travel, Tourism and Hospitality: Theory, Practice and Cases*. Great Britain, Ashgate. Ch. 9.

Hargittai, E., & Litt, E. (2012). Becoming a tweep: How prior online experiences influence twitter use. *Information, Communication & Society*, 15(5), pp. 680–702.

Hassan, S. B. (2013). Social media and destination positioning: Egypt as a case study. *European Journal of Tourism, Hospitality and Recreation*, 4(1), pp. 98–103.

Huberman, B., Romero, D., & Wu, F. (2009). Social networks that matter: Twitter under the microscope, *First Monday*, 14(1), http://firstmonday.org/article/view/2317/2063 [Accessed 21 November 2013].

Katsoni, V., & Venetsanopoulou, M. (2013). ICTs Integration into Destination Marketing Organizations (DMOs) Tourism Strategy. *3rd International Conference on Tourism and Hospitality Management*. Athens, Greece, June 27–29, pp. 173–182.

Kavoura, A., & Stavianea, A. (2014). Economic and social aspects from social media's implementation as a strategic innovative marketing tool in the tourism industry. *Procedia: Economics and Finance*, 148, pp. 32–39.

Kavoura, A., & Stavianea, A. (2015). Following and belonging to an online travel community in social media, its shared characteristics and gender differences. *Procedia: Social and Behavioral Sciences*, 175, February, pp. 515–521.

Kozinets, R. V. (2002). The field behind the screen: Using netnography for marketing research in online communities. *Journal of Marketing Research*, 39, February, pp. 61–72.

Krackhardt, D. (1996). Social networks and the liability of newness for managers. In C. L. Cooper & D. M. Rousseau (eds.) *Trends in Organizational Behavior*. New York, NY, John Wiley and Sons, Ltd. Ch. 9, pp. 179–191.

Krishnamurthy, B., Gill, P., & Arlitt, M. (2008). A few chirps about twitter. In *WOSN'08*. Seattle, Washington, August 18.

Kwak, H., Lee, C., Park, H., & Moon, S. (2010). What is twitter, a social network or a news media? In *WWW 2010*. Raleigh NC, April 26–30, pp. 591–600.

Marwick, A., & boyd, d. (2010). To see and be seen: Celebrity practice on twitter. *Convergence*, 17(2), pp. 139–158.

McPherson, M., Smith-Lovin, L., & Cook, J. (2001). Birds of a feather: Homophily in social networks. *Annual Review of Sociology*, 27, August, pp. 415–444.

Milgram, S. (1967). The small-world problem, *Psychology Today*, 1(1), pp. 61–67.

Milwood, P., Marchiori, E., & Zach, F. (2013). A Comparison of social media adoption and use in different countries: The case of the United States and Switzerland. *Journal of Travel & Tourism Marketing*, 30(1–2), pp. 165–168.

Musiał, K., & Kazienko, P. (2013). Social networks on the Internet. *World Wide Web*, 16, pp. 31–72.

Newman, M. E. J. (2000). Models of the small world: A review. *Journal of Statistical Physics*, 101(3–4), pp. 819–841.

Nguyen, V. H., & Wang, Z. (2012). *Practice of online marketing with social media in tourism destination marketing: The case study of VisitSweden, Sweden*, Master thesis. Södertörns University.

O'Connor, B., Balasubramanyan, R., Routledge, B., & Smith, N. (2010). From tweets to polls: Linking text sentiment to public opinion time series. In *International AAAI Conference on Weblogs and Social Media*. Washington, DC, May 23–26, pp. 122–129.

Pike, S., & Page, S. (2014). Destination marketing organizations and destination marketing: A narrative analysis of the literature. *Tourism Management*, 41, April. pp. 202–227.

Rudat, A., & Buder, J. (2015). Making retweeting social: The influence of content and context information on sharing news in Twitter. *Computers in Human Behavior*, 46, May, pp. 75–84.

Sevin, E. (2013). Places going viral: Twitter usage patterns in destination marketing and place branding. *Journal of Place Management and Development*, 6(3), pp. 227–239.

Sotiriadis, M., & van Zyl, C. (2013). Electronic word-of-mouth and online reviews in tourism services: The use of twitter by tourists. *Electronic Commerce Research*, 13(1), pp. 103–124.

Staab, S. (2005). Social networks applied. *IEEE Intelligent systems*, 20(1), pp. 80–82.

Stepchenkova, S., Kirilenko, A., & Kim, H. (2013). Grassroots branding with twitter: Amazing Florida. In L. Cantoni & X. P. Xiang (eds.) *Information and Communication Technologies in Tourism 2013*. Berlin Heidelberg, Springer-Verlag. pp. 144–156.

Travers, J., & Milgram, S. (1969). An experimental study of the small world problem. *Sociometry*, 32(5), pp. 425–443.

Van Noort, V., Snel, B., & Huynen, M. (2004). The yeast coexpression network has a small-world, scale-free architecture and can be explained by a simple model. *EMBO Reports*, 5(3), pp. 280–284.

Vrana V., Kydros D., & Theocharidis, A. (2014). A network analysis of Greek tech blogs: A lonely road. *Social Networking*, 3(1), pp. 1–8.

Vrana, V., & Zafiropoulos, K. (2011). Associations between USPs and design characteristics of Mediterranean countries. *Journal of Hospitality Marketing & Management*, 20(7), pp. 766–790.

Vrana, V., Zafiropoulos, K., & Vagianos, D. (2013). Authority groups among popular wine blogs. *Journal of Quality Assurance in Hospitality & Tourism*, 14(2), pp. 142–162.

Wang, X. F., & Chen, G. (2003). Complex networks: Small-world, scale-free and beyond. *IEEE Circuits and Systems Magazine*, 1st Quarter, pp. 6–20.

Watts, D., & Strogatz, S. (1998). Collective dynamics of 'small-world' networks. *Nature*, 393, pp. 440–442.

Xiang, Z., & Gretzel, U. (2010). Role of social media in online travel information search. *Tourism management*, 31(2), pp. 179–188.

Zafarani, R., Abbasi, M. A. & Liu, H. (2014). Influence and homophily. In R. M. A. Abbasi & H. Liu (eds.) *Social Media Mining: An Introduction*. New York, Cambridge University Press. Ch.8.

Conclusion

Ulrike Gretzel and Marianna Sigala

Social media are an evolving phenomenon and require constant adaptation from hospitality and tourism marketers, general users and social media researchers. Platforms can rapidly arise and disrupt the existing social media ecosystem (e.g. Snapchat and WeChat). Others disappear or start occupying niches. New technologies embedded in social media can change expectations, use behaviors (e.g. livestreaming and augmented reality) and customers' working patterns and lifestyles. Growth, shifts in user demographics or changes to business models can have tremendous impact on the culture of a platform, its contents and the way users interact (e.g. Facebook) and engage in value co-creation (e.g. sharing economy platforms, open innovation). Greater connectivity and mobile social media use on the go lead to a growing emphasis on visual, localized and contextualized (i.e. based on the time, occasion, companionship and environment) tourism contents and services (Gretzel, 2016). New ways in which data can be created and harnessed (e.g. Facebook Insights, Amazon Mechanical Turk or Twitter brand surveys) arise, which in turn means that successful marketing practices need to shift from "make-and-sell" strategies to "sense-and-response" strategies (Haeckel, 2013; Knuz et al., 2017). Emerging devices (e.g. Oculus, Google Cardboard, wearable devices/cameras, drones) promise different ways of creating and engaging with social media contents and additional touchpoints that travellers can use for interacting and accessing services during all stages of the customer journey (Sigala, 2017a). Overall, the goal of technology exploitation is not only to customize tourism experiences but also involve, empower and motivate the travellers to participate in the customization of their tourism experiences so that they fit their needs and expectations (Sigala, 2017a). Ever-greater integration of social media and e-commerce, m-commerce or augmented-commerce offer business opportunities but also mean more pressure on marketers to "crack the code" of social media marketing and demonstrate return on social media investments.

While these dynamics are exciting and challenging at the same time, they also demand a certain way of approaching social media research. Though descriptive research of new phenomena is informative, it is deep conceptualization, hypotheses testing, longitudinal research, comparative analyses and in-depth cultural understandings that foster the development of a stable body of knowledge regarding not only the types of social media use, but more importantly of the drivers of social media use and its impacts on travellers' behavior, value co-creation processes and the structure and operations of value chain systems. Fundamental theories and frameworks like value co-creation (Ranjan & Read, 2016) but also value co-destruction (Sigala, 2017b), open innovation (Egger et al., 2016), customer engagement (Brodie et al., 2013; Khan, 2017), gamification (Sigala, 2015) and persuasion (Gass & Seiter, 2015) are needed to investigate underlying drivers of social media perceptions, usage and behaviors. Profound understanding of the tourism experience is also paramount to gauging social media impacts (Kim & Fesenmaier, 2017). Especially in the context of social media marketing, there is a dearth of theory that could help depict and explain phenomena beyond the specific platform or case study (Felix et al., 2017). For instance, the field is in dire need of a new theory of brands and branding as social media make it ever more difficult to pinpoint what a brand is and what branding involves. Indeed, there is an emerging stream of research looking into how co-creation, customer engagement and interactions contribute to brand identity development, brand value and image (Ramaswamy & Ozcan, 2016; Hajli et al., 2017; Black & Veloutsou, 2017). What is also needed is research for better understanding how different actors (e.g. platforms and organizations, not just consumers) co-create but also co-destruct value by exchanging various resources through market practices at various levels (individual, dyadic, network, platform etc.) (Sigala, 2017b; Breidbach & Maglio, 2016). The chapters in this book also warn of oversimplification – greater complexity in social media demands a nuanced understanding of users, engagement platforms and uses.

Moreover, changes in social media require agility in terms of social media research approaches and methodologies. To stay relevant, social media researchers need to take advantage of the growing amount of data that is available, use the ever bigger array of existing tools for social media monitoring, and most importantly, grapple with the opportunities but also challenges big data approaches offer to tourism researchers (Xiang & Fesenmaier, 2017; Gandomi & Haider, 2015). Commercial interests in protecting data make data extraction increasingly problematic. Privacy and ethical concerns are often not even discussed. Big data veracity is a huge issue but is currently conveniently neglected, while the value of data-driven marketing practices is still to be proven and provided with a robust way to measure their effectiveness (Wedel & Kannan, 2016). A particular challenge in the context of big data and social media research lies in the need to visualize the results, which is not easy and currently not commonplace in tourism and hospitality research. Further, collaborations with industry partners such as telecommunications companies are sometime necessary in order to gain access to data and computing power, typically putting a damper on what can be researched but at the same time providing opportunities for innovation through exposure to different perspectives and techniques. However, while big data analytics are important for identifying larger patterns and trends, they cannot fill the gap in our understanding of social media use as highly individual and culturally embedded. Approaches like netnography (Kozinets, 2015) seek to provide guidance in what forms such deep dives into social media data can assume and to which kinds of understandings they can lead.

Essential to future social media research in tourism and hospitality will be the recognition that social media are not only a global phenomenon but also highly localized. While the chapters in the book cover different countries, they do currently not provide a full picture of differences in social media meanings and practices across different national cultures. And, cultural understandings should go beyond national culture. Social media use is, to a great extent, embedded in youth cultures, leisure and work cultures, media cultures, community cultures, platform cultures as well as users' personalities and religious background. Better contextualization of social media use in tourism and hospitality is therefore required. In addition, to better develop and interpret marketing analytics research, one should adopt more multi-and inter-disciplinary research including theoretical frameworks and approaches used in mathematics, econometrics, economics, psychometrics, psychology, computer science, religion, consumer culture theory, marketing, management and organizational behavior research. To that end, it is envisioned that theory building will increasingly rely on studies that use a mixture of theoretical frameworks and methodologies to describe, diagnose and predict the usage, drivers and outcomes of social media practices.

The book chapters tried to capture some of the emerging social media trends. We see as one of the biggest frontiers of social media research and marketing practice the increasing integration of social media use with physical infrastructure in the realm of smart tourism (Gretzel et al., 2015). The "Internet of Things" (Whitmore et al., 2015), when successfully implemented, can enable new ways of accessing and interacting with social media, new sources of data streams, new levels of context awareness and personalization of social media contents, as well as new ways of actors' participation in value co-creation or co-destruction. Of importance is also the notion of social media users being increasingly non-human. This phenomenon is most prominently visible in the form of news bots that already flood the social media universe with posts (Lokot & Diakopoulos, 2016) as well as in the increased use of anthropomorphic technologies in service settings (Fan et al., 2016). Such developments will make it even more important to also humanize interactions (Ge, 2016), but the marketing theory currently provides little insight into how this can happen and what its potential effects on consumers' behavior may be (Yuan & Dennis, 2017).

Social media is an extremely fast moving phenomenon and by the time this book will be printed, some of the specific statements presented by the authors will already be dated and maybe even obsolete. However, we are confident that the frameworks, the theoretical lenses and the techniques presented as well as the questions raised by the chapters will stay relevant for quite some time. Whatever the specific platforms or technologies may be, value co-creation, value co-destruction, customer engagement and experiences, use behaviors, commercial applications and social media analytics are topic areas that will need to be continuously explored.

References

Black, I., & Veloutsou, C. (2017). Working consumers: Co-creation of brand identity, consumer identity and brand community identity. *Journal of Business Research, 70*, pp. 416–429.

Breidbach, C. F., & Maglio, P. P. (2016). Technology-enabled value co-creation: An empirical analysis of actors, resources, and practices. *Industrial Marketing Management, 56*, 73–85.

Brodie, R. J., Ilic, A., Juric, B., & Hollebeek, L. (2013). Consumer engagement in a virtual brand community: An exploratory analysis. *Journal of Business Research, 66*, pp. 105–114.

Egger, R., Gula, I., & Walcher, D. (Eds.). (2016). *Open Tourism: Open Innovation, Crowdsourcing and Co-Creation Challenging the Tourism Industry*, New York, Springer International Publishing.

Fan, A., Fan, A., Wu, L., Wu, L., Mattila, A. S., & Mattila, A. S. (2016). Does anthropomorphism influence customers' switching intentions in the self-service technology failure context? *Journal of Services Marketing, 30*(7), pp. 713–723.

Felix, R., Rauschnabel, P. A., & Hinsch, C. (2017). Elements of strategic social media marketing: A holistic framework. *Journal of Business Research, 70*, pp. 118–126.

Gandomi, A., & Haider, M. (2015). Beyond the hype: Big data concepts, methods, and analytics. *International Journal of Information Management, 35*(2), pp. 137–144.

Gass, R. H., & Seiter, J. S. (2015). *Persuasion: Social influence and compliance gaining*, Oxon, UK: Routledge.

Ge, J. (2016). 4 Ways DMOs Use Weibo to Humanize Their Brands. DestinationThink!, Accessed online (December 10, 2016) at: https://destinationthink.com/4-ways-chinese-dmos-use-weibo-humanize-brands/.

Gretzel, U. (2016). The visual turn in social media marketing. In *Tourismos*, forthcoming.

Gretzel, U., Sigala, M., Xiang, Z., & Koo, C. (2015). Smart tourism: Foundations and developments. *Electronic Markets, 25*(3), pp. 179–188.

Haeckel, S. H. (2013), *Adaptive Enterprise: Creating and Leading Sense-and-Respond Organizations*, Cambridge, MA: Harvard Business Press.

Hajli, N., Shanmugam, M., Papagiannidis, S., Zahay, D., & Richard, M. O. (2017). Branding co-creation with members of online brand communities. *Journal of Business Research, 70*, pp. 136–144

Khan, M. L. (2017). Social media engagement: What motivates user participation and consumption on YouTube? *Computers in Human Behavior, 66*, pp. 236–247.

Kim, J. J., & Fesenmaier, D. R. (2017). Tourism experience and tourism design. In D. R. Fesenmaier & Z. Xiang (eds.) *Design Science in Tourism*. New York, Springer International Publishing, pp. 17–29.

Knuz, W., Aksoy, L., Bart, Y., Heinonen, K., Kabadayi, S., Ordenes F. V., Sigala, M., Diaz, D., & Theodoulidis, B. (2017). Customer engagement in a big data world. *Journal of Services Marketing, 31*(2), 161–171.

Kozinets, R. V. (2015). *Netnography: Redefined*. Thousand Oaks, CA, Sage.

Lokot, T., & Diakopoulos, N. (2016). News bots: Automating news and information dissemination on twitter. *Digital Journalism, 4*(6), pp. 682–699.

Ramaswamy, V., & Ozcan, K. (2016). Brand value co-creation in a digitalized world: An integrative framework and research implications. *International Journal of Research in Marketing, 33*(1), pp. 93–106.

Ranjan, K. R., & Read, S. (2016). Value co-creation: concept and measurement. *Journal of the Academy of Marketing Science*, 44(3), pp. 290–315.

Sigala, M. (2015). The application and impact of gamification funware on trip planning and experiences: The case of TripAdvisor's funware. *Electronic Markets*, 25(3), 189–209.

Sigala, M. (2017a). Social media and the co-creation of tourism experiences. In M. Sotiriadis & D. Gursoy (eds.) *Managing and Marketing Tourism Experiences: Issues, Challenges and Approaches*. Bingley, UK: Emerald Publishing, pp. 85–111.

Sigala, M. (2017b). How bad are you? Justification and normalization of online deviant behavior. Proceedings of the ENTER 2017 eTourism Conference, 24–26 January, 2017, Rome, Italy.

Wedel, M., & Kannan, P. K. (2016). Marketing analytics for data-rich environments. *Journal of Marketing*, 80, pp. 97–121.

Whitmore, A., Agarwal, A., & Da Xu, L. (2015). The Internet of Things – A survey of topics and trends. *Information Systems Frontiers*, 17(2), 261–274.

Xiang, Z., & Fesenmaier, D. R. (2017). Big data analytics, tourism design and smart tourism. In Z. Xiang & D. R. Fesenmaier (eds.) *Analytics in Smart Tourism Design*. New York: Springer International Publishing, pp. 299–307.

Yuan, L., & Dennis, A. (2017). Interacting like humans? Understanding the effect of anthropomorphism on consumer's willingness to pay in online auctions. In *Proceedings of the 50th Hawaii International Conference on System Sciences*, pp. 537–546. Retrieved online January 7, 2017, from http://scholarspace.manoa.hawaii.edu/bitstream/10125/41215/1/paper0066.pdf

Index

For Product Safety Concerns and Information please contact our EU
representative GPSR@taylorandfrancis.com
Taylor & Francis Verlag GmbH, Kaufingerstraße 24, 80331 München, Germany